Study Guide

For Garrett's

Brain and Behavior

Sheila Steiner
Jamestown College

THOMSON
WADSWORTH

Australia • Canada • Mexico • Singapore • Spain • United Kingdom • United States

Printed in Canada
1 2 3 4 5 6 7   07 06 05 04 03

Printer: Webcom

0-534-51336-0

For more information about our products, contact us at:
Thomson Learning Academic Resource Center
1-800-423-0563

For permission to use material from this text, contact us by:
Phone: 1-800-730-2214
Fax: 1-800-731-2215
Web: http://www.thomsonrights.com

Asia
Thomson Learning
5 Shenton Way #01-01
UIC Building
Singapore 068808

Australia/New Zealand
Thomson Learning
102 Dodds Street
Southbank, Victoria 3006
Australia

Canada
Nelson
1120 Birchmount Road
Toronto, Ontario M1K 5G4
Canada

Europe/Middle East/South Africa
Thomson Learning
High Holborn House
50/51 Bedford Row
London WC1R 4LR
United Kingdom

Latin America
Thomson Learning
Seneca, 53
Colonia Polanco
11560 Mexico D.F.
Mexico

Spain/Portugal
Paraninfo
Calle/Magallanes, 25
28015 Madrid, Spain

Contents

How To Use This Study Guide

The purpose of this study guide is to assist you in mastering the material in the textbook, *Brain and Behavior*. Each chapter contains several features that require you to rehearse the material in some way. These features are described below.

Chapter Outline and Learning Objectives

I have incorporated detailed learning objectives into the outline of each chapter. As you read the chapter, write your responses to these learning objectives in the space provided or on separate paper. Be sure that you understand the definitions of terms in **bold print**. Rather than simply copying the author's words, try to restate the main ideas in your own words.

After completing each major section of a chapter in the textbook, you should complete the Summary and Guided Review and Short Answer and Essay Questions sections of the corresponding study guide chapter.

Summary and Guided Review

These sections contain comprehensive summaries of each major section of each chapter. In writing these summaries, I have tried to "boil down" the author's ideas to the main points in my own words. As you read each summary, there are fill-in-the-blank items for you to complete. For the most part, the answers to these items come from the textbook.

Short Answer and Essay Questions

I have written these items in order to promote more sophisticated thinking about the material (beyond memorization). For example, some of these items require application of the material to new situations, and some require you to explain the reasoning behind the research discussed in the book.

Post-Test

These sections contain about 40 multiple-choice items and should be completed after you have finished the entire textbook chapter. These items are designed to help you review for an in-class multiple-choice exam.

Answers and Explanations

These sections contain answers to the fill-in-the-blank, sample answers to the short answer and essay questions, and answers with explanations to the post-test questions. Ideally, you should check your answers only after you have completed a section of the study guide.

Chapter 1: What is Biopsychology?

Chapter Outline and Learning Objectives

As you read the chapter, use these learning objectives to guide your studying. You should be able to define the key terms from the text, which are shown in boldface type below.

1) The Origins of Biopsychology
    - Discuss the significance of the "decade of the brain."

    - Define **neuroscience** and **biopsychology**.

    - What kinds of research questions do biological psychologists attempt to answer?

    a) Prescientific Psychology and the Mind-Brain Problem
        - What is the **mind-brain question**? Compare the positions of **monism, materialistic monism**, and **dualism**.

        - Describe Descartes' hydraulic **model** of brain activity.

    b) Discovering the Brain's Role in Behavior
        - How did scientists learn that nerves operate by electricity? What information did Helmholtz contribute?

        - What did the cases of Phineas Gage and Broca's patient suggest about **localization** of functions within the brain?

2) Science, Research, and Theory
    - Define **empiricism**.

    a) Empiricism: How to Answer Scientific Questions
        - Why is it important that scientific observations be **objective**?

        - Define **experiment**; distinguish between **independent** and **dependent variables**.

        - What is the primary advantage of an experimental study?

- Explain what a **confounded** variable is.

- How does a **correlational** study differ from an experiment?

b) Theory and the Uncertainty of Science
   - Why are scientists careful about drawing firm conclusions from their research?

   - Define **theory** and **hypothesis**, and describe how they are related.

3) Nature and Nurture
   - What is the **nature versus nurture** question?

a) The Genetic Code
   - Explain how genes and chromosomes are arranged in human cells, including the sex cells.

   - Define **zygote**, **embryo**, and **fetus**.

   - Describe the structure of **deoxyribonucleic acid**.

   - What is the function of genes?

   - Distinguish between **dominant** and **recessive** genes.

   - What is an **X-linked trait**?

   - Define **homozygous** and **heterozygous**.

   - Distinguish between **genotype** and **phenotype**.

   - What does it mean to say that someone is a **carrier** for a trait?

   - What is a **polygenic** trait?

b) Genes and Behavior
- Describe how genes are thought to influence behaviors.

c) Investigating Heredity
  i) Genetic Similarities: The Correlational Approach
  - Distinguish between **family**, **adoption**, and **twin studies**.

  - Distinguish between **fraternal (dizygotic)** and **identical (monozygotic) twins**.

  - What do **correlations** and **concordance rates** measure in studies of inheritance?

  ii) Genetic Engineering: The Experimental Approach
  - What is **genetic engineering**? How are **transgenic** and **knockout mice** created?

  - How does **antisense RNA** technology work?

  - How has genetic engineering been used to treat immunodeficiency in humans?

  iii) The Human Genome Project
  - What is the goal of the **Human Genome Project**? What benefits are expected to come from it?

  - What difficulties have those working on this project encountered?

d) Heredity: Destiny or Predisposition?
  i) Genes and Individuality
  - Explain the importance of variability in traits for **natural selection**.

  - Give some examples that show how genes are flexible in their effects on traits.

  ii) Heredity, Environment, and Vulnerability
  - What is **heritability**, and how is it measured?

  - Give some examples of traits that show low, moderate and high heritability.

- What do behavioral geneticists mean when they say that "we inherit dispositions, not destinies?" How does the **vulnerability** model of schizophrenia demonstrate this?

4) Research Ethics
   a) Plagiarism and Fabrication
- Why are **plagiarism** and **fabrication** of results unethical practices?

   b) Protecting the Welfare of Research Subjects
      i) Research with Humans
- What is **informed consent**?

- Under what circumstances may researchers use **deception**?

      ii) Research with Animals
- Why are animals used in behavioral and medical research?

- What are the responsibilities of researchers in caring for animals?

- What effects has the animal welfare movement had on regulations surrounding animal research?

   c) New Technology, New Ethical Concerns
      i) Gene Therapy
- What are the ethical concerns surrounding gene therapy research?

      ii) Using Human Embryos
- What are **stem cells**, and why do they have such great potential for treating various diseases?

- What are the controversies surrounding stem cell research?

- What are some alternatives to stem cell research?

The Origins of Biopsychology

Summary and Guided Review

After studying this section in the text, fill in the blanks of the following summary. The answers are found on p. 17.

During the 1990s, also known as the _____ ___ ____ _____ (1), numerous advances were made in understanding the role of biology in behavioral problems, including mental illness, drug addiction, and memory impairment. Currently, neuroscience includes researchers from psychology, chemistry, computer science, and many areas of the biological and health sciences, so it is a _____ (2) approach to understanding the nervous system. A psychologist who studies the relationship between the brain and _____ (3) is called a _____ (4) psychologist.

Historically, biopsychology is a new science, but it addresses a rather old problem: the _____ - _____ (5) question. Philosophers and scientists have long struggled to determine if the mind is physical like the body, a position called _____ _____ (6), or if it is separate and immaterial, a position called _____ (7). Among the ancient Greek philosophers, Democritus and _____ (8) were monists, whereas _____ (9) was a dualist. The 17th century French philosopher _____ (10), a dualist, used the _____ (11) model to explain how the brain operates. He suggested that when the mind willed the body to action, the _____ (12) gland pumped _____ _____ (13) through the nerves, which he believed were hollow tubes, to the muscles, resulting in movement. Although his model was wrong and did not ultimately contribute to the understanding of the nervous system, it set a precedent for appealing to physical explanations for behavior.

Important principles of nervous system anatomy and physiology were discovered during the 1700s and 1800s. Work by several European physiologists showed that nerves operated via _____ (14) , not Descartes' "animal spirits." However, the German physiologist _____ (15) performed experiments indicating that nerve conduction was not as fast as electricity conducted through wires, which suggested that something more than just electricity was occurring in the nervous system. Helmholtz also contributed to the understanding of vision and _____ (16). In the 1800s, well-documented cases of brain injury suggested that specific parts of the brain have specific functions, a concept known as _____ (17). One such case was Phineas Gage, who underwent extreme changes in personality following an accident in which an iron rod was driven through his skull and _____ (18) lobes. Another case was reported by the French physician _____(19); his patient was unable to speak, and after the patient died, it was discovered that he had damage in the left hemisphere.

Currently, brain researchers know that to a certain degree brain functions are localized, and that the brain is involved in all behaviors. In explaining the connection between the mind and brain, most neuroscientists are _____ _____ (20).

Short Answer & Essay Questions

Answer the following questions. See p. 18 for sample answers.

1. Give two examples of the types of research questions that biological psychologists might ask.

2. What does the author mean when he writes that "there is no such thing as mind?"

3. Regarding the mind-brain question, compare monism and dualism. What are (or were) the problems with each position?

4. How did 18th and 19th century physiologists learn that the nervous system works by conducting electrical impulses?

5. Why was the case of Phineas Gage important for brain science? What did it reveal about the localization of function issue?

6. How do most modern neuroscientists explain the relationship between the brain and mind?

Science, Research, and Theory

Summary and Guided Review

After studying this section in the text, fill in the blanks of the following summary. The answers are found on p. 17.

Science requires that information be derived from observation, a concept known as _____ (21). Scientific observations should be _____ (22), so that two or more people watching the same event will describe it in the same way. Non-experimental observational methods used by scientists include naturalistic observation, _____ _____ (23), and survey. An experiment is a study in which the researcher(s) manipulate at least one _____ _____ (24) and measure its/their effects on one or more _____ _____ (25). Because researchers control the IV, it is possible to determine if the IV _____ (26) changes in a DV. A _____ (27) group is used to compare the effects of a treatment with no treatment or a placebo. Although _____ (28) variables, which are variables that cannot be manipulated, such as gender or age, are usually a problem for researchers, they can be investigated in _____ (29) studies. Such studies can reveal that variables are related to one another, but do not tell us if one causes the other. When two variables are found to be correlated, there may be a _____ (30) variable that accounts for the relationship between the two. Although experimental studies are most useful for determining cause-effect relationships, other types of studies may be more practical or ethical. The best approach for studying the causes of behavior may use a combination of types.

Like many other scientists, biological psychologists are careful about the way they _____ (31) their research results. One reason is because of the _____ (32) of behavior and the nervous system, and another is because knowledge often undergoes _____ (33) over time. What is thought of as a "fact" today may be shown to be incorrect in the future. Many scientists use _____ (34) to explain observations and guide their research. They generate _____ (35), which are testable predictions derived from theories; they suggest how two or more variables should be related. If a hypothesis is found to be incorrect, then the theory must be revised. This is one way in which theories change over time.

Short Answer & Essay Questions

Answer the following questions. See pp. 18-19 for sample answers.

7. A new drug is developed to treat depression. The company that manufactures the drug wants to find out if it is more effective than current drug treatments. Describe how they might do a study to test this, and be sure to describe the types of groups that would be needed. What measure could they take to ensure that any differences in outcome were due to the different treatments and not because of differences between people in the groups?

8. If experimental studies are the only ones that allow us to determine cause-effect relationships, why are other studies used at all? What are the limitations of experimental studies?

9. Why do researchers avoid using words like "truth" and "proof" when they discuss the results of their work?

10. Discuss how the dopamine theory of schizophrenia has evolved. What observations led to the dopamine theory? How was it tested? What were the results of these tests? What is the current status of the theory?

Nature and Nurture

Summary and Guided Review

After studying this section in the text, fill in the blanks of the following summary. The answers are found on pp. 17-18.

Evidence is accumulating that many behaviors have a genetic or _____ (36) component, although this does not mean that behaviors are influenced by genes alone. Genes are located in all human cells. Genes are located on _____ (37), which are paired. The sex of an individual is determined by the sex chromosomes: females are ___ ___(38), and males are ___ ___(39). Most body cells have _____ (40), but _____ (41) and egg cells have 23. When conception occurs, the fertilized egg, or _____ (42), contains half of each parent's genetic material. For the first 8 weeks following conception, the developing baby is considered an _____ (43), and then it is a _____ (44) until it is born.

Genes are composed of a double strand of molecules known as _____ _____ (45) (DNA). The strands are connected by pairs of base molecules (adenine, _____ (46), guanine, and _____ (47)) that carry instructions for producing _____ (48). Only ___ % (49) of humans' genes are believed to differ between individuals. Genes that are paired may be in different forms, and one form may be _____ (50) over the other. In order for a _____ (51) gene to be expressed, there must be two copies of it. Individuals who possess two copies of a dominant gene (homozygous) will have the same _____ (52) as those who possess one dominant and one recessive gene (_____ (53)). If a recessive gene is located on the X chromosome, the trait it influences is more likely to be seen in _____ (54); red-green color blindness is an example of an ___ - _____ (55) trait.

Not all traits follow the pattern of dominance seen with eye color. For example, _____ _____ (56) is a trait in which genes may blend their effects. Furthermore, traits such as height and intelligence are _____ (57), meaning they are influenced by more than one gene. The effects of genes on complex traits such as behavior are complicated. Because genes are only responsible for the production of proteins, they influence behavior indirectly, for example through the structure and function of the _____ _____ (58).

The heredity of behavior in humans may be studied through _____ (59) studies, such as family, adoption, and _____ (60) studies. By comparing the behaviors of related individuals, researchers can determine the extent to which heredity influences traits between related individuals. For example, family studies have revealed that between parents and their children there is a _____ (61) of about .42 in the IQ scores, and a _____ (62) rate of about 13% for schizophrenia in the offspring of schizophrenic parents. However, _____ (63) studies reveal a correlation of IQ scores of .22, indicating that some of the similarity between parents and children stems from the environment. One of the best ways of examining the influence of heredity on behavior in humans is through twin studies. Because _____ (64) twins share the same genetic material, any differences between them must be due to environmental influences. Such studies reveal correlations of IQ scores to be around ___ (65), suggesting a strong genetic component to intelligence.

At present, the experimental manipulation of genes, or _____ _____ (66), is done mostly with non-human animals, particularly mice. One way of changing mice's genetic makeup is by inserting foreign DNA into mouse embryos and then breeding the offspring, thus creating

_____ (67) mice. _____ ____ (68) technology is used to alter a gene's activity by blocking the protein building activity of _____ (69) acid. Gene therapy is currently being tested for treatment of human disorders, including cancer and autoimmune diseases. In fact, three children with _____ - _____ (70) have been successfully treated using this technology.

Locating genes that influence traits is difficult and time-consuming. However, in 2001 several genetics laboratories published a rough draft of the human _____ (71), which will be useful in locating specific genes. Such knowledge may eventually lead to genetic-based treatment of many more disorders.

The notion that offspring are like clones of their parents is incorrect. Because of the 60-70 trillion possible _____ (72) of genes resulting from sexual reproduction, no two individuals are alike (unless they are identical twins!). This _____ (73) of traits is the cornerstone of Darwin's theory of natural selection, which states that organisms possessing traits that are most conducive to survival are more likely to pass their genes on to offspring. _____ (74) are quite flexible in their operation. They are not all active at the same time. They may produce more proteins at some times than at others. They may become active under certain _____ (75) conditions, such as when an organism is learning. Clearly genes are not the sole dictators of behavior.

Monozygotic and _____ (76) twins are used for calculating the percentage of variation in characteristics due to heredity, or _____ (77). It appears that heritability for height and _____ (78) is higher than that for intelligence. Personality characteristics show a heritability of _____ - _____% (79). If half of the variation in behaviors is due to genetics, then the other half must be due to _____ (80). However, it is important to understand that the more similarity there is between people's environment, the _____ (81) the degree of heritability. The _____ (82) model of schizophrenia demonstrates the importance of the environment, even for traits that are highly heritable. Genes result in a predisposition for schizophrenia, but the disorder will emerge only under certain _____ (83) conditions. Clearly both factors are important.

Short Answer & Essay Questions
Answer the following questions. See p. 19 for sample answers.

11. If brown eyes is a dominant trait, explain how a couple, both of whom have brown eyes, can have a child with blue eyes.

12. Distinguish between adoption and family studies. Why are adoption studies generally better for studying heredity of traits than family studies?

13. The concordance rate for autism is about .65 for MZ twins and about .08 for DZ twins. What can we conclude about the relative contributions of genes and environment to this disorder? How is this similar to the vulnerability model of schizophrenia?

14. Do geneticists have a clear picture of what the human genome looks like? Explain your answer.

15. Janet and Charles are expecting their first baby. They are both highly intelligent, and assume that their child will inherit their intelligence through the genes it shares with them. They feel that the environment has little or no impact on intelligence. After having read the section on the heredity of behavior, what would you tell this couple about the scientific evidence for their claim?

Research Ethics

Summary and Guided Review

After studying this section in the text, fill in the blanks of the following summary. The answers are found on p. 18.

Scientists must adhere to guidelines for ethical conduct. These guidelines cover many aspects of scientists' work, including publishing information, and using humans and animals in research. One type of ethical violation involves claiming someone else's ideas as one's own; this is known as _____ (84). A more serious violation, in which false or misleading data are published, is _____ (85). These types of violations are potentially damaging for the scientific community.

Scientists are also obligated to treat their human research participants with dignity and respect, and to obtain their _____ _____ (86) before participating in research. This means that participants are fully aware of any risks or potential risks involved in the research. Some behavioral studies, such as the one by Albert Ax described in the book, employ _____ (87), which involves withholding information or giving false information at the outset of a study. This type of research is acceptable only under certain circumstances.

Many of the recent advances in medicine would not have been possible without animal research. Animals are used as research subjects for a variety of reasons. Many procedures that are potentially dangerous to humans can be performed on animals. Animals' environments and genetic makeup can be controlled. Consequently, it is easier to subject them to _____ (88) procedures than humans. Most laboratory animals are _____ (89), with only about 3.5% being _____ (90). Animal rights _____ (91), people who work on behalf of the welfare of research animals, may cooperate with animal researchers to improve conditions for research animals, or they may damage or destroy labs and threaten to harm or actually harm the researchers themselves. Scientists who use animals in research are obligated to treat them _____ (92). They must be well cared for, and pain and suffering should be _____ (93). However, as the Silver _____ (94) case demonstrates, there are different ways of interpreting the rules regarding animal welfare. Overall, treatment of research animals seems to be improving, and many researchers are using alternative methods such as tissue _____ (95) and _____ (96) simulations.

Perhaps the most controversial area of medical research using humans is in _____ (97) research. Such research involves altering the genetic makeup or genetic activity of individuals in order to treat specific problems. As the result of a research participant's death in 1999, _____ (98) guidelines for such research are expected. There are other ethical concerns with this type of research as well, including its impact on successive generations of human beings.

The use of human _____ (99) has also been a controversial area of research. One procedure that has been somewhat successful involves transplanting the immature brain cells from aborted fetuses into the brains of people with _____ (100) disease. However, many people believe that it is morally wrong to use the cells of aborted fetuses in this way. Another line of research which shows great promise is the use of stem cells, which are _____ (101) cells with the potential for becoming any type of cell. In animals whose nervous systems were damaged, stem cells put into the _____ (102) and spinal cord have resulted in improvement in movement. Stem cell research in humans is also controversial because the most common source of them is from embryos, but they may also be taken from adult animals or generated from unfertilized _____ (103). This latter option appears to be the most ethically sound.

Short Answer & Essay Questions

Answer the following questions. See pp. 19-20 for sample answers.

16. Describe the study by Albert Ax. Why was this study ethically controversial? Would researchers be able to do this study now? Why or why not?

17. If medical research is done to benefit humans, why are animals used as research subjects?

18. What is speciesism?

19. In what way is current genetic research similar to the premise of the movie *GATTACA*?

20. What is the major ethical controversy of human stem-cell research?

Post-Test

Use these multiple choice questions to check your understanding of the chapter. The answers, along with explanations, are found beginning on p. 20.

1. Which of the following did NOT occur during the Decade of the Brain?
    a. Genes contributing to the development of Alzheimer's disease were identified.
    b. It was discovered that neurons conduct electricity.
    c. Drugs that block addiction were discovered.
    d. New treatments for depression were developed.

2. All scientists who study the nervous system are
    a. biopsychologists.
    b. physiologists.
    c. neuroscientists.
    d. neurologists.

3. Dr. Locke is a philosopher who believes that there is no distinction between the physical brain and the mind. This position is known as
    a. materialistic monism.
    b. idealistic monism.
    c. dualism.
    d. materialistic dualism.

4. Which of the following philosophers was/were dualist(s)? More than one answer may be correct.
    a. Aristotle
    b. Plato
    c. Democritus
    d. Descartes

5. Descartes believed that the "seat of the soul" was located in
    a. the frontal lobes of the brain.
    b. animal spirits.
    c. the pineal gland.
    d. the left hemisphere.

6. Through their experiments, Fritsch and Hitzig showed that
    a. the muscle in a frog's leg can be made to move by stimulating the nerve connected to it.
    b. the rate of nerve conduction is about 90 feet per second.
    c. the left hemisphere controls speech.
    d. muscle movement is the result of brain stimulation.

7. Who discovered that nerves conduct electricity at a rate significantly slower than the speed of light?
    a. Hermann von Helmholtz
    b. Rene Descartes
    c. Luigi Galvani
    d. Phineas Gage

8. Broca's mute patient had damage to his
    a. pineal gland.
    b. frontal lobes.
    c. left hemisphere.
    d. motor cortex.

9. A detailed study of a single person showing interesting behavior is called a(n)
    a. case study.
    b. experiment.
    c. survey.
    d. correlational study.

10. A study which allows researchers to determine if a cause-effect relationship exists between two variables is a(n)
    a. correlational study.
    b. experiment.
    c. naturalistic observational study.
    d. none of the above.

11. Dr. Hagen performs a study in which participants are given different amounts of alcohol, and then are tested on a driving simulation. In this study, alcohol is the
    a. dependent variable.
    b. correlational variable.
    c. confounded variable.
    d. independent variable.

12. The scores of female and male college students on a variety of verbal and mathematical tests are compared. This describes a(n)
    a. experiment.
    b. independent variable.
    c. correlational study.
    d. none of the above.

13. Which of the following statements is a biological psychologist LEAST likely to make?
    a. These results suggest that people who drink heavily may suffer from memory loss.
    b. These results show that some people who drink heavily will suffer from memory loss.
    c. These results prove that heavy drinking results in memory loss.
    d. From these results, it appears that memory loss may be a result of heavy drinking.

14. The dopamine theory of schizophrenia
    a. suggests that the disorder is a result of over activity of dopamine in the brain.
    b. was developed after some researchers noticed drug users showing signs of schizophrenia.
    c. does not account for all cases of schizophrenia.
    d. all of the above.

15. With the exception of egg and sperm cells, all human body cells have
    a. 23 chromosomes.
    b. 46 chromosomes.
    c. 23 genes.
    d. 46 genes.

16. Females have
    a.   two X chromosomes.
    b.   two Y chromosomes.
    c.   one X and one Y chromosome.
    d.   one X chromosome.

17. At six weeks after conception, a developing human is known as a(n)
    a.   zygote.
    b.   ova.
    c.   embryo.
    d.   fetus.

18. How many different bases make up DNA?
    a.   20
    b.   10
    c.   5
    d.   4

19. Enzymes
    a.   are proteins.
    b.   are produced as a result of genetic mechanisms.
    c.   modify chemical reactions in the body.
    d.   all of the above.

20. Sharon and John both have blue eyes. What color will their children's eyes be?
    a.   All brown
    b.   Some brown, some blue
    c.   All blue
    d.   Not enough information is given to answer the question

21. Which of the following is FALSE regarding red-green color blindness?
    a.   It is an X-linked trait.
    b.   A female cannot be red-green color blind.
    c.   Males are more likely to have it.
    d.   It is a recessive trait.

22. George is heterozygous for brown eyes, and his son Jason is homozygous for brown eyes. Which of the following statements is true?
    a.   George and Jason have the same phenotype, but different genotypes.
    b.   George and Jason have the same phenotype and the same genotype.
    c.   George and Jason have different phenotypes, but the same genotype.
    d.   George and Jason have different phenotypes and different genotypes.

23. A trait is polygenic if
    a.   it is influenced by a gene on the X chromosome.
    b.   it is influenced by a gene on the Y chromosome.
    c.   it is influenced by more than one gene.
    d.   it is influenced only by a single gene.

24. The effects of heredity and environment on behavior are MOST confounded in
    a. family studies.
    b. adoption studies.
    c. twin studies.
    d. genetic engineering studies.

25. A correlation of -.75 indicates
    a. a weak relationship between two variables.
    b. a strong relationship between two variables.
    c. no relationship between two variables.
    d. a mistake; correlations cannot be negative.

26. When researchers look at the IQ scores of children raised by adoptive parents, there is a correlation of about _____ with the IQ scores of their biological parents.
    a. .42
    b. .47
    c. .60
    d. .22

27. Compared to monozygotic twins, dizygotic twins show _____ concordance rate for schizophrenia.
    a. a higher
    b. a lower
    c. the same
    d. no

28. The _____ technique of genetic engineering involves preventing or reducing the expression of a particular gene by occupying the cell's ribonucleic acid with a synthetic strand of DNA.
    a. antisense DNA
    b. transgenic
    c. antisense RNA
    d. knockout

29. People with SCID-XI
    a. may die if exposed to cold viruses.
    b. suffer from severe mental disorders.
    c. may be aided by genetic engineering.
    d. a and c.

30. Which of the following is TRUE of the human genome?
    a. It has been completely mapped.
    b. Most of our DNA is directly involved in coding for proteins.
    c. The specific locations of genes are not all known.
    d. There are about 80,000 genes.

31. Which of the following is NOT true of gene activity?
    a. Once a gene becomes inactive, it remains inactive.
    b. Genes may fluctuate in the amount of protein they code for at different times.
    c. A gene may become active at only a certain time of the life cycle.
    d. The activity of a gene may be influenced by environmental events.

32. Which of the following traits has the highest degree of heritability?
    a. Intelligence
    b. Schizophrenia
    c. Height
    d. Alzheimer's disease

33. If the environment is kept constant, then heritability of a trait
    a. will be low.
    b. will be high.
    c. will be negligible.
    d. will be impossible to determine.

34. Jennifer is a graduate student studying the effects of electrical stimulation on the cingulate gyrus in rat's brains. Her initial results are not what she expected, and because she is worried about finishing her dissertation on time, she changes some of her data so that it fits her hypothesis. Jennifer has engaged in
    a. plagiarism.
    b. deception.
    c. fabrication.
    d. breaking the law.

35. Researchers who use humans as participants
    a. are barred from intentionally deceiving them.
    b. may withhold information from them, but cannot lie to them.
    c. must fully inform them about all details of a procedure beforehand.
    d. cannot withhold information about risks or discomfort that might occur.

36. What percent of laboratory animals are primates?
    a. More than 90%
    b. About 50%
    c. Between 10 and 15%
    d. Fewer than 5%

37. Regarding animal research guidelines, which of the following is FALSE?
    a. Procedures involving pain may not be performed on primates.
    b. Stress should be minimized.
    c. Procedures must be approved by an Institutional Animal Care and Use Committee.
    d. Researchers must provide humane housing and medical care.

38. The researcher Edward Taub, whose laboratory at Silver Springs, Maryland, made national headlines in the 1980s,
    a. is currently serving a prison sentence for animal abuse.
    b. received an award from the American Psychological Society.
    c. was able to complete his research after his grant was reinstated by the National Institutes of Health.
    d. none of the above.

39. Which of the following statements regarding gene therapy research is true?
    a. No human has died from gene therapy research.
    b. Some humans have been treated for diseases using gene therapy research.
    c. Gene therapy research with humans is illegal in the United States.
    d. Genetic "superhumans" have been created.

40. In Sweden, Parkinson's patients implanted with fetal brain cells
    a. show about a 50% reduction of symptoms.
    b. usually die from the procedure.
    c. reject all of the implanted cells.
    d. are completely cured.

41. Which of the following statements regarding stem cells is FALSE?
    a. They may be obtained from embryos.
    b. They may be obtained from adult cells.
    c. They have been used to grow human organs for transplant.
    d. They have the potential to become any kind of body cell.

Answers and Explanations

Guided Review

1. Decade of the Brain
2. inter- or multi-disciplinary
3. behavior
4. biological
5. mind-brain
6. materialistic monism
7. dualism
8. Aristotle
9. Plato
10. Descartes
11. hydraulic
12. pineal
13. animal spirits
14. electricity
15. Helmholtz
16. hearing
17. localization
18. frontal
19. Broca
20. material monists
21. empiricism
22. objective
23. case study
24. independent variable
25. dependent variables
26. causes
27. control
28. confounded
29. correlational
30. third
31. interpret
32. complexity
33. change
34. theories
35. hypotheses
36. heritable
37. chromosomes
38. XX
39. XY
40. 46
41. sperm
42. zygote
43. embryo
44. fetus
45. deoxyribo-nucleic acid
46. thymine
47. cytosine
48. proteins
49. 0.1%
50. dominant
51. recessive
52. phenotype
53. heterozygous
54. males
55. X-linked
56. blood type
57. polygenic
58. nervous system
59. correlational
60. twin
61. correlation
62. concordance
63. adoption
64. monozygotic
65. .86
66. genetic engineering
67. transgenic
68. Antisense RNA
69. ribonucleic
70. SCID-X1
71. genome
72. combinations
73. variability
74. Genes
75. environmental
76. dizygotic
77. heritability

78. schizophrenia
79. 40-50
80. environment
81. greater
82. vulnerability
83. environmental
84. plagiarism
85. fabrication

86. informed consent
87. deception
88. experimental
89. rodents
90. primates
91. activists
92. humanely
93. minimized
94. Springs

95. cultures
96. computer
97. genetic
98. stricter
99. embryos
100. Parkinson's
101. undifferentiated
102. brain
103. ova

Short Answer & Essay Questions

1. There are lots of possible answers, but all must mention that biological psychologists look for a connection between the nervous system and a specific behavior or set of behaviors.

2. The mind is really a term used to describe different functions of the brain, including consciousness, emotions, learning, etc. The mind has no physical make-up. It is analogous to the concept of weather. Rain, sunshine, and snow are all physical features of the environment, but they are referred to as weather.

3. Monism assumes that the mind and brain are composed of the same thing or substance. Most monists are materialistic, meaning that they believe everything, including the mind, is physical, and therefore has no separate existence. Dualists, however, believe that while the brain is physical, the mind is also real, although not material, and exists separately from the brain. The problem with dualism is that it cannot explain how something non-physical (the mind) can affect something physical (the body). The problem with monism is explaining how the brain causes subjective, mental experience.

4. Galvani used electricity to stimulate a nerve, causing a frog's leg muscle to twitch. Fritsch and Hitzig caused movement in dogs by electrically stimulating the brain. Because these behaviors looked like the behaviors that the animals would spontaneously emit, it was concluded that electricity was responsible for the operation of nerves.

5. It was important because it showed that damage to a particular part of the brain resulted in disruption of some types of functions, but not others. Following his accident, Gage was still able to speak and move normally, and showed no change in memory or intelligence, but his personality changed and he became impulsive and hard to deal with. This suggested that the part of the brain damaged by his injury was involved in some types of behaviors, but not in others.

6. Most modern neuroscientists are materialistic monists. They believe that the mind is not a real entity, but rather a concept we use to describe what our brains are doing. Therefore, the mind really is the brain.

7. They would need at least two groups, one receiving the new drug and one receiving an established drug. They could include several groups, depending on how many drugs they want to test the new one against. They should also employ a placebo group, one that receives no drug therapy. They should also try to find ways of matching participants in groups; for example the groups should be similar in terms of sex, age, and extent of depression.

8. There are many types of questions that cannot be answered using experimental procedures. Researchers are bound by ethical and legal rules that forbid the use of humans for many types of potentially interesting studies. Also, there are many variables that researchers are unable to manipulate, such as age, sex, and other factors that are inherent to individuals.

9. Knowledge, or what we think we know to be true, changes. Many ideas which are currently accepted as fact may someday be shown to be incorrect. Therefore, scientists are usually careful about drawing such conclusions from their research. They prefer to be tentative about their conclusions.

10. The theory was first developed when some researchers noticed that people using certain drugs that increase dopamine activity in the brain showed symptoms of schizophrenia (but these symptoms disappeared when the drugs wore off). It was suggested that schizophrenia is caused by excess dopamine. One hypothesis used to test this theory was that schizophrenics should improve when given drugs that decrease dopamine activity. However, not all schizophrenics show this expected result, and therefore the dopamine theory is recognized as being an incomplete explanation of schizophrenia.

11. If both parents are heterozygous, that is they both have one dominant and one recessive gene, then it is likely that about 25% of their children will have blue eyes, because approximately 25% of their children will inherit the recessive gene from each parent.

12. The difference between adoption and family studies is that adoption studies look at children raised in homes by adoptive parents, whereas family studies look at children in intact families. Family studies are inherently confounded because not only do individuals share genes, they also share environment. Therefore, any similarities between them may be due to either, or more likely both, factors.

13. It is highly heritable. The fact that there is such a large difference in concordance rates between the two types of twins, with a very low concordance among the DZ twins, suggests that genetic influences are very important in the development of this disorder. However, the fact that the concordance rate is not perfect (1.0) among MZ twins also suggests that environmental influences play a role. In other words, if the environment did not contribute to autism, then the concordance rate would be 1.0. This suggests that, just as in schizophrenia, an individual inherits a predisposition for a disorder. Whether or not the disorder develops depends on the environment.

14. What they have is a "rough draft" of the genome. They know roughly what the sequence of DNA on the different chromosomes is, but there are gaps. Also, it is difficult to tell just how much DNA makes up a particular gene. Furthermore, most of the DNA in our cells does not apparently contribute to protein synthesis. Finally, although many genes have been identified, researchers don't know what their protein products are for.

15. The evidence suggests that genes and environment are both important. Identical twins tend to have very similar, but not perfectly similar IQs. The environmental differences between them account for the differences in intelligence. Additionally, the IQ scores of children raised by adoptive parents are less strongly correlated with their birth parents' IQ scores than children raised by their biological parents. This suggests that some degree of the similarity between parents and children is due to being in a similar environment.

16. Albert Ax studied the physiological changes accompanying emotions. One part of Ax's experimental set-up involved convincing some of his participants that they were in physical danger (which they weren't) in order to induce fear. Many of the participants indeed seemed very afraid during the procedure, and one must question whether it was ethical to do this. Although they were in no real danger, they did not know this at the time. There are two major reasons why this was ethically

19

questionable. First of all, human research participants should be able to give their informed consent before participating in a research project. This means that they are informed ahead of time of any risks inherent in the procedure, and that with this knowledge they voluntarily agree to participate. The second, related, problem is that the participants were deceived. Deception is now allowed in research, but only when the potential benefits of the study outweigh the costs of using it. At the time of the study, standards for deception and informed consent did not exist. It is not likely that such a study would be conducted now, since it involved such an extreme manipulation of fear.

17. There are many procedures that would be unethical to perform on humans. For this reason, procedures that may eventually be used on humans are tested first on animals. Also, the laboratory animal's environment may be controlled, so it is easier to perform experimental manipulations on animals (because many potentially confounding variables can be eliminated).

18. It is the assumption that animals have fewer rights than humans.

19. The movie *GATTACA* was about a society in which superior genetically engineered individuals were more privileged than others. Although the movie was science fiction, some people in our society are concerned that genetic engineering of humans could lead to something similar to this, particularly if the rich and powerful are allowed to use genetic engineering to select the most beneficial traits for their offspring.

20. The primary reason why the use of human stem cells in research is controversial is because most of them come from embryos that have been discarded from fertility clinics.

Post-Test

All page references in this section pertain to the textbook.

1. a. Wrong
    b . Correct; Galvani in the 18th century and Fritsch and Hitzig in the 19th century did work that showed that nerves operate by electricity; all of the other choices describe events that occurred during the 1990s, the Decade of the Brain.
    c. Wrong
    d. Wrong

2. a. Wrong; this is a branch of psychology that involves the study of the brain. Not all brain researchers are psychologists.
    b. Wrong; this is a branch of the biological sciences.
    c. Correct; this term is applied to anyone who studies the brain, regardless of academic discipline.
    d. Wrong; this is a medical doctor who specializes in the nervous system.

3. **a. Correct**; anyone who believes that the brain and mind are physically the same thing is a materialistic monist.
    b. Wrong; while idealistic monists believe that there is no distinction between the mind and brain, they argue that everything is actually nonmaterial.
    c. Wrong; dualists believe that the mind and the brain are separate, although they may interact.
    d. Wrong; there is no position called materialistic dualism.

4. a. Wrong; Aristotle was a monist.
   b. Correct
   c. Wrong; Democritus was a monist.
   d. Correct

5. a. Wrong
   b. Wrong; this was the fluid that filled the brain, which Descartes believed was responsible for operation of the nerves and muscles.
   c. Correct; this was the part of the brain that Descartes believed was responsible for controlling the rest of the body.
   d. Wrong

6. a. Wrong; Galvani did this work.
   b. Wrong; Helmholtz did this work.
   c. Wrong; Broca did this work.
   d. Correct

7. **a. Correct**
   b. Wrong; Descartes was unaware that nerves operate via electricity. He thought they were hollow tubes filled with "animal spirits."
   c. Wrong; Galvani was one of the first scientists to show that nerves work via electricity by stimulating a frog's leg, but he did not actually measure the speed of conduction.
   d. Wrong; this was a man whose personality changed radically after a brain injury.

8. a. Wrong
   b. Wrong; this is the part of the brain that was damaged in Phineas Gage's case.
   c. Correct; there was apparently no damage to any of the other parts of the brain.
   d. Wrong

9. **a. Correct**
   b. Wrong; an experiment involves several participants, and also involves direct manipulation of some variable of interest.
   c. Wrong; a survey is usually given to several people.
   d. Wrong; a correlational study involves making comparisons of people who differ by a variable such as age or sex on other measures such as intelligence.

10. a. Wrong; correlational studies can reveal if relationships between variables exist, but not the nature of the relationship.
    b. Correct; in order to determine if a causal relationship exists between variables, researchers must be able to manipulate the suspected causal variable (IV). This is the only procedure that involves manipulation of variables.
    c. Wrong; naturalistic observation by itself involves no manipulation.
    d. Wrong

11. a. Wrong; the dependent variable is the variable that is measured to see if the independent variable has any effect on it.
    b. Wrong
    c. Wrong; this is a variable that the researcher cannot control which may effect another variable.
    d. Correct; the IV is the variable manipulated by the researcher.

12. a.   Wrong; no IV exists in this study. There is no manipulation of variables.
    b.   Wrong; no manipulation.
    c.   **Correct**; because no manipulation is done, but groups are compared on some measure, this is a correlational study.
    d.   Wrong

13. a.   Wrong
    b.   Wrong
    c.   **Correct**; scientists rarely say that they have proven anything. Scientists are careful not to overinterpret their results. A scientist may make such a statement only if all other possibilities have been exhausted.
    d.   Wrong

14. a.   Wrong
    b.   Wrong.
    c.   Wrong
    d.   **Correct**; choices a-c are true of the dopamine hypothesis.

15. a.   Wrong; there are 23 pairs of chromosomes in body cells, and 23 chromosomes in sex cells.
    b.   Correct
    c.   Wrong; each chromosome contains many genes.
    d.   Wrong

16. **a.   Correct**; females receive an X chromosome from each parent.
    b.   Wrong; because females are XX, they can only pass on an X to their children of either sex.
    c.   Wrong; males receive an X from the mother and a Y chromosome from the father.
    d.   Wrong; this doesn't usually happen (when it does, it is called Turner's syndrome).

17. a.   Wrong; this is what the fertilized egg is called.
    b.   Wrong; this is an unfertilized egg cell.
    c.   **Correct**; once the organism begins dividing, until 8 weeks after conception, it is considered to be an embryo.
    d.   Wrong; the organism is only considered to be a fetus after 8 weeks post-conception.

18. a.   Wrong
    b.   Wrong
    c.   Wrong
    d.   **Correct**; all DNA is composed of adenine, thymine, guanine, and cytosine.

19. a.   Wrong
    b.   Wrong
    c.   Wrong
    d.   **Correct**; choices a-c are true of enzymes.

20. a.   Wrong; none of their children will have brown eyes.
    b.   Wrong
    c.   **Correct**; because the only way each of them could have blue eyes is if each has two copies of the recessive gene, then that is the only form of the gene that they can pass on. All of their children will have two copies of the recessive gene as well.
    d.   Wrong; if you understand the principle of dominance and recessive inheritance, you can answer the question.

21. a. Wrong
    b. **Correct**; although they are more rare than males who have this form of color-blindness, females can inherit it (they need two copies of the recessive gene, one from each parent, whereas males only need one copy). All of the other choices are true.
    c. Wrong
    d. Wrong

22. **a.** **Correct**; the genotype refers to the actual genes an individual possesses, whereas the phenotype refers to the trait expressed. The two have the same trait (brown eyes) but different genes.
    b. Wrong
    c. Wrong
    d. Wrong

23. a. Wrong; while some polygenic traits may be influenced by genes on the X chromosome, there are many that are not.
    b. Wrong; while some polygenic traits may be influenced by genes on the Y chromosome, there are many that are not.
    c. **Correct**; by definition, a polygenic trait is influenced by several genes (*poly* means "many").
    d. Wrong

24. **a.** **Correct**; because family studies look at individuals who are biologically related and living in the same household, the effects of genes and environment are commingled and cannot be separated.
    b. Wrong; adoption studies look at individuals living in the same household who are not related, so it is easier to identify the extent of genetic influence. However, because many adoptive households are of the same type (mostly middle class), environment may be somewhat confounded with heredity.
    c. Wrong; if we look at identical twins, because they have the same genetic makeup, any differences between them must be due to the environment.
    d. Wrong; these studies are typically done under tightly controlled experimental conditions in non-human animals.

25. a. Wrong; the negative sign simply indicates that an inverse correlation exists.
    b. **Correct**; if a perfect correlation is 1.0 or -1.0, and no correlation is 0, then -.75 is quite strong.
    c. Wrong
    d. Wrong

26. a. Wrong; this is the correlation between parents and children in family studies.
    b. Wrong; this is the correlation between siblings in family studies.
    c. Wrong; this is the correlation between dizygotic twins.
    d. **Correct**; see p. 12.

27. a. Wrong
    b. **Correct**; the concordance rate of schizophrenia for monozygotic twins is 48%, and 17% for dizygotic twins.
    c. Wrong
    d. Wrong

28. a. Wrong; refer to c below.
   b. Wrong; this technique refers to introducing new genes into an organism.
   c. Correct; the technique involves "tying up" the RNA by providing cells with synthetic DNA. The DNA is not actually incorporated into the organism's genome.
   d. Wrong; this technique involves introducing genetic material that will disrupt the function of existing genes.

29. a. Wrong; c is also correct.
   b. Wrong; there is no mention of mental disorders associated with this disorder.
   c. Wrong; a is also correct.
   d. Correct; this is a disorder of the immune system that is potential fatal, and there have been cases of it being treated successfully in humans.

30. a. Wrong; there are gaps in the "map." It is more of a "working draft" than a "final draft."
   b. Wrong; about 98% of our DNA does NOT appear to be directly involved in protein synthesis.
   c. Correct; although the basic sequence of DNA has been worked out, researchers still have not identified all of the genes within that sequence. It is not clear where a sequence of DNA that corresponds to a functional gene begins and ends.
   d. Wrong; researchers estimate 26,000 – 40,000 genes.

31. **a. Correct**; this statement is false. Genes may "turn" on and off several times. All of the other choices are true.
   b. Wrong
   c. Wrong
   d. Wrong

32. a. Wrong; its heritability is estimated around 50%.
   b. Wrong; its heritability is estimated around 60-70%.
   c. Correct; its heritability is estimated around 90%.
   d. Wrong; its heritability is less than 60% (Figure 1.12 indicates a concordance rate of about .6 for MZ and .3 for DZ twins).

33. a. Wrong
   b. Correct; if animals that are reared and maintained in the same environment differ, those differences must be due to their genetic makeup.
   c. Wrong
   d. Wrong; variation can be mathematically represented by genetic and environmental influences. If the environment is the same, then any variation observed must be due to genetic differences.

34. a. Wrong; plagiarism involves passing off someone else's work or ideas as one's own.
   b. Wrong; while in the general sense she has engaged in deception, this term more accurately refers to misleading or withholding information from research participants.
   c. Correct; see p. 19.
   d. Wrong; what she has done is not necessarily illegal, but it is unethical.

35. a.   Wrong; deception may be used if it is adequately justified.
b.   Wrong; both forms of deception may be used.
c.   Wrong; when using deception, details must obviously be omitted, as long as the deception poses no threat. However, participants should be debriefed following the procedure about the deception and why it was used.
d.   Correct; in order for a person to give their informed consent to participate in research, they must be made aware of any potential risks. If a deception might pose risk to the participants, then it should not be done.

36. a.   Wrong
b.   Wrong
c.   Wrong
d.   Correct; the book states that 3.5% of laboratory animals are primates.

37. **a.   Correct**; this statement is false. As long as they are justified, painful procedures are allowed. All of the other choices are true.
b.   Wrong
c.   Wrong
d.   Wrong

38. a.   Wrong; while he was convicted of animal abuse, there was no mention of whether or not he served jail time, and furthermore his conviction was overturned.
b.   Correct; he received the William James Award.
c.   Wrong; NIH revoked his funding, and new rules bar him from performing his procedure on the surviving monkeys.
d.   Wrong

39. a.   Wrong; an 18-year old died in 1999 while undergoing treatment for liver enzyme deficiency.
b.   Correct; for example, the book mentions the three children treated successfully for SCID-X1.
c.   Wrong; there are currently several experimental treatment programs operating.
d.   Wrong; the technology for this does not yet exist.

40. **a.   Correct**; see p. 23.
b.   Wrong; there is no mention of mortality.
c.   Wrong; although most of the cells are rejected, a few do survive (about 5-10%).
d.   Wrong; this is not stated in the book.

41. a.   Wrong; stem cells can be retrieved from embryos.
b.   Wrong; there is a relatively new procedure that allows stem cells to be grown from adult cells.
c.   Correct; while this is something that may happen in the future, it has not been done yet.
d.   Wrong; this is true of stem cells.

Chapter 2: Communication within the Nervous System

Chapter Outline and Learning Objectives

As you read the chapter, use these learning objectives to guide your studying. You should be able to define the key terms from the text, which are shown in boldface type below.

1) The Cells That Make Us Who We Are
   a) Neurons
      - What are **neurons**, and what are their major functions?

      i) Basic Structure: The Motor Neuron
         - Be able to locate and describe the functions of the following parts of a neuron: **soma**, **dendrites**, **axon**, **terminals**, and **synapse**.

         - Describe neurons in terms of their size (diameter and length).

      ii) Other Types of Neurons
         - Distinguish between **motor neurons**, **sensory neurons**, **interneurons**, and **projection neurons**.

      iii) The Neural Membrane
         - Describe the structure and function of the **neural membrane**.

         - What is the significance of selective permeability of the neural membrane?

         (1) The Resting Potential
         - Describe the distribution of **ions** inside and outside of the neuron, and explain how these contribute to the **resting potential**.

         - Distinguish between **concentration gradient** and **electrical gradient**.

         - What is the **sodium-potassium pump**, and what is its role in maintaining the resting potential?

         (2) The Action Potential
         - Describe the ionic (chemical and electrical) changes that produce an **action potential**.

- What electrochemical events occur on the neural membrane following an action potential? How is the resting potential restored?

- Explain how an action potential is transmitted down the length of an axon.

- Compare action potentials and **graded potentials**. What is the **all-or-none law**?

- What are **neurotoxins**, and how may their functions be useful in designing new drugs?

    iv) Refractory Periods
- What is the **absolute refractory period**? What effects does it have on neuron cellular function?

- What is the **relative refractory period**? What role does it play in **intensity coding**?

b) Glial Cells
- What is the relationship between an axon's diameter and the rate at which it can transmit action potentials?

    i) Myelination and Conduction Speed
- What is **myelin**? Why do myelinated neurons transmit impulses more quickly than unmyelinated neurons?

- Explain the function of the **nodes of Ranvier** in **saltatory conduction**.

- What happens when myelin is destroyed (which occurs in the disease **multiple sclerosis**)?

    ii) Other Glial Functions
- What other functions do **glial** cells perform?

2) How Neurons Communicate with Each Other
- What is the **synaptic cleft**, and how was it discovered?

a) Chemical Transmission at the Synapse
- How did Otto Loewi discover that neurons use chemicals to communicate?

- Describe the events that occur in the **presynaptic** and **postsynaptic** neurons once an action potential arrives at the synapse.

i) Excitation and Inhibition
- Distinguish between **hypopolarization** and **hyperpolarization**.

- Why is inhibition of neurons important?

- Distinguish between **excitatory postsynaptic potential** and **inhibitory postsynaptic potential**. What ions are involved in each? How do they affect the firing rate of the neuron?

- How does the stimulant drug Ritalin demonstrate the complexity of neural excitation and inhibition?

ii) Postsynaptic Integration
- Distinguish between **spatial summation** and **temporal summation**.

- Explain how summation accounts for changes in firing rates in a neuron.

- Why is a neuron considered to be an **integrator** and a **decision maker**?

iii) Terminating Synaptic Activity
- Describe how synaptic transmitters are inactivated. Why is it important for this to occur?

b) Synaptic Modulation
- Explain how **presynaptic excitation** and **presynaptic inhibition** occur.

- How is synaptic functioning affected by **autoreceptors**, glial cells, and **postsynaptic receptors**?

c) Neurotransmitters
- How do **nicotinic** and **muscarinic** acetylcholine receptors differ?

- What is **Dale's principle**? What is now known about neurotransmitter release that shows this principle to be incorrect?

- What is the significance of a single neuron releasing both excitatory and inhibitory neurotransmitters?

- Distinguish between **agonists** and **antagonists**, and discuss drugs that have these effects.

d) Computer Models of Neural Processing
- Distinguish between **serial** and **parallel processing**.

- Describe an **artificial neural network**. How do such networks "learn?"

- How are artificial neural networks similar to brains?

- What are the uses of artificial neural networks?

The Cells that Make Us Who We Are

Summary and Guided Review

After studying this section in the text, fill in the blanks of the following summary. The answers are found on p. 40.

The human brain consists of about 100 million _____ (1), cells that carry messages and underlie our thoughts, feelings, and behaviors. It also contains many more _____ (2) cells, which have a variety of functions.

Neurons exist in many different forms, but they all share common structures and functions. The _____ (3), or cell body, is where the cell's DNA is located, and where most metabolic functions occur. Branching out from the cell body are _____ (4), structures that receive _____ (5) from other cells. A single tail-like structure called the _____ (6) extends away from the cell body and carries messages to other neurons. Many axons are insulated by _____ (7), which speeds neural conduction. The axon _____ (8) contain neurotransmitters, chemicals that are used for _____ (9) with other cells. Neurons are not physically connected to one another, but rather transfer information across a _____ (10). Each neuron receives signals from and sends signals to several other neurons, so that the connections in the nervous system are quite complex.

29

_____ (11) neurons carry information to muscle and gland tissue, whereas _____ (12) neurons are stimulated by environmental events and transmit information about those events to the _____ (13) nervous system. Neurons with short or no axons that transmit information between adjacent neurons are called _____ (14), and they are the most abundant type. _____ (15) neurons also transmit information between other neurons, but they do so over longer distances.

The membrane of a neuron is composed of two layers of _____ (16), or fat molecules, and _____ (17). Fluid is found both inside and outside the cell. Because the membrane is selectively _____ (18), it controls what gets into and out of the cell. Some molecules, such as oxygen, can pass through the membrane, while others are prevented from getting in. The _____ _____ (19) in the membrane control the passage of other substances.

Because ions are distributed in different concentrations on each side of the membrane, the membrane is _____ (20) (electrically charged). When the cell is at rest, the inside is _____ (21) charged relative to the outside. This is known as the _____ (22) potential, and it forms an electrical gradient. ____ (23) and Cl⁻ ions are more concentrated outside, and K⁺ ions and ____ (24) (protein anions) are more concentrated inside. Ions are attracted to the side of the membrane where their type is least abundant, forming a _____ (25) gradient. An electrical gradient is also formed, because ions are also attracted to the side of the membrane with the opposite charge (so positively charged ions are attracted to the _____ (26) of the cell). The _____ - _____ _____ (27) helps to maintain the balance of ions within and outside of the cell.

Na⁺ ions are attracted inside the cell by both the electrical and concentration _____ (28), but they are kept out because they cannot pass through the membrane. However, if the membrane is stimulated by an activating stimulus, then _____ _____ (29) within the membrane will open, allowing Na⁺ into the cell. This results in the cell becoming _____ (30), and the inside is less negative than before. If enough Na⁺ enters the cell, its polarity will reach threshold and the cell will generate an _____ _____ (31), during which Na⁺ ions enter so rapidly that the cell becomes suddenly _____ (32) charged at the site of the depolarization. Shortly after this, the sodium channels close, and _____ (33) channels open. The loss of K⁺ ions results in the resumption of the _____ _____ (34). All of this occurs in about one _____ (35). Once it occurs, an action potential spreads down an axon because it causes adjacent _____ _____ (36) to open and depolarize another portion of the membrane. The ions are restored to their "resting" locations by the sodium-potassium pump.

Depolarizations and action potentials are not identical. Whereas the initial depolarization is _____ (37), the action potential is not. Action potentials occur according to the ____ - ___ - _____ _____ (38), which means that a cell's action potentials are all of the same strength. Also, whereas

30

depolarizations are _____ (39), or lose strength, action potentials maintain their strength until they reach the axon terminal.

Immediately after an action potential occurs, the sodium channels are unable to open again and therefore the cell is unable to produce another action potential right away. This is known as the _____ _____ _____ (40), and it limits the frequency of action potentials. The cell is also subject to a relative refractory period, when the _____ (41) channels are still open and the inside is slightly more _____ (42) charged for a short time. In order for an action potential to occur at this time, the stimulus must be _____ (43) than normal. This accounts for the rate law: more intensive stimuli will produce more _____ (44) action potentials. Neurons with larger axons conduct action potentials more _____ (45) than those with smaller axons.

Glial cells are an important component of the nervous system. For example, the fatty substance _____ (46) also increases conduction speed. In the central nervous system, myelin is made up of _____ (47), while _____ (48) cells produce myelin outside the brain and spinal cord. Both of these are types of glial cells. Action potentials only occur at the gaps between myelin cells known as _____ ____ _____ (49), and the action potential jumps from one gap to the next rather than traveling down the entire length of the axon. This is known as _____ (50) conduction, and it is faster and more efficient than conduction in unmyelinated neurons. When myelin is destroyed, as in the disease _____ _____ (51), the neurons cease to function properly.

Glial cells, which are _____ (52) numerous than neurons, also perform a number of other important functions. They support and _____ (53) developing neurons. They support and keep mature neurons functioning properly. When deprived of glial cells, neurons lose their _____ (54).

Short Answer & Essay Questions

Answer the following questions. See pp. 40-41 for sample answers.

1. How are sensory and motor neurons different in terms of their functions and structure?

2. What does it mean that the neural cell membrane is selectively permeable? How do water, oxygen, and carbon dioxide molecules enter the cell? How do ions and other substances necessary for functioning enter the cell?

3. Of all the ions involved in neuronal depolarization, Na^+ are most strongly attracted across the membrane. Give TWO reasons for this.

4. When an axon is depolarized to threshold, it fires an action potential at the site of depolarization. How does that action potential spread to the rest of the axon? Why does that action potential spread in only one direction (toward the axon terminals)?

5. The intensity of a stimulus is coded or represented in the sensory neuron by the frequency with which action potentials are generated. For example, a more intense stimulus produces more action potentials per second than a less intense one, although the action potentials themselves are of the same strength. What role does the relative refractory period play in this effect?

6. Explain why action potentials are conducted more quickly, and more efficiently in terms of energy used, in myelinated cells than in unmyelinated cells.

How Neurons Communicate with Each Other

Summary and Guided Review

After studying this section in the text, fill in the blanks of the following summary. The answers are found on p. 40.

The fact that neurons are not physically attached to one another was discovered by _____ _____ (55) in the 19th century. In the 20th century, _____ _____ (56) showed that neurons communicate with one another chemically. He did this by first stimulating the vagus nerve of one frog heart, which resulted in the heart rate _____ (57). Then he collected the fluid from the first heart and administered it to another heart, which also _____ (58). These chemical transmitters are called _____ (59), and they are located in _____ (60), small sacs in the axon terminals. When an action potential reaches the axon terminal, _____ (61) ions enter the cell and cause the vesicles to fuse with the presynaptic cell membrane, dumping their contents into the synaptic cleft. The neurotransmitter molecules then attach to receptors on the _____ (62) membrane, causing changes in the polarity of this cell and changing its rate of firing by directly or indirectly opening _____ (63) ion channels. The postsynaptic cell can be either hyperpolarized (inhibited), or _____ (64) (excited) in the form of graded potentials. Both EPSPs and _____ (65) play an important role in the functioning of the nervous system.

Because a single cell is continuously receiving messages from many other cells, the effects of excitation and inhibition are quite complex. The incoming information is integrated in the postsynaptic neuron. When two or more postsynaptic potentials arrive simultaneously but at different parts of the cell, _____ (66) summation occurs. Because the effect of a graded potential takes a while to dissipate, when postsynaptic potentials arrive in close succession, _____ (67) summation can occur. A good way of thinking about the neuron is that it integrates incoming information from a variety of sources and then makes a _____ (68) about whether it will fire and at what rate.

Once it has attached to the postsynaptic receptor and had its effect on the postsynaptic cell, the _____ (69) is inactivated in some way. Often this is accomplished through _____ (70),

32

in which the presynaptic cell absorbs it. It may also be broken down by _____ (71), or absorbed by
_____ (72) cells. Drugs may affect behavior by interfering with these mechanisms in some way.

Synaptic transmission can be altered by the presence of _____ (73) synapses, which
affect the release of the neurotransmitter from the presynaptic neuron through presynaptic _____ (74)
or inhibition. Additionally, _____ (75) on the presynaptic axon terminal can monitor the amount
of neurotransmitter in the synapse and adjust the cell's release of it. Glial cells _____ (76) synaptic
activity as well. And postsynaptic _____ (77) may become more or less sensitive to presynaptic
input.

There are many different types of neurotransmitters, and each type may have different effects
through different receptor types. For example, at _____ (78) receptors, acetylcholine has an
excitatory effect, while at _____ (79) receptors it may have excitatory or inhibitory effects. A
single neuron can release more than one type of neurotransmitter at the same synapse. One of these may be
_____-_____ (80) and have an immediate effect on the postsynaptic cell while the others
enhance the effects of the first through more prolonged mechanisms. Some cells appear to release two fast-
acting transmitters at the same time, and some release both excitatory and inhibitory transmitters at
different _____ (81). This may allow for detection of movement of visual stimuli.

Many drugs affect neural functioning. Nicotine, for example is an _____ (82) of
acetylcholine, stimulating receptors for this transmitter. _____ (83), an acetylcholine antagonist, is
used by Amazonian Indians to paralyze animals.

Neural connections are highly complex, and it is difficult to understand how neural activity
contributes to behavior by examining only a _____-_____ _____ (84). Instead,
neuroscientists are turning to computer models to help them understand neural processing. However, such
models have been limited by the fact that computers are generally _____ _____ (85),
whereas humans are parallel processors. One type of model that employs parallel processing is the
_____ _____ _____ (86). This model includes "cells" responsible for
input and output, as well as one or more layers of _____ (87) cells where the actual processing
takes place. Through feedback about its performance, the network can gradually "learn" to approximate
output similar to human behavior. During learning, the hidden units change in terms of the _____ (88)
of their connections while output improves. Such models have been "taught" or programmed to do such
things as produce spoken English in response to text, and seem to mimic the way that humans and other
animals learn. They may also have practical applications in medicine and other technology.

Short Answer & Essay Questions

Answer the following questions. See p. 41 for sample answers.

7. Describe the experiment by Otto Loewi. How did he arrive at the conclusion that neurons communicate via chemical transmission?

8. What happens to a cell's polarity and firing rate when an IPSP occurs? Why does the firing rate change?

9. Why are models composed only of a single chain of neurons inadequate for understanding how the brain works? Give two reasons.

10. What does it mean when we say that information is "distributed" in an artificial neural network? What are the advantages of information being distributed rather than localized?

Post-Test

Use these multiple-choice questions to check your understanding of the chapter. The answers, along with explanations, are found beginning on p. 41.

1. Scientists estimate that there are about _____ neurons in the brain.
    a. 1 million
    b. 100 million
    c. 1 billion
    d. 100 billion

2. In the nervous system, which of the following types of cells is most numerous?
    a. Glia
    b. Motor neurons
    c. Sensory neurons
    d. Interneurons

3. Dendritic spines
    a. give structural support to dendrites as they develop.
    b. increase the number of synapses a neuron may have.
    c. are only found on interneurons.
    d. all of the above.

4. The nucleus of a neural cell is located in the
    a. axon.
    b. dendrites.
    c. soma.
    d. axon hillock.

5. A neuron that transmits information between the central nervous system and a muscle is called a(n)
   a. motor neuron.
   b. sensory neuron.
   c. interneuron.
   d. projection neuron.

6. A(n) _____ neuron has an axon and several dendrites projecting away from the cell body.
   a. bipolar
   b. multipolar
   c. unipolar
   d. monopolar

7. Which of the following statements regarding interneurons is TRUE?
   a. They receive input directly from the external environment.
   b. They send information across long distances.
   c. They may have no axon at all.
   d. They are found only in the brain.

8. The neural membrane is selectively permeable to all of the following substances EXCEPT
   a. sodium.
   b. potassium.
   c. oxygen.
   d. chloride.

9. When a neuron is at rest, _____ ions are more plentiful outside of the cell.
   a. Na^+
   b. K^+
   c. A^-
   d. All of the above

10. The **typical** resting potential of a neuron is
    a. −70 V.
    b. −35 mV.
    c. 70 mV.
    d. −70 mV.

11. When the cell is at rest, K^+ ions are strongly attracted across the cell membrane because of the
    a. electrical gradient.
    b. concentration gradient.
    c. both the electrical and concentration gradients.
    d. neither the electrical nor the concentration gradients.

12. All of the following are able to pass through the membrane under certain conditions except:
    a. Na^+
    b. Cl^-
    c. K^+
    d. A^-

13. Which of the following statements regarding the sodium-potassium pump is FALSE?
    a. It requires a lot of energy.
    b. It works against the concentration gradient.
    c. It pumps sodium into the cell.
    d. It helps maintain the resting potential.

14. Neurons undergo depolarization when
    a. K^+ enter the cell.
    b. Na^+ enter the cell.
    c. either K^+ or Na^+ enter the cell.
    d. Cl^- leave the cell.

15. Depolarization is MOST similar to
    a. hypopolarization.
    b. hyperpolarization.
    c. action potential.
    d. electrical gradient.

16. When the cell is at rest, Na^+ ions are strongly attracted across the cell membrane because of the
    a. electrical gradient.
    b. concentration gradient.
    c. both the electrical and concentration gradients.
    d. neither the electrical nor the concentration gradients.

17. A neuron will fire an action potential when it is
    a. depolarized by 10 mV.
    b. hyperpolarized by 10 mV.
    c. depolarized by 5 mV.
    d. depolarized to its threshold.

18. At what point during an action potential do potassium channels open?
    a. After the sodium channels close
    b. At the same time as the sodium channels open
    c. At the same time as the sodium channels close
    d. Before the sodium channels close

19. The outflow of K^+ ions during an action potential results in
    a. hypopolarization.
    b. hyperpolarization.
    c. depolarization.
    d. another action potential.

20. Which of the following is true regarding the action potentials generated by a neuron?
    a. They are always the same strength.
    b. They always occur at the same frequency.
    c. They are graded.
    d. They are decremental.

21. Which of the following statements regarding the absolute refractory period is FALSE?
    a. The potassium channels are closed and cannot be opened.
    b. The sodium channels are closed and cannot be opened.
    c. An action potential cannot be generated.
    d. The absolute refractory period ensures that the action potential will only travel in one direction.

22. During the relative refractory period,
    a. the neuron is hyperpolarized.
    b. a stronger stimulus may result in another action period.
    c. potassium channels are open.
    d. all of the above.

23. The maximum speed at which a neuron can conduct an action potential seems to be about
    a. 10 m/hour.
    b. 1000 m/hour.
    c. 120 m/hour.
    d. 1.2 m/hour.

24. The _____ the axon, the _____ the action potential.
    a. thicker, slower
    b. thicker, faster
    c. longer, slower
    d. thinner, faster

25. In the brain, myelin is formed by
    a. Schwann cells.
    b. protein.
    c. oligodendrocytes.
    d. vesicles.

26. On myelinated axons,
    a. action potentials occur along the entire length of the axon.
    b. action potentials occur only at the nodes of Ranvier.
    c. action potentials occur only where the myelin is in contact with the axon.
    d. only graded potentials occur.

27. Myelination results in all of the following EXCEPT
    a. increased capacitance.
    b. increased speed of conduction.
    c. saltatory conduction.
    d. less work required by the sodium-potassium pump.

28. Glial cells have been shown to perform all of the following functions EXCEPT
    a. releasing neurotransmitters.
    b. guiding developing axons.
    c. assisting in the development of synapses.
    d. transmitting action potentials between neurons.

29. Who discovered that neurons are not in contact with each other?
    a. Ramon y Cajal
    b. Golgi
    c. Loewi
    d. Dale

30. Who demonstrated that synaptic transmission is chemical?
    a. Ramon y Cajal
    b. Golgi
    c. Loewi
    d. Dale

31. When an action potential reaches an axon terminal, _____ ions enters the cell and trigger the release of the neurotransmitter.
    a. Na^+
    b. K^+
    c. Cl^-
    d. Ca^{++}

32. Under normal circumstances, the neurotransmitter molecules released by a single neuron can do all of the following EXCEPT
    a. cause ion channels to open.
    b. trigger a graded depolarization.
    c. trigger an action potential.
    d. inhibit the postsynaptic cell.

33. An IPSP will occur if
    a. sodium channels open.
    b. potassium channels open.
    c. chloride channels open.
    d. b or c.

34. Action potentials are first produced
    a. in the axon hillock.
    b. in the soma.
    c. in the dendrites.
    d. in the axon terminals.

35. In order for spatial summation to occur,
    a. several EPSPs must arrive at the same time.
    b. several EPSPs and/or IPSPs must arrive at the same time.
    c. several EPSPs must arrive in quick succession to one another.
    d. EPSPs and IPSPs must arrive in quick succession to one another.

36. If a neuron has a threshold of 10mV, which of the following combinations of simultaneous postsynaptic potentials will result in an action potential?
    a. 15 EPSPs of 1 mV each and 20 IPSPs of 1 mV each.
    b. 50 EPSPs of .5 mV each and 20 IPSPs of .5 mV each.
    c. 50 EPSPs of .2 mV each and 15 IPSPs of .2 mV each.
    d. 25 EPSPs of 1 mV each and 20 IPSPs of 1 mV each.

37. Acetylcholine is inactivated by
    a. reuptake by the presynaptic neuron.
    b. absorption by the postsynaptic neuron.
    c. enzymatic deactivation.
    d. absorption by glial cells.

38. Neurotransmitters can fit into receptor sites
    a. on both the presynaptic and postsynaptic membrane.
    b. on neither the presynaptic nor the postsynaptic membrane.
    c. on the presynaptic membrane only.
    d. on the postsynaptic membrane only.

39. Which of the following statements regarding nicotinic receptors is FALSE?
    a. They are inhibitory.
    b. They are stimulated by acetylcholine.
    c. They are found in the brain.
    d. They are found in muscles.

40. Regarding the types of neurotransmitters that a neuron can release, which of the following statements is FALSE?
    a. A neuron may release more than one fast-acting neurotransmitter.
    b. A neuron may release only excitatory or only inhibitory neurotransmitters.
    c. A neuron may release one fast-acting and one slower acting neurotransmitter.
    d. A neuron may release one fast-acting and several slower acting neurotransmitters.

41. Which of the following is an antagonist of acetylcholine?
    a. Nicotine
    b. Muscarine
    c. Naloxone
    d. Curare

42. In an artificial neural network, most of the processing occurs in which layer of neurons?
    a. Input
    b. Hidden
    c. Output
    d. Excitatory

43. Which of the following statements about artificial neural networks is FALSE?
    a. They can be taught to read and speak English.
    b. Information is distributed within them.
    c. They can be used to identify precancerous cells.
    d. They work exactly like a human brain.

Answers and Explanations

Guided Review

1. neurons
2. glial
3. soma
4. dendrites
5. information or signals
6. axon
7. myelin
8. terminals
9. communication
10. synapse
11. Motor
12. sensory
13. central
14. interneurons
15. Projection
16. lipids
17. protein
18. permeable
19. protein channels
20. polarized
21. negatively
22. resting
23. Na^+
24. A^-
25. concentration
26. inside
27. sodium-potassium pump
28. gradients
29. protein channels
30. depolarized
31. action potential
32. positively
33. potassium
34. resting potential
35. millisecond
36. sodium channels
37. graded
38. all-or-none law
39. decremental
40. absolute refractory period
41. K^+
42. negatively
43. stronger
44. frequent
45. quickly
46. myelin
47. oligodendro-cytes
48. Schwann
49. nodes of Ranvier
50. saltatory
51. multiple sclerosis
52. more
53. guide
54. synapses
55. Santiago Ramon y Cajal
56. Otto Loewi
57. decreasing
58. decreased
59. neurotransmit-ters
60. vesicles
61. Ca^{++}
62. postsynaptic
63. ion
64. hypopolarized
65. IPSPs
66. spatial
67. temporal
68. decision
69. (neuro)transmit-ter
70. reuptake
71. enzymes
72. glial
73. axoaxonic
74. excitation
75. autoreceptors
76. modulate
77. receptors
78. nicotinic
79. muscarinic
80. fast-acting
81. terminals
82. agonist
83. Curare
84. single-neuron chain
85. serial processors
86. artificial neural network
87. hidden
88. strength

Short Answer & Essay Questions

1. Sensory neurons carry information about environmental stimuli to the central nervous system, whereas motor neurons carry messages away from the central nervous system to the muscle and glandular cells of the body. Structurally, sensory neurons are usually bipolar or unipolar. Motor neurons are usually multipolar, with several dendritic branches extending in several directions.

2. A membrane that is selectively permeable allows only certain substances to pass through it. Neurons can be readily permeated by water, oxygen, and carbon dioxide, but not by other substances that they need for proper functioning. Proteins channels embedded within the membrane control the flow of ions and other molecules. These substances can only get in when the protein channels are open.

3. Na$^+$ ions are more concentrated on the outside of the cell, so they are attracted across the membrane because of the concentration gradient. Also, because they are positively charged, they are also attracted into the cell because the inside of it is negative relative to the outside.

4. The action potential spreads because it causes the sodium channels near it to open, thereby depolarizing the adjacent part of the membrane to threshold. This propagates the action potential across the length of the axon. The action potential cannot spread backward toward the soma because once the sodium channels at the site of depolarization close, they cannot be opened for a brief period (the absolute refractory period).

5. During the relative refractory period, a neuron is slightly more negative inside than while at rest, and so it requires a stronger stimulus to initiate an action potential. Therefore, stimuli of stronger intensities will have a greater effect than those of weak intensities. The cell's rate of firing will be greater when the stronger stimulus, which is better able to depolarize the cell to its threshold, is present.

6. The axons of myelinated cells contain gaps between the myelin where the action potential actually occurs. In between those gaps, the cell undergoes a graded depolarization that spreads more quickly than an action potential. This depolarization then triggers the action potential at the next gap. Because the action potential is generated at fewer points along the axon and transmission is faster between nodes, it travels more quickly. Furthermore, fewer ions are exchanged, and therefore the cell does not have to work as hard (via the sodium-potassium pump) to restore the resting potential.

7. First he isolated the hearts of two frogs and kept them beating. Then he stimulated the vagus nerve of one heart, which caused it to slow down. He transferred fluid from this heart to the other heart, which also slowed down. Then he caused the first heart to speed up, and repeated the procedure of transferring fluid. The second heart also increased its rate of contractions. He concluded that something in the fluid, some chemical released by the nerve he stimulated, had caused the change in heart rate.

8. The cell becomes slightly hyperpolarized, and this results in the neuron reducing the frequency of action potentials. This is because in order for the cell to be depolarized to threshold, a stronger than normal stimulus (perhaps in the form of several EPSPs) is required.

9. First of all, a single postsynaptic neuron may receive information from more than one presynaptic neuron, and possibly thousands of them. Therefore, its activity is a result of the integration of information it receives from all of these different sources. Secondly, synaptic activity may be modulated by a number of mechanisms, including glial cells, autoreceptors, and presynaptic excitation or inhibition from a third neuron.

10. This means that information is not stored in a single location (neuron), but rather in the connections between neurons that are found in different locations. If some neurons are damaged, the information may not be lost if the remaining ones can compensate. Furthermore, this is an efficient way of storing information because a single neuron can "contribute" to the storage of many different pieces of information through its connections with different neurons.

Post-Test

All page references in this section pertain to the textbook.

1. a. Wrong
   b. Wrong
   c. Wrong
   d. **Correct**; see p. 33.

2. **a.** **Correct**; 90% of the cells in the brain are non-neural glial cells.
    b. Wrong; this is a type of neuron.
    c. Wrong; this is a type of neuron.
    d. Wrong, although it is the most common type of neuron.

3. a. Wrong; this may be done by glial cells.
    b. **Correct**; dendritic spines are small outgrowths of the dendrite that increase the surface area of the cell and therefore allow for more synapses.
    c. Wrong; this is not stated in the book.
    d. Wrong

4. a. Wrong
    b. Wrong
    c. **Correct**; see p. 34.
    d. Wrong

5. **a.** **Correct**
    b. Wrong; sensory neurons transmit information from the external environment to the central nervous system.
    c. Wrong; interneurons transmit information between neurons.
    d. Wrong; projection neurons transmit information between neurons.

6. a. Wrong; a bipolar neuron has a single branch of dendrites.
    b. **Correct**
    c. Wrong; a unipolar neuron has a single process that branches into dendrites and an axon.
    d. Wrong; the book does not mention such a neuron.

7. a. Wrong; this is true of sensory neurons.
    b. Wrong; their effects are on nearby neurons. Projection neurons connect other neurons across longer distances.
    c. **Correct**; some have short axons, while others have no axon.
    d. Wrong; the book describes interneurons in the spinal cord.

8. a. Wrong
    b. Wrong
    c. **Correct**; oxygen passes freely across the membrane. All of the others pass through channels.
    d. Wrong

9. **a.** **Correct**; see p. 36.
    b. Wrong; K^+ is more concentrated inside the cell.
    c. Wrong; A^- are found only inside the cell.
    d. Wrong

10. a. Wrong
    b. Wrong
    c. Wrong
    d. **Correct**; see p. 37.

11. a.   Wrong; because the inside is negative while the cell is at rest, they should not be attracted to the positively charged environment outside.
    b.   Correct; there is more K^+ inside, and so they are compelled to diffuse across the membrane if possible.
    c.   Wrong
    d.   Wrong

12. a.   Wrong
    b.   Wrong
    c.   Wrong
    d.   Correct; these are too large to pass across or fit any of the channels. All of the other substances pass through channels.

13. a.   Wrong; this is true.
    b.   Wrong; this is true.
    c.   Correct; it actually pumps sodium out of the cell, against the concentration gradient (which requires a lot of energy).
    d.   Wrong; this is true. After a cell fires an action potential, although it is repolarized and may fire again, the pump is responsible for restoring the concentration gradient.

14. a.   Wrong; when K^+ channels open, these ions are attracted out of the cell, and it becomes hyperpolarized.
    b.   Correct; see p. 38.
    c.   Wrong
    d.   Wrong; when Cl^- channels open, these ions are attracted inside the cell (because of the concentration gradient), and it becomes hyperpolarized.

15. **a.   Correct**; both terms mean that the inside of the cell becomes less negatively charged.
    b.   Wrong; this means that the cell becomes more negatively charged.
    c.   Wrong; while action potentials are depolarizations, not all depolarizations are action potentials (only a depolarization that reaches threshold can trigger an action potential).
    d.   Wrong

16. a.   Wrong; b is also correct.
    b.   Wrong; a is also correct.
    c.   Correct
    d.   Wrong

17. a.   Wrong; although this is the typical threshold change required, some neurons have other thresholds.
    b.   Wrong; hyperpolarizing a neuron would make it MORE negative, and reduce the likelihood of an action potential occurring.
    c.   Wrong
    d.   Correct; thresholds of different neurons vary.

18. a.   Wrong
    b.   Wrong
    c.   Wrong
    d.   Correct; see pp. 38-39.

19. a. Wrong; the loss of positive ions makes the inside more, not less, negatively charged.
    b. Correct
    c. Wrong
    d. Wrong; this actually inhibits another action potential from being generated.

20. **a. Correct**; they conform to the all-or-none law.
    b. Wrong; a neuron's firing rate changes according to excitatory and inhibitory input.
    c. Wrong; action potentials are by definition not graded potentials.
    d. Wrong; this is a characteristic of graded potentials. Action potentials do not lose their strength as they pass along the axon.

21. **a. Correct**; the K$^+$ are in fact open during this time.
    b. Wrong; this is true.
    c. Wrong; this is true.
    d. Wrong; this is true.

22. a. Wrong; b and c are also correct.
    b. Wrong
    c. Wrong
    d. Correct; see p. 39.

23. a. Wrong
    b. Wrong
    c. Correct; see p. 41.
    d. Wrong

24. a. Wrong
    b. Correct; see p. 41.
    c. Wrong; the length of an axon has no effect on the speed of action potentials. Two neurons with different length axons may conduct action potentials at the same speed.
    d. Wrong

25. a. Wrong; these are the cells that form myelin in the periphery (outside the brain and spinal cord).
    b. Wrong; myelin cells are actually a form of fat cell.
    c. Correct; see p. 41
    d. Wrong; these are the sacs inside the axon terminals that contain neurotransmitter.

26. a. Wrong; graded potentials occur along the portions that are myelinated.
    b. Correct; see p. 41.
    c. Wrong
    d. Wrong

27. **a. Correct**; capacitance is the tendency to resist movement of ions, and myelin reduces this, making it easier for ions to move. All of the other choices are true of myelin.
    b. Wrong
    c. Wrong
    d. Wrong

28. a. Wrong
    b. Wrong
    c. Wrong
    d. Correct; this is a function only carried out by neurons. All of the other choices are true of glial cells.

29. **a. Correct**; see p. 43.
    b. Wrong; he developed the staining technique used by Ramon y Cajal.
    c. Wrong; he lived after Ramon y Cajal.
    d. Wrong

30. a. Wrong; he did not study synaptic transmission.
    b. Wrong
    c. Correct; see p. 43.
    d. Wrong

31. a. Wrong
    b. Wrong
    c. Wrong
    d. Correct; see p. 44.

32. a. Wrong
    b. Wrong
    c. Correct; a single cell can cause only a very small depolarization, not enough to trigger an action potential. All of the other choices are true.
    d. Wrong

33. a. Wrong; this would result in an EPSP or depolarization.
    b. Wrong; c is also correct.
    c. Wrong; b is also correct.
    d. Correct; allowing either K^+ out or Cl^- in would drive the inside of the cell to become more negative.

34. **a. Correct**; see p. 45.
    b. Wrong
    c. Wrong
    d. Wrong

35. a. Wrong; b is the more complete answer.
    b. Correct
    c. Wrong; this is temporal summation.
    d. Wrong; this is temporal summation.

36. a. Wrong; this would result in a net change of +5 mV.
    b. Correct; this would result in a net change of +15mV.
    c. Wrong; this would result in a net change of 7 mV.
    d. Wrong; this would result in a net change of 5 mV.

37. a. Wrong; although it does reabsorb choline, the molecule is first broken down by acetylcholine esterase.
    b. Wrong
    c. **Correct**; see pp. 46-47.
    d. Wrong

38. a. **Correct**; some presynaptic neurons contain autoreceptors which are responsive to the neurotransmitters they release.
    b. Wrong
    c. Wrong
    d. Wrong

39. a. **Correct**; they are excitatory (see p. 49). All of the other choices are true.
    b. Wrong
    c. Wrong
    d. Wrong

40. a. Wrong
    b. **Correct**; a single neuron may release both types, but at different synapses (see p. 49). All of the other choices are true.
    c. Wrong
    d. Wrong

41. a. Wrong; it is an agonist.
    b. Wrong; it is an agonist.
    c. Wrong; it is an antagonist of opiate, not acetylcholine, receptors.
    d. **Correct**; see p. 49.

42. a. Wrong
    b. **Correct**; see p. 52.
    c. Wrong
    d. Wrong; this is not a layer of neurons in the network. Individual neurons may be excitatory or inhibitory.

43. a. Wrong
    b. Wrong
    c. Wrong
    d. **Correct**; they represent an approximation of how brains work, but no one knows for sure if they operate in the exact same way. All of the other choices are true.

Chapter 3: The Functions of the Nervous System

Chapter Outline and Learning Objectives

As you read the chapter, use these learning objectives to guide your studying. You should be able to define the key terms from the text, which are shown in boldface type below.

1) The Central Nervous System (CNS)
- Distinguish between the following terms: **CNS** and **PNS**; **neuron, nerve,** and **tract**; **nucleus** and **ganglion**.

  a) The Forebrain
  - What are the major structures of the **forebrain**?

    i) The **Cerebral Hemispheres**
    - Describe the structure of the cortex in terms of its **gyri** (ridges), **sulci** (grooves), and **fissures**. What is the significance of the convolutions of the cortex?

    - Describe the organization of the cortex, distinguishing between **gray matter** and **white matter**.

    - Discuss the relationship between brain size and intelligence. What structural factors of brains are better indications of intelligence?

    ii) The Four Lobes
    - Be able to locate the **frontal, temporal, parietal,** and **occipital lobes**.

    - Know the definitions of the following directional terms: **anterior/posterior, superior/inferior, ventral/dorsal,** and **medial/lateral**.

    - Where is the **motor cortex**? What is the significance of the **homunculus**? With what other brain areas does the motor cortex work?

    - Where is **Broca's area**, and in what behaviors is it involved?

    - Where is the **prefrontal cortex**? Describe its functions. What are the implications of damage to this area?

- Discuss the use of **lobotomies** to treat mental disorders.

- Describe the case of Phineas Gage, and discuss what information it has contributed, even recently, to our understanding of the brain.

- Where is the **somatosensory cortex**, and what does it do?

- What are the functions of the **association cortex**? What are the consequences of damage to this area?

- Locate the **auditory cortex** and **Wernicke's area**, and describe their functions.

- What are the functions of the **inferior temporal cortex**, and what are the consequences of damage to this area?

- Describe the procedure used by Penfield to map his patients' brains. What sorts of experiences did his patients report when different areas were stimulated?

- Describe the **visual cortex**, including the distinction between the functions of the **primary** and **secondary** areas.

iii) The Thalamus and Hypothalamus
- Where is the **thalamus**, and what are its functions?

- Where is the **hypothalamus**? What is its relation to the **pituitary gland?** What are the functions of these areas?

- What are the structures of the **limbic system**? What types of behaviors and experiences do these contribute to?

- Where is the **pineal gland**, and what does it do?

iv) Other Forebrain Structures
   (1) The **Cerebral Commissures**
- What is the function of the **corpus callosum**? What are the consequences of severing it?

(2) The Ventricles
- Describe the **ventricles** and **cerebrospinal fluid**. Why are these important?

b) The **Midbrain** and **Hindbrain**
- Where is the **tectum**? What are the functions of the **superior** and **inferior colliculi**?

- Where is the **tegmentum**? What do the nuclei (e.g. the **substantia nigra**) in this structure do?

- Where are the **medulla** and the **pons**? What are their functions?

- What is the **reticular formation**?

- Describe the structure and functions of the **cerebellum**. What are the consequences of damage to this area?

c) Localization
- What was **phrenology**, and why was it incorrect?

- Distinguish between the concepts of **localization of function** and **equipotentiality**. To what extent is each correct?

d) The Spinal Cord
- What are the general functions of the **spinal cord**?

- Distinguish between the sensory and motor components of the spinal cord (including the **dorsal root**, **ventral horns**, and **ventral roots**).

- What is a **reflex**?

e) Protecting the CNS
- How is the brain protected by the **meninges** and the **cerebrospinal fluid**?

- What is the **blood-brain barrier**, and how does it protect the brain? Why is it significant that some areas of the brain, such as the **area postrema**, are not protected by the blood-brain barrier?

2) The Peripheral Nervous System (PNS)
- Be able to define the following terms: **cranial nerves, spinal nerves, somatic nervous system**, and **autonomic nervous system**.

a) The Cranial Nerves
- Among the cranial nerves, why are the **optic** and **olfactory** nerves considered special?

- What are the significant features of the **optic chiasm**?

b) The Autonomic Nervous System (ANS)
- Distinguish between the functions of the **sympathetic** and **parasympathetic nervous systems**.

- What is the significance of the **sympathetic ganglion chain** for the activity of the sympathetic nervous system?

3) Development and Change in the Nervous System
a) The Stages of Development
- What processes occur during **proliferation** and **migration**? How are **radial glial cells** involved in migration?

- Describe the stage of **circuit formation**, including the roles of the **growth cone**, the chemical environment of the developing nervous system, and **pioneer neurons**.

- What happens during **circuit pruning**? What is the role of neural **plasticity** in this process?

- How does circuit pruning occur before birth in the visual system?

- What effects can exposure to alcohol or radiation during fetal development have on neural development (e.g. **fetal alcohol syndrome**)?

- Describe the time pattern of myelination in the nervous system. What are the implications of some areas being myelinated before others?

b) How Experience Modifies the Nervous System
- What is **reorganization**? Give some examples.

- What is the **doctrine of specific nerve energies**? How is it violated by neural reorganization in people blind from birth?

- Give some examples of how reorganization can be harmful or deleterious (e.g. as in **phantom pain**).

c) Damage and Recovery in the CNS
  i) Limitations on Recovery
  - Describe the process of **regeneration** in the mammalian PNS. Why are damaged neurons in the CNS in mammals unable to regenerate?

  - Where does **neurogenesis** occur in the mammalian CNS? What are the problems with the new neurons that are produced?

  ii) Compensation
  - What mechanisms does the mature CNS use to **compensate** for damage?

  - What is **constraint-induced-therapy**, and how does it help stroke victims recover limb function?

  - Discuss the role of reorganization in recovery from brain damage, including cases in which an entire hemisphere is removed.

  - Why are special cases of **periventricular heterotopia** and **hydrocephalus** challenging for neuroscientists?

  iii) Possibilities for CNS Repair
  - Describe the potential therapies for repairing damage to the brain and spinal cord.

The Central Nervous System (CNS)

Summary and Guided Review

After studying this section in the text, fill in the blanks of the following summary. The answers are found on p. 65.

In the central nervous system (CNS), which is composed of the brain and _____ (1), a bundle of axons is called a _____ (2) and a group of cell bodies is known as a _____ (3). In the peripheral nervous system (PNS), which is composed of the _____ (4) and spinal nerves, an axon bundle is a _____ (5) and a group of cell bodies is a _____ (6). Early in development the CNS begins as a hollow tube and quickly differentiates into a spinal cord and three brain areas, the _____ (7), which in humans becomes the largest, the midbrain, and the _____ (8).

The forebrain contains two _____ _____ (9), which are separated by the longitudinal _____ (10). For the most part, each hemisphere receives information from and controls movement in the _____ (11) side of the body. The outer layer of the cerebral hemispheres, the _____ (12), is wrinkled in appearance, and contains many _____ (13) (ridges) and _____ (14) (grooves). The surface is composed mostly of _____ _____ (15), which accounts for its gray appearance. Its convoluted structure allows for greater _____ _____ (16) and better connections for axons. The interior of the cortex, composed mostly of axons, appears _____ (17). The overall size of the brain is in proportion to the body, with larger animals having larger brains. The intelligence of a species appears to be more related to the _____ (18) of the brain rather than its size.

Each hemisphere is divided into four lobes, and each contributes to somewhat different functions. One function that the _____ (19) lobe is involved in is movement. Different parts of the body are mapped onto areas of the _____ _____ (20), or primary motor cortex, such that the parts of the body that are capable of fine motor movements (such as the fingers) are represented by a larger portion of the brain. The primary motor cortex also works with the _____ (21) motor cortex and _____ _____ (22) in the planning of movement. _____ (23) area, another frontal lobe structure, is involved in _____ (24) and grammar. The _____ _____ (25), the largest area in the human brain, contributes to a number of cognitive functions. Damage to this area can lead to a number of problems, including an inability to plan or organize actions, learn from experience, use working memory, of make decisions. In the 1940s and 1950s, it was common practice to "disconnect" the prefrontal cortex from the rest of the brain through a procedure known as _____ (26). Over 40,000 of these were performed in the United States on people with mental illnesses of various types. The

success of this procedure was limited, and it eventually fell into disfavor, especially when effective
_____ (27) treatments become available in the 1950s.

The parietal lobe contains the _____ (28) gyrus, which includes the
_____ _____ (29), where the skin and body position/movement senses are
projected. This area is structured to represent the body in much the same way as the primary motor cortex.
The parietal lobe's _____ _____ (30) provides further processing of sensory
information, and a person with damage to this area may experience _____ (31) affecting the opposite
side of the body. The _____ (32) lobe contains the auditory cortex and on the left hemisphere,
_____ (33) area, which is involved in language comprehension and production. Visual
identification is carried out in the _____ _____ (34) cortex; people with damage to this
area have difficulty recognizing objects by sight, including familiar people. During brain surgery, when
stimulated in parts of the temporal cortex, people have reported experiencing specific events or memories.
The entire occipital lobe is devoted to the sense of _____ (35). Area V1 is organized like a map of
the retina. The remainder of the occipital cortical areas process different components of images, such as
color, form, and movement. This information is then sent to the _____ (36) lobe for further
processing.

Other major structures of the forebrain include the _____ (37), which serves as a
relay station for sensory information, and the _____ (38), which regulates the internal
environment partly via the _____ (39) gland, which in turn controls the _____ (40)
system . Along with the hypothalamus, the _____ _____ (41) is involved in motivation,
learning, and _____ (42). Bodily cycles such as sleep are controlled in part by the
_____ _____ (43).

The hemispheres communicate via _____ (44). The largest of these, the
_____ _____ (45), is found at the bottom of the longitudinal fissure. In cases of severe
epilepsy, the commissures may be surgically disconnected. People who have had this procedure can lead
normal lives, but they show that to a certain extent the two hemispheres have different functions, the left
hemisphere being more involved in _____ (46) and the right in _____ _____ (47)
and recognizing faces. Fluid-filled cavities called _____ (48) are located in the forebrain.
The _____ (49) fluid transports nutrients to and _____ (50) away from the CNS.

The lower structures of the brain, the midbrain and hindbrain, compose the tubular-shaped brain
_____ (51). The midbrain is composed of the _____ (52) on the dorsal side and the
_____ (53) on the ventral side. In the tectum, the _____ _____ (54) are involved
in vision while the _____ _____ (55) are involved in hearing. The _____
_____ (56) in the tegmentum is involved in movement. The degeneration of cells in this nucleus is

implicated in _____ (57) disease. The hindbrain includes the _____ (58), which is involved in vital functions such as respiration and keeping the heart beating, and the pons, which includes part of the _____ _____ (59), which is involved in sleep and arousal. The _____ (60), which physically resembles the cerebral cortex, is essential in a number of motor and cognitive activities, and contains _____ (61) of all of the neurons in the brain.

To a certain extent, _____ (62) are localized within specific areas of the brain. However, we must be careful not to assign too much localization to the brain, just as we should not assume that the opposite position of _____ (63) is correct. Most of our capacities are controlled by numerous areas of the brain working in conjunction with one another.

The spinal cord and cranial nerves link the _____ (64) with the rest of the body. The spinal cord contains _____ _____ (65), motor programs for repetitive behaviors such as walking, and is responsible for certain reflexive behaviors. The spinal cord contains ascending _____ (66) tracts, which enter the spinal cord through the _____ (67) roots, and descending _____ (68) tracts, which exit the cord through the _____ (69) roost. The cell bodies of sensory neurons are located outside the spinal cord in the _____ _____ _____ (70), while those of motor neurons are located inside the spinal cord in the _____ _____ (71). Some of the sensory neurons form connections with _____ (72) and then motor neurons, which allow for spinal reflexes.

The CNS is protected in a number of ways. It is covered by the _____ (73), and the ventricles are filled with _____ _____ (74), which cushions the brain. Harmful substances are prevented from entering the brain by the _____-_____ (75) barrier. The walls of many of the _____ (76) serving the brain are tightly packed, which keeps many substances from passing through them. One area of the brain that is not protected in this way is the area _____ (77), and when toxins are detected here, _____ (78) occurs.

Short Answer & Essay Questions

Answer the following questions. See p. 66 for sample answers.

1. What are TWO advantages of the convoluted structure of the cerebral cortex?

2. Why is brain size alone not a good indication of intelligence of different species of animals (e.g. humans and elephants)? What is a better indication?

3. How are the primary motor and somatosensory cortices organized in relation to the body areas they receive information from or send information to? What determines how much space on the cortex is devoted to a particular area of the body?

4. What is the condition known as *neglect*? What is the likely cause of it?

5. What is the *binding problem*?

6. Why is the blood-brain barrier important? Explain how the structure of the blood-brain barrier helps keep some harmful substances out of the brain. Why is it advantageous that the area postrema NOT be protected by the barrier?

The Peripheral Nervous System (PNS)

Summary and Guided Review

After studying this section in the text, fill in the blanks of the following summary. The answers are found on p. 65.

The peripheral nervous system includes _____ (79) pairs of cranial nerves and 31 pairs of

_____ (80) nerves; it can be divided into the _____ (81) nervous system, which is

involved in the control of movement and carries sensory information to the CNS, and the autonomic

nervous system (ANS), which is involved in the control of _____ (82) and glands.

Among the cranial nerves, the _____ (83) nerve, which carries information about

smell, and the _____ (84) nerve, which carries information about vision, are sometimes considered to

be part of the brain. The two optic nerves converge at the _____ _____ (85), where some

information crosses over to the other side of the brain.

The ANS has two divisions: the sympathetic, which _____ (86) bodily resources, and the

_____ , (87) which helps to restore energy. The sympathetic nervous system is highly

coordinated, due to the _____ _____ _____ (88). Most of the affected

organs are stimulated almost simultaneously when this system is activated. In general, the two branches of

the ANS have opposite effects on organs. For example, sympathetic activation _____ (89) heart

rate, while parasympathetic activation _____ (90) it. However, both branches are active at the

same time, but one may have a stronger effect at one time than the other.

Short Answer & Essay Questions

Answer the following questions. See pp. 66-67 for sample answers.

7. From the information provided in Figure 3.20 (p. 77 in the textbook), which cranial nerves appear to be involved in eye movement? Which are probably involved in speaking?

8. Why is the sympathetic nervous system able to act in a more coordinated fashion than the parasympathetic? What advantage is there for the quick, coordinated action of the sympathetic nervous system?

Development and Change in the Nervous System

Summary and Guided Review

After studying this section in the text, fill in the blanks of the following summary. The answers are found on p. 65.

Once the neural tube has formed, the nervous system develops in stages. During the first stage, _____ (91), new neurons are formed at a high rate in the _____ _____ (92) of the neural tube. Then, with the support of _____ _____ _____ (93), the new neurons migrate toward the outer layers of the tube. During this time, the neurons are quite flexible and have the potential to become many different types of neurons. The next stage is _____ _____ (94), during which axons find their way to target cells and form synapses with them. Axons are directed by the chemical environment of the developing nervous system; they are attracted to certain locations and repelled from others by the chemicals present. _____ (95) neurons are also instrumental in helping neurons find their connections. Without them, other neurons cannot make connections. Once connections have been made, these neurons die. The nervous system produces many more neurons than it needs, and during the last stage of development, _____ _____ (96), neurons die. This process removes the synapses and cells that are the least useful, leaving the nervous system in a more organized state. A neuron is more likely to survive this stage if it fires at the same time as its _____ (97). Once connections have been formed and strengthened, some cells retain their _____ (98), or ability to undergo change. This ability is important for the organism to modify its behavior according to its experiences, since the nervous system provides the basis for such learning. Circuit pruning may occur before birth, even in the absence of environmental input. In the visual system, for example, waves of activity sweep through the _____ (99), strengthening the connections that have been formed.

During the formation of the nervous system, disruption of development can have serious consequences. For example, periventricular _____ (100), a genetic disorder, produces a _____ (101) cortex, which usually results in severe epilepsy and mental _____ (102). Prenatal exposure to _____ (103) may result in neurons migrating to the wrong place or failing to become appropriately organized. Babies with fetal alcohol syndrome often have _____ (104) brains and are mentally retarded. _____ (105) is another environmental agent that can interfere with proliferation and migration, particularly if the mother is exposed between the 8th and 15th week of pregnancy.

The nervous system is not considered fully mature until _____ (106) is complete, which happens sometime in late _____ (107) or adulthood. This process begins with the lower areas of the brain, and the last areas to mature are the _____ _____ (108), which may explain why certain cognitive skills are not achieved until adolescence or adulthood.

Throughout the lifespan, the nervous system may undergo _____ (109) in response to experience. Through this process, some synapses may be lost while others are formed, and areas of the brain devoted to specific functions may actually expand. Reorganization can even violate the doctrine of _____ _____ _____ (110), which states that input to a particular sensory area will always result in the same type of sensation. In the blind, for example, the visual cortex is apparently taken over by the _____ (111) system. Sometimes reorganization can have detrimental effects, such as when a limb is amputated and the somatosensory neurons from nearby body parts take over the part of the cortex that was devoted to the missing limb; this is thought to be responsible for _____ _____ (112) that amputees sometimes experience. Experiments with cats have revealed that if an animal sees only horizontal stripes during early development, it will not be able to later detect objects that oriented _____ (113).

Recovery from damage in the nervous system is limited. Although in some species, such as _____ (114), damaged neurons easily regenerate, this is not true in all animals. In mammals, regeneration involving the regrowth of a severed _____ (115) occurs in the _____ (116) nervous system with the help of myelin. In the CNS, however, regrowth is _____ (117) because of the chemical environment, scar tissue, and the presence of glial and _____ (118) cells. Also, in most parts of the nervous system new cells are not produced once proliferation ends. Exceptions are the _____ (119) and the olfactory bulb, although it is not clear that the new neurons can functionally replace lost neurons.

Many people who suffer brain damage do recover some of the functions lost initially from the damage through the process of _____ (120), in which healthy neurons take over the connections that were lost due to the damage. _____ - _____ (121) therapy, which requires limiting the use of a functional body part so the one affected by the damage can be exercised, has shown promising results. Reorganization may also occur, such as in the case of _____ (122) (language impairment). Occasionally, researchers encounter a person who suffers from profound structural damage but who shows no apparent behavioral impairment. Examples from the text include cases of periventricular heterotopia, which has been discussed previously, and _____ (123), a condition in which blockage of CSF can lead to severe retardation if untreated. These cases demonstrate that the nervous system is capable of compensating for even extensive damage, although the processes involved are not understood.

There are some other promising forms of therapy that may result in repairing CNS damage. Some, including the use of stem cells, have already been discussed. Others involve counteracting the mature nervous system's features that inhibit regeneration. Based on some success with experimental animals, neuroscientists are hopeful that in the future, people with spinal cord and brain injuries will be able to recover some of their lost capacities.

Short Answer & Essay Questions

Answer the following questions. See p. 67 for sample answers.

9. During neural development, axons often have to grow over extensive distances in order to reach their target postsynaptic cells. How is this accomplished? Include in your answer the roles of growth cones and pioneer neurons.

10. It is clear that the nervous system starts out with a lot more neurons than it needs. Why do you think it is advantageous for the nervous system to have so many neurons to start with, if many of them are only going to be lost? Keep in mind that the environment an animal encounters is at least somewhat unpredictable.

11. Maria was exposed to high levels of ionizing radiation during her 32nd week of pregnancy. She is concerned that this will have profound negative effects on her fetus, particularly its nervous system. What would you tell her?

12. What is *syndactyly*? How does surgical correction of syndactyly and the resulting changes in the brain demonstrate neural reorganization?

13. What is phantom pain, and how do neuroscientists explain its occurrence?

14. Describe three ways in which the CNS can compensate at the level of the synapse for the loss of neurons in specific locations.

15. Describe five possible treatments that may be used in the future to correct brain and spinal cord injuries.

Post-Test

Use these multiple-choice questions to check your understanding of the chapter. The answers, along with explanations, are found beginning on p. 68.

1. Which of the following is NOT a characteristic of individuals with periventricular heterotopia?
   a. They often have epilepsy.
   b. They are usually male.
   c. They are usually lissencephalic.
   d. They are usually mentally retarded.

2. A _____ is the name for a bundle of neurons in the PNS.
   a. nerve
   b. tract
   c. nucleus
   d. ganglion

3. The cranial nerves are BEST considered part of the _____ nervous system.
   a. central
   b. autonomic
   c. peripheral
   d. sympathetic

4. Which of the following is the largest division of the mature CNS in humans?
   a. Forebrain
   b. Midbrain
   c. Hindbrain
   d. Spinal cord

5. The cerebral hemispheres are separated by the:
   a. lateral fissure.
   b. anterior commissure.
   c. central sulcus.
   d. longitudinal fissure.

6. The surface of the cortex appears gray because it is composed mostly of
   a. unmyelinated axons.
   b. unmyelinated cell bodies.
   c. myelinated axons.
   d. myelinated cell bodies.

7. On the cortex, a ridge is called a
   a. fissure.
   b. gyrus.
   c. commissure.
   d. sulcus.

8. What is the name of the 19th century European anatomist who argued that because women have smaller brains than men, they are less intelligent?
   a. Penfield
   b. Gall
   c. Bischoff
   d. Sperry

9. Animals species that are the most intelligent tend to have
   a. bigger brains overall.
   b. more convolutions on the cortex.
   c. a proportionately larger forebrain.
   d. b and c.
   e. a, b and c.

10. The directional term *anterior* means:
   a. in front of.
   b. behind.
   c. above.
   d. below.

11. The brain area controlling fine motor movement is located on the
    a.   prefrontal cortex.
    b.   precentral gyrus.
    c.   postcentral gyrus.
    d.   central sulcus.

12. The area of the motor cortex devoted to which of the following body areas is probably the smallest?
    a.   Lips
    b.   Tongue
    c.   Thumb
    d.   Thigh

13. Damage to the prefrontal cortex is LEAST likely to result in problems with
    a.   decision making.
    b.   working memory.
    c.   speech.
    d.   behavioral inhibition.

14. Which of the following was a proponent of lobotomies as a treatment for mental illness?
    a.   Penfield
    b.   Sperry
    c.   Freeman
    d.   Bischoff

15. Which of the following statements regarding lobotomies is FALSE?
    a.   They are no longer performed.
    b.   They often resulted in profound personality changes.
    c.   They became less common when effective psychiatric drugs were developed.
    d.   They were often ineffective at treating mental illness.

16. The somatosensory cortex is located in the _____ lobe.
    a.   frontal
    b.   occipital
    c.   temporal
    d.   parietal

17. Identifying objects by touch is a function of the
    a.   somatosensory cortex.
    b.   association cortex.
    c.   visual cortex.
    d.   inferior temporal cortex.

18. Modern computer studies of the skull of Phineas Gage have revealed that he suffered damage to the
    a.   frontal lobes.
    b.   corpus callosum.
    c.   parietal lobes.
    d.   brain stem.

19. Which of the following is NOT a function of the temporal lobes?
    a. Processing auditory information
    b. Language comprehension
    c. Fine motor control
    d. Visual identification of objects

20. Electrical stimulation of the association areas of the temporal lobe may result in the patient experiencing
    a. intense pain.
    b. buzzing sounds.
    c. bright lights.
    d. vivid memories.

21. The occipital lobe processes _____ information.
    a. visual
    b. auditory
    c. somatosensory
    d. a and b
    e. a, b and c

22. The thalamus receives information from all of the sensory systems EXCEPT
    a. vision.
    b. hearing.
    c. smell.
    d. taste.
    e. touch.

23. The hypothalamus is located _____ the thalamus.
    a. above
    b. below
    c. behind
    d. in front of

24. The _____ is the body's "master" endocrine gland.
    a. pituitary
    b. pineal
    c. hypothalamus
    d. pons

25. The sleep-inducing hormone melatonin is released by the
    a. pituitary gland.
    b. pineal gland.
    c. hypothalamus.
    d. pons.

26. Which statement regarding the corpus callosum is FALSE?
    a. It consists of neuron tracts connecting the two hemispheres.
    b. It is the only place in the brain where information crosses from one side to the other.
    c. It may be severed in order to prevent severe epileptic seizures.
    d. It allows the left side of the brain to control the right side of the body.

27. Studies of split-brain patients have shown that
    a. the right side of the brain is specialized for language.
    b. the left side of the brain is specialized for recognition of faces.
    c. people cannot talk after their corpus callosum has been severed.
    d. the right side of the brain is specialized for spatial tasks.

28. Which of the following structures is NOT part of the brain stem?
    a. Lateral ventricle
    b. Midbrain
    c. Pons
    d. Medulla

29. All of the following structures are located in the midbrain EXCEPT the
    a. tectum
    b. tegmentum
    c. pons
    d. substantia nigra.

30. Heart rate and breathing are controlled by the
    a. pons.
    b. cerebellum
    c. superior colliculi.
    d. medulla.

31. A person with damage to the cerebellum may
    a. be blind.
    b. be unable to recognize familiar objects.
    c. be insensitive to pain.
    d. have problems with movement.

32. Which of the following was a leading proponent of phrenology?
    a. Muller
    b. Gall
    c. Penfield
    d. Bischoff

33. Which of the following statements regarding reflexes is FALSE?
    a. The neurons controlling them may be located in the spinal cord.
    b. The neurons controlling them may be located in the brain.
    c. Any behavior that can be executed without thought is a reflex.
    d. They are the result of direct sensory-motor connections.

34. The cerebrospinal fluid protects the brain in all of the following ways EXCEPT
    a. it provides nourishment to brain cells.
    b. it cushions the brain.
    c. it removes waste products from the CNS.
    d. it prevents toxins from entering the CNS.

35. The skeletal muscles are most directly controlled by the _____ nervous system.
    a.   autonomic
    b.   somatic
    c.   sympathetic
    d.   central

36. Which of the following cranial nerves is sometimes considered part of the CNS rather than the PNS?
    a.   oculomotor
    b.   auditory
    c.   vagus
    d.   optic

37. Which of the following is more a result of parasympathetic than sympathetic activation?
    a.   increased digestive activity
    b.   increased heart rate
    c.   increased blood pressure
    d.   increased respiration

38. The stage of neural development in which axons grow toward their target connections is called
    a.   proliferation.
    b.   migration
    c.   circuit formation.
    d.   circuit pruning.

39. Cell proliferation occurs
    a.   in the innermost layer of the neural tube.
    b.   in the outermost layers of the neural tube.
    c.   throughout the neural tube.
    d.   in the location of a neuron's final destination.

40. Cells that form a scaffold for neural migration are called
    a.   pioneer neurons.
    b.   radial glial cells.
    c.   myelin cells.
    d.   ladder cells.

41. During the first three weeks of life, the neurons in a monkey's corpus callosum
    a.   triple in number.
    b.   increase by about 8 million.
    c.   decrease by about 8 million.
    d.   undergo very little change.

42. Neural plasticity in adulthood retained to the greatest extent in which of the following brain areas?
    a.   the primary visual cortex
    b.   somatosensory cortex
    c.   primary motor cortex
    d.   association cortex

43. Which of the following is NOT a result of fetal exposure to alcohol?
    a. improper migration of cells
    b. failure of cells to form myelin
    c. small brain size
    d. mental retardation

44. Which of the following brain areas is among the last to undergo myelination?
    a. frontal cortex
    b. occipital cortex
    c. spinal nerves
    d. medulla

45. Which of the following is NOT an example of brain reorganization?
    a. larger area of the somatosensory cortex devoted to the index finger in people who read Braille
    b. the occipital cortex of people blind from birth responding to somatosensory information
    c. phantom limb pain following amputation of a leg
    d. regrowth of a severed spinal motor neuron

46. Regeneration is least likely to occur in the
    a. CNS of a frog.
    b. PNS of a frog.
    c. CNS of a mammal.
    d. PNS of a mammal.

47. In the adult mammal, neurogenesis is most likely to occur in the
    a. spinal cord.
    b. medulla.
    c. hippocampus.
    d. hypothalamus.

48. Following brain injury in adults, which of the following functions is most likely to be responsible for recovery of functions? (more than one answer may be correct)
    a. compensation
    b. reorganization
    c. regeneration
    d. neurogenesis

49. Which of the following is NOT TRUE of hydrocephalus?
    a. It results from a blockage of the CSF.
    b. It can be treated using a drainage shunt.
    c. Even without treatment, individuals are likely to have normal intelligence.
    d. It affects the development of the CNS.

Answers and Explanations

Guided Review

1. spinal cord
2. tract
3. nucleus
4. cranial
5. nerve
6. ganglion
7. forebrain
8. hindbrain
9. cerebral hemispheres
10. fissure
11. opposite
12. cortex
13. gyri
14. sulci
15. cell bodies
16. surface area
17. white
18. complexity
19. frontal
20. precentral gyrus
21. secondary
22. basal ganglia
23. Broca's
24. speech
25. prefrontal cortex
26. lobotomy
27. drug
28. postcentral
29. somatosensory cortex
30. association cortex
31. neglect
32. temporal
33. Wernicke's
34. inferior temporal
35. vision
36. temporal
37. thalamus
38. hypothalamus
39. pituitary
40. endocrine
41. limbic system
42. emotion
43. pineal gland
44. commissures
45. corpus callosum
46. language
47. spatial tasks
48. ventricles
49. cerebrospinal
50. wastes
51. stem
52. tectum
53. tegmentum
54. superior colliculi
55. inferior colliculi
56. substantia nigra
57. Parkinson's
58. medulla
59. reticular formation
60. cerebellum
61. half
62. functions
63. equipotentiality
64. brain
65. pattern generators
66. sensory
67. dorsal
68. motor
69. ventral
70. dorsal root ganglia
71. ventral horn
72. interneurons
73. meninges
74. cerebrospinal fluid
75. blood-brain
76. capillaries
77. postrema
78. vomiting
79. 12
80. spinal
81. somatic
82. organs
83. olfactory
84. optic
85. optic chiasm
86. activates or mobilizes
87. parasympathetic
88. sympathetic ganglion chain
89. increases
90. decreases
91. proliferation
92. ventricular zone
93. radial glial cells
94. circuit formation
95. Pioneer
96. circuit pruning
97. neighbors
98. plasticity
99. retina
100. heterotopia
101. smooth
102. retardation
103. alcohol
104. smaller
105. Radiation
106. myelination
107. adolescence
108. frontal lobes
109. reorganization
110. specific nerve energies
111. somatosensory
112. phantom pain
113. vertically
114. amphibians or frogs
115. axon
116. peripheral
117. inhibited
118. immune
119. hippocampus
120. compensation
121. constraint-induced
122. aphasia
123. hydrocephalus

Short Answer & Essay Questions

1. One advantage is that it increases the surface area of the brain without increasing its size a great deal. This means more cortex can be packed into a small area. Another advantage is that it allows the axons to be organized more efficiently.

2. If we compare between species, brain size is more related to body size than intelligence; the largest animals tend to have the largest brains. A good way of representing the connection between brain and intelligence is its complexity, particularly the degree to which the forebrain is developed. Humans' forebrains are larger and more extensively convoluted than apes', which are larger and more convoluted than monkeys', etc.

3. These areas of the brain are organized like maps of the body. Sensory neurons from particular areas of the body project to specific areas of the somatosensory cortex, and neurons from specific parts of the motor cortex control movement in particular areas of the body. Areas of the body which are either especially sensitive (because they contain a lot of sensory receptors) or capable of fine motor movement are represented by a larger area of the cortex than areas that are less sensitive or not involved in fine motor movement. For example, the fingers are represented to a greater extent in both cortices than the back.

4. This is often the result of damage to the association cortex in the parietal lobe. It occurs because this part of the brain is involved in various spatial tasks, such as being able to tell where things are in the environment, and also being able to locate one's own body in space. If a person suffers damage to this area on the right hemisphere, s/he may not pay attention to things on the left side of the body, or may not even recognize that an arm or leg belongs to her or him.

5. Our subjective experiences are based on brain activity, although often this activity involves several areas of the brain. The binding problem refers to our lack of understanding of HOW the brain is able to integrate all this activity so that we experience it as a cohesive, whole event.

6. The main route for toxins and other substances to get into different organs is through the blood stream. The brain is served by capillaries that allow nutrients in and remove waste products. Because the brain is especially vulnerable (that it, because adult neurons do not for the most part replicate), it is especially important to keep toxins out of the brain. In many parts of the brain the capillaries are structured to do just that. The cells that make up the capillary walls are tightly packed together, so that very few substances can pass through them without going through special channels. And the special channels are selective in what they allow through. However, not all brain areas are protected in this manner. In the area postrema, toxins can get in, and it is actually beneficial that they do in some cases. If a toxin is detected in this area, it triggers the vomiting response, and if the source of the toxin is in the stomach, it will be removed from the body.

7. Cranial nerves III (oculomotor), IV (trochlear), and VI (abducens) control eye movement. Cranial nerves X (vagus), and XII (hypogloassal) are probably involved in speech.

8. The sympathetic nervous system consists of components of several of the spinal nerves serving various internal organs. The activity of its neurons is coordinated by the fact the many of them form synapses within the sympathetic ganglion chain just outside the spinal cord,

which allows for a fast, coordinated response. No such structure exists in the parasympathetic division. The advantage of the fast action of the sympathetic division is that because it is responsible for mobilizing the body's resources in times of stress, it is able to ensure a quick physical response to those stressors.

9. First of all, axons contain a growth cone, which is used to find the correct pathway. The cone is sensitive to the external chemical environment, and is attracted to certain places and repelled from others. The sensitivity of the growth cone to different chemicals can also change over time as the axon grows into different areas. Also, pioneer neurons are those that "pave the way" for subsequent neurons to follow.

10. By initially overproducing neurons, the nervous system allows for streamlining (elimination of unused and retention of used connections) in response to the particular environmental stimuli the organism encounters. Because the environment is somewhat unpredictable, it is impossible to determine ahead of time which connections will be the most important. Therefore, environmental input essentially selects the important connections at the expense of other, less important ones.

11. While there may be some detrimental effects, they would probably be worse if she had been exposed earlier, between 8 and 15 weeks, because that is when proliferation and migration are occurring at high rates.

12. Syndactyly is a condition in which the fingers are connected by a web, are of limited usefulness, and are mapped onto overlapping areas of the somatosensory cortex. Within a week following surgical separation, patients' brains showed dramatic changes in that the separated fingers were now represented in distinct locations on the somatosensory cortex.

13. Phantom pain is pain that seems to occur in a body part that is missing. When a limb (arm or leg) is amputated, the part of the somatosensory cortex devoted to it is taken over by neurons from neighboring areas of the body. When these neurons are activated, they can result in the sensation of pain stemming from the missing limb.

14. Healthy presynaptic neurons can form new terminals to create replacement connections. Postsynaptic cells can create new synapses to compensate for less presynaptic input. And "silent" collaterals, terminals that were inactive, may become active almost immediately following injury.

15. One possibility is introducing new neurons, either from fetal cells or stem cells. The other possibilities involve manipulating the environment of the mature CNS so that it does not inhibit axon regeneration. These mechanisms include providing the NS with substances that can promote neural growth, inhibit those substances that inhibit neural growth, serve as "scaffolds" for developing axons, and/or block the immune response that may be harmful to developing axons.

Post-Test

All page references in this section pertain to the textbook.

1. a. Wrong
   b. Correct; males with this disorder usually die shortly before or after birth. All of the other choices are true of periventricular heterotopia.
   c. Wrong
   d. Wrong

2. **a. Correct**
   b. Wrong; this is a bundle of axons in the CNS.
   c. Wrong; this refers to a group of cell bodies in the CNS.
   d. Wrong; this refers to a group of cell bodies in the PNS.

3. a. Wrong; although a couple of the cranial nerves are sometimes considered part of the CNS (see p. 76), in general they are treated as part of the PNS.
   b. Wrong; some of the cranial nerves contain ANS nerves, but not all.
   c. Correct
   d. Wrong

4. **a. Correct**; see p. 60.
   b. Wrong
   c. Wrong
   d. Wrong

5. a. Wrong; this separates the temporal lobes from the frontal and parietal lobes.
   b. Wrong; this consists of axons that connect the two hemispheres.
   c. Wrong; this is not as deep as the longitudinal fissure, and it runs across both hemispheres, perpendicular to the longitudinal fissure.
   d. Correct

6. a. Wrong
   b. Correct
   c. Wrong; this makes up the white matter under the surface.
   d. Wrong; axons, not cell bodies, are typically myelinated.

7. a. Wrong; this is the name for a very deep groove or sulcus.
   b. Correct
   c. Wrong; this refers to a band of fibers connecting the hemispheres.
   d. Wrong; this is a groove.

8. a. Wrong; Penfield was a 20th century neurosurgeon.
   b. Wrong; Gall was a phrenologist.
   c. Correct
   d. Wrong; Sperry was a 20th century neuroscientist.

9.   a.   Wrong; the brain of an animal is more reflective of its body size than its intelligence.
     b.   Wrong; c is also correct.
     c.   Wrong; b is also correct.
     d.   Correct
     e.   Wrong

10.   **a.   Correct**; see Figure 3.8 on p. 64.
     b.   Wrong; this is what posterior means.
     c.   Wrong; this is what superior means.
     d.   Wrong; this is what inferior means.

11.   a.   Wrong; this is anterior to the primary motor cortex.
     b.   Correct
     c.   Wrong; this is posterior to the primary motor cortex and is the somatosensory cortex.
     d.   Wrong; this is the groove separating the pre- and postcentral gyri.

12.   a.   Wrong
     b.   Wrong
     c.   Wrong
     d.   Correct; see Figure 3.9 on p. 65.

13.   a.   Wrong
     b.   Wrong
     c.   Correct; speech is controlled in other parts of the frontal lobe (e.g. Broca's area). All of the other choices refer to functions controlled by the prefrontal cortex.
     d.   Wrong

14.   a.   Wrong; he was a neurosurgeon, but the book does not discuss his performing lobotomies.
     b.   Wrong; he performed split-brain procedures to treat severe epilepsy.
     c.   Correct
     d.   Wrong; he was a 19th century anatomist.

15.   **a.   Correct**; they are still performed, although rarely (see p. 65). All of the other choices are true.
     b.   Wrong
     c.   Wrong
     d.   Wrong

16.   a.   Wrong
     b.   Wrong
     c.   Wrong
     d.   Correct; see p. 65.

17.   a.   Wrong; this is a primary sensory area, not directly involved in recognition.
     b.   Correct
     c.   Wrong
     d.   Wrong; this is involved in the visual recognition of objects.

18. **a.** **Correct**; see p. 67.
    b. Wrong
    c. Wrong
    d. Wrong

19. a. Wrong
    b. Wrong
    c. **Correct**; this is handled by the frontal lobe. All of the other choices are functions of the temporal lobe.
    d. Wrong.

20. a. Wrong; because it has no pain receptors, the brain itself is insensitive to pain.
    b. Wrong; this would be more likely to occur if the primary auditory cortex were stimulated.
    c. Wrong; this would be more likely to occur if the primary visual cortex were stimulated.
    d. **Correct**

21. **a.** **Correct**
    b. Wrong; this is handled in the temporal lobe.
    c. Wrong; this is handled in the parietal lobe.
    d. Wrong
    e. Wrong

22. a. Wrong
    b. Wrong
    c. **Correct**; see p. 68.
    d. Wrong
    e. Wrong

23. a. Wrong
    b. **Correct**; *hypo* means below.
    c. Wrong
    d. Wrong

24. **a.** **Correct**
    b. Wrong; this secretes melatonin and is involved mainly in sleep and wake cycles.
    c. Wrong; this is not an endocrine gland, although it controls the other endocrine glands.
    d. Wrong; this is not responsible for secreting hormones.

25. a. Wrong
    b. **Correct**; see p. 69.
    c. Wrong
    d. Wrong

26. a. Wrong
    b. **Correct**; information also crosses at the anterior commissure and the optic chiasm. All of the other choices are true.
    c. Wrong
    d. Wrong

27. a. Wrong; the left hemisphere controls most language functions in most people.
    b. Wrong; facial recognition involves the right hemisphere.
    c. Wrong; this is not true. In fact, split-brain patients show very few problems.
    d. Correct

28. **a. Correct**; all of the other choices are part of the brain stem.
    b. Wrong
    c. Wrong
    d. Wrong

29. a. Wrong
    b. Wrong
    c. Correct; this is part of the hindbrain. All of the other choices are midbrain structures.
    d. Wrong

30. a. Wrong
    b. Wrong
    c. Wrong
    d. Correct; see p. 71.

31. a. Wrong
    b. Wrong
    c. Wrong
    d. Correct; see pp. 31-32.

32. a. Wrong; Muller postulated the doctrine of specific nerve energies, but he was not a phrenologist.
    b. Correct
    c. Wrong
    d. Wrong

33. a. Wrong
    b. Wrong
    c. Correct; the book defines a reflex as a behavior that is controlled by a direct sensory-motor connection or sensory-inter-motor neuron connection. All of the other choices are true of reflexes.
    d. Wrong

34. a. Wrong
    b. Wrong
    c. Wrong
    d. Correct; this is accomplished by the blood-brain barrier. All of the other choices are true of the CSF.

35. a. Wrong; this controls glands and organs.
    b. Correct
    c. Wrong; this is a subdivision of the ANS.
    d. Wrong; although motor control begins in the CNS, it is the motor nerves of the PNS that actually physically control the skeletal muscles.

36. a. Wrong
    b. Wrong
    c. Wrong
    d. Correct; see p. 76.

37. **a. Correct**; all of the other choices are the result of sympathetic activation.
    b. Wrong
    c. Wrong
    d. Wrong

38. a. Wrong; this is when new neurons are formed.
    b. Wrong; this is when neurons migrate.
    c. Correct
    d. Wrong; this is when synapses and neurons are lost.

39. **a. Correct**; see p. 79.
    b. Wrong
    c. Wrong
    d. Wrong

40. a. Wrong; these are the first set of neurons that send axonic projections to postsynaptic targets, which are then followed by axons of other neurons.
    b. Correct
    c. Wrong; these cells wrap themselves around axons after migration and growth have occurred.
    d. Wrong; no such cells are mentioned in the text.

41. a. Wrong
    b. Wrong
    c. Correct; see p. 81.
    d. Wrong

42. a. Wrong
    b. Wrong
    c. Wrong
    d. Correct; although the other areas may remain somewhat plastic, the association areas, which are responsible for learning, are probably the most plastic throughout the lifespan.

43. a. Wrong
    b. Correct; there is no mention of this in the text. All of the other choices are true of FAS.
    c. Wrong
    d. Wrong

44. **a. Correct**
    b. Wrong; this is actually the first part of the cortex to be myelinated.
    c. Wrong; these are myelinated early.
    d. Wrong; as a subcortical structure important for sustaining life, it is mature quite early.

45. a. Wrong
    b. Wrong
    c. Wrong
    d. Correct; this exemplifies regeneration. All of the other choices are examples of reorganization.

46. a. Wrong
    b. Wrong
    c. Correct; once mature, CNS neurons in mammals are inhibited from regenerating. All of the other choices represent neurons that may regenerate following damage.
    d. Wrong

47. a. Wrong
    b. Wrong
    c. Correct; see p. 85.
    d. Wrong

48. **a. Correct**; there are many examples in the text.
    b. Correct; there are many examples in the text.
    c. Wrong; this is currently unlikely to happen in the mature human brain.
    d. Wrong; this is currently unlikely to happen in the mature human brain.

49. a. Wrong
    b. Wrong
    c. Correct; the person described in the book who was an untreated hydrocephalic and who had above normal intelligence was the exception to the rule. Left untreated, this disorder usually results in mental retardation. All of the other choices are true.
    d. Wrong

Chapter 4: Drugs and Addiction

Chapter Outline and Learning Objectives

As you read the chapter, use these learning objectives to guide your studying. You should be able to define the key terms from the text, which are shown in boldface type below.

1) Psychoactive Drugs
- Describe the **agonistic** and **antagonistic** effects of **psychoactive drugs**.

- Distinguish between **addiction, withdrawal**, and **tolerance**.

   a) Opiates
- Describe the **analgesic, hypnotic**, and **euphoric** effects of **opiates**.

- Distinguish between opium, morphine, **heroin**, and codeine.

- What are the therapeutic uses of opiates?

- Why is heroin so addictive?

- Explain conditioned tolerance.

- What is the relationship between the **ligands endorphins** and opiates?

   b) Depressants
- Describe the **sedative** and **anxiolytic** effects of **depressants**.

   i) Alcohol
- Describe the central nervous system effects of **alcohol** at different concentrations.

- What are the health consequences of alcohol withdrawal, including **delirium tremens**, and long-term alcohol abuse?

- What effects does alcohol have on neurotransmitters?

- Discuss the cause and symptoms of **fetal alcohol syndrome**.

ii) Barbiturates and Benzodiazepines
- Describe the general effects and clinical uses of **barbiturates** and **benzodiazepines**, as well as their potential for abuse.

- Compare the effects of barbiturates and benzodiazepines on neurotransmitters.

c) Stimulants
- Describe the effects of **stimulants**.

i) Cocaine
- Describe the effects of **cocaine**, including behavioral effects, effects on neurotransmitters, and negative effects on the nervous system.

- What were some of the early uses of cocaine?

- Discuss the addictive potential of cocaine and the effectiveness of treating addiction.

- Discuss the evidence that prenatal cocaine exposure leads to problems with central nervous system development.

ii) Amphetamine
- Describe the effects of **amphetamines**, including behavioral effects and effects on neurotransmitters. Which type is the most potent?

- Describe the psychotic effects of amphetamine.

iii) Nicotine
- Describe the effects of **nicotine** at different doses.

- What are the withdrawal symptoms of nicotine? How likely is someone to successfully quit smoking?

- What are the health problems caused by long-term cigarette smoking?

- What long-term effects does smoking during pregnancy have on the fetus?

- How does nicotine affect neurotransmitters and cells in the nervous system?

    iv) Caffeine
- Describe the behavioral and neurotransmitter effects of **caffeine**.

- Discuss the symptoms of caffeine withdrawal.

d) Psychedelics
- Describe the perceptual distortions caused by **psychedelic** drugs.

- What effects do psychedelic drugs have on neurotransmitters?

- What are the potential harmful effects of MDMA on the nervous system?

- Why are researchers interested in PCP?

e) Marijuana
- Distinguish between **marijuana**, THC, and **hashish**.

- What is the relationship between THC and **anandamide**?

- What parts of the brain contain cannabinoid receptors?

- What effects may prenatal exposure to THC have on child development?

- Discuss the controversies surrounding legalization of marijuana and its status as an addictive substance.

2) Addiction
- Discuss the problems with the assumption that addiction occurs as a result of avoidance of withdrawal symptoms.

a) The Neural Basis of Addiction
   - Discuss the role of the periaqueductal gray in withdrawal.

   - Discuss the role of the **mesolimbic dopamine system** in addiction. What is the significance of the **nucleus accumbens (NAcc)** and the **ventral tegmental area (VTA)**?

b) Dopamine and Reward
   - Why do researchers suspect that drugs that increase dopamine levels in the mesolimbic dopamine system lead to **reward** and addiction?

   - Discuss the role of **electrical brain stimulation (ESB)** in the study of reinforcement. What is the significance of the **medial forebrain bundle (MFB)**?

   - What evidence is there that reinforcement from ESB and drugs involves similar mechanisms?

   - What naturally occurring behaviors seem to result in activation of some mesolimbic dopamine system areas? Why might this be?

   - What evidence is there that PCP's effect involves both dopamine and glutamate?

   - Discuss the role that learning may play in addiction.

c) Ending Dependency on Drugs
   - Discuss the difficulties people face when trying to quit using drugs.

   i) Pharmacological Treatments
      - Discuss the use of the following drug treatments, including their advantages and disadvantages: drug **agonists**, including **methadone**; drug **antagonists**, including **Naltrexone**; **aversive treatment**, including **Antabuse**; and **anti-drug vaccines**.

   ii) Other Treatment Options
      - Discuss the use of drugs to treat drug addiction. What are the moral/ethical and practical implications of this approach?

3) The Neural and Genetic Bases of Alcoholism
- Discuss why researchers rely on the study of alcoholism more than any other form of addiction to understand drug addiction.

a) The EEG as a Diagnostic Tool
- What is an **electroencephalogram (EEG)**? An **evoked potential (EP)**?

- How do alcoholics and those predisposed to alcoholism differ in EEG and evoked potential responses from nonalcoholics?

b) Two Kinds of Alcoholism
- Describe Cloninger's method for studying genetic and environmental contributions to alcoholism. Why is his approach more valid than previous studies?

- Distinguish between the characteristics of **early-** and **late-onset alcoholics**.

c) Dopamine and Serotonin Irregularities
- Discuss the role of the A1 dopamine **allele** in alcoholism. How do the brains of individuals with this allele differ from other people's? How does this explain the fact that alcoholics are often less sensitive to alcohol's effects than nonalcoholics?

- What role does **aldehyde dehydrogenase (ALDH)** play in alcoholism? Why are people with a deficiency in this enzyme unlikely to become alcoholics?

- Discuss the role of serotonin in alcoholism. How are serotonin and dopamine thought to interact in producing the rewarding effects of drugs?

d) Implications of Alcoholism Research
- What can the study of alcoholism tell us about the biological and environmental determinants of other behaviors?

___

Psychoactive Drugs

Summary and Guided Review

After studying this section in the text, fill in the blanks of the following summary. The answers are given on pp. 91-92.

Drugs, substances that _____ (1), can have _____ (2) effects in which they mimic the effects of neurotransmitters, or _____ (3) effects in which they block or reduce the effects of neurotransmitters. _____ (4) drugs alter psychological functioning. Individuals who become obsessed with obtaining a drug or use it compulsively are showing signs of _____ (5). When a person stops taking a drug, she or he may experience symptoms of _____ (6), usually opposite in effect of the drug. With repeated use, the brain may develop tolerance to a drug, a result of a reduction in quantity or _____ (7) of receptors.

Opiates are drugs that come from opium poppies; these drugs have powerful psychoactive effects, including analgesic, _____ (8), and euphoric effects. Derivatives of opium include morphine, which may be used for _____ _____ (9) in cancer patients and others, and _____ (10), which has been used as a cough suppressant. _____ (11) is the opiate most commonly abused, because of its intense effects on the nervous system. In a long-term study of heroin addicts, the most common cause of death (25%) was _____ _____ (12), and about _____ (13) of those surviving were still using heroin. Overdose may also be common because of _____ _____ (14). The body actually produces _____(15), which are ligands that affect the same receptors as opiates.

Drugs that have inhibitory effects on the central nervous system are called _____ (16). Alcohol, the most commonly abused drug, is produced by a process called _____ (17). Its effects include impairments in _____ (18) and motor functions, and someone with a blood-alcohol level of _____ (19) is considered too intoxicated to drive. At concentrations of 0.5%, a person may suffer _____ (20). Severe withdrawal symptoms such as hallucinations, delusions, and seizures, also known as _____ _____ (21), may occur following prolonged alcohol abuse. Health problems associated with long term use of alcohol include cirrhosis of the _____ (22) and brain damage due to a deficiency in _____ (23). Alcohol affects the central nervous system by inhibiting _____ (24) receptors and by enhancing GABA$_A$ at its receptors, which results in _____ (25) of the neurons. Exposure to alcohol during prenatal development may result in _____ _____ (26), irritability, attention problems, and facial anomalies, a cluster of symptoms called _____ _____ _____ (27). The drugs

79

that have been commonly used to treat anxiety are barbiturates and _____ (28), which are safer, although still _____ (29).

Stimulants are drugs that produce arousal and _____ (30) and enhance _____ (31). Cocaine, which is derived from the _____ (32) plant, produces euphoria as well as relief from _____ (33). Pure cocaine, in the form of freebase or _____ (34), produces especially rapid, intense effects. Cocaine blocks the reuptake of _____ (35) and serotonin, which results in removal of cortical _____ (36) of lower structures. Although in the past cocaine was not considered dangerous, it is now recognized as being quite addictive, especially when injected or _____ (37). Among cocaine addicts, _____ (38) disorders are common, a fact which makes treatment difficult. Other problems associated with cocaine use include _____ _____ (39), psychotic symptoms, and _____ (40), which result from increased sensitivity to the drug with prolonged use. Although cocaine's prenatal effects on babies may be confounded with environmental factors such as _____ (41) and neglect, animal studies reveal brain damage resulting from prenatal exposure, and a controlled adoption study revealed that children exposed to cocaine prenatally had lower IQs and problems with _____ (42) and attention. Due to their tendency to enhance alertness, even in sleepy individuals, _____ (43) such as Benzedrine and methamphetamine are often used to stay awake for long periods of time. These drugs cause an increase in the release of and then _____ (44) of _____ (45) and dopamine. Psychotic symptoms of prolonged use include hallucinations and _____ (46) similar to those seen in paranoid schizophrenics. Nicotine, the addictive psychoactive ingredient in tobacco, has _____ (47) effects when taken in short puffs, but _____ (48) effects when deeply inhaled. Extremely large doses can cause nausea and vomiting, and in extreme cases _____ (49). Most people find that when they quit smoking, the withdrawal effects such as anxiety and _____ (50) are unpleasant, and many return to smoking. Long-term health problems in smokers include respiratory diseases, lung cancer, and _____ _____ (51), which results in poor circulation to the extremities and possibly requires amputation. Children exposed to nicotine prenatally have more problems with _____ _____ (52) than other children. In the central nervous system, _____ (53) - releasing neurons are activated by nicotine, leading to cortical arousal. Caffeine, a milder stimulant than cocaine and amphetamine, affects the nervous system by blocking _____ (54) receptors, which results in an increase in the release of dopamine and _____ (55). Withdrawal symptoms are mild, but common; the most problematic symptom seems to be _____ (56).

Psychedelic drugs cause _____ _____ (57) in users, such as intensification or changes of visual stimuli, and cross-modality perceptions in which light produces _____ (58) sensations. Ecstasy is another effect of some of these drugs. LSD and drugs derived from the *Psilocybe mexicana* _____ (59) resemble and stimulate the same receptors as the neurotransmitter _____ (60). Mescaline comes from the _____ _____ (61), and may be used legally for religious practices by some Native Americans. MDMA, otherwise known as _____ (62), stimulates the release of serotonin and dopamine, and may lead to the destruction of _____ (63) neurons. Phencyclidine (PCP), which often triggers _____ (64) like symptoms and therefore may be useful in studying psychosis, shows indications of being an addictive substance.

The psychoactive ingredient in marijuana and hashish is _____ (65), a substance that binds to the same cannabinoid receptors as the endogenous substance _____ (66). Cannabinoid receptors are found on _____ (67) and axon _____ (68), and are located throughout the central nervous system. Marijuana's effects on cognition and time perception may be due to its effects on the _____ (69) cortex, whereas the memory impairment seen with marijuana use probably results from its effects on the _____ (70). Prenatal exposure to marijuana has been linked to various cognitive problems in school-aged children. Marijuana may have beneficial uses, such as relieving _____ (71) and _____ (72), and is legal to use for medical purposes in some states. Marijuana's status as an addictive substance is controversial. While most people suffer no withdrawal symptoms when they stop using the drug, some cases of anxiety, _____ (73), and stomach cramps have been reported. More importantly, monkeys will _____-_____ (74) THC when given the opportunity to do so, suggesting that it is an addictive substance.

Short Answer & Essay Questions

Answer the following questions. See pp. 92-93 for sample answers.

1. Jerry recently began shooting heroin. After the first few times, he noticed that the same dose had less of an effect, and he had to use more heroin to achieve the same high he experienced the first time he tried it. Explain what is happening to Jerry.

2. What evidence is there that heroin use may lead to conditioned tolerance?

3. Explain why alcohol has stimulant properties at low doses.

4. What are the different methods by which cocaine is used currently as a drug of abuse?

5. All of the stimulants discussed in the chapter increase or enhance dopamine, which results in heightened arousal. Explain how this happens. Include in your answer the relationship between cortical and subcortical structures.

6. Joan smoked marijuana for most of the time that she was pregnant with her son Rick. Now that Rick is 18 months old, Joan has noticed no signs of mental or physical impairment, and feels confident that he will suffer no long lasting effects. Is she right? Defend your answer.

Addiction

Summary and Guided Review

After studying this section in the text, fill in the blanks of the following summary. The answers are found on p. 92.

In the past, addiction researchers assumed that people became addicted to drugs because they wanted to avoid _____ _____ (75). However, there are many problems with this explanation. Also, the concept of _____ _____ (76) is difficult to understand because it implies a non-physical basis to addiction.

Work with animals has shown that while the _____ _____ (77) is involved in withdrawal symptoms, it is not implicated in addiction. Rats will learn to self-administer drugs into both the _____ _____ (78) and the ventral tegmental area, indicating that these are _____ (79) centers.

Many drugs that have rewarding effects have been shown to increase _____ (80) levels in certain areas of the brain. Furthermore, drugs that are dopamine _____ (81) tend to reduce the euphoric effects of _____ (82). If an experimental animal receives _____ _____ _____ (83) to the medial forebrain bundle as a reward for pressing a lever, it will continue to press the lever at a high rate over a long period of time, indicating that this stimulation is highly reinforcing. This may be related to the reward experienced from drug use because dopamine release in the _____ _____ (84) occurs with ESB. The function of reward centers of the brain may be related to _____ (85) activities such as eating and reproductive activities, as evidenced by the fact that stimulation of some areas in which ESB is effective leads to eating or sexual activity.

Dopamine is apparently not the only _____ (86) involved in addiction. The rewarding effects of some drugs, such as _____ (87) and PCP, may involve other neurotransmitter systems. In addition to directly triggering an increase of dopamine in the nucleus accumbens, PCP causes cells in the _____ (88) cortex to release _____ (89).

Other factors are important in explaining addiction. In cocaine addicts, the sight of drug paraphernalia evokes _____ (90), which coincides with an increase of activity in the brain areas involved in learning and _____ (91). In rats, stimulation of the hippocampus has been shown to _____ (92) a lever-press response that was once associated with receiving a drug reward. Researchers believe that the use of addictive drugs leads to long-term changes in the brain.

Quitting an addictive substance can be very difficult. When a person stops taking a drug, the body rids itself of the drug, a process called _____ (93). Withdrawal symptoms can be intense, and in the case of alcohol withdrawal, _____ (94) may be given to relieve some of the symptoms. Once the withdrawal symptoms have subsided, abstaining from a drug may involve the therapeutic use of other drugs. For example, _____ (95) is an opiate agonist given to heroin users that has milder effects and can be obtained legally. Naltrexone is used as an _____ _____ (96) of both opiate and _____ (97) addiction. _____ (98) is an aversive treatment for alcohol addiction; it works by making the person violently ill if alcohol is consumed. A promising area of research involves the use of _____ - _____ _____ (99), which work by stimulating the immune system to produce antibodies for a drug, thereby disabling it. This treatment is expected to have fewer _____ _____ (100) and be longer lasting than current pharmacological treatments. Addiction has been correlated with reduced _____ (101), and drugs that increase the level of this neurotransmitter are useful in treating both alcohol and _____ (104) addiction. Additionally, drugs that indirectly affect the reward mechanism may be useful in treating addiction. For example, a drug that enhances _____ (105) reduces alcohol cravings. The use of pharmacological treatments for addiction is controversial. However, studies suggest that the combination of drug treatment with _____ (106) is quite effective.

Short Answer & Essay Questions

Answer the following questions. See pp. 93-94 for sample answers.

7. What are the problems with explaining addiction as the avoidance of withdrawal symptoms?

8. Ken uses cocaine on a regular basis. He is currently taking a medication that blocks dopamine receptors. He notices that he no longer feels the euphoric effects of cocaine, even when he takes a slightly larger dose than normal. Explain what is happening.

9. Why are dopamine antagonists ineffective in completely blocking the rewarding effects of PCP in the nucleus accumbens?

10. Compare the mechanisms of methadone and naltrexone treatments for opiate addiction. What are the drawbacks of each treatment?

11. How might the immune system be manipulated to treat drug addiction? What are the advantages of this approach?

12. Why are pharmacological treatments for drugs controversial? Do you think they should be used? Why or why not?

The Neural and Genetic Bases of Addiction

Summary and Guided Review

After studying this section in the text, fill in the blanks of the following summary. The answers are found on p. 92.

_____ (105) addiction has been more thoroughly studied than any other form of addiction. Furthermore, because most drug addictions share common elements, alcoholism provides a useful model for understanding all drug addiction.

Research using the EEG has shown that male alcoholics and their sons have more _____ _____ (106) waves than those not at risk for alcoholism. Sons of alcoholic men also show _____ (107) EEG responsiveness when given a small amount of alcohol; this is most pronounced in sons of alcoholics who later become _____ (108). Furthermore, alcoholics and their children show less responsiveness in the _____ _____ (109) in response to novel stimuli than nonalcoholics and their children.

Based on twin and adoption studies, there appears to be a strong _____ (110) component to alcoholism. The results of _____ (111)'s comprehensive study of Swedish adoptees suggested that there are early- and late-onset alcoholics, although the differences between them are not entirely clear-cut. In _____ - _____ (112), or Type I alcoholics, problem drinking usually emerges after age _____ (113), and these people may alternate between abstinence and _____ _____ (114). They tend to feel _____ (115) about drinking, and they are cautious and _____ _____ (116). Type 2, or early-onset alcoholics, may begin drinking in adolescence, and display a host of personality traits characteristic of _____ (117) personality disorder, including impulsiveness and emotional _____ (118). _____ (119) - onset alcoholics are more likely to be hospitalized, and have therefore been over represented in studies of alcoholism. Furthermore, the environment seems to have a greater impact on the development of alcoholism in _____ (120) -onset alcoholics.

The exact role of genetics in alcoholism is beginning to be understood. Alcoholics and people addicted to other drugs often have different _____ (121) for D_2 receptors than nonalcoholics, and they also show _____ (122) of these receptors when examined at autopsy. People who become alcoholics report that prior to becoming addicted they were often able to consume large amounts of alcohol with few effects. This reduced _____ (123) to alcohol may be a result of having fewer D_2 receptors. Addiction to alcohol then may result in part from consuming large quantities of it in order to feel its effects. This explanation is supported by the fact that people who inherit _____ _____ (124), which leads to nausea and other unpleasant effects when drinking, rarely become alcoholics. Serotonin may also play a role in alcoholism and drug abuse. Alcohol _____ (125) serotonin pathways and enhances serotonin activity and mood. In turn, serotonin may enhance the rewarding effects of _____ (126). Serotonin _____ (127) reduce many of the effects of alcohol, making it easier to recover from addiction.

Alcoholism research has a number of applications. It provides a model for understanding the role of genetics in _____ (128); and it demonstrates how genes and _____ (129) may interact in producing behavior, as well as the complexity of the neural basis of behavior.

Short Answer & Essay Questions

Answer the following questions. See pp. 94-95 for sample answers.

13. Describe three ways in which the EEG patterns of alcoholics and those at risk for becoming alcoholics differ from nonalcoholics. Why might the EEG be a useful tool for determining who is most at risk for becoming an alcoholic?

14. Distinguish between early- and late-onset alcoholics in terms of (1) the developmental pattern of the addiction and (2) the personality characteristics of each type.

15. Why did Cloninger's studies of hereditary and environmental factors in alcoholism suggest that environment is sometimes important, whereas previous studies did not show that environment is important?

16. Many alcoholics report that when they started drinking, alcohol seemed to affect them less than others. What genetic and neurological differences may account for this?

17. Gretchen is currently undergoing outpatient treatment for alcohol addiction. As part of her recovery process, she takes a prescription drug that blocks serotonin. She notices that when she drinks alcohol now, it doesn't feel as good as it used to. Explain why she experiences reduced effects.

18. Imagine that you are a scientist who studies the biological basis of alcoholism. You are in the process of seeking a multi-million dollar grant to fund additional research in this area. The granting agency wants to know why alcoholism should be studied so intensely, when there are many other forms of addiction. How would you respond in a way that justifies your continued study of alcoholism?

Post-Test

Use these multiple choice questions to check your understanding of the chapter. The answers, along with explanations, are found beginning on p. 95.

1. Which of the following is NOT true of heroin use?
   a. It may lead to an addiction that is difficult to overcome.
   b. It may lead to withdrawal symptoms that are quite severe.
   c. Users experience intense euphoria followed by relaxation.
   d. It may lead to conditioned tolerance.

2. Arlene has been smoking marijuana three to four times a week for two years. She often worries about running out, and occasionally steals small amounts from her friends who smoke. She recently tried to quit, but started again after one month of being off the drug. Arlene is experiencing
   a. withdrawal.
   b. tolerance.
   c. addiction.
   d. depression.

3. Alcohol is BEST classified as a _____ drug.
   a. depressant
   b. stimulant
   c. opiate
   d. psychedelic

4. Jerry, a 45-year-old chronic alcoholic, has recently begun experiencing memory loss and coordination problems. His doctor informs him that he may be suffering from _____ as a result of his long-term alcohol abuse.
   a. delirium tremens
   b. conditioned tolerance
   c. Korsakoff's syndrome
   d. psychosis

5. Which of the following drugs enhances the activity of GABA?
   a. alcohol
   b. barbiturates
   c. benzodiazepines
   d. all of the above

6. Which of the following is NOT TRUE regarding the early historical use of cocaine?
   a. The freebase form was used by South American Indians for centuries.
   b. It was an ingredient in Coca-Cola until 1906.
   c. In the 1800's it was used as a local anesthetic.
   d. Sigmund Freud recommended it to his family and friends.

7. Prenatal exposure to cocaine has been linked to which of the following problems?
   a. seizure disorders in children
   b. poor cognitive development
   c. facial abnormalities
   d. all of the above

8. The most potent form of amphetamine is
   a. Benzedrine.
   b. Dexedrine.
   c. methamphetamine.
   d. dextroamphetamine.

9. What percentage of people who quit smoking are able to abstain for at least 2 years?
   a. 10%
   b. 20%
   c. 50%
   d. 80%

10. Which of the following is NOT a health problem associated with cigarette smoking or tobacco use?
    a. Buerger's disease
    b. cancer of the mouth
    c. emphysema
    d. Korsakoff's syndrome

11. Which stimulant affects dopamine levels indirectly through its effects on adenosine?
    a. Caffeine
    b. Cocaine
    c. Nicotine
    d. Amphetamine

12. Which of the following psychedelic drugs is found in a cactus?
    a. Ecstasy
    b. Angel dust
    c. Mescaline
    d. Psilocybin

13. Which of the following psychedelic drugs is most closely related to amphetamines?
    a. Ecstasy
    b. Angel dust
    c. LSD
    d. Mescaline

14. The psychoactive ingredient in marijuana affects the same receptor sites as which of the following ligand?
    a. Endorphin
    b. Anandamide
    c. Dopamine
    d. Glutamate

15. The cognitive deficits seen in children exposed to marijuana prenatally seem most likely due to impairment of which part of the brain?
    a. Hippocampus
    b. Basal ganglia
    c. Cerebellum
    d. Prefrontal cortex

16. The MOST compelling reason to believe that marijuana is an addictive substance is that
    a. some people experience withdrawal symptoms when they stop using it.
    b. many people use it for years.
    c. animals will self-administer it.
    d. it has negative effects on the fetus.

17. Rats will learn to press a lever in order to inject drugs into which of the following brain structures?
    a. Periaqueductal gray
    b. Ventral tegmental area
    c. Striate nucleus
    d. Ventromedial hypothalamus

18. Addictive drugs may produce euphoric effects by
    a. blocking the reuptake of dopamine.
    b. blocking dopamine receptors.
    c. eliminating dopamine from the synapse.
    d. inhibiting the release of dopamine.

19. ESB has its greatest effect
    a. on animals missing a specific subtype of dopamine receptor.
    b. when an animal is also given cocaine or amphetamine.
    c. in brain areas where dopaminergic neurons are highly concentrated.
    d. in brain areas where serotonergic neurons are highly concentrated.

20. An animal with lesions in the ventral tegmental area will
    a. have about a 94% increase in dopamine.
    b. be more sensitive to dopamine.
    c. learn to self-administer drugs like cocaine and amphetamine.
    d. lever-press for ESB at a very low rate.

21. A male rat that is presented with a sexually receptive female shows an increase of dopamine in the
    a. ventral tegmental area.
    b. nucleus accumbens.
    c. medial forebrain bundle.
    d. prefrontal cortex.

22. Opiates are implicated in the rewarding effects of which drug?
    a. Alcohol
    b. Cocaine
    c. Amphetamine
    d. Nicotine

23. PCP has an antagonistic effect on
    a. dopamine.
    b. glutamate.
    c. serotonin.
    d. endorphins.

24. When a rat that has learned to press a lever in order to receive a drug reward no longer receives the reward, it will stop pressing the lever. However, stimulation of the _____ reinstates the lever pressing.
    a. nucleus accumbens
    b. ventral tegmental area
    c. hippocampus
    d. lateral hypothalamus

25. Freud suffered from lifelong addiction to
    a. cocaine.
    b. alcohol.
    c. heroin.
    d. nicotine.

26. Sharon was recently admitted to the hospital because she was suffering severe withdrawal symptoms, including seizures. She was given benzodiazepine to reduce the severity of her symptoms. Which of the following drugs is Sharon MOST likely addicted to?
    a. alcohol
    b. heroin
    c. nicotine
    d. cocaine

27. Nicotine gum is an example of an _____ treatment for drug addiction.
    a. antagonist
    b. aversive
    c. agonist
    d. anti-drug

28. Naltrexone may be used to block opiate receptors in people who abuse
    a. nicotine.
    b. cocaine.
    c. amphetamines.
    d. alcohol.

29. Methadone was developed as an analgesic during World War II when _____ was in short supply.
    a. morphine
    b. heroine
    c. codeine
    d. endorphin

30. The major disadvantage of antagonistic pharmacological treatments for drug addiction is that
    a. the person becomes addicted to the replacement drug.
    b. they usually make the person violently ill.
    c. their effects are unpleasant.
    d. they are prohibitively expensive.

31. Which of the following statements is NOT true of anti-drug vaccines?
    a. They lead to the destruction of drug molecules before they can reach the brain.
    b. They are more effective than other pharmacological treatments in humans.
    c. They result in fewer side-effects than other pharmacological treatments.
    d. Their effects may be longer lasting than other pharmacological treatments.

32. Drugs that affect which neurotransmitters have shown promise in treating alcohol addiction?
    a. serotonin and glutamate
    b. GABA and glutamate
    c. GABA and serotonin
    d. serotonin, glutamate, and GABA

33. For heroin addicts,
    a. methadone treatment alone is the most effective treatment option.
    b. counseling alone has a high rate of success.
    c. no treatment method has more than a 50% success rate.
    d. methadone plus counseling is quite effective.

34. Which of the following statements regarding EEG and alcoholism studies is NOT true?
    a. Sons of male alcoholics show the same EEG response patterns as nonalcoholics.
    b. Children of alcoholics show abnormal P300 wave responses.
    c. When under the influence of alcohol, alcoholics show reduced EEG responding compared to nonalcoholics.
    d. Male alcoholics show more high frequency EEG waves than nonalcoholics.

35. The P300 wave
    a. shows promise for diagnosing those at risk for alcoholism.
    b. occurs in response to a novel stimulus.
    c. occurs in similar ways among family members.
    d. all of the above.

36. The heritability for alcoholism is
    a. 5-10%.
    b. 20-30%.
    c. 50-60%.
    d. 80-90%.

37. Which of the following characteristics typifies early-onset alcoholics?
    a. They tend to feel guilty about drinking.
    b. They tend to be novelty seekers.
    c. They may abstain from alcohol for long periods of time.
    d. They are often emotionally dependent.

38. Which of the following is a characteristic of Type 1 alcoholics?
    a. They begin having problems with alcohol in adolescence.
    b. They tend to behave aggressively when drinking.
    c. They are quite cautious.
    d. All of the above

39. Cloninger's study of early- and late-onset alcoholics indicates that
    a. exposure to alcoholism in the home has more of an impact on the children of late-onset alcoholics than the children of early-onset alcoholics.
    b. exposure to alcoholism in the home has more of an impact on the children of early-onset alcoholics than the children of late-onset alcoholics.
    c. exposure to alcoholism in the home has about the same effect on the children of early- and late-onset alcoholics.
    d. late-onset alcoholics are most likely to have children who are early-onset alcoholics.

40. Compared to people with the A2 allele for dopamine receptors, those with the A1 allele
    a. have fewer D_2 receptors.
    b. have more D_2 receptors.
    c. are more sensitive to dopamine.
    d. are more sensitive to alcohol.

41. Which of the following is NOT a predictor of alcoholism?
    a. being the child of an alcoholic
    b. feeling fewer effects of alcohol when drinking
    c. having ALDH deficiency
    d. showing a delayed P300 wave

42. ALDH is an enzyme that
    a. breaks down dopamine.
    b. blocks serotonin receptors.
    c. has an agonistic effect on alcohol.
    d. breaks down alcohol.

43. Which of the following statements about serotonin is TRUE?
    a. It inhibits the dopamine reward system.
    b. Its activity is stimulated by alcohol.
    c. Its antagonists enhance the effects of alcohol.
    d. It is involved in alcoholism, but not other forms of drug addiction.

Answers and Explanations

Guided Review

1. change the body or its functioning
2. agonistic
3. antagonistic
4. Psychoactive
5. addiction
6. withdrawal
7. sensitivity
8. hypnotic
9. pain relief
10. codeine
11. Heroin
12. drug overdose
13. half (or 50%)
14. conditioned tolerance
15. endorphins
16. depressants
17. fermentation
18. cognitive
19. 0.08-0.10
20. death
21. delirium tremens
22. liver
23. vitamin B_1
24. glutamate
25. hyperpolarization
26. mental retardation
27. fetal alcohol syndrome
28. benzodiazepines
29. addictive
30. alertness
31. mood

32. coca
33. fatigue
34. crack
35. dopamine
36. inhibition
37. smoked/
   inhaled
38. psychological
39. brain damage
40. seizures
41. poverty
42. language
43. amphetamines
44. depletion
45. norepi-
   nephrine
46. delusions
47. stimulating
48. tranquilizing/
   depressant
49. death
50. drowsiness/
   lightheaded-
   ness/
   headaches
51. Buerger's
   disease
52. impulse
   control
53. dopamine
54. adenosine
55. acetylcholine
56. headache
57. perceptual
   distortions
58. auditory
59. mushroom

60. serotonin
61. peyote cactus
62. ecstasy
63. serotonergic
64. schizophrenia
65. THC
66. anandamide
67. dendrites
68. terminals
69. prefrontal
70. hippocampus
71. nausea
72. glaucoma
73. irritability
74. self-administer/inject
75. withdrawal symptoms
76. psychological
   dependence
77. periaqueductal gray
78. nucleus accumbens
79. reward
80. dopamine
81. antagonists
82. amphetamines
83. electrical brain
   stimulation
84. nucleus accumbens
85. survival
86. neurotransmitter
87. alcohol
88. frontal
89. glutamate
90. craving
91. emotion
92. reinstate
93. detoxification
94. benzodiazepines

95. methadone
96. antagonist treatment
97. Alcohol
98. Antabuse
99. anti-drug vaccines
100. side effects
101. serotonin
102. nicotine
103. GABA
104. counseling
105. alcohol
106. high-frequency
107. less
108. alcoholic or addicted
109. P300 wave
110. genetic or hereditary
111. Cloninger
112. late-onset
113. 25
114. binge drinking
115. guilty
116. emotionally dependent
117. antisocial
118. detachment
119. Early
120. late
121. alleles
122. fewer
123. sensitivity
124. ALDH deficiency
125. stimulates
126. dopamine
127. antagonists
128. addictions
129. environment

Short Answer & Essay

1. He is experiencing tolerance. His brain has been altered by the use of heroin, either through a loss of receptors affected by the drug, or a reduction in their sensitivity.

2. When rats are given a large dose of heroin in an environment in which they have received heroin before, they are less likely to die than those given the large dose in a novel environment (32% versus 64% of rats in each group died). Likewise, human heroin addicts may be more likely to overdose when they take the same amount of drug in a novel setting. This is thought to occur because the environmental cues present during administration of the drug may elicit tolerance, so the body withstands some of the effects of the drug. When in a different environment, those cues that trigger the tolerance response are no longer present, and the same dose may have a more powerful effect.

3. At any dose, alcohol acts mainly by inhibiting activity in different parts of the central nervous system. At low doses, it inhibits cortical inhibition (disinhibition), which leads to more excited behavior. For example, someone who is normally quiet around strangers may become quite talkative.

4. Cocaine may be processed with hydrochloric acid into powder form, which is snorted. Freebase and crack cocaine are the result of removing the hydrochloric acid. When inhaled, this pure cocaine has a rapid, intense effect on the brain.

5. The cortex tends to inhibit activity in the subcortex. Dopamine is an inhibitory neurotransmitter for much of the central nervous system. High levels of dopamine in the cortex results in LOWER levels of activity here, which REMOVES some of the inhibitory control that the cortex has over the subcortex. It is this removal of inhibition of subcortical structures which is believed to result in euphoria and increased arousal.

6. No, Rick MAY suffer problems a little later in childhood. Some research has shown that children exposed to marijuana prenatally begin manifesting problems around age 4, including problems with visual perception, attention, memory, and language comprehension.

7. One problem is that withdrawal symptoms often don't occur until a person becomes dependent; in the early stages of addiction, they don't experience the symptoms of withdrawal. Therefore, avoidance of withdrawal cannot be the mechanism that maintains early drug use. Second, addicts intentionally go through withdrawal to adjust their tolerance level. Third, many addicts start using a drug again after having quit for a long period of time, and are presumably no longer experiencing withdrawal. Finally, the power of addiction of a drug is not related to the severity of withdrawal. For example, alcohol can cause severe withdrawal symptoms, but heroin or stimulants may not.

8. Normally, when a person takes cocaine, it causes an increase in the release of dopamine in the reward centers of the brain. This is believed to be responsible for the pleasurable sensation associated with using the drug. However, because the second drug Ken is taking blocks those dopamine receptors, he does not feel the rush, even though dopamine is being released at a higher level.

9. PCP has effects on both dopamine and glutamate. Dopamine antagonists can block the effects of dopamine in the nucleus accumbens, but they have no influence on the effects of glutamate. Glutamate and dopamine have opposite effects on certain cells in the nucleus accumbens. When dopamine is present, rewarding effects are experienced, but glutamate inhibits this effect. Because PCP inhibits the glutamate receptors on these neurons, it has the same net effect as the presence of dopamine.

10. Methadone is an opiate agonist; it has similar, although milder effects, to opiates like heroin. Therefore, a heroin addict would probably not experience withdrawal symptoms or cravings while using methadone. However, methadone is addictive, and therefore may not be a good alternative. Naltrexone is an opiate antagonist; it blocks opiate receptors. This prevents any opiates the addict takes from producing their effects, which may lead to a reduction in drug use. However, addicts tend not to like the effect of naltrexone, so they may not continue to use it.

11. Currently, anti-drug vaccines are being tested on animals. These vaccines provide an animal's body with the means of producing antibodies to destroy the drug. They appear to be quite effective, and may soon be available for use with humans. The advantages of these drugs are that they do not result in the side-effects common to drugs that interfere with neurotransmitters, and their effects may be quite long lasting.

12. Pharmacological treatments are controversial because they involve treating drug addiction by giving a person another drug. In the case of methadone, this means substituting a less problematic addiction for a more problematic one. However, not all drug treatments lead to addiction (such as Naltrexone and Antabuse). Also, some people believe that addiction should be overcome by sheer will power, and that relying on other drugs to do it is taking the easy way out.

13. First of all, when not under the influence of alcohol, male alcoholics and their sons show more high frequency waves than nonalcoholics. Second, when given a small amount of alcohol, nonalcoholics show an increase in EEG responding, but the sons of alcoholics show less EEG responsiveness. Finally, alcoholics and their children, who are probably at risk for alcoholism, show reduced P300 waves in response to novel stimuli. These techniques may be useful for determining who is most at risk for alcoholism, since children of alcoholics, who are not alcoholics themselves, often show the same pattern of responses as their parents. In the case of reduced EEG responsiveness when under the influence of alcohol, those sons who showed the most pronounced reduction in responsiveness were most likely to become alcoholics later.

14. Early-onset alcoholics usually begin drinking prior to the age of 25, many of them in their teens. They are more likely to be male, and often display impulsive, aggressive, and reckless behavior, while being socially and emotionally detached from others. This pattern of characteristics is associated with antisocial personality disorder. Late-onset drinkers usually begin having problems with alcohol after the age of 25, following a period of social drinking. They tend to binge drink, which results in guilt feelings; they may abstain from alcohol for long periods of time. They tend to be cautious and emotionally dependent.

15. Cloninger's work was instrumental in identifying the two types of alcoholics, early- and late-onset. His study sample included all people adopted in early childhood to nonrelatives in Stockholm, Sweden, during a 20-year period. Previous studies tended to focus on groups of people hospitalized for alcoholism. The characteristics of these groups are more similar to early-onset alcoholics, and thus do not represent all alcoholics. Because early-onset alcoholism does not seem to be influenced by the rearing environment, these early studies concluded that environment was not an important factor in the development of alcoholism. In Cloninger's study, early-onset alcoholics tended to resemble their biological parents rather than their adoptive parents with respect to alcoholism. Cloninger's late-onset alcoholics, however, were more likely to be raised in an adoptive home in which alcohol was present.

16. Alcoholics who have the A1 allele for D_2 (dopamine) receptors may actually have fewer of these receptors. Because alcohol stimulates dopamine activity, which is experienced as pleasant or rewarding, such individuals would have to consume more alcohol to feel the same level of effect as someone with more D_2 receptors. Greater consumption puts them more at risk for becoming addicted.

17. Serotonin may be involved in alcohol addiction along with dopamine. Alcohol stimulates serotonin activity, which results in elevated mood and also enhances dopamine activity. Therefore, drugs that block serotonin, specifically at the 5-HT$_3$ receptor, limit the mood-enhancing effects of alcohol. They also seem to reduce cravings, which may make it easier to quit.

18. Alcoholism is a good model for studying drug addiction. Many of the addictive drugs have very similar effects in the brain, mostly through their effects on the dopamine reward system. Therefore, any discoveries made about the genetic and neurological bases of alcohol addiction may be applicable to other forms of addiction. Furthermore, alcoholism is the most problematic addiction in our society. Its use is linked to violence, traffic accidents, and other serious behavior problems. Because it is a legal drug, there are more alcoholics than people addicted to other drugs. Consequently, it makes sense to attempt to understand and perhaps control or even eradicate it. In doing so, it may be possible to treat other forms of addiction as well.

Post-Test

All page references in this section pertain to the textbook.

1. a. Wrong
   b. Correct; heroin withdrawal symptoms are similar to flu symptoms. All of the other choices are true of heroin (addiction may be long term, its effects include intense euphoria and relaxation, and it leads to conditioned tolerance).
   c. Wrong
   d. Wrong

2. a. Wrong; withdrawal is a negative physical reaction that occurs when the drug is stopped.
   b. Wrong; tolerance occurs when a person needs more of a drug to achieve the same effect.
   c. Correct
   d. Wrong; she is not showing symptoms of depression.

3. **a. Correct**
   b. Wrong; stimulants include cocaine, amphetamine, nicotine, and caffeine; although alcohol has some stimulant-like properties, especially at low doses, its general function is inhibition of central nervous system activity.
   c. Wrong; opiates include morphine, codeine, and heroin.
   d. Wrong; psychedelics include LSD, psilocybin and psilocin, peyote, mescaline, ecstacy, and PCP.

4. a. Wrong; delirium tremens is a withdrawal symptom of alcohol abuse.
   b. Wrong; conditioned tolerance refers to the nervous system compensating for the presence of a drug.
   c. Correct
   d. Wrong; psychosis is typically a state of acute psychological distress, which may include hallucinations and delusions, that is more commonly associated with amphetamine use.

5. a. Wrong
    b. Wrong
    c. Wrong
    d. **Correct**; all of these depressants work on the GABA receptor complex, although each works slightly differently.

6. a. **Correct**; all of the other choices are true of early cocaine use. South American Indians chewed coca leaves, but freebasing is a modern procedure.
    b. Wrong
    c. Wrong
    d. Wrong

7. a. Wrong; seizures are not mentioned in this part of the text; seizures may be more common in adults who abuse cocaine.
    b. **Correct**
    c. Wrong; facial abnormalities are a sign of fetal alcohol syndrome, but not cocaine use during pregnancy.
    d. Wrong

8. a. Wrong; Benzedrine is the least potent form of amphetamine.
    b. Wrong; Dexedrine is less potent than methamphetamine.
    c. **Correct**
    d. Wrong; dextroamphetamine is the generic form of Dexedrine.

9. a. Wrong
    b. **Correct**; see p. 103.
    c. Wrong
    d. Wrong

10. a. Wrong
    b. Wrong
    c. Wrong
    d. **Correct**; the other choices are associated with tobacco use. Korsakoff's syndrome is associated with chronic alcohol abuse.

11. a. **Correct**
    b. Wrong; cocaine directly blocks the reuptake of dopamine.
    c. Wrong; nicotine directly stimulates dopamine release (neurons that release dopamine contain nicotinic receptors).
    d. Wrong; amphetamine directly causes cells to release more dopamine.

12. a. Wrong; Ecstasy is similar in structure to amphetamine and was originally developed as a weight loss drug.
    b. Wrong; angel dust (PCP) was developed as a veterinary anesthetic.
    c. **Correct**
    d. Wrong; psilocybin in found in the *Psilocybe mexicana* mushroom.

13. a. **Correct**; see pp. 104-105.
    b. Wrong
    c. Wrong
    d. Wrong

14. a.   Wrong; while endorphins are produced in the body, opiates are the drugs that affect their receptors.
    b.   Correct
    c.   Wrong; it is believed that activation of the cannabinoid receptor by THC or anandamide leads to an increase in dopamine.
    d.   Wrong; there is no mention of glutamate in this section of the text.

15. a.   Wrong; it is believed that memory problems experienced by users during intoxication may be due to temporary impairment of the hippocampus.
    b.   Wrong; the basal ganglia are associated with movement.
    c.   Wrong; the cerebellum is also associated with movement.
    d.   Correct

16. a.   Wrong; not everyone suffers from these, and withdrawal symptoms alone are not sufficient evidence of addiction.
    b.   Wrong; while many people do use it for a long period of time, it seems that some of these people can stop without any problems.
    c.   Correct
    d.   Wrong; prenatal effects of a drug have no bearing on whether or not it is addictive.

17. a.   Wrong; although when rats who have received opiate injections to the PAG are given naloxone they do show withdrawal symptoms, they will not learn to self-administer the drug to this location.
    b.   Correct
    c.   Wrong; this area is not mentioned in this part of the text.
    d.   Wrong; this area is not mentioned in this part of the text.

18. **a.   Correct**; the other mechanisms described would lead to reduced dopamine activity at the synapse, which would not produce euphoria.
    b.   Wrong
    c.   Wrong
    d.   Wrong

19. a.   Wrong; these animals are actually less sensitive to euphoria-producing drugs.
    b.   Wrong; there is no mention of the combined effects of ESB and drugs.
    c.   Correct; see p. 109.
    d.   Wrong

20. a.   Wrong; there is actually a 94-99% decrease in dopaminergic neurons.
    b.   Wrong; they are less sensitive to dopamine, especially in that area.
    c.   Wrong; this is not mentioned in the text, but it is unlikely, since they have reduced sensitivity to dopamine, which both of these drugs would increase.
    d.   Correct

21. a.   Wrong; while the VTA is implicated in some rewarding behaviors, sexual activity was not mentioned in the text.
    b.   Correct
    c.   Wrong; while the MFB is implicated in some rewarding behaviors, sexual activity was not mentioned in the text.
    d.   Wrong; although the NAcc sends projections to the frontal cortex, the text does not mention what neurotransmitters are involved.

22. **a.** **Correct**; see p. 110.
    b.   Wrong
    c.   Wrong
    d.   Wrong

23. a.   Wrong; it probably facilitates the release of dopamine.
    b. **Correct**
    c.   Wrong; there is no mention of a relationship between PCP and serotonin.
    d.   Wrong; there is no mention of a relationship between PCP and endorphins.

24. a.   Wrong; in this situation, the stimulation of the hippocampus is necessary to elicit
    activity in the NAcc.
    b.   Wrong; this area is not mentioned as being related to memory and reward.
    c. **Correct**
    d.   Wrong; this area is not mentioned as being related to memory and reward.

25. a.   Wrong; although he used cocaine for a while, he stopped when he realized it was
    dangerous.
    b.   Wrong; this was not mentioned in the text.
    c.   Wrong; this was not mentioned in the text.
    d. **Correct**

26. **a.** **Correct**; benzodiazepines are sometimes given to help people undergoing alcohol
    detoxification and withdrawal because the symptoms are so severe that sometimes people
    die.
    b.   Wrong; withdrawal symptoms are not severe, more flu-like.
    c.   Wrong; although nicotine may produce one of the most difficult addictions to
    overcome, the withdrawal symptoms are not severe or life-threatening.
    d.   Wrong; withdrawal from cocaine is not as severe as withdrawal from alcohol.

27. a.   Wrong; an antagonist treatment interferes with the addictive substance's effects on
    neurotransmitters.
    b.   Wrong; an aversive treatment leads to unpleasant effects if the addictive drug is taken.
    c. **Correct**
    d.   Wrong; this refers to anti-drug vaccines, which stimulate the immune system to
    destroy addictive drug molecules.

28. a.   Wrong; nicotine addiction does not appear to involve opiate receptors.
    b.   Wrong; cocaine addiction does not appear to involve opiate receptors.
    c.   Wrong; amphetamine addiction does not appear to involve opiate receptors.
    d. **Correct**

29. **a.** **Correct**
    b.   Wrong; although similar in structure to morphine and methadone, heroin was not used
    clinically for pain relief.
    c.   Wrong; codeine is a less powerful analgesic, and it was probably in short supply as
    well, given that it is derived from the same source as morphine.
    d.   Wrong; endorphins are endogenous opiates – they cannot be manufactured.

30. a. Wrong; because they have the opposite (usually unpleasant) effect as the addictive drug, it isn't likely that a person would become addicted.
    b. Wrong; although their effects are unpleasant, they are not as bad as some aversive treatments (e.g. compare Naltrexone to Antabuse).
    c. Correct
    d. Wrong; there is no mention of this.

31. a. Wrong; this is true of anti-drug vaccines.
    b. Correct; they have not yet been tested in humans.
    c. Wrong; same as a.
    d. Wrong; same as a.

32. a. Wrong; while serotonin is involved in alcohol addiction, there is no evidence that glutamate is; glutamate is involved in the effects of PCP, however.
    b. Wrong; GABA, but not glutamate, is involved in alcohol addiction.
    c. Correct
    d. Wrong; see a and b.

33. a. Wrong; this is not stated.
    b. Wrong; the success rate of counseling alone is 10-30%.
    c. Wrong; the success rate of methadone plus counseling is 60-80%.
    d. Correct

34. **a. Correct**; sons of alcoholics tend to show the same response patterns as their fathers, even if they are not themselves alcoholics.
    b. Wrong; this is true.
    c. Wrong; same as b.
    d. Wrong; same as b.

35. a. Wrong; b and c are also correct.
    b. Wrong
    c. Wrong
    d. Correct; see p. 114.

36. a. Wrong
    b. Wrong
    c. Correct; see p. 115.
    d. Wrong

37. a. Wrong; more likely to be true of late-onset alcoholics.
    b. Correct
    c. Wrong; same as a.
    d. Wrong; same as a.

38. a. Wrong; describes Type 2, or early-onset alcoholics.
    b. Wrong; same as a.
    c. Correct
    d. Wrong; because a and b are incorrect.

39. **a. Correct**
    b. Wrong; Cloninger showed there was little effect of environment on children of early-onset alcoholics.
    c. Wrong
    d. Wrong; no mention of this was made in the text.

40. **a. Correct**
    b. Wrong; people with the A1 allele have fewer D_2 receptors.
    c. Wrong; because they have fewer D_2 receptors, they are less sensitive to dopamine.
    d. Wrong; because alcohol enhances dopamine activity, and because they have fewer D_2 receptors, they are less sensitive to alcohol's effects via dopamine.

41. a. Wrong; this is a predictor of alcoholism.
    b. Wrong; same as a.
    c. Correct; people with ALDH deficiency do not tolerate even small amounts of alcohol well, and are unlikely to become addicted to it.
    d. Wrong; same as a.

42. a. Wrong; it is not directly involved in dopamine metabolism.
    b. Wrong; there is no evidence for this.
    c. Wrong; it is not an agonist; its effects are similar to the aversive treatment antabuse.
    d. Correct

43. a. Wrong; it actually stimulates dopamine activity.
    b. Correct
    c. Wrong; because it is stimulated by alcohol, blockers of serotonin actually reduce the effects of alcohol.
    d. Wrong; because the mechanism of addiction is similar across substances, serotonin is most likely involved in other forms of addiction.

Chapter 5: Motivation and the Regulation of Internal States

Chapter Outline and Learning Objectives

As you read the chapter, use these learning objectives to guide your studying. You should be able to define the key terms from the text, which are shown in boldface type below.

1) Motivation and Homeostasis
   - Why is the concept of **motivation** useful for explaining behavior?

   a) Theoretical Approaches to Motivation
      - What is an **instinct**? What are the problems associated with using this concept to explain human behavior?

      - Explain **drive theory**. What is the role of **homeostasis** in this theory?

      - How does **incentive theory** differ from drive theory?

      - What is **arousal theory**?

      - What are the advantages of considering drives as brain states rather than body tissue states?

   b) Simple Homeostatic Drives
      - How does the concept of **set point** help us understand homeostasis?

      i) Temperature Regulation
         - Distinguish between the temperature regulation mechanisms of **homeothermic** and **endothermic** animals.

         - Discuss the role of the **preoptic area** of the hypothalamus in temperature regulation.

      ii) Thirst
         - Explain the role of the **organum vasculosum lamina terminalis (OVLT)** in **osmotic thirst**.

- Explain the role of **baroreceptors** and **angiotensin II** and the **subfornical organ (SFO)** in **hypovolemic thirst**.

- Discuss the mechanisms for **satiety** in thirst.

2) Hunger: A Complex Drive
    - How is the hunger drive different from the temperature and thirst drives?

   a) The Role of Taste
       - Compare the diets of **herbivores**, **carnivores**, and **omnivores**. What are the advantages and disadvantages of being an omnivore?

       - What are the five basic tastes, and how are they useful in helping select appropriate and avoid inappropriate foods?

       - Describe the taste receptors. What route does taste information take into the brain?

      i) Sensory-Specific Satiety: Varying the Choices
          - What is **sensory-specific satiety**, and how does it influence eating?

          - What is the role of the **nucleus of the solitary tract (NST)** in sensory-specific satiety?

      ii) Learned Taste Aversion: Avoiding Dangerous Foods
          - What is a **learned taste aversion**? What are the advantages and disadvantages of this type of learning?

          - How can learned taste aversion be used to decrease predation on domestic animals?

      iii) Learned Taste Preferences: Selecting Nutritious Foods
          - What is a **learned taste preference**? Give some examples.

   b) Regulating Food Intake
      i) The Digestive Process
          - Discuss the process of digestion, including what occurs in the mouth, stomach, and **duodenum**.

- What mechanisms help to ensure that ingested toxins do not remain in the body?

- What are the consequences when the autonomic nervous system disrupts digestion?

(1) The Absorptive Phase
- What occurs during the **absorptive phase** of digestion?

- What is the importance of **insulin** in getting nutrients to the cells?

- How are nutrients that are not immediately used stored in the body?

(2) The Fasting Phase
- How are nutrients distributed during the **fasting phase**?

ii) Signals That Start a Meal
- Discuss the role of the liver in hunger.

- Discuss the role of the medulla, including the area postrema (AP) and NST, in hunger.

- What is the role of the **paraventricular nucleus (PVN)** in the hypothalamus in hunger?

- What are the effects of **neuropeptide Y (NPY)** on behavior?

iii) Signals That End a Meal
- How does the stomach signal satiety? **Cholecystokinin (CCK)?** Nutrients?

c) Long-Term Controls
- Describe Hervey's experimental procedure and results.

- Discuss the role of **leptin** in eating.

3) Eating Disorders
   a) Obesity
- What are the health implications of obesity?

- How is the **body mass index (BMI)** calculated? What level is considered risky?

i) The Myths of Obesity
   - What popular beliefs about the causes of obesity are not supported by research?

ii) The Contribution of Heredity
   - To what extent does heredity contribute to one's BMI?

   - Discuss the role of leptin in obesity in mice.

iii) Obesity and Reduced Metabolism
   - Discuss the role of **basal metabolism** in obesity; how does weight change affect one's BMR?

   - What role does the body's response to overeating have in obesity?

iv) Treating Obesity
   - How does exercise contribute to weight loss?

   - What problems have been associated with obesity drugs?

   - Discuss the possible role of serotonin in obesity.

   - Discuss how leptin treatment and FAS inhibitors may work to reduce obesity.

b) Anorexia and Bulimia
   - Describe the characteristics of **anorexia nervosa**. Distinguish between **purgers** and **restrictors**.

   - What are the health consequences of anorexia?

   - What are the characteristics of **bulimia nervosa**?

i) Environmental and Genetic Contributions
   - Discuss the environmental factors that are believed to contribute to anorexia and bulimia.

- What is the evidence for a genetic basis of anorexia and bulimia?

ii) The Role of Serotonin
- Discuss how serotonin levels may be related to anorexia and bulimia.

- Discuss the complexities of serotonin treatment for anorexics and bulimics.

- What role may season of birth play in anorexia?

Motivation and Homeostasis

Summary and Guided Review

After studying this section in the text, fill in the blanks of the following summary. The answers are found on p. 118.

_____ (1) refers to various internal forces that cause an organism to behave in certain ways. Throughout history, philosophers, and more recently scientists, have proposed various explanations for motivation. The ancient Greeks, for example, proposed that humans are motivated by _____ (2), automatic or unlearned behaviors. More recently, early 20th century psychologists like _____ (3) proposed that many human behaviors are instinctive. However, saying that a behavior is instinctive doesn't tell us anything about its causes. Currently, in order for a behavior to be considered instinctive, it must meet certain strict criteria.

Another explanation for motivation is _____ (4) theory, which proposes that the body attempts to maintain _____ (5), or balance. This explanation assumes that each bodily system has a range of states, some of which are more comfortable than others. For example when body temperature is too low, shivering, putting on additional layers of clothing, and turning up the heat help to restore the system to an optimal level. While this theory helps explain some behaviors, it does not explain behaviors that do not satisfy bodily needs, such as pursuing achievement, status, etc. _____ (6) theory accounts for the fact that people are often motivated by external stimuli. Another theory, _____ (7) theory, suggests that people are also motivated to maintain a preferred level of stimulation, although this level varies from person to person. Perhaps the best way to think about drives is to assume that they represent _____ (8) rather than bodily states. This is supported by the fact that many stimuli can motivate a behavior, even in the absence of tissue needs. For example, someone who has recently eaten a meal and is not hungry may suddenly feel the need to eat a preferred food like cookies or ice cream if it becomes available.

A useful way of representing homeostasis and the preferred state of a particular system is the _____ _____ (9). When conditions deviate too far from this point, the nervous system becomes operative to restore it. For example, all animals must maintain their body temperature within a particular range, or they will die. Different types of animals have different ways of doing this. _____ (10) animals like reptiles rely on the temperature of the external environment, whereas _____ (11) like mammals and birds have internal mechanisms that regulate body temperature, although they can also manipulate their environment to maintain a comfortable state. In mammals, body temperature is controlled by the _____ _____ (12) of the _____ (13). Here, warm and _____ - _____ (14) cells respond to the temperature of the blood and to temperature receptors in other parts of the body by altering their firing rates, which results in physiological changes to counteract temperatures that are too high or too low. For example, an animal that is too warm may sweat, reduce its _____ (15), and _____ (16) or enlarge the peripheral blood vessels to let off heat.

Another drive that nicely fits the homeostatic model is thirst. Because water makes up about _____ (17) % of the body, is essential for the proper function of most if not all bodily systems, and is continually lost through secretion and excretion, it is especially important to maintain sufficient liquids in the body. Without water, a person would die in a matter of _____ (18). The most common signs of thirst are dry mouth or throat, but how much liquid is ingested depends on the amount and type of water deprivation. _____ (19) thirst is a result of low intracellular fluid, which can happen after one eats a salty meal (a high concentration of salt in the blood draws water out of the cells). The loss of _____ (20) fluid, through sweating, vomiting, diarrhea, or blood loss, results in _____ (21) thirst. While these two types of thirst may occur at the same time, they are controlled by different mechanisms. Osmotic thirst is regulated by cells in the _____ (22), along the third ventricle, that detect low levels of intracellular fluid and initiate drinking. There are at least two mechanisms regulating hypovolemic thirst. Pressure receptors, also known as _____ (23), in the heart detect low blood volume, and signal the hypothalamus via the _____ (24) nerve. The _____ (25) respond to low blood volume by releasing renin; this increases the level of _____ ____ (26), which stimulates the _____ _____ (27) and induces drinking. Homeostasis is not achieved immediately after ingesting water, so there must be some kind of _____ (28) mechanism that recognizes when enough water has been taken. One possibility is that water intake is monitored by receptors in the _____ (29), and there may be water or pressure receptors in the _____ (30) as well.

Short Answer & Essay Questions

Answer the following questions. See p. 119 for sample answers.

1. What is the cause, and what are the consequences, of Prader-Willi syndrome?

2. Why has instinct theory been largely abandoned as an explanation for human behavior?

3. Why is drive theory alone insufficient to account for motivation?

4. What mechanisms for temperature regulation do homeothermic and endothermic animals have in common?

5. Compare the mechanisms responsible for managing osmotic and hypovolemic thirst. How do researchers know they operate independently?

Hunger: A Complex Drive

Summary and Guided Review

After studying this section in the text, fill in the blanks of the following summary. The answers are found on p. 118.

As a drive, hunger shares many characteristics with other drives such as thirst. However, it is also more complicated because the _____ _____ (31) can undergo dramatic changes, and because there are so many different types of _____ (32) that the body needs.

Humans eat a variety of plant and animal foods, meaning that we are _____ (33). In order to remain healthy, we need to eat a varied diet and at the same time carefully select foods that are not toxic or spoiled. People from different cultures solve the problem of what to eat in different ways, and for the most part these different diets provide adequate nutrition.

The sense of _____ (34) helps us select good foods and avoid bad ones. We have _____ (35) primary taste sensations, each of which seems to indicate different qualities of food. Foods that taste _____ (36), such as fruits, and those that taste salty are highly preferred. These types of food typically provide nutrients necessary for survival. A recently discovered taste, _____ (37), may be an indication of the presence of amino acids in food. The other qualities, _____ (38) and _____ (39), often indicate that food is either spoiled or toxic, and should therefore be avoided. Sensory information about taste is transmitted from the taste buds located in the _____ (40) of the tongue, through the nucleus of the solitary tract in the _____ (41), to the primary _____ (42) cortex.

Foods that have an appealing taste can become less appealing as we eat more of them, a phenomenon known as _____ - _____ (43) satiety . This is probably an important mechanism for ensuring that we eat a variety of foods. A study by Davis showed that even infants will select a variety of healthy foods if given the opportunity to do so. This form of satiety seems to be controlled by the _____ _____ _____ _____ _____ (44) (NST); rats given a glucose injection showed less of a response in this region to glucose on the tongue than those only receiving glucose orally.

Taste is an important cue for learning which foods to avoid. Experiments with rats have shown that if a certain taste becomes associated with illness, they will avoid items with that taste in the future. Humans also demonstrate these _____ _____ (45) aversions, although the bouts of sickness are often not caused by the foods they become associated with, as in the case of children undergoing _____ (46) who learned to avoid a particular flavor of ice cream. This form of aversion learning has been used successfully by ranchers who wish to reduce predation on their livestock. For example, wolves or coyotes that ate some of a tainted sheep carcass become ill, and thereafter avoided sheep. There is even some evidence that rats will form an aversion to a diet _____ (47) in thiamine.

Taste is also an important cue for learning which foods to eat when the nutrients themselves may not be detected. For example, rats deprived of a specific _____ (48) learned to eat a food enriched with it and flavored with anise. When a different anise-flavored food was offered, the rats switched to that food, which indicated that they had learned to _____ (49) the anise flavor with the benefits of consuming the needed nutrient. Unfortunately, modern day _____ _____ (50), which are often high in fat and lack other nutrients, contain flavors that we find appealing, and many people eat these foods and pass up more nutritious foods. Even rats prefer to eat this type of food!

Human digestion and metabolism are complex processes. Because we eat at different times throughout the day, our bodies must do different things with the nutrients we have ingested, depending on the amount of time that has passed since our last meal.

During and after eating, food is _____ (51). This process begins in the mouth, where _____ (52) is added to food, and continues in the stomach and small intestine. In the stomach, _____ _____ (53) and pepsin are added to food to break it down. If food contains toxins that irritate the stomach too much, this stimulates _____ (54). Toxins that make it into the blood stream may trigger regurgitation when they reach the _____ _____ (55). The first segment of the small intestine, the _____ (56), is where most food is digested. Here, carbohydrates are converted into _____ (57) such as glucose and proteins into _____ (58) acids. Fats are converted to fatty acids and _____ (59) in the intestines and _____ (60). These basic nutrients are then _____ (61) into the bloodstream and taken to the liver by the _____ _____ _____ (62). Excess water is reabsorbed in the _____ _____ (63). Digestion is controlled by the _____ (64) nervous system, and can be disrupted by arousal, which may lead to nausea, constipation, or _____ (65).

During the first few hours after a meal, the _____ (66) phase of the feeding cycle, recently ingested nutrients provide fuel for the body. This is managed by the parasympathetic nervous system, which is activated by _____ (67) levels of glucose. Insulin is secreted by the _____ (68), allowing glucose to be used by the cells. _____ _____ (69) is a result of not having enough insulin or being less responsive to it. Glucose is also converted to _____ (70) for short-term storage. Excess glucose and proteins are converted to fat. Fat is stored in _____ (71) tissue.

When glucose levels in the blood decline, the body enters the _____ (72) phase of the feeding cycle. Sympathetic activity replaces parasympathetic activity, resulting in the secretion of _____ (73). This substance is instrumental in the conversion of glycogen to _____ (74), and fat into fatty acids and _____ (75), the latter of which is converted into glucose by the _____ (76). The decrease in the level of nutrients stimulates hunger.

Blood levels of glucose and fatty acids are monitored by the liver; when these levels are low, a message is carried to the medulla via the _____ (77) nerve. Glucose levels in the brain are monitored directly by the _____ (78). Next the message is carried to the _____ _____ (79), which triggers the release of neuropeptide Y, a substance that increases appetite and conserves _____ (80).

There are a number of satiety signals. The stomach contains _____ _____ (81) that become active when the stomach is full. The hormone _____ (82) initiates a signal in the vagus nerve to the medulla to stop eating. The arrival of foods that are relatively higher in nutrients in the duodenum will also trigger satiety. There are also long-term mechanisms for the control of eating. Rats with lesions in the _____ (83) hypothalamus overeat because insulin production is increased, which results in nutrients being stored rather than utilized. In _____ (84) rats in which one was lesioned and one was not, the normal rat reduced its eating in response to a satiety signal that the lesioned rat was insensitive to. The satiety signal turned out to be the hormone _____ (85), low levels of which trigger the release of neuropeptide Y. Obese individuals have higher blood levels of this hormone, as well as higher levels of insulin. Overeating may be a result of fewer receptors for these substances.

Short Answer & Essay Questions

Answer the following questions. See pp. 119-120 for sample answers.

6. As a drive, why is hunger more complex than the drives of thirst and temperature regulation?

7. Why is it advantageous for us to like sweet and salty foods and to dislike sour and bitter foods?

8. How does sensory-specific satiety help explain the tendency for some people to overeat at potluck meals or banquets where many different types of foods are available?

9. As a child, Shirley became ill and threw up several times in one night. Her family had eaten chili for dinner that day. Shirley was the only one who became sick, so there must have been some other cause for her illness. However, for the next ten years, Shirley refused to eat chili, and even the sight of it made her nauseous. Explain why Shirley stopped eating chili.

10. Why do diabetics feel hungry, even when their blood sugar is high? What is the role of insulin in this?

11. Why may a diet high in sugar and/or protein lead to weight gain?

12. What happens when rats are given injections of neuropeptide Y? What effects does it have on appetite? On energy consumption?

Eating Disorders

Summary and Guided Review

After studying this section in the text, fill in the blanks of the following summary. The answers are found on p. 118.

In 1994, the rate of _____ (86) in the United States was at 22.5%, and is increasing in many countries, in part because of the availability of junk food. Obesity contributes to a number of health problems, including diabetes, heart disease, and some types of cancer. The degree of obesity is calculated by dividing weight by squared height, which yields the _____ _____ _____ (87). A BMI of 26 or more may indicate an increased risk.

The causes of obesity are more complicated than many people assume. It is commonly believed that obesity results from overeating due to poor impulse control or is learned in the family environment, but there is little evidence to support these assumptions. If obesity runs in families, it is more likely due to _____ (88) than environment, as evidenced by the fact that identical twins raised apart share a BMI correlation of _____ (89), only slightly lower than the .74 correlation for those raised together. However, the role of inheritance is complicated, as there are several genes involved.

The genetics of obesity have been studied experimentally in mice. Coleman used the parabiotic technique described earlier to study the effects of abnormal recessive genes on food intake and weight. The results showed that diabetic and obese mice both gained weight, but for different reasons. The *db/db* mice produced a signal to stop eating but were insensitive to it, while the _____ (90) mice were sensitive to the signal but did not produce it. Later, it was discovered that _____ (91) was the substance responsible for inhibiting eating.

Metabolism, or the rate of energy expenditure, is an important component in weight control. Some overweight people who try to lose weight but fail may underestimate their food intake or overestimate the amount of _____ _____ (92) they engage in. A person's _____ _____ (93) largely determines how much food is needed to maintain weight. Someone with a higher BMR needs to take in more calories than someone with a lower BMR. Even when on a restrictive diet, some individuals cannot lose weight, presumably because of a low BMR, which seems to have a heritable component. When a person gains or loses weight, the BMR often changes as well (_____ (94) in the case of weight gain and decreasing in the case of weight loss), and for many people this keeps their weight fairly steady. However, because the body has a greater tendency to _____ (95) than expend energy, many people will gain weight when conditions are conducive for it (such as having plentiful food). When overfed, the increase in metabolism is variable. People who engage in more _____ _____ (96) such as fidgeting seem to expend more energy and gain less weight than others. Another factor that may make weight loss difficult is that after a person gains weight, she or he may develop a new _____ _____ (97). If this happens, extreme dieting and/or exercise may result in additional weight loss.

Exercise seems to be an important part of losing weight, more because of its effects on one's _____ (98) than because of the calories expended during the exercise itself. Some medications have been used to treat obesity, but one of these, _____ (99), was recalled in 1997 because of serious health risks. Currently approved drugs affect the neurotransmitters _____ (100) and serotonin. Serotonin enhancement seems to work in some individuals because it reduces _____ (101) intake, but this is not true of all overweight people. Experimental drugs have shown some success in reducing appetite, for example through increasing leptin in those deficient in it, or inhibiting _____ _____ _____ (102), which is responsible for converting other substances to fatty acids.

About 3% of women suffer from anorexia or _____ (103) at some point in their lives, and there are _____ (104) times as many women with these types of eating disorders as men. _____ (105) nervosa is characterized by maintaining weight at an unhealthy low level, which can lead to serious health problems and even death. Anorexics who binge eat and control their weight by vomiting or using _____ (106) are called _____ (107), while _____ (108) are those who simply eat very little food. Individuals with bulimia are usually of _____ (109) weight.

The environment plays a role in anorexia and bulimia, particularly exposure to media. In _____ (110), after satellite TV became available in 1995, almost 75% of the teenage girls reported feeling fat, and the number of those who admitted to vomiting to control their weight rose from 3% to _____ (111). However, the long history of anorexia/bulimia as well as heritability studies indicate that the environment is not the only factor. The neurotransmitter _____ (112) seems to be implicated in some cases. Drugs that enhance the activity of this neurotransmitter may treat some bulimics through their effects on many behavioral systems, including mood, anxiety, and impulsiveness. For anorexics, those who are _____ (113) may be less likely to be helped by antidepressant drugs. Purgers, on the other hand, may respond better to these drugs because they are affected by low levels of serotonin in ways similar to _____ (114).

Short Answer & Essay Questions

Answer the following questions. See p. 120 for sample answers.

13. Distinguish between malnourishment and undernourishment. Which is a characteristic of obesity?

14. Why is it easier to gain than lose weight?

15. Kelly, who does not exercise, recently moved in with a roommate who likes to cook. Before this, Kelly lived by herself and ate small meals at dinner. Now, because of her roommate's influence, she eats lavish dinners and consumes about 500 more calories per day than she used to. However, she is not gaining weight. What, according to the textbook, might account for her increased energy expenditure?

16. Discuss the role that serotonin may play in eating disorders, including obesity, bulimia, and purging and restrictive anorexia. Be sure to include what evidence exists for these relationships.

Post-Test

Use these multiple-choice questions to check your understanding of the chapter. The answers, along with explanations, are found beginning on p. 120.

1. Christopher, the person described in the introduction to the chapter, exhibited all of the following EXCEPT
    a. poor impulse control.
    b. short stature.
    c. mental retardation.
    d. violent outbursts.

2. Which of the following statements regarding motivation is TRUE?
    a. Motivation is controlled by the hypothalamus.
    b. Motivations are best thought of as instinctive drives.
    c. Motivation refers to bodily states of need.
    d. Motivation is sometimes confused with emotion.

3. The fact that some people have higher optimum levels of arousal than others is best explained by _____ theory.
    a. incentive
    b. arousal
    c. drive
    d. instinct

4. Which of the following animals is homeothermic?
   a. Elephant
   b. Chicken
   c. Cow
   d. Snake

5. Endothermic animals can reduce their body temperature by
   a. burrowing into the ground.
   b. finding shade.
   c. sweating.
   d. a and b
   e. a, b, and c

6. Warm-sensitive and cold-sensitive cells that help mammals regulate their body temperature are found in the _____ of the hypothalamus.
   a. preoptic area
   b. area postrema
   c. ventromedial nucleus
   d. nucleus of the solitary tract

7. Jason has just eaten an entire bag of potato chips, and suddenly feels thirsty. What type of thirst is he experiencing?
   a. hypovolemic
   b. osmotic
   c. hypervolemic
   d. endothermic

8. Which of the following does NOT result in loss of extracellular water?
   a. Exercise
   b. Blood loss
   c. Ingesting a lot of salt
   d. Vomiting

9. Osmotic thirst
   a. results from activation of baroreceptors in the heart.
   b. results from the release of renin by the kidneys.
   c. is controlled by the subfornical organ.
   d. is disrupted when the OVLT is lesioned.

10. Which of the following statements is true?
    a. The set point for temperature is less variable than the set point for hunger.
    b. The set point for thirst is more variable than the set point for hunger.
    c. The set point for temperature is more variable than the set point for hunger.
    d. Once we reach adulthood, the set point for hunger becomes stable.

11. A species of animal that eats only berries and leaves is a(n)
    a. carnivore.
    b. omnivore.
    c. herbivore.
    d. endovore.

12. Of all of the primary taste qualities, _____ is the most recently discovered.
    a. umami
    b. sour
    c. bitter
    d. salty
    e. sweet

13. Foods that provide the ions necessary for neural transmission are most likely to be found in foods that taste
    a. sweet
    b. salty
    c. bitter
    d. sour
    e. umami

14. Foods that contain toxins tend to taste
    a. sweet.
    b. sour.
    c. salty.
    d. bitter.
    e. umami.

15. The taste buds send signals to the _____ area of the cortex.
    a. olfactory
    b. auditory
    c. gustatory
    d. somatosensory

16. Learned taste aversion accounts for all of the following EXCEPT
    a. bait shyness in rats.
    b. coyotes that refuse to eat lamb after having consumed a tainted carcass.
    c. rats' decreased responsiveness to glucose placed on the tongue after receiving a glucose injection.
    d. children avoiding certain flavors of ice cream eaten while undergoing chemotherapy.

17. Which of the following statements regarding taste preferences is true?
    a. Rats are better at "listening to what their bodies need" than humans.
    b. Rats deprived of a vitamin can develop a preference for a food high in that vitamin.
    c. Rats don't seem to notice when their diet is missing critical nutrients.
    d. Rats find the taste of cinnamon aversive.

18. Which of the following is released by the stomach when food is present?
    a. pepsin
    b. leptin
    c. insulin
    d. cholecystokinin

19. Most of digestion occurs in the
    a. large intestine.
    b. small intestine.
    c. liver.
    d. stomach.

20. Glycerol is a product of the transformation of
    a. fats.
    b. proteins.
    c. carbohydrates.
    d. all of the above.

21. After nutrients are absorbed into the bloodstream, they are transported to the _____ by the hepatic portal vein.
    a. kidneys
    b. liver
    c. brain
    d. large intestine

22. During the absorptive phase of the feeding cycle,
    a. recently eaten food may be stored.
    b. recently eaten food is used for energy.
    c. the parasympathetic nervous system is activated.
    d. b and c
    e. a, b, and c

23. Which of the following statements regarding insulin is true?
    a. Brain cells can import glucose without it.
    b. All body cells can import glucose without it.
    c. Diabetics produce too much of it.
    d. Its production is activated by the sympathetic nervous system.

24. Which of the following is stored in the body as fat?
    a. Excess protein
    b. Excess glucose
    c. Fat
    d. a, b, and c
    e. a and c

25. Which of the following statements regarding glucagons is FALSE?
    a. It is secreted by the pancreas.
    b. It transforms proteins to fatty acids.
    c. It transforms glycogen to glucose.
    d. It converts stored fat to glycerol.

26. A rabbit injected with 2-deoxyglucose into its hepatic portal vein will
    a. start eating, but only a small amount.
    b. not eat for several hours.
    c. start eating, and eat more than usual.
    d. enter a diabetic coma.

27. The brain structure that monitors glucose and fatty acid levels is the
    a. hypothalamus.
    b. subfornical organ.
    c. medulla.
    d. OVLT.

28. Which of the following statements regarding neuropeptide Y is FALSE?
    a. It is released by the preoptic area of the hypothalamus.
    b. It stimulates eating.
    c. It is released in response to low glucose.
    d. It may help an animal conserve energy.

29. Satiety in hunger may be signaled by
    a. stretch receptors in the stomach.
    b. the release of cholecystokinin.
    c. the presence of nutrients in the liver.
    d. all of the above.
    e. none of the above.

30. Rats injected with CCK over several days will
    a. gain a lot of weight.
    b. lose a lot of weight.
    c. stay at the same weight.
    d. lose a little bit of weight, but then gain it back when the injections are withheld.

31. In Hervey's parabiotic rats, the rat without a lesion lost weight because
    a. the lesioned rat was digesting all of the food that both rats consumed.
    b. the lesioned rat continually produced a satiety signal that inhibited eating only in the non-lesioned rat.
    c. the non-lesioned rat became insensitive to hunger cues.
    d. the lesioned rat refused to eat.

32. As leptin _____ , neuropeptide Y _____ .
    a. increases; increases
    b. increases; decreases
    c. decreases; decreases
    d. increases; remains the same

33. Which of the following is NOT a health risk associated with obesity?
    a. Loss of bone density
    b. Breast cancer
    c. Gall bladder disease
    d. Heart disease
    e. Diabetes

34. A body mass index (BMI) of _____ is considered moderately risky.
    a. 20
    b. 30
    c. 26
    d. 36

35. Correlations for BMI are highest for
    a. identical twins raised together.
    b. identical twins raised apart.
    c. same-sex fraternal twins raised together.
    d. same-sex fraternal twins raised apart.

36. In which of the following parabiotic mouse pairs is weight the LEAST abnormal?
    a. *db/db* – normal
    b. *db/db* – *ob/ob*
    c. *db/db* – *db/db*
    d. *ob/ob* – normal

37. Basal metabolism accounts for energy used for
    a. exercise.
    b. digestion.
    c. maintaining body temperature.
    d. physical activity.

38. Mavis, who does not exercise, has reduced her calorie intake by 25%, and expects to lose a lot of weight. What is likely to happen?
    a. She will lose as much weight as she wants.
    b. She will increase her metabolism.
    c. She will decrease her metabolism.
    d. It is impossible to predict.

39. Someone who responds to increased caloric consumption by fidgeting a lot
    a. will probably gain a lot of weight.
    b. may gain little or no weight.
    c. will probably lose weight.
    d. may develop other nervous habits.

40. In some obese people, carbohydrate consumption may
    a. elevate mood.
    b. lead to depression.
    c. reduce serotonin levels.
    d. a and c.

41. Serotonin enhancing drugs are least likely to be useful for treating
    a. obesity.
    b. bulimia.
    c. purging anorexia.
    d. restrictive anorexia.

42. Leptin seems to
    a. increase appetite.
    b. increase metabolism.
    c. decrease appetite.
    d. a and b
    e. b and c

43. The difference between bulimics and purging anorexics is that
    a. bulimics are usually of normal weight.
    b. purging anorexics purge by using laxatives, whereas bulimics rely on vomiting.
    c. purging anorexics are usually male.
    d. bulimics, but not purging anorexics, tend to be impulsive.

Answers and Explanations

Guided Review

1. Motivation
2. instinct
3. McDougall
4. drive
5. homeostasis
6. Incentive
7. arousal
8. brain
9. set point
10. Homeothermic
11. endothermic
12. preoptic area
13. hypothalamus
14. cold-sensitive
15. metabolism
16. dilate
17. 70
18. days
19. Osmotic
20. extracellular
21. hypovolemic
22. OVLT
23. baroreceptors
24. vagus
25. kidneys
26. angiotensin II
27. subformical organ
28. satiety
29. stomach
30. liver
31. set point
32. nutrients
33. omnivores
34. taste
35. 5
36. sweet
37. umami
38. sour

39. bitter
40. papillae
41. medulla
42. gustatory
43. sensory-specific
44. nucleus of the solitary tract
45. learned taste
46. chemotherapy
47. deficient
48. vitamin
49. associate
50. junk foods
51. digested
52. saliva
53. hydrochloric acid
54. vomiting or regurgitation
55. area postrema
56. duodenum
57. sugars
58. amino
59. glycerol
60. liver
61. absorbed
62. hepatic portal vein
63. large intestine
64. autonomic
65. diarrhea
66. absorptive
67. increased or higher
68. pancreas
69. Diabetes mellitus
70. glycogen
71. adipose
72. fasting
73. glucagon
74. glucose
75. glycerol
76. liver

77. vagus
78. medulla
79. periventricular nucleus
80. energy
81. stretch receptors
82. cholecystokinin
83. ventromedial
84. parabiotic
85. leptin
86. obesity
87. body mass index
88. genes or heredity
89. .62
90. *ob/ob*
91. leptin
92. physical activity
93. basal metabolism
94. increasing
95. conserve
96. spontaneous activity
97. set point
98. BMR
99. dexfenfluramine
100. norepinephrine
101. carbohydrate
102. fatty acid synthase
103. bulimia
104. ten
105. Anorexia
106. laxatives
107. purgers
108. restrictors
109. normal
110. Fiji
111. 15%
112. serotonin
113. restrictors
114. bulimics

Short Answer & Essay Questions

1. This disorder is caused by the failure of a section of the father's chromosome 15 to be incorporated into the fertilized egg. The results of this missing genetic material include a number of impulsive behaviors (such as extreme overeating), short stature, and learning disabilities.

2. First of all, many people believe that human behavior is not instinctive in the sense that it is highly automatic and hardwired by our genetic makeup. Because it is so variable, human behavior is thought to be mostly learned (although some theorists argue for some behaviors to be considered instinctive). Secondly, saying that a behavior occurs because it is instinctive is not a very good explanation. It doesn't tell us <u>why</u> a particular behavior occurs.

3. Drive theory explains behaviors resulting from tissue deficits, such as eating and drinking, but not other forms of behavior that seem to be at least partially internally driven, such as sex, striving for achievement, thrill seeking, and even eating when we are not hungry. Most researchers conceptualize motivation in terms of brain states, which can account for all of these forms of motivation.

4. Both types of animals can perform behaviors to alter their body temperatures. Reptiles, for example, can move to warmer or colder areas, depending on what their needs are. Birds and mammals can do the same, and they can also construct shelters which allow them to remain warmer or cooler.

5. Osmotic thirst is regulated by cells in the OVLT that detect low levels of intracellular fluid. An animal whose OVLT is lesioned and who is given an injection of salt water will increase its water intake to a lesser degree than one without the OVLT lesion. Hypovolemic thirst is regulated by receptors in the heart, which signals the hypothalamus via the vagus nerve, and the kidneys, which initiates increases in renin and then angiotensin II, which in turn stimulates the SFO. An animal whose SFO is lesioned will not drink in response to the presence of angiotensin II, but will drink if its intracellular fluid levels fall too low.

6. First of all, the set point for hunger fluctuates to a greater extent than that for the others. The second difference has to do with the fact that thirst is satiated by water, while satiation of hunger requires a variety of nutrients.

7. Naturally sweet foods are generally nutritious, and those that are salty contain salt, which is converted to ions that we need. Sour foods are often rotten or spoiled. Bitter foods contain toxins. In both cases, we could become sick from eating them.

8. When we eat a lot of the same food, it becomes less appealing. However, having a variety of foods (and tastes) available seems to maintain one's appetite, and therefore interest in eating. For example, the study by Rolls et. al. suggested that more food will be consumed if a greater variety of food is offered.

9. Shirley developed a learned taste aversion to chili. Her illness, although not caused by the chili, was associated with it because she happened to get sick within a few hours of eating it. In order to avoid becoming ill again, she learned to avoid the chili.

10. People with diabetes mellitus either have low levels of insulin or are less sensitive to it than others. Because insulin is needed to allow cells to utilize glucose, diabetics cannot use glucose as efficiently as other people. Therefore, they essentially "starve" their cells of glucose, even though it is available in the blood.

11. Because excess amounts of either of these types of nutrients is stored as fat.

12. This stimulates the appetite, and they will eat more than normal. There is also evidence that it may reduce energy consumption, since these rats gained weight disproportionately to the amount of food they ate. Under severe deprivation conditions, NPY can reduce body temperature and inhibit sexual behavior, thereby conserving energy.

13. Malnourishment is frequently a characteristic of obesity. Some people are obese because they eat too much of the wrong types of food (junk food in particular, which contains very little nutrients). Undernourished individuals simply don't have enough food.

14. The body seems to be programmed to hold on to weight. For the most part, this is adaptive because in times of deprivation, the body would conserve fat. Although the body for the most part maintains weight around a set point, it is less likely to inhibit weight gain than weight loss.

15. According to information presented in the text (see p. 146), spontaneous activity such as casual walking, fidgeting, and posture maintenance, may contribute to an increase in energy expenditure. It is possible that her level of spontaneous activity has increased, which would increase her BMR. The extra calories might get used up due to this.

16. In some people, obesity may in part be a result of low levels of serotonin. When given drugs that enhance serotonin, obese people who crave carbohydrates reduce their carbohydrate intake. Serotonin may be involved in bulimia and purging anorexia in similar ways. People with these disorders tend to have impulsive personalities, which may be a result of low serotonin. Serotonin enhancing drugs seem to reduce the behaviors associated with these eating disorders. Finally, restrictive anorexics may actually be keeping serotonin low (by undereating) in response to an obsessive disorder. These people respond better to drugs that decrease rather than enhance serotonin activity.

Post-Test

All page references in this section pertain to the textbook.

1. a. Wrong
    b. Wrong
    c. Correct; in the text, it specifically states that he was of normal intelligence (see p. 125). All of the other choices are true of his condition.
    d. Wrong

2. a. Wrong; while some areas of the hypothalamus are involved in motivation, it is not entirely devoted to the control of motivation. Also other brain areas are involved.
    b. Wrong; the concept of instinct is not very useful in explaining behavior, because it doesn't tell us why a behavior occurs. Furthermore, most of human behavior is most likely NOT instinctive in the sense that it is entirely determined by our genetic makeup.
    c. Wrong; while this is true of some forms of motivation, such as thirst, other forms of motivation, such as sexual needs and sensation seeking, are not really bodily need states (stemming from deprivation), but rather are best thought of as brain states.
    d. Correct

3. a. Wrong; this theory suggests that people are motivated by external stimuli such as money or fame.
   b. Correct; see p. 127.
   c. Wrong; drive theory deals with internal, tissue needs.
   d. Wrong; instinct theory has largely been discredited (see the explanation for question 2 choice b above).

4. a. Wrong; elephants are mammals, and mammals are endothermic.
   b. Wrong; chickens are birds, and birds are endothermic.
   c. Wrong; cows are mammals.
   d. Correct; see p. 127.

5. a. Wrong; b and c are also true.
   b. Wrong; a and c are also true.
   c. Wrong; a and b are also true.
   d. Wrong
   e. Correct; endothermic animals may use all of the above mechanisms to regulate body temperature.

6. **a. Correct**; see p. 128.
   b. Wrong; this is actually part of the medulla.
   c. Wrong; the ventromedial nucleus is involved in eating.
   d. Wrong; this is part of the medulla.

7. a. Wrong; hypovolemic thirst is triggered by low blood volume or loss of extracellular water. Eating salty potato chips will result in loss of water within the cells.
   b. Correct; osmotic thirst is a result of too little water within the cells. If Jason eats food with a lot of salt, this will draw water out of the cells.
   c. Wrong; there is no such thing.
   d. Wrong; this is a term used to describe animals capable of regulating their own body temperature.

8. a. Wrong; if one sweats during exercise, extracellular fluid is lost.
   b. Wrong; losing blood means losing water.
   c. Correct; this will cause water to be drawn from the cells into the bloodstream.
   d. Wrong; vomiting often reduces the amount of liquid in the body, and can lead to dehydration.

9. a. Wrong; this is true of hypovolemic thirst.
   b. Wrong; this is true of hypovolemic thirst.
   c. Wrong; this is true of hypovolemic thirst.
   d. Correct; rats OVLT lesions drink less when injected with saline than those without the lesion.

10. **a. Correct**; while there is some fluctuation in preferred body temperature, the set point for hunger can be affected by many more factors and is more variable.
    b. Wrong; thirst is a unitary need, whereas hunger is more multifaceted because of the different forms of nutrition we need. This means that while thirst may always be satiated with water, hunger may be satiated by different types of foods at different times.
    c. Wrong; see the explanation for a above.
    d. Wrong; long periods of overeating or starvation may reset the set point, even in adults.

11. a. Wrong; carnivores eat meat.
    b. Wrong; omnivores may eat berries and leaves, but will eat other foods as well, including animal protein.
    c. **Correct**; an herbivore is an animal that eats only plant products. Although the animal described here, is an herbivore, do not assume that all herbivores are limited to these types of plant foods.
    d. Wrong; there is not such thing.

12. **a.** **Correct**; see p. 131.
    b. Wrong
    c. Wrong
    d. Wrong
    e. Wrong

13. a. Wrong; sweet foods are high in sugars.
    b. **Correct**; salty foods are high in Na, K, or other components of salt that become ions.
    c. Wrong; bitter foods usually contain toxins.
    d. Wrong; sour foods usually indicate spoilage.
    e. Wrong; this taste may indicate the presence of amino acids.

14. a. Wrong
    b. Wrong
    c. Wrong
    d. **Correct**; see the answers for question 13.
    e. Wrong

15. a. Wrong; this is the area for smell.
    b. Wrong; this is the area for hearing.
    c. **Correct**; see p. 133.
    d. Wrong; this is the area for touch.

16. a. Wrong; this is an example of learned taste aversion.
    b. Wrong; this is an example of learned taste aversion.
    c. **Correct**; this is related to the rats tendency to seek novel foods rather than avoid toxic ones.
    d. Wrong; this is an example of learned taste aversion.

17. a. Wrong; rats will overeat on human junk food.
    b. **Correct**; see p. 133.
    c. Wrong; they actually may develop an aversion to food that is missing a critical nutrient.
    d. Wrong; this seems to be a flavor they prefer.

18. **a.** **Correct**; see p. 134.
    b. Wrong; this is secreted by fat cells.
    c. Wrong; this comes from the pancreas.
    d. Wrong; this hormone is released when food passes into the duodenum.

19. a.   Wrong; water is reabsorbed here, but by the time food reaches the large intestine, most nutrients have been taken out.
    b.   **Correct**; see p. 134.
    c.   Wrong; the liver is somewhat involved in digestion, but not to the same extent as the small intestine.
    d.   Wrong; a few nutrients may be absorbed into the blood stream by the stomach, but most of this occurs in the small intestine.

20. **a.**   **Correct**; see p. 134.
    b.   Wrong; proteins are broken down into amino acids.
    c.   Wrong; carbohydrates are broken down into sugars.
    d.   Wrong

21. a.   Wrong; the kidneys play a larger role in water regulation than digestion.
    b.   **Correct**; see p. 134.
    c.   Wrong
    d.   Wrong

22. a.   Wrong; b and c are also correct
    b.   Wrong; a and c are also correct
    c.   Wrong; a and b are also correct
    d.   Wrong
    e.   **Correct**; see p. 135.

23. **a.**   **Correct**; see p. 135.
    b.   Wrong; all body cells, with the exception of brain cells, need insulin to use glucose.
    c.   Wrong; diabetics either don't produce enough, or they are less sensitive to it.
    d.   Wrong; insulin production is activated by parasympathetic activity.

24. a.   Wrong; b and c are also correct.
    b.   Wrong; a and c are also correct.
    c.   Wrong; a and b are also correct.
    d.   **Correct**; any nutrients not used immediately for fuel can be stored as fat.

25. a.   Wrong; this is true of glucagon.
    b.   **Correct**; proteins are not transformed to fatty acids.
    c.   Wrong; this is true of glucagon.
    d.   Wrong; this is true of glucagon.

26. a.   Wrong; it will eat a lot.
    b.   Wrong
    c.   **Correct**; see p. 136.
    d.   Wrong; there is no mention of this in the text.

27. a.   Wrong; while parts of the hypothalamus are involved in feeding, this is a function of the medulla.
    b.   Wrong; this structure is involved in the regulation of hypovolemic thirst.
    c.   **Correct**; the area postrema and the nucleus of the solitary tract, both of which are in the medulla, seem to be crucial in monitoring the levels of these nutrients.
    d.   Wrong; this area is involved in the regulation of osmotic thirst.

28. **a.** **Correct**; it is released by the periventricular nucleus of the hypothalamus.
    b. Wrong; this is true of NPY.
    c. Wrong; this is true of NPY.
    d. Wrong; this is true of NPY.

29. a. Wrong; b and c are also correct.
    b. Wrong; a and c are also correct.
    c. Wrong; a and b are also correct.
    d. **Correct**; there is evidence that all of these mechanisms play a role in satiety.
    e. Wrong

30. a. Wrong; their weight stays about the same.
    b. Wrong; although they eat less at each meal, they eat more meals and maintain their weight.
    c. **Correct**; see p. 138.
    d. Wrong

31. a. Wrong; the rats share blood supply, but not food supply.
    b. **Correct**; see p. 144.
    c. Wrong; the normal rat starved because it was sensitive to the satiety cues being produced by the lesioned rat. The lesioned rat, however, was insensitive to these cues.
    d. Wrong; this did not happen. The lesioned rat overate.

32. a. Wrong
    b. **Correct**; see p. 139.
    c. Wrong
    d. Wrong

33. **a.** **Correct**; this is a risk associated with anorexia, but the book does not mention a link between obesity and bone density problems.
    b. Wrong; this is true of NPY.
    c. Wrong; this is true of NPY.
    d. Wrong; this is true of NPY.

34. a. Wrong; this is not in the risky range.
    b. Wrong; this is above the level of moderate risk.
    c. **Correct**; see p. 140.
    d. Wrong; this is above the level of moderate risk.

35. **a.** **Correct**; the correlation is .74.
    b. Wrong; the correlation is .62.
    c. Wrong; the correlation is .33.
    d. Wrong; this group was not included or not reported.

36. a. Wrong; in these pairs, the *db/db* mouse became obese and the normal mouse starved.
    b. Wrong; in these pairs, the *db/db* mouse became obese and the *ob/ob* mouse starved.
    c. Wrong; these pairs were not included or not reported.
    d. **Correct**; although the *ob/ob* mice did not produce leptin, they were somewhat affected by the leptin signal produced by the normal mice, and had a lower rate of weight gain.

37. a.   Wrong; this is not part of basal metabolism.
    b.   Wrong; this is not part of basal metabolism.
    c.   Correct; basal metabolism includes energy used to maintain body temperature and provide fuel for the body's organs.
    d.   Wrong; this would be considered exercise.

38. a.   Wrong; because her metabolism is likely to decrease, she will probably not lose much weight.
    b.   Wrong; unless she increases her activity level, there is likely to be a drop in her metabolism.
    c.   Correct; see pp. 142-144.
    d.   Wrong

39. a.   Wrong; this spontaneous activity might increase metabolism, enough to compensate for the additional calories.
    b.   Correct; see p. 144.
    c.   Wrong; while a person might be able to maintain their weight, the book does not mention that they could lose weight.
    d.   Wrong; there is no mention of this.

40. **a.   Correct**; see p. 145.
    b.   Wrong; in those who don't experience mood elevation, it may lead to sleepiness.
    c.   Wrong; it probably increases serotonin.
    d.   Wrong; a is correct, but not c.

41. a.   Wrong; for some obese people, these seem to work.
    b.   Wrong; there have been successes with bulimics.
    c.   Wrong; there have been successes with this type of anorexics.
    d.   Correct; restrictive anorexics seem to respond better to drugs that reduce serotonin.

42. a.   Wrong; it inhibits eating, at least in most cases.
    b.   Wrong; while this is true, c is true also.
    c.   Wrong; b is also true.
    d.   Wrong; a is not true.
    e.   Correct

43. **a.   Correct**; see p. 146.
    b.   Wrong; both forms of purging may be used by either.
    c.   Wrong; most individuals with anorexia and bulimia are female.
    d.   Wrong; both tend to be impulsive.

Chapter 6: The Biology of Sex and Gender

Chapter Outline and Learning Objectives

As you read the chapter, use these learning objectives to guide your studying. You should be able to define the key terms from the text, which are shown in boldface type below.

1) Sex as a Form of Motivation
   - Compare sex with other forms of motivation. What are the similarities and differences?

   a) Arousal and Satiation
      - Describe what events occur during each phase of the sexual response. What are the differences between males and females?

   b) The Role of Testosterone
      - What effects does **castration** have on sexual motivation in non-human mammals? In humans?

      - Discuss the role of hormones in sexual motivation in women. How is a woman's reproductive cycle related to her level of sexual activity?

   c) Brain Structures and Neurotransmitters
      - How are the following brain areas related to sexual motivation and behavior in animals: **MPOA**, **medial amygdala**, **SDN**, and the **ventromedial nucleus** of the hypothalamus.

      - Discuss the role of neurotransmitters in sexual motivation.

   d) Sensory Stimuli in Sexual Behavior
      i) The Nose as a Sex Organ
         - What is the **MHC**? What is the possible relationship between body odor and MHC?

         - How does the olfactory system work? What structures are involved? How are we able to identify odors?

         - What is the **VNO**? What brain areas does it project to?

         - What evidence is there that humans can detect **pheromones**?

- What evidence is there that pheromones influence sexual motivation and behavior in humans?

    ii) Body Symmetry, Fitness, and Fertility
- What is the relationship between body symmetry, fitness, and fertility?

2) The Biological Determination of Sex
- Distinguish between **sex**, **gender role**, and **gender identity**.

  a) Chromosomes and Hormones
- How does a fetus with two X chromosomes develop into a female?

- How does a fetus with XY chromosomes develop into a male?

- Distinguish between organizing and activating effects of hormones.

- What hormonally driven changes occur in puberty in females and males?

  b) Prenatal Hormones and the Brain
- How does early exposure to hormones affect the sexual behavior of adult rats?

3) Gender-Related Behavioral and Cognitive Differences
  a) Some Demonstrated Male-Female Differences
- What consistent sex differences did Maccoby and Jacklin find when they reviewed the research in this area? How extensive are these differences?

  b) Origins of Male-Female Differences
- What evidence supports the role of experience or environment as the source of sex differences?

- What evidence supports a biological basis for sex differences in verbal ability?

- What evidence supports a biological basis for sex differences in spatial ability?

- What evidence supports a biological basis for sex differences in aggression?

4) Sexual Anomalies
   a) Male Pseudohermaphrodites
      - Distinguish between a true hermaphrodite and a **pseudophermaphrodite**.

      - What can lead to the development of male pseudohermaphrodites?

      - What are the effects of **androgen insensitivity syndrome**?

   b) Female Pseudohermaphrodites
      - What mechanisms can lead to the development of female pseudohermaphrodites?

      - What is **CAH**? How can it be treated?

   c) Sex Anomalies and the Brain
      - What evidence from studies of CAH females supports the premise that prenatal exposure to hormones influences subsequent sex- and gender-related behavior?

      - What evidence from studies of AI males supports the premise that prenatal exposure to hormones influences subsequent sex- and gender-related behavior?

      - What evidence from studies of **DES** females supports the premise that prenatal exposure to hormones influences subsequent sex- and gender-related behavior?

   d) Ablatio Penis: A Natural Experiment
      - Compare the arguments of neutral-at-birth and sexuality-at-birth theories of gender identity.

      - Describe the outcomes of the sex reassignment cases described in the text.

5) Sexual Orientation
      - Describe the different ways that the term "homosexual" may be used? What does **bisexual** mean?

      - How common is homosexuality thought to be?

      - Discuss the issue of gender identity in homosexual and **transsexual** individuals.

a) The Social Influence Hypothesis
    • Discuss the evidence for a social basis of homosexuality.

b) The Biological Hypothesis
    • What is **gender noncomformity**? How is it related to homosexuality?

    i) Genetic Influence
        • What evidence is there supporting a genetic basis for homosexuality?

    ii) Hormonal Influence
        • What evidence is there for hormonal influences on sexual behavior in animals?

        • Discuss the occurrence of homosexual behavior in sheep and gulls.

    iii) Brain Structures
        • What brain areas seem to be different in homosexual men compared to heterosexual men? What conclusions can be drawn about these differences?

        • Discuss the relationship of the **BSTc** with gender identity.

        • What are the limitations we face in understanding the role of early exposure to hormones on sexual orientation and gender identity?

    iv) The Challenge of Female Homosexuality
        • What evidence exists for a biological basis of homosexuality in women?

    v) Social Implications of the Biological Model
        • What are the social implications of assuming that homosexuality has a biological basis?

        • Discuss the complexities of chromosomal testing of female athletes. Why might it be unfair to ban a male-to-female transsexual or an AI male from competing with women?

Sex as a Form of Motivation

Summary and Guided Review

After studying this section in the text, fill in the blanks of the following summary. The answers are found on p. 145.

Although sex shares some similarities with other forms of _____ (1), such as cycles of arousal and _____ (2), and regulation by hormones and specific brain areas, there are differences as well. For example, sexual arousal is linked to external stimuli to a greater extent than are hunger and thirst. Additionally, there is no tissue need for _____ (3). Finally, sexual arousal is a state we tend to seek, whereas we usually do not seek to be hungry or thirsty.

The cycle of sexual arousal and satiation in humans was studied extensively by _____ _____ _____ (4) in the 1960's. They described four phases: _____ (5), during which physiological arousal increases sharply; _____ (6), during which arousal levels off; _____ (7), during which _____ (8) occurs in males, vaginal contractions occur in females, and an intense pleasurable feeling is experienced; and _____ (9), during which the body returns to its resting state. Whereas _____ (10) can reenter the excitement phase immediately after orgasm, _____ (11) have a refractory phase during which time they cannot be aroused. The refractory phase is highly variable. For example, in some animals when a male is presented with a novel female he may become aroused sooner than if he is exposed to the same female. This is known as the _____ _____ (12).

The role of hormones in sexual behavior is often studied in non-human animals, in part because hormones control their behavior to a greater extent than in humans. The method of _____ (13) involves removing the _____ (14), the source of sex hormones like testosterone; this is done to determine what effects exposure to hormones has on behavior. Occasionally humans undergo castration, and those that do often experience a _____ (15) in sexual interest and behavior, although there is a great deal of variability. (This is true for both men and women.)

Some male criminals have volunteered to undergo castration (and produce much less _____ (16)) in order to curb their violent or sexual behavior; additionally, drugs that block testosterone are quite effective in reducing harmful sexual behaviors. Apparently in human males, just a small amount of testosterone is needed to maintain sexual interest and behavior. There is evidence that an individual's testosterone level is related to recent, or perhaps even anticipated future, sexual activity.

Sexual behavior in females may be regulated by more than just testosterone levels. In many species, females will only mate while they are in _____ (17) (when they are ovulating) and estrogen levels are high. Human females will engage in sex throughout the reproductive cycle, although they tend to be more likely to initiate sex around the time of _____ (18), which corresponds with peaks in the hormones _____ (19) and testosterone. Postmenopausal women produce less estrogen, and at that point sexual activity is closely related to testosterone levels, so this hormone appears to work similarly in men and women.

Research with animals has revealed several brain areas involved in sexual behavior that probably work in conjunction with one another. The _____ _____ _____ (20) of the hypothalamus is active during copulation in both male and female rats, and studies with monkeys indicate that it is more involved in sexual _____ (21) than motivation (the lesioned monkeys would masturbate but not _____ (22)). The _____ _____ (23) is responsive to sexual stimuli and is also active during copulation. In male rats, when the _____ _____ _____ (24) (which is larger in male rats) of the MPOA is lesioned, the result is reduced sexual activity. In female rats, when the _____ _____ (25) of the hypothalamus is lesioned, they are less likely to copulate.

Many neurotransmitters are involved in sexual functioning. _____ (26) and serotonin activity in the MPOA increases during sexual activity. Studies with humans show that norepinephrine levels rise during sex, and _____ (27) seem to be involved in the reinforcing properties of arousal and orgasm. Dopamine activity in the _____ _____ (28) may be responsible for the Coolidge effect, as a recently mated male presented with a new female will show an increase in activity here.

Both internal and external factors are involved in sexual motivation and behavior. One external factor for humans that has recently received research attention is bodily scent. There is evidence that humans may use the scent of others to recognize relatives or people with similar genes, in particular the _____ _____ _____ (29) (which is involved in immune functioning and may be related to fertility), and avoid selecting them as mates. Odors are detected by the _____ (30) system, which is composed of receptors within the lining of the _____ _____ (31) that respond to inhaled odorant molecules. Our ability to recognize over _____ (32) different odors seems to be a result of the combination of activity in a few hundred different receptor types. But we can also detect _____ (33), which are chemicals that other members of the species respond to in specific ways. Although the receptors for pheromones are located near the olfactory system, pheromones are detected by the _____ _____ (34), whose receptors are influenced by different genes than the olfactory system, and which sends messages to the _____ (35) and the ventromedial hypothalamus. Pheromones do not activate olfactory receptors, but exposure to them has been shown to result in autonomic changes such as decreased _____ _____ (36) and increased sweat gland activity.

Studies indicate that pheromones are involved in a number of sex-related events in humans. For example, _____ (37) found that when women were exposed to other women's underarm secretions, their menstrual cycles became _____ (38), whereas those who engaged in weekly sexual activity with men had more regular cycles. Other studies indicate that pheromones play a role in sexual attraction. For example, men exposed to suspected _____ (39) pheromones rate women as more attractive, and men and women seem to be able to identify attractive members of the other sex by their scent. Furthermore, men wearing aftershave containing a suspected pheromone reported more _____ _____ (40) with women than men wearing a control aftershave.

Physical appearance is another external factor related to sex. There is some evidence that a _____ (41) body is related to health and fitness. For example, in Belize men who were more symmetrical had more _____ (42) and were healthier. The number of _____ _____ (43) among college students is positively related to body symmetry. And during _____ (44), women preferred the scent of symmetrical men.

Short Answer & Essay Questions

Answer the following questions. See pp. 146-147 for sample answers.

1. Compare hunger and sex as forms of motivation. Point out their similarities and differences.

2. What role does testosterone play in sexual motivation in men and women? Discuss the research that indicates this hormone's importance for sexual arousal and behavior men and for women.

3. What is the Coolidge effect? How is dopamine release in the nucleus accumbens related to this effect?

4. What is the major histocompatibility complex? Why might it be disadvantageous for a person to be sexually attracted to someone with a similar MHC?

5. How were researchers able to establish that humans have a functional VNO that is independent of the olfactory system?

The Biological Determination of Sex/ Gender-Related Behavioral and Cognitive Differences

Summary and Guided Review

After studying these sections in the text, fill in the blanks of the following summary. The answers are found on p. 145.

When describing individuals as female or male, the word "sex" should not be confused with

_____ _____ (45), which refers to the set of behaviors deemed appropriate for

males and females, or _____ _____ (46), which is the sex an individual

identifies her or himself as being. Sometimes a person's gender and sex do not perfectly match.

The first step in the determination of sex occurs during _____ (47), when the egg

and sperm cells, each containing only 1 chromosome of each of the 23 pairs of chromosomes, combine.

The sex of the fetus is determined by the makeup of the sex chromosomes. The mother always contributes

an _____ (48) chromosome. If the sperm cell contains an X chromosome, the fetus will be _____ (49),

and if it contains a Y chromosome, the fetus will be _____ (50). Fetuses of both sexes possess

internal tissue, including gonads and two sets of ducts, and external structures that will later differentiate

into sex organs. In XX fetuses, the primitive gonads become _____ (51), the Mullerian ducts

become the _____ (52), the _____ _____ (53) are reabsorbed, and the

external structures form the _____ (54), part of the vagina, and the _____ (55). The ovaries

produce _____ (56), but this has no effect on the sexual development of the fetus. In XY

fetuses, the _____ (57) gene on the Y chromosome transforms the gonads to become _____ (58).

The testes then produce _____ _____ _____ (59), which causes

these ducts to degenerate, and _____ (60), which transforms the Wolffian ducts into the

_____ _____ (61) and vas deferens. _____ (62)

causes the external structures to form into a penis and _____ (63).

These effects of male hormones are called _____ (64) effects because they occur

early in development and produce changes that will last throughout the lifespan. Hormones also have

_____ (65) effects, which cause reversible changes in physiology and behavior later in

development. In humans, sexual maturation is completed during _____ (66), when gonadal

hormones are again released in high concentrations. Both organizing effects, such as maturation of the

_____ (67), and activating effects, such as _____ (68) and muscle development

and the production of egg and sperm cells, occur at puberty.

In many species, sex hormones are largely responsible for sexual behavior. There are

_____ _____ (69) during development when exposure to a particular hormone alters the brain and thus influences future behavior. In rats, for example, a newborn male that is castrated will be more likely to engage in female-typical sexual behavior _____ (70) as an adult. A young female rat exposed to _____ (71) will perform male-typical mounting more often as an adult. Early exposure to sex hormones also organizes the brain in ways that contribute to sex differences in nonsexual behaviors such as play and _____ (72).

Behavioral sex differences in humans are less clear than they are in other animals, in part because of the limitations of research in this area. However, _____ _____ _____ (73) published a review of the research literature in 1974 and concluded that there were consistent differences between males and females. In cognitive performance, girls tended to be better at _____

_____ (74), whereas boys tended to be better at visual-spatial tasks and _____ (75). Boys were also found to be more _____ (76) than girls. More recent cognitive studies have narrowed down the areas of difference to an advantage in verbal fluency and _____ (77) for girls, and advantages in _____ _____ (78) and standardized math tests in boys. These differences are not absolute, and much _____ (79) between the performances of boys and girls exists.

The source of these differences has been debated. There is evidence that experience contributes to them, in that the differences have been decreasing over the last few decades, particularly in the area of _____ (80). However, there is evidence that biological factors contribute to some of the differences, particularly verbal and _____ (81) abilities, and aggression. For example, the advantage in verbal skills observed in females may be a result of a larger _____ (82), which may result in greater interhemispheric communication, and exposure to _____ (83). The male advantage in spatial skills may be a function of _____ (84) or one or more genes on the X chromosome. Although laboratory studies of aggression indicate small sex differences, in reality men are _____ (85) times more likely to kill than women. A moderate correlation in aggression between identical twins reared apart suggests that _____ (86) is somewhat heritable. Testosterone plays a role in aggression, but its exact influence is unclear.

Short Answer & Essay Questions

Answer the following questions. See p. 147 for sample answers.

6. Which of the different sex organs and structures in females and males develop from the same primitive tissue? What factors are responsible for transforming these primitive structures into the male-typical structures? Be sure to include both internal and external structures.

7. Distinguish between organizing and activating effects of hormones, and give an example of each.

8. Compare the sexual behavior of normal female rats to those that have been "masculinized."

9. Why does the fact that the sex difference in math scores has been declining over the last several decades suggest that experience is an important factor in this sex difference? What specific social factors may be responsible for the change?

10. Why does the author refer to males and females as "other" rather than "opposite" sexes?

Sexual Anomalies

Summary and Guided Review

After studying this section in the text, fill in the blanks of the following summary. The answers are found on pp. 145-146.

Studies of people with naturally-occurring variations in human sexual development can reveal valuable information about the roles of experience and biology on sex and gender. For example, many of the physical differences between males and females are clearly the result of the effects of hormones on development. _____ (87) are born with ambiguous genitalia, although these individuals have _____ (88) that match their chromosomal sex. (True hermaphrodites, who possess both _____ (89) and testicular tissue, are extremely rare.) One cause of male pseudohermaphroditism in males is the lack of the enzyme _____ (90) that converts testosterone into _____ (91); males with this condition appear female at birth, but undergo some masculinization at puberty due to _____ (92). A similar condition, caused by the lack of 5α-reductase, has a genetic basis; many individuals with this condition live in the _____ _____ (93). In most cases, the individual is raised as a girl, but begins questioning her gender during childhood. When masculine characteristics develop in puberty, most of these individuals will adopt a male gender role. Although this suggests that hormones are largely responsible for our sense of gender, the fact that males are more valued in this society indicates that _____ (94) may play a role as well. A third condition that produces male pseudohermaphrodites is _____ _____ _____(95); due to a genetic mutation, these individuals lack androgen receptors, and develop as apparent females, although they have undescended _____ (96). They undergo further feminization at puberty, developing _____ (97) for example.

Female pseudohermaphroditism typically results from exposure to high levels of _____ (98) during fetal development. These individuals have internal female structures, but externally they resemble males; the clitoris is enlarged, resembling a _____ (99), and the

_____ (100) may be partially or completely fused. One cause of female pseudohermaphroditism is

_____ _____ _____ (101), which involves excessive androgen production by the adrenal glands. Parents may decide to raise the baby as a boy or a girl, and reconstructive surgery may be performed to alter the appearance of the genitals to match the baby's assigned sex. Some researchers believe that we need to include more categories for sex than two, including _____ (102) categories for male and female pseudohermaphrodites.

Hormones may be involved in behavioral differences as well, through their influence on brain development. Studies of CAH females suggest that they are somewhat more likely to display

_____ (103) characteristics and have sexual contact with _____ (104) than controls. Cognitively, they tend to have better _____ _____ (105) than other women. Androgen insensitive males tend to have many feminine characteristics, including a strong desire for _____ (106). They also tend to have better _____ (107) than spatial skills. While some claim that these differences are due entirely to rearing factors, the fact that AI males perform _____ (108) on spatial tasks than their normal sisters and other females strongly supports the role of androgens in the development of spatial skills. Furthermore, women exposed to

_____ (109) (a substance that masculinizes the SDN but not the genitals of rats) during fetal development score higher on measures of _____ (110) than controls.

But what about gender identity in individuals without hormonal abnormalities?

_____ _____ (111) argued that our gender identity is determined by our early rearing environment, and that chromosomal sex and hormones do not matter that much. On the other hand, _____ _____ (112) argues that biological factors are more important than early experience. This debate is played out in the case of a young boy whose penis was accidentally destroyed during _____ (113). At the age of 17 months, the child underwent corrective surgery and was reassigned and reared as a girl. Money, who followed this case, reported that "Brenda" was a well-adjusted, feminine child. However, when "Brenda" discovered the truth at the age of 14 after several years of feeling like a male, he began living as a male named David, and adopted a typically masculine role. Another case of _____ _____ (114) had a different outcome, indicating that experience may have played some role. This individual, who underwent

_____ (115) from male to female at 7 months of age and whose mother showed less of the ambivalence displayed by Brenda's mother about the change, adopted a female role; however, she also showed some masculine traits and was _____ (116). It is important to keep in mind that these are _____ (117) studies, and we must be careful about any conclusions we draw from them. While they may be interesting, they do not tell us with certainty whether gender identity is influenced more by biology or experience.

Short Answer & Essay Questions

Answer the following questions. See p. 147 for sample answers.

11. If androgen insensitive males are raised as females, look female even after puberty, and typically adopt a female gender identity without question, how may their condition be discovered?

12. Will a female with CAH have a uterus? Why or why not?

13. What accounts for the fact that androgen insensitive males perform more poorly on tests of spatial skills than their sisters and other females?

14. Does CAH cause women to engage in homosexual activity? Support your answer.

15. Why are the conclusions that can be drawn about the influence of biology and experience on gender from the ablatio penis studies so limited?

Sexual Orientation

Summary and Guided Review

After studying this section in the text, fill in the blanks of the following summary. The answers are found on p. 146.

Identifying the basis of sexual orientation is difficult. However, if we can understand why some people are attracted to members of the same sex, this may tell us something about why people are generally attracted to members of the other sex. Gay men and lesbians are usually exclusively _____ (118). People who are not exclusively heterosexual or homosexual are _____ (119). It is important to understand that many more people have homosexual experiences than are considered homosexuals. The rate of homosexuality in the population is not known, although it is probably less than 3% for men and less than 1.5% for women. Although homosexuals are often stereotyped as displaying characteristics of the other sex, this is not always the case. Furthermore, homosexuals usually adopt a _____ _____ (120) that matches their sex. _____ (121), individuals who live as the other gender and often undergo surgery in order to look more like the sex they have adopted, are sometimes, but not always attracted to members of their biological sex. Clearly, gender role, gender identity, and _____ _____ (122) are somewhat independent.

Much research has focused on one or more biological mechanisms for homosexuality. This model assumes that sexual orientation is largely predetermined at birth by genetic and/or _____ (123) influences. If this is true, then there may be some differences between children and adolescents who will eventually be homosexual, and those who will be heterosexual. Although there is no basis for comparison among heterosexuals, about _____ (124) % of homosexuals recall feeling different in their early years,

137

suggesting that for many, same-sex attraction is a life-long pattern. Those who become homosexual are more likely to display _____ _____-_____ (125), preferring companions of the other sex and activities typical of the other sex.

There is strong evidence for a genetic component to homosexuality. Researchers estimate its heritability between 31-_____ (126) %, and identical twins show higher concordance rates than other sibling pairs. One researcher, Hamer, claims to have found an area of DNA on the _____ (127) chromosome that contributes to homosexuality in males. Hamer's study group included pairs of gay brothers with gay _____ (128) relatives, and _____ (129) % of the brother pairs had identical genotypes in the region in question. However, even if this area contributes to homosexuality in the cases discovered, it cannot be the only explanation, because many of the sibling pairs did not have the same genotype here.

Some animal studies support early hormonal influences on later homosexuality. Experimental manipulation of hormone levels in other species can produce homosexuality, although critics argue that these animals display homosexuality only when isolated from members of the other sex. However, a few studies indicate that homosexuality can occur naturally in some species, such as _____ (130) and gulls. The evidence for hormonal influences in humans is weak, but there is evidence that early hormonal factors may alter the structure and _____ (131) of the brain, which in turn may contribute to homosexuality.

In gay males, two brain structures have been found which appear more female-like. Simon _____ (132) found that the third interstitial nucleus of the _____ _____ (133) is smaller in gay men and heterosexual women than in heterosexual men. The _____ _____ (134) shows this pattern as well. Additionally, the _____ _____ (135) is larger in gay men than in heterosexual men. In animal studies, both the INAH 3 and the SCN have been implicated in sexual behavior, although how these might contribute to sexual behavior in humans is unclear. The differences in the size of the anterior commissure are correlated with differences between gay and heterosexual men on cognitive tasks; gay men tend to score higher on _____ (136) tasks and lower on _____ (137) tasks than heterosexual men. A final brain difference is seen in transsexuals in the central bed nucleus of the stria terminalis. The BSTc in _____-_____-_____ (138) transsexuals was smaller, resembling those of women, and in the only female-to-male transsexual studied, the BSTc was larger, similar to _____ (139). However, these differences were not related to the _____ _____ (140) of the individual. The brains of gay men and male-to-female transsexuals may be _____ (141) at different stages of prenatal development. However, it is difficult to draw firm conclusions about the roles of these structures in sexual orientation and gender identity for several reasons. First, many of the studies are case studies. Second, if these differences are consistent, we still don't know how they contribute to sexual orientation. Finally, the nature of the samples (often brains from older gay men or those who have died from _____ (142)), is limiting. New imaging techniques of live, intact brains may provide better information.

Understanding female homosexuality also represents a challenge. Twin studies indicate that the _____ _____ (143) for homosexuality in women is 48% for identical and 16% for fraternal twins. But, aside from the evidence that _____ (144) and DES women are more likely to display homosexuality, there is little evidence that the brains of lesbians have been _____ (145). Two ways in which lesbians resemble heterosexual men have been discovered: their _____-_____-_____ _____ (146) ratios, and the strength of the click-evoked otoacoustic emissions. Because both of these traits are influenced by prenatal exposure to _____ (147), it may be that the timing of exposure results in masculinization of mechanisms for sexual orientation but not _____ (148) skills.

The social implications of the biological model are important. If sexual preference is something that can be _____ (149), then those who display homosexuality do not qualify for special civil rights status. However, if sexual preference is not chosen, as many homosexuals claim, then their status should be protected. Although the majority of homosexuals believe that one is born being homosexual or heterosexual, some are opposed to the _____ (150) model because of its association with a disease explanation, and fear of efforts to "cure" homosexuality at the _____ (151) level. Other homosexuals embrace the biological model because they think it will make homosexuality more _____ (152) in society, an assumption that has some empirical support.

Short Answer & Essay Questions

Answer the following questions. See p. 148 for sample answers.

16. What can studying homosexuality tell us about heterosexuality?

17. What evidence is presented for the social learning hypothesis of homosexuality? What are the problems with interpreting this evidence?

18. Why do researchers think that the BSTc is related to gender identity, but not sexual orientation?

19. One criticism of the studies of brain differences in homosexuals is that they rely too much on older individuals and those who have died from AIDS. Why is this a problem? What limitations do these samples place on the conclusions that can be drawn from the results?

20. Why are some members of the homosexual community opposed to the biological model of homosexuality?

___

Post-Test

Use these multiple-choice questions to check your understanding of the chapter. The answers, along with explanations, are found beginning on p. 148.

1. As forms of motivation, how are hunger and sex different?
   a. Sex, but not hunger, involves arousal and satiation.
   b. Hunger, but not sex, is under the influence of hormones.
   c. Hunger, but not sex, represents a homeostatic tissue need.
   d. Sex, but not hunger, is entirely under the control of external stimuli.

2. Penile and clitoral erection first occurs in the _____ phase of the sexual response.
   a. excitement
   b. plateau
   c. orgasm
   d. resolution

3. Which of the following statements regarding the refractory phase of the sexual response is true?
   a. Females have a shorter refractory phase than males.
   b. During the refractory phase, orgasm cannot occur.
   c. Males typically have a refractory phase of 3-5 hours.
   d. All of the above

4. Following castration,
   a. men, but not women undergo a decrease in sexual desire.
   b. women, but not men undergo a decrease in sexual desire.
   c. men are completely incapable of having erections.
   d. adrenal androgens may contribute to sexual desire.

5. Antiandrogen drugs
   a. may block the production of testosterone.
   b. may reduce deviant sexual behaviors.
   c. may reduce sexual fantasies.
   d. b and c.
   e. a, b, and c.

6. Which of the following statements regarding sexual activity in females is true?
   a. Only female humans will engage in sexual activity when they are not ovulating.
   b. Women on birth control pills are less likely to initiate sex mid-cycle than at other times.
   c. In women, the increased likelihood of initiating sex corresponds with an increase in sex hormone levels.
   d. Women are less likely to engage in sexual intercourse during ovulation than at other times of the cycle.

7. Which of the following brain areas seems to be involved in sexual activity in female, but not male, rats?
   a. Medial preoptic area
   b. Medial amygdala
   c. Sexually dimorphic nucleus
   d. Ventromedial nucleus

8. Which of the following neurotransmitters increases in the nucleus accumbens during sexual activity?
   a. Dopamine
   b. Serotonin
   c. Norepinephrine
   d. Endorphin

9. Which of the following statements regarding the major histocompatibility complex is FALSE?
   a. Couples with similar MHCs may have more fertility problems.
   b. People who are unrelated are more likely to have similar MHCs.
   c. The MHC includes genes involved in the immune system.
   d. Animals often avoid inbreeding by selecting mates with different MHCs.

10. Olfactory receptors
   a. respond to odors, but not pheromones.
   b. respond to pheromones, but not odors.
   c. respond to both odors and pheromones.
   d. respond to neither odors nor pheromones.

11. Receptors in the VNO project to which TWO areas of the hypothalamus?
   a. Lateral geniculate nucleus
   b. Sexually dimorphic nucleus
   c. Medial preoptic area
   d. Ventromedial

12. Which of the following statements regarding pheromones in humans is FALSE?
   a. Women's menstrual cycles may be synchronized by pheromones.
   b. Men rate women more attractive when exposed to vaginal pheromones.
   c. Pheromones have been linked to sexual attraction, but not sexual behavior.
   d. Exposure to pheromones produces changes in autonomic arousal.

13. Among humans, those with symmetrical bodies
   a. tend to be more intelligent.
   b. are rated as more attractive.
   c. show indications of better health.
   d. b and c
   e. a, b, and c.

14. A woman who feels more like a man than a woman has a _____ that does not match her sex.
   a. gender role
   b. gender identity
   c. sexual orientation
   d. b and c

15. Which of the following statements regarding egg cells is TRUE?
    a. They contain both X and Y chromosomes.
    b. They contain only Y chromosomes.
    c. They contain only X chromosomes.
    d. They contain either an X or a Y chromosome.

16. Which of the following internal structures must be actively inhibited in order for the normal pattern of male genitalia to form?
    a. Mullerian ducts
    b. Wolffian ducts
    c. Ovaries
    d. Testes

17. The penis in males and the _____ in females develop from the same embryonic tissue.
    a. vagina
    b. labia
    c. uterus
    d. clitoris

18. What hormone(s) is/are responsible for masculinization of the external genitalia in males?
    a. Testosterone
    b. Dihydrotestosterone
    c. Mullerian inhibiting hormone
    d. a and b
    e. a, b, and c

19. Which of the following represents an activating effect of a hormone?
    a. Maturation of the genitals at puberty
    b. The enlargement of the SDN in male rats
    c. Release of a mature egg cell during ovulation
    d. Masculinization of the genitals during prenatal development

20. Which of the following statements regarding sexual behavior in rats is TRUE?
    a. Among male rats, only those castrated shortly after birth will display lordosis.
    b. Androgenized females will mount other rats, but do not display lordosis.
    c. Castrated males do not display mounting.
    d. Normal females occasionally mount other females.

21. Which of the following gender differences has NOT been consistently found in the research literature?
    a. Females are more emotional than males.
    b. Females tend to score better on verbal tasks than males.
    c. Males tend to score better on spatial tasks than females.
    d. Males tend to be more aggressive than females.

22. Evidence of an environmental contribution to sex differences is strongest for which of the following?
    a. Mental rotation
    b. Verbal fluency
    c. Mathematics
    d. Reading comprehension

23. The posterior portion of the corpus callosum is
    a. larger in females, but only in adults.
    b. larger in males, but only in adults.
    c. larger in females prior to birth.
    d. larger in males prior to birth.

24. Which hormone may be linked to enhanced verbal fluency?
    a. Testosterone
    b. Estrogen
    c. Progesterone
    d. Dihydrotestosterone

25. Which hormone may be linked to enhanced spatial skills?
    a. Testosterone
    b. Estrogen
    c. Progesterone
    d. Dihydrotestosterone

26. Which of the following statements regarding sex differences in aggression is FALSE?
    a. Studies indicate that aggression in males is more acceptable than aggression in females.
    b. Studies indicate that males are much more likely than females to kill another person.
    c. Studies indicate that aggression is moderately heritable.
    d. Studies indicate that testosterone is related to aggression.

27. Which of the following will NOT result in male pseudohermaphroditism?
    a. 17β-hydroxysteroid deficiency
    b. androgen insensitivity syndrome
    c. 5α-reductase deficiency
    d. congenital adrenal hyperplasia

28. Which of the following statements regarding female pseudohermaphrodites is TRUE?
    a. They are always raised as girls.
    b. They have ovaries.
    c. They have a penis instead of a clitoris.
    d. They lack a uterus.

29. Which of the following groups tends to score the lowest on spatial tasks?
    a. CAH females
    b. AI males
    c. Normal females
    d. Normal males

30. Which of the following statements regarding DES females is TRUE?
    a. Their spatial task scores are better than most males' scores.
    b. They report more homosexual fantasies, but no more homosexual contact, than other women.
    c. They are more likely to describe themselves as homosexual than other women.
    d. They have masculinized genitalia.

31. Regarding the case of "Bruce-Brenda-David," which of the following is TRUE?
    a. Brenda chose to become a boy without knowing her true sex.
    b. Brenda was comfortable with her feminine role until adolescence.
    c. Brenda's mother had no problem about her child making the switch from male to female.
    d. This case clearly demonstrated that the "neutral-at-birth" position is incorrect.

32. Which of the following statements regarding sexual orientation is TRUE?
    a. Gay men are more likely to be bisexual than lesbians.
    b. Lesbians make up a larger proportion of the population than do gay men.
    c. Gay men and lesbians are usually bisexual to a certain degree.
    d. Many more people engage in homosexual behavior than are considered homosexual.

33. Transsexuals
    a. have the gender identity but not necessarily the sexual orientation of members of the other sex.
    b. have the gender identity and the sexual orientation of members of the other sex.
    c. have the sexual orientation but not necessarily the gender identity of members of the other sex.
    d. none of the above.

34. Gender non-conformity includes
    a. early homosexual experiences.
    b. a preference for friends of the other sex.
    c. a preference for activities usually associated with the other sex.
    d. a, b, and c
    e. b and c

35. The concordance rate for homosexuality is
    a. much higher in lesbians than gay men.
    b. about the same in lesbians and gay men.
    c. much higher in gay men than lesbians.
    d. low in both gay men and lesbians.

36. Homosexuality in other species
    a. occurs only under controlled laboratory conditions.
    b. results only from the manipulation of hormones during development.
    c. resembles heterosexuality in some ways (e.g. pair bonding, parenting).
    d. is rarely, if ever, observed.

37. The INAH 3 is largest in
    a. heterosexual males.
    b. homosexual males.
    c. heterosexual females.
    d. homosexual females.

38. The BSTc has been linked to
    a. both sexual orientation and gender identity.
    b. neither sexual orientation nor gender identity.
    c. sexual orientation only.
    d. gender identity only.

39. Lesbians resemble heterosexual men in which of the following ways?
    a. They perform more poorly on verbal tasks than heterosexual women.
    b. They perform better on spatial tasks than heterosexual women.
    c. They have a larger anterior commissure than heterosexual women.
    d. They have a greater ring-to-index finger ratio than heterosexual women.

40. About what percentage of the general public believes that homosexuality is inborn?
    a. 80-90%
    b. 50-75%
    c. 35-50%
    d. 10-15%

Answers and Explanations

Guided Review

1. motivation
2. satiation
3. homeostasis
4. Masters and Johnson
5. excitement
6. plateau
7. orgasm
8. ejaculation
9. resolution
10. women
11. men
12. Coolidge effect
13. castration
14. gonads
15. decline
16. testosterone
17. estrus
18. ovulation
19. estrogen
20. medial preoptic area
21. performance
22. copulate
23. medial amygdala
24. sexually dimorphic nucleus
25. ventromedial nucleus
26. Dopamine
27. endorphins
28. nucleus accumbens
29. major histocompatibility complex
30. olfactory
31. nasal cavity
32. 10,000
33. pheromones
34. vomeronasal organ
35. MPOA
36. skin temperature
37. McClintock
38. synchronized
39. vaginal
40. sexual intercourse
41. symmetrical
42. children
43. sexual partners
44. ovulation
45. gender role
46. gender identity
47. conception
48. X
49. female
50. male
51. ovaries
52. uterus
53. Wolffian ducts
54. clitoris
55. labia
56. estrogen
57. SRY
58. testes
59. Mullerian inhibiting hormone
60. testosterone
61. seminal vesicles
62. Dihydrotestosterone
63. scrotum
64. organizing
65. activating
66. puberty
67. genitals
68. breast
69. critical periods
70. lordosis
71. testosterone
72. learning
73. Maccoby and Jacklin
74. verbal tasks
75. mathematics
76. aggressive
77. writing
78. mental rotation
79. overlap
80. mathematics
81. spatial
82. splenium
83. estrogen
84. testosterone
85. 30
86. aggression
87. Pseudohermaphrodites
88. gonads

89. ovarian
90. 17β-hydroxysteroid
91. dihydrotestosterone
92. testosterone
93. Dominican Republic
94. environment
95. androgen insensitivity syndrome
96. testes
97. breasts
98. androgens
99. penis
100. labia
101. congenital adrenal hyperplasia
102. intersexual
103. masculine
104. women
105. spatial skills
106. children
107. verbal
108. worse
109. diethylstilbesterol
110. homosexuality
111. John Money
112. Milton Diamond
113. circumcision
114. ablatio penis
115. reassignment
116. bisexual
117. case
118. homosexual
119. bisexual
120. gender identity
121. Transsexuals
122. sexual orientation
123. hormonal
124. 70
125. gender non-conformity
126. 74
127. X
128. maternal
129. 64
130. sheep
131. function
132. LeVay
133. anterior hypothalamus
134. anterior commissure
135. suprachiasmatic nucleus
136. verbal
137. spatial
138. male-to-female
139. men
140. sexual orientation
141. feminization
142. AIDS
143. concordance rate
144. CAH
145. masculinized
146. ring-to-index finger
147. testosterone
148. cognitive
149. chosen
150. biological
151. genetic
152. acceptable

Short Answer & Essay

1. Sex and hunger are similar in that they are under the regulation of the brain and hormones, and they both involve arousal and satiation. However, there are important differences. Usually, we eat to reduce hunger, but we seek out stimuli that will increase sexual arousal. Hunger is also more controlled by internal conditions, whereas sexual arousal is relatively more responsive to external conditions.

2. Testosterone seems to be required for sexual motivation in both men and women, although only at a low level. However, sexual activity also increases testosterone levels, so the picture is somewhat complicated. In both men and women, castration leads to a reduction of sexual functioning. Men who are voluntarily castrated or are given testosterone-blocking drugs show reduced aggression and sexual tendencies. In women, testosterone levels are correlated with initiating sexual activity. When given testosterone, women show more sexual responsiveness.

3. The Coolidge effect occurs when a male animal that has mated with one female shows renewed sexual arousal in the presence of a different female. It is correlated with changes within the nucleus accumbens. During copulation, dopamine release in the NAcc is high, and then decreases, even with the female's continued presence. When the male encounters a novel female, dopamine release in the NAcc increases again, and remains high during copulation. However, as the book points out, these changes in behavior and brain activity are "parallel" (see pp. 159-160), and do not necessarily imply cause and effect.

4. The MHC refers to a group of genes involved in immune system functioning. Couples with similar MHCs have more fertility problems than those whose MHCs are different.

5. When stimulated with suspected pheromones, the receptors in the VNO produced potentials. These receptors did not respond to odors, and the olfactory receptors did not respond to the pheromones.

6. Internally, the gonads develop into either ovaries or testes; development of testes is dependent on the presence of the SRY gene on the Y chromosome. Without the presence of dihydrotestosterone, the external genitalia will become a clitoris, lower portion of the vagina, and labia, which is typical for females. If dihydrotestosterone is present, as it is in males, then the external structures become a penis and scrotum.

7. Organizing effects typically occur when the developing individual is first exposed to the hormone, either before or shortly after birth. This exposure leads to permanent changes in bodily structures. One example is how dihydrotestosterone changes the primitive external genital structures into a penis and scrotum, but there are many other examples in the book. Activating effects can occur any time in the lifespan after the initial exposure when hormone levels change, and they are reversible. An example is the development of breast tissue in females during puberty, but there are other examples in the book as well.

8. Normal female rats typically engage in lordosis, although they will occasionally mount other females. In females who have been masculinized, mounting occurs much more frequently.

9. If the difference were solely or mostly biologically influenced, we would not expect to see a rapid change over time. The narrowing gap has corresponded with a change in gender roles, particularly for women, and perhaps this loosening of restrictions on females' occupational choices and education is largely responsible for their improved math scores.

10. He uses the term "other" to reflect the fact that males and females are not really opposite. There are some consistent differences, but in these there is a great deal of overlap between the sexes. Overall, males and females share more similarities than they do differences.

11. Since they do not have ovaries, they do not menstruate, and they certainly cannot become pregnant. So during adolescence or early adulthood, they would probably discover their condition if they try to determine the source of problems with their reproductive systems.

12. Yes, because the development of the uterus is determined by the absence of Mullerian inhibiting hormone, which CAH females are not exposed to.

13. They are insensitive to the effects of masculinizing hormones. Normal females are exposed to small amounts of these hormones, which are probably enough to alter the brain structures responsible for mental rotation to a certain degree, but because AI males lack receptors for androgens, their brains will not develop in the same way.

14. It may influence some women, as evidenced by the fact that more CAH women reported homosexual contact than a control group of women. However, we can't ignore that some of the normal women behaved like the minority of the CAH women who had homosexual contact, and that most of the CAH women did not report homosexual contact. Clearly, CAH is not the only factor.

15. Each case involves only a single individual, so generalizing to others is very difficult. Another problem is that these were not experiments, and there was virtually no control over the many factors influencing gender.

16. Studying those whose orientation differs from the majority of humans, in particular the ways in which their brains differ, can tell us not only why some people are homosexual, but also why others are heterosexual.

17. The social learning hypothesis suggests that people who have early homosexual experiences will be more likely to become homosexual later. There is evidence for this; for example, individuals who reported having other-sex friends, masturbating in the presence of or being masturbated by a same-sex partner, and having homosexual contact prior to age 18, were more likely to be homosexual as adults. But an alternative interpretation is that these experiences are early manifestations of an underlying homosexual tendency rather than the origin of homosexuality.

18. The BSTc is smaller in women than men. In one female-to-male transsexual, his BSTc resembled the male pattern. The BSTc is also smaller in male-to-female transsexuals, men who have a female gender identity. But, its size was unrelated to the sexual orientation of these men.

19. A problem with studying the brains of older homosexuals is that they have been practicing homosexual behavior for a longer period of time. Gay men who have died from AIDS may have brains that look different as a result of the disease.

20. They are concerned that if a biological basis to homosexuality is discovered, it will be understood in terms of a physical abnormality that can be corrected to "cure" or prevent homosexuality.

Post-Test

All page references in this section pertain to the textbook.

1. a. Wrong; both involve arousal and satiation.
    b. Wrong; both are influenced by hormones.
    c. **Correct**; whereas we cannot live without food, we can live without sex.
    d. Wrong; particularly in humans, sex may be more controlled by external stimuli, but hunger can be elicited by the sight of food, and internal factors (such as hormones) influence sex.

2. a. **Correct**; see p. 156.
    b. Wrong
    c. Wrong
    d. Wrong

3. a. Wrong; females have no refractory phase.
    b. **Correct**; see p. 156.
    c. Wrong; the length of the refractory phase is highly variable, and may be influenced by external stimuli.
    d. Wrong

4. a. Wrong; both men and women experience a decline in sexual desire.
    b. Wrong; both men and women experience a decline in sexual desire.
    c. Wrong; some, but not all men may experience this.
    d. **Correct**; adrenal testosterone may have a similar effect.

5. a. Wrong; b and c are also correct.
    b. Wrong; a and c are also correct.
    c. Wrong; a and b are also correct.
    d. Wrong; a is also correct.
    e. Correct; see p. 157.

6. a. Wrong; although most other species only mate during estrus, the females of some primate species will mate when they are not ovulating.
    b. Wrong; the book does not state this, but says that they are not MORE likely to initiate sex midcycle.
    c. Correct; an increase in sex hormones is linked to ovulation, and this is the time when women not on birth control pills are more likely to initiate sex (but not necessarily participate in sex).
    d. Wrong

7. a. Wrong; this is involved in sexual activity in both males and females.
    b. Wrong; this is involved in sexual activity in both males and females.
    c. Wrong; this is involved in male sexual activity, but is not mentioned as being related to female sexual activity.
    d. Correct; see p. 159.

8. **a. Correct**; see pp. 159-160. This may be similar to the mechanism responsible for the rewarding experience associated with drugs.
    b. Wrong; although serotonin may increase during sexual activity, the book does not indicate that this is occurring in the nucleus accumbens.
    c. Wrong; this is involved in sexual activity, but no mention of it in the NA is made.
    d. Wrong; this is involved in sexual activity, but no mention of it in the NA is made.

9. a. Wrong; this is true.
    b. Correct; MHC genes are probably MORE similar among relatives than nonrelatives.
    c. Wrong; this is true.
    d. Wrong; this is true.

10. **a. Correct**; see p. 163.
    b. Wrong; they do not respond to pheromones.
    c. Wrong
    d. Wrong

11. a. Wrong
    b. Wrong
    c. Correct; see p. 163.
    d. Correct; see p. 163.

12. a. Wrong; this is true.
    b. Wrong; this is true.
    c. Correct; men who were given a pheromone reported more sexual intercourse (implying that they found partners) but not more masturbation (implying that they were not more motivated) than men in the control condition.
    d. Wrong; this is true.

13. a. Wrong; this is not stated in the text.
    b. Wrong; c is also correct.
    c. Wrong; b is also correct.
    d. Correct; see p. 164.
    e. Wrong

14. a. Wrong; this is the set of behaviors that society dictates appropriate for the different sexes.
    b. Correct; this refers to the sex one identifies with.
    c. Wrong; gender identity and sexual orientation are not always related.
    d. Wrong

15. a. Wrong; each normally contains only a single X chromosome.
    b. Wrong; see a.
    c. Correct; see p. 165.
    d. Wrong; see a.

16. **a. Correct**; without Mullerian inhibiting hormone, these will develop into female structures.
    b. Wrong; in females, these disintegrate on their own because of the lack of exposure to androgens. In males, their development is normal.
    c. Wrong; these will form in the absence of a Y chromosome.
    d. Wrong; these will form in the presence of a Y chromosome, and are part of the normal male pattern.

17. a. Wrong; this arises in part from the Mullerian ducts.
    b. Wrong; this is from the same tissue as the scrotum.
    c. Wrong; this arises from the Mullerian ducts.
    d. Correct; see p. 166.

18. a. Wrong; it is the derivative of testosterone, dihydrotestosterone, that is responsible.
    b. Correct; see p. 166.
    c. Wrong; this affects internal, but not external, structures.
    d. Wrong
    e. Wrong

19. a. Wrong; this is an organizing effect (it is irreversible).
    b. Wrong; this is an organizing effect (it is irreversible).
    c. Correct; this is a temporary fluctuation in hormone level.
    d. Wrong; this is an organizing effect (it is irreversible).

20. a. Wrong; the book states that castrated males are more likely to display lordosis, implying normal males do it less frequently.
    b. Wrong; they are more likely to mount than normal females, but the book implies that they will also perform lordosis.
    c. Wrong; the book implies that they mount less frequently than normal males.
    d. Correct; although mounting occurs more frequently in masculinized females, it also occurs in normal females.

21. **a. Correct**; this was not mentioned in the text.
    b. Wrong; this is a consistently observed difference.
    c. Wrong; this is a consistently observed difference.
    d. Wrong; this is a consistently observed difference.

22. a.   Wrong; this difference has remained consistent over time.
    b.   Wrong; this difference has remained consistent over time.
    c. **Correct**; this difference has particularly declined, suggesting that females are getting better math education than they used to.
    d.   Wrong; there is no consistent difference found in this area.

23. a.   Wrong
    b.   Wrong
    c. **Correct**; see p. 169. This difference is apparent about 26 weeks after conception.
    d.   Wrong

24. a.   Wrong
    b. **Correct**; men taking estrogen supplements scored higher on verbal fluency tests.
    c.   Wrong
    d.   Wrong

25. **a.** **Correct**; men's spatial scores improve when they are taking testosterone supplements.
    b.   Wrong
    c.   Wrong
    d.   Wrong

26. **a.** **Correct**; at least one study shows that this is not the case, so the picture is unclear.
    b.   Wrong; this is true.
    c.   Wrong; this is true.
    d.   Wrong; this is true, although a causal mechanism is not understood.

27. a.   Wrong; this reduces the level of androgens.
    b.   Wrong; these males lack receptors for androgens.
    c.   Wrong; this reduces the level of androgens.
    d. **Correct**; this was discussed as leading to female, but not male, pseudohermaphroditism.

28. a.   Wrong; the extent of masculinization of the genitals often determines whether they are raised as boys or girls.
    b. **Correct**; the gonads match the chromosomal sex.
    c.   Wrong; although some CAH girls may be born with penis-like clitorises, not all are.
    d.   Wrong; although not stated, the text implies that their Mullerian ducts can mature normally.

29. a.   Wrong; they actually score higher than normal women.
    b. **Correct**; their spatial scores are the lowest of all groups, perhaps as a result of the complete insensitivity to androgens.
    c.   Wrong; they score higher than AI males.
    d.   Wrong; they are among the highest scoring.

30. a.   Wrong
    b.   Wrong; they report more homosexual fantasies AND more homosexual contact than other women.
    c. **Correct**; see p. 173.
    d.   Wrong

31. **a.** **Correct**; she decided at age 14 to switch to a boy, and then her parents revealed the truth.
b. Wrong; she displayed many masculine characteristics and reported being uncomfortable with herself as a girl.
c. Wrong; her mother displayed some ambivalence about the sex change.
d. Wrong; although it argues against this position, it is only one case, and Bruce did not become Brenda until about 18 months of age.

32. a. Wrong; lesbians are actually more likely to be bisexual.
b. Wrong; gay men make up slightly more of the population of men than lesbians do of women.
c. Wrong; both are usually exclusively homosexual.
d. **Correct**; many people who consider themselves heterosexual report having had homosexual experiences.

33. **a.** **Correct**; for example, some male-to-female transsexuals are attracted to men, whereas some are attracted to women.
b. Wrong
c. Wrong
d. Wrong

34. a. Wrong; while this is more common among homosexuals, it is not part of the pattern of gender non-conformity.
b. Wrong; c is also correct.
c. Wrong; b is also correct.
d. Wrong
e. **Correct**; see p. 177.

35. a. Wrong
b. **Correct**; it is about 52% in men and 48% in women.
c. Wrong; although it is slightly higher in men, the difference is not great.
d. Wrong; this is a moderately strong concordance rate.

36. a. Wrong; it does occur in the wild as well.
b. Wrong; in the cases of wild animals displaying homosexuality, the role of hormones is unknown.
c. **Correct**; in species such as gulls that display "lesbianism," the couple behave very similarly to heterosexual couples.
d. Wrong; castration and androgenization produces it in laboratory animals, so it can't really be considered rare. This option does not state that only wild populations are being considered.

37. **a.** **Correct**; see p. 179.
b. Wrong; this group resembled the smaller heterosexual women.
c. Wrong
d. Wrong; this group was not included in the study.

38. a. Wrong; in male-to-female transsexuals, it was found to be smaller (like women's) regardless of their sexual orientation.
b. Wrong
c. Wrong
d. **Correct**; see p. 180.

39. a. Wrong; there is no difference in verbal ability between lesbian and heterosexual women.
    b. Wrong; there is no difference in spatial ability between lesbian and heterosexual women.
    c. Wrong; gay men have a larger anterior commissure than heterosexual men, but no difference was discussed in women.
    d. Correct; these seem to be an indication of masculinization of some type.

40. a. Wrong
    b. Wrong
    c. Correct; see p. 182.
    d. Wrong

Chapter 7: Emotion and Health

Chapter Outline and Learning Objectives

As you read the chapter, use these learning objectives to guide your studying. You should be able to define the key terms from the text, which are shown in boldface type below.

1) Emotion and the Nervous System
    a) Autonomic and Muscular Involvement in Emotion
    - How does the autonomic nervous system (both branches) contribute to emotion?

        i) Two Competing Theories
        - How, according to the **James-Lange theory**, does emotion occur? What are the criticisms of this theory?

        - How does the **cognitive theory** explain emotion?

        ii) Cognitive Aspects of Emotion
        - Describe the studies by Schachter and Singer (1962) and Dutton and Aron (1974). How do the result of these studies support the cognitive theory of emotion?

        iii) Physical Patterns of Emotional Response
        - What types of physiological responses can be measured using a **polygraph**?

        - What evidence supports the James-Lange assumption that the autonomic nervous system is instrumental in determining the experience of emotion?

        - Discuss the role of facial expressions in emotion. How does this evidence fit with the James-Lange theory?

        - How might a thermal camera be used as a lie detector?

        iv) What We Have Learned
        - Describe the gambling task discussed in the introduction to this chapter. What does it tell us about the role of arousal and cognition in emotional behavior? Which theory of emotion does it support?

        - Discuss how the autonomic and behavioral components of emotional responses may be adaptive.

b) The Brain and Emotion
- What are the advantages and disadvantages of using humans to study the role of the brain in emotion? Of using animals?

i) The Limbic System
- What does Heath's research tell us about the role of the **limbic system**, and in particular the hypothalamus and septum, in emotions in humans?

ii) The Amygdala
- What structures does the **amygdala** receive information from and project to?

- What are the emotional and behavioral consequences of damage to the amygdala?

iii) The Prefrontal Cortex
- What role does the **prefrontal cortex** play in emotion?

- What does the case of Jane, described in the introduction to this chapter, reveal about the importance of this area of the brain for emotion, learning, and decision making?

iv) The Right Hemisphere
- Discuss the role of the right hemisphere in emotion. What are the consequences of right hemisphere damage?

2) Stress, Immunity, and Health
- What are two different ways that psychologists define **stress**?

a) Stress as an Adaptive Response
- What are the components of the **HPA**, and what happens when it is activated? What effects do the stress hormones epinephrine, norepinephrine, and cortisol have on bodily systems?

- Describe the function of each of the following **immune system** cells: **leucocytes**, **macrophages**, **T cells**, **B cells**, and **natural killer cells**.

- What are the consequences of **autoimmune disorders** like multiple sclerosis?

b) Negative Effects of Stress
   - What evidence is there that prolonged stress impairs the immune system, and consequently contributes to poor health?

   - What evidence is there that stress contributes to cardiovascular disease and **sudden cardiac death**?

   - What evidence is there that stress contributes to brain damage? What is the likely cause of this type of brain damage?

   - What evidence is there that reducing stress improves health?

c) Social and Personality Variables
   - What evidence is there that social support and personality factors are involved in stress-related health problems?

   - What does the relationship between extraversion and immune system activity demonstrate about personality variables and health?

d) Pain as an Adaptive Emotion
   - What is the result of congenital insensitivity to pain? What does this tell us about the adaptive benefits of pain?

   - What influence do culture and other situational variables have on the experience of pain?

   - What structures contribute to the emotional component of pain perception? How do researchers know that the sensation and emotion of pain are separate reactions?

3) Biological Origins of Aggression
   - Distinguish between **offensive, defensive,** and **predatory aggression**.

   a) Hormones
      - What evidence suggests that the sex hormones are related to aggression? What is the nature of this relationship?

   b) The Brain
      - What are the pathways involved in defensive and predatory aggression in cats?

- What brain areas seem to be involved in aggression in humans?

- What are the characteristics of people with **antisocial personality disorder**? What may be the cause of their impulsiveness?

c) Serotonin
  i) Inhibition of Aggression
    - How is serotonin activity typically measured? What form of aggression is low serotonin activity associated with?

    - What is the possible link between prenatal exposure to nicotine and aggression?

    - What experimental evidence is there that low serotonin increases aggression in humans and animals?

  ii) Alcohol and Serotonin
    - What is the relationship between alcohol, serotonin, and aggression? What type of people seem to be more at risk for being aggressive while under the influence of alcohol?

  iii) Serotonin and Testosterone
    - How do monkeys with high testosterone differ from those with low 5-HIAA in terms of aggression? What about monkeys with both high testosterone and low 5-HIAA?

d) Heredity and Environment
    - What evidence is there for a genetic contribution to aggression?

    - What environmental characteristics are associated with violent aggression?

Emotion and the Nervous System

Summary and Guided Review

After studying this section in the text, fill in the blanks of the following summary. The answers are found on p. 169.

Emotions involve subjective "feelings," expressions, and behavior, all of which are rooted in the

_____ _____ (1). For example, the autonomic nervous system is intimately involved in emotional responding; activation of the _____ (2) branch produces arousal, and the _____ (3) branch helps to reduce activity and restore bodily resources. However, just how the sympathetic nervous system contributes to emotional experience has been an issue for debate for over 100 years.

The _____-_____ (4) theory of emotion, developed in the late 19th century, suggests that physiological arousal occurs in response to a stimulus and precedes emotional experience, and that different emotions are the result of different patterns of autonomic arousal. This theory was challenged beginning in the 1920's, when _____ (5) argued that the nervous system reacts the same way during different emotions, so the particular feeling of arousal was not alone responsible for emotion – there must be some additional factor.

After several decades of practically ignoring emotions, experimental psychologists took up the issue again in the 1960's. _____ _____ _____ (6) cognitive theory suggested that arousal and cognitive appraisal occurred simultaneously, and that the appraisal component was more important for determining exactly what emotion was experienced, whereas arousal accounted for the _____ (7) of an emotion. Some research supports this theory. For example, _____ _____ _____ (8) demonstrated that men interviewed by a woman were more likely to be attracted to her if they were interviewed while on a suspension bridge than if they were interviewed after crossing the bridge. This indicated that the arousal many men experienced while crossing the bridge was attributed to sexual attraction.

There is also evidence in support of the James-Lange theory. For example, when Ax induced negative emotions in his research subjects, those experiencing fear showed a different pattern of physiological responses as measured by a _____ (9) than those experiencing anger. Other research indicates that feedback from the _____ (10) muscles may be even more important in determining emotional experience than autonomic feedback. For example, when participants were instructed to produce particular facial expressions (but were not aware of the specific expression they were being asked to make), their _____ (11) arousal patterns differed with each expression, and they reported feeling the associated emotion.

Another way of approaching the study of emotions is to ask what emotions are for. Emotions serve _____ (12) functions such as communication and preparing the body for physical challenges. Some recent research even suggests that emotions help us make adaptive _____ (13). In a gambling task in which participants could select cards from risky piles (with lower overall payoff) or safe piles (with greater overall payoff), after several rounds participants showed an increase in the _____ _____ _____ (14), an indication of autonomic arousal, before selecting a card from a _____ (15) pile. Many of them switched to the safe pile, even though they were consciously unaware of the relative risk of each pile.

There are several brain structures that play important roles in emotions. Many of these areas are located in the _____ (16) system, which also contributes to learning, memory, and motivation. In humans undergoing brain surgery, electrical stimulation of the _____ (17) elicited autonomic arousal, and patients reported feeling different emotions, depending on the placement of the electrode. Sexual pleasure seems to be at least in part a result of stimulation of the _____ (18) area. The _____ (19), another limbic structure, is highly interconnected with other brain areas; it receives input from the senses and sends messages to several other brain areas involved in different aspects of emotion. It seems to be most intensively involved in the related emotions of fear and _____ (20). Rats with damage to the amygdala display no fear of _____ (21), and humans with damaged amygdalas are very trusting of others and have difficulty identifying _____ (22) facial expressions in others. Furthermore, they seem incapable of learning to recognize harmful situations or experiencing emotional responses to rewards and _____ (23). Normal people, on the other hand, show _____ (24) activity in the amygdala when presented with pictures of people displaying fearful expressions, and stimulation of the amygdala produces fear. _____- _____ (25) drugs have effects in this area. The amygdala sends information to the _____ (26) cortex, which uses emotional information for making decisions. Individuals with damage to the _____ _____ (27) area can learn to avoid performing behaviors that are immediately harmful, but not those with _____-_____ (28) harmful consequences.

The right hemisphere, which mediates _____ (29) arousal, seems to be somewhat specialized for specific emotional functions. Right hemisphere damage has been linked to impairment of emotional responses and perception of emotions in others, perhaps because people with such damage are essentially disconnected from autonomic _____ (30).

Short Answer & Essay Questions

Answer the following questions. See pp. 169-170 for sample answers.

1. Many people draw a distinction between human capacities for rationality and emotion, treating them independently, and often assuming that decisions based on rationality are superior to those based on emotion. After reading this section of the chapter, do you agree that rationality and emotion are independent? Why or why not?

2. What was Walter Cannon's criticism of the James-Lange theory of emotion?

3. Describe the method used by Schachter and Singer to study the cognitive component of emotion. What was their hypothesis, and how were they able to test it?

4. What limitations exist in human studies of the brain's role in emotion? Why are we unable to draw firm conclusions from these studies?

5. Give an example of how emotional experiences are adaptive (how they promote survival).

Stress, Immunity, and Health

Summary and Guided Review

After studying this section in the text, fill in the blanks of the following summary. The answers are found on p. 169.

The term _____ (31) is used to refer to external events that challenge an organism as well as internal changes associated with meeting challenges. The internal experience of stress is highly variable; not everyone feels stress under the same conditions.

Usually, the internal changes associated with stress are _____ (32). These include activation of the _____-_____-_____ (33) axis, a mechanism responsible for the release of _____ (34) that prepare the body for "fight or flight" via their effects on circulation and energy availability. For example, the stress hormone _____ (35) converts proteins to glucose, and increases fat availability and _____ (36); this provides for more energy for a longer period of time than _____ (37) arousal alone. Changes also occur in the _____ (38) system, such as increases in leukocyte and _____ _____ _____ (39) activity. These cells are the first line of defense in fighting off invading microorganisms, such as those that could be introduced into the body during injury. If the stress response continues over a long period of time, however, considerable harm can occur, including _____ (40) of memory, motivational changes, mood changes, and immune system impairment. Some evidence suggests that chronic stress can also lead to _____ (41) risk of disease, due to the effect on the immune system. For example, studies have shown that long-term unemployment and _____ _____ (42) are associated with illness, and recently _____ (43) women are more subject to illness than controls. Cardiovascular disease may also be a result of chronic stress, as evidenced by the fact that children who were more reactive to the _____ _____ (44) were more likely to have high blood pressure as adults. There is even evidence that acute stress can lead to _____ (45). For example, on the day of the 1994 earthquake in Southern California, the number of deaths due to _____ _____ (46) was five times higher than average. Stress may also contribute to brain damage, particularly in the _____ (47), perhaps due to prolonged exposure to cortisol.

If chronic stress impairs health, then stress _____ (48) or prevention may improve health. Meditation, _____ (49) training, and social skills training have been linked to health gains in people at risk for health problems, such as the elderly, and AIDS and cancer patients. However, due to methodological limitations, it is not known if these health benefits were a result of improved _____ (50) function.

Several social and _____ (51) variables are linked to stress-related health problems as well. For example, Three Mile Island residents with greater _____ _____ (52) tended to have lower levels of stress hormones. People who experience a lot of _____ (53) are more likely to suffer from heart disease. Among _____ (54) patients, those who lose hope or accept their disease have a lower survival rate than those who fight. However, these results are mostly correlational, and in each case a _____ _____ (55) may be operating. For example, low extraversion is associated with _____ (56) natural killer cell activity, but both of these may be a result of high levels of stress hormones.

Like stress, _____ (57) is in many ways an adaptive response. People with congenital _____ (58) to pain have difficulty learning to avoid injuries, and may die prematurely. Pain can be considered an _____ (59) as well as a sensation. How people experience pain varies on an individual and cultural basis. For example, in the United States _____ (60) is considered more painful than it is in other cultures. A study of WWII soldiers wounded in combat revealed that they reported very little pain, compared with patients undergoing _____ (61). Some people will voluntarily undergo torture-like procedures apparently without experiencing debilitating pain, as in the case of Indians who are hung by steel hooks sunk into their backs. Pathways that carry messages about pain connect with the _____ (62) cortex, the anterior cingulate cortex, and various limbic structures. Studies suggest that it is the _____ (63) that is involved in the emotional component of pain. The _____ (64) cortex is also involved in emotional responses to pain, and is implicated in cases of pain insensitivity disorders in which people are able to feel pain, but are not bothered by it.

Short Answer & Essay Questions

Answer the following questions. See p. 170 for sample answers.

6. List the four types of immune cells discussed in the book, and explain the function of each.

7. According to the immunoredistribution hypothesis, why is the redistribution adaptive?

8. Discuss the role of personality factors in cancer survival. Why is it difficult to determine if having a "fighting spirit" causes one to have a better chance of surviving?

9. Why is pain considered to be adaptive? What would your life be like if you could not feel, or were not bothered by, pain?

10. Discuss the role of the ACC in pain. How do researchers know that it is involved in the emotional response to, but not the sensation of, pain?

Biological Origins of Aggression

Summary and Guided Review

After studying this section in the text, fill in the blanks of the following summary. The answers are found on p. 169.

Aggression is sometimes, but not always, an adaptive response, involving both motivation and

_____ (65). Although there are many different forms of aggression, they can be

thought of as belonging to one of three categories: _____ (66) aggression, which is

characterized as an unprovoked attack on another individual; _____ (67)

aggression, which involves responding physically to a threat; and _____ (68)

aggression, which occurs when an animal kills another for food. Different motivational and emotional

states accompany each type, and each probably has different underlying _____ (69)

and anatomical roots as well.

The _____ (70) hormones seem to be involved in offensive aggression, particularly in rats.

In humans, studies suggest that increased aggression is linked to _____ (71)

syndrome in some women, and violent male criminals have higher _____ (72)

levels. However, the exact relationship between hormones and aggression is not clear, since it has been

shown that testosterone _____ (73) following competition.

Defensive and predatory aggression in cats involve different behaviors and different brain

pathways in the amygdala, hypothalamus, and _____ _____ (74).

In humans, the hypothalamus, septal region, and amygdala are involved in aggression. For example,

seizures in the _____ (75) are linked to increased aggression, whereas damage is

linked to decreased aggression. There appears to be more activity in the amygdala in murderers. Cognitive

impairment and impulsiveness are also associated with increased aggression, suggesting a link to the

_____ _____ (76).

Serotonin activity, which can be measured via _____ (77) in the cerebrospinal fluid, is also related to aggression. Compared with premeditated violence, _____ (78) violence is correlated with low serotonin activity. Evidence for serotonin's causal role in aggression comes from a study in which men deprived of _____ (79), a serotonin precursor, displayed more aggression than controls. Also, rats with lesions reducing serotonin in the _____ (80) displayed more aggression towards intruders, suggesting that inhibition of aggression by the prefrontal cortex involves serotonin. In people with low serotonin, _____ (81) may facilitate aggression, perhaps because it reduces serotonin even further. Drugs such as fluoxetine that _____ (82) serotonin uptake facilitate alcohol treatment and also reduce _____ (83) and aggression. Serotonin and testosterone levels may interact in aggression. Monkeys with _____ (84) levels of testosterone and _____ (85) serotonin were the most aggressive.

Aggression appears to be moderately heritable; the genetic contribution may involve _____ (86) -mediated impulsiveness. The environment also plays a role in aggression. For example, low-quality _____ (87) may contribute to impulsive aggression.

Short Answer & Essay Questions

Answer the following questions. See pp. 170-171 for sample answers.

11. Distinguish between offensive, defensive, and predatory aggression. Give an example of each.

12. Identify the specific nuclei of the amygdala, hypothalamus, and PAG involved in defensive and predatory aggression.

13. What are the characteristics of people with antisocial personality disorder?

14. Describe how Moeller and colleagues demonstrated a causal relationship between low serotonin levels and aggression in humans. From this study, can we say for sure that low serotonin causes aggression in humans? Why or why not?

15. Explain how serotonin and alcohol may interact in contributing to aggression.

Post-Test

Use these multiple-choice questions to check your understanding of the chapter. The answers, along with explanations, are found beginning on p. 171.

1. In the gambling task described in the introduction to this chapter, individuals with prefrontal damage
    a. learn an SCR response to the risky piles, but do not learn to avoid choosing from the risky card piles.
    b. do not learn an SCR response, but learn to avoid choosing from the risky card piles anyway.
    c. do not learn an SCR response, and do not learn to avoid choosing from the risky card piles.
    d. learn an SCR response, and learn to avoid choosing from the risky card piles.

2. Sympathetic arousal involves all of the following EXCEPT
    a. increased heart rate.
    b. increased blood pressure.
    c. increased respiration.
    d. increased digestion.

3. According to the James-Lange theory, emotional experiences occur in which order?
    a. stimulus → arousal → emotion
    b. stimulus → emotion → arousal
    c. stimulus → appraisal → emotion
    d. stimulus → arousal/appraisal → emotion

4. In the study by Dutton and Aron in which men were interviewed by a woman while or after crossing a bridge,
    a. the men interviewed on the bridge were more likely to call the woman afterwards.
    b. the men interviewed after crossing the bridge included more sexual content in stories.
    c. the men interviewed on the bridge showed higher SCR.
    d. the men interviewed after crossing the bridge were more likely to ask the woman out on a date.

5. Polygraph studies indicate that in negative emotions,
    a. there are no differences in autonomic arousal patterns.
    b. blood pressure increases more during anger.
    c. heart rate increases more during sadness than fear.
    d. fear involves less motor activation than sadness.

6. Facial expressions
    a. are probably less important in emotional feedback than autonomic arousal.
    b. are all learned from one's family.
    c. can be manipulated without the participant's awareness.
    d. none of the above.

7. Which of the following structures is NOT considered part of the limbic system?
    a. fornix
    b. cingulate gyrus
    c. parahippocampal gyrus
    d. medulla

8. In humans, stimulation of the septal area seems to evoke
    a. pleasure.
    b. fear.
    c. anxiety.
    d. sadness.

9. Someone with heightened activity in the amygdala would be most likely to experience
    a. pleasure.
    b. anxiety.
    c. anger.
    d. sadness.

10. People with damage to the amygdala
    a. are completely fearless.
    b. often exhibit fits of rage.
    c. have difficulty learning to avoid harmful situations.
    d. suffer from antisocial personality disorder.

11. People with prefrontal damage are LEAST likely to:
    a. experience any emotion at all.
    b. learn to avoid venomous snakes.
    c. experience negative emotions.
    d. learn to avoid risky investments.

12. People with right hemisphere damage have difficulty with all of the following EXCEPT
    a. recognizing facial expressions in others.
    b. recognizing emotion in others' voices.
    c. understanding verbal descriptions of emotion.
    d. displaying nonverbal signs of emotion.

13. ACTH is released by the
    a. hypothalamus.
    b. pituitary gland.
    c. adrenal glands.
    d. all of the above.

14. Cortisol is responsible for all of the following EXCEPT
    a. increased oxygen transport to muscle cells.
    b. conversion of protein to glucose.
    c. increase in fat availability.
    d. increase in metabolism.

15. Immune system cells that work by ingesting foreign substances and then displaying their antigens are called
    a. T cells.
    b. B cells.
    c. macrophages.
    d. natural killer cells.

16. Antibodies are produced by
    a. T cells.
    b. B cells.
    c. macrophages.
    d. natural killer cells.

17. Following the Three Mile Island accident, nearby residents displayed
    a. reduced immune cells.
    b. a higher cancer rate.
    c. reduced ability to concentrate.
    d. a and c.
    e. a, b, and c.

18. Increased susceptibility to cold virus infections is associated with all of the following EXCEPT
    a. stress that lasts 2-3 weeks.
    b. unemployment.
    c. marital difficulties.
    d. underemployment.

19. The cold-pressor test in children can predict
    a. cancer in children.
    b. cancer in adults.
    c. high blood pressure in children.
    d. high blood pressure in adults.

20. Sudden cardiac death may be linked to
    a. fear.
    b. bereavement.
    c. joy.
    d. a and b.
    e. a, b, and c.

21. On the day of a major earthquake in Southern California, the number of people who died from a heart attack was _____ times the average.
    a. 50
    b. 25
    c. 5
    d. 1/5

22. Brain damage in chronic stress may be due to
    a. increased cortisol.
    b. increased norepinephrine.
    c. increased epinephrine.
    d. all of the above.

23. In cancer patients, stress reduction is most clearly linked to
    a. longer survival.
    b. better immune functioning.
    c. lower recurrence rates.
    d. all of the above.

24. The personality factor of hostility is most strongly associated with
    a. cancer.
    b. heart disease.
    c. ulcers.
    d. reduced immune functioning.

25. Low extraversion is associated with
    a. increased natural killer cell activity.
    b. higher levels of stress hormones.
    c. higher cancer rates.
    d. a and b.
    e. a, b, and c.

26. Which of the following statements regarding pain is FALSE?
    a. It is both a sensation and an emotion.
    b. Situational factors may influence how strongly it is felt.
    c. The ability to experience pain is not adaptive.
    d. Some people are unable to experience pain.

27. Pain messages are probably routed to the limbic system via the
    a. medial amygdala.
    b. anterior cingulate cortex.
    c. parahippocampal gyrus.
    d. septal area.

28. People who underwent prefrontal lobotomy for pain that failed to respond to other treatments
    a. no longer experienced pain.
    b. were no longer bothered by pain.
    c. experienced more pain than before the procedure.
    d. were often paralyzed as well as rendered insensitive to pain.

29. Which of the following is an example of offensive aggression?
    a. Two male elk fighting over a female in estrus
    b. A cheetah chasing down and killing an antelope
    c. A woman killing an attacker in self defense
    d. A man hunting deer for meat

30. Among prisoners, testosterone was found to be lowest in those convicted of which of the following crimes?
    a. Drug offenses
    b. Rape
    c. Murder
    d. Armed robbery

31. Which of the following statements regarding hormones and aggression in humans is FALSE?
    a. The hormonal changes accompanying PMS may be associated with increased aggression in women.
    b. Winning a sporting event increases testosterone.
    c. High testosterone is linked to aggression in men, but not women.
    d. Male prisoners with higher testosterone are rated as tougher by their peers.

32. Which of the following structures is NOT part of the pathway for predatory aggression in cats?
    a. amygdala
    b. hypothalamus
    c. thalamus
    d. periaqueductal gray

33. In humans, aggression is linked to
    a. excessive prefrontal activity.
    b. seizures in the amygdala.
    c. hypothalamic tumor.
    d. b and c.
    e. a, b, and c.

34. In humans, affective, but not premeditated, murder is linked to
    a. underactivity in the prefrontal cortex.
    b. tumors in the hypothalamus.
    c. seizures in the amygdala.
    d. tumors in the septal area.

35. The impulsiveness displayed by people with antisocial personality disorder may result from abnormalities of the
    a. amygdala.
    b. prefrontal cortex.
    c. medial hypothalamus.
    d. lateral hypothalamus.

36. 5-HIAA is a(n) _____ of serotonin.
    a. precursor
    b. antagonist
    c. metabolite
    d. agonist

37. Men who drank a substance that inhibited tryptophan
    a. were more likely to physically attack their opponents.
    b. were more likely to lose points to their opponents.
    c. were more likely to take points away from their opponents.
    d. showed reduced 5-HIAA levels.

38. Prozac reduces all of the following EXCEPT
    a. alcohol cravings.
    b. serotonin levels.
    c. aggression.
    d. alcohol consumption.

39. Monkeys with high testosterone
    a. tend be behave impulsively.
    b. tend to be extremely aggressive.
    c. engage in dominance-related aggression.
    d. show little hostility toward other monkeys.

40. Heredity accounts for about _____% of the variability in aggression.
    a. 50
    b. 75
    c. 25
    d. 15

Answers and Explanations

Guided Review

1. nervous system
2. sympathetic
3. parasympathetic
4. James-Lange
5. Cannon
6. Schachter and Singer's
7. intensity
8. Dutton and Aron
9. polygraph
10. facial
11. autonomic
12. adaptive
13. decisions
14. skin conductance response
15. risky
16. limbic
17. hypothalamus
18. septal
19. amygdala
20. anxiety
21. cats
22. fearful
23. punishment
24. increased
25. Anti-anxiety
26. prefrontal
27. ventromedial prefrontal
28. long-term
29. autonomic
30. feedback or responding
31. stress
32. adaptive
33. hypothalamus-pituitary-adrenal
34. hormones
35. cortisol
36. metabolism
37. sympathetic
38. immune
39. natural killer cells
40. impairment
41. increased
42. interpersonal problems
43. widowed
44. cold pressor test
45. death
46. heart attack
47. hippocampus
48. reduction
49. relaxation
50. immune
51. personality
52. social support
53. hostility
54. cancer
55. third variable
56. increased
57. pain
58. insensitivity
59. emotion
60. childbirth
61. surgery
62. somatosensory
63. ACC
64. prefrontal
65. emotion
66. offensive
67. defensive
68. predatory
69. physiological
70. sex
71. premenstrual syndrome
72. testosterone
73. increases
74. periaqueductal gray
75. amygdala
76. prefrontal cortex
77. 5-HIAA
78. Impulsive
79. tryptophan
80. forebrain
81. alcohol
82. inhibit
83. hostility
84. high
85. low
86. serotonin
87. parenting

Short Answer & Essay

1. Answers may vary on this question. However, the author makes a compelling argument against the distinction between rationality and emotion. In particular, the studies of people whose emotional capacities are impaired suggest that without emotion, we would not make very good decisions. For example, people like Jane who have prefrontal damage seem to be unable to learn from many of the emotions that accompany rewards and punishment, and so their behavior is often impulsive.

2. Cannon's primary criticism was that the nervous system responded in similar ways during different emotional experiences, contrary to what the James-Lange theory suggested.

3. The hypothesis was that aroused individuals who were unaware of the reason for their arousal would attribute it to the environmental context they were in. They tested this by injecting participants with epinephrine, and informing some that they would experience jitteriness, but telling the others nothing. After encountering either a euphoric or an angry accomplice, the informed participants should have attributed their emotional state to the injection, but the uninformed should have attributed their arousal to the emotional state of the accomplice.

4. Most studies in this area on humans involve people with brain damage, something that obviously cannot be controlled by researchers. When someone suffers from a stroke or other brain injury, the damage may be limited to a small area, or it may involve many structures. The resulting behavioral changes may be due to damage to one or more of the areas involved, but it is difficult to pinpoint which one.

5. There are many possible answers, but a correct response should refer to the role of emotions in decision making, communication, or learning.

6. Macrophages are a type of leucocyte that engulf and ingest invading microorganisms, and then display the antigen code of the invader, attracting T cells. The T cells than multiply and destroy invaders with the specific antigens displayed by the macrophages. B cells produce antibodies that fight off specific intruders. Natural killer cells are more general in their attack: they target cancer cells and virus-infected cells.

7. The immunoredistribution hypothesis suggests that during stress, it is more adaptive for the immune system to concentrate its efforts near the surface of the body where injury from fighting may occur, rather than protecting the internal organs.

8. People with cancer who display a fighting spirit seem to have a better survival rate than those who accept the disease or become hopeless. However, we cannot say for certain that the "fighting spirit" is the causal factor in better survival rates. It may be that people who display this attitude in some fundamental way differ physiologically from those who do not, and this physiological difference may be what keeps them alive longer.

9. Pain is adaptive because it lets us know when we have done something that is harmful, and therefore we can learn to avoid such behaviors. People who are insensitive to or not bothered by pain have difficulty learning not to do things that can lead to injury.

10. When a painful stimulus is presented several times and participants feel increasing unpleasantness (but the stimulus remains the same), there are changes in the ACC but not the somatosensory cortex. Also, when participants under hypnosis are instructed that a painful stimulus is becoming more unpleasant (again, without any change in the stimulus), the same result occurs.

11. Offensive aggression involves an unprovoked attack, such as when a mother animal attacks an intruder. Defensive aggression involves a response to a threat or attack, and is motivated by fear. An example of this is when an animal attacks another animal that has threatened it. Predatory aggression involves killing another animal for food, and generally lacks the emotional components seen in the other forms of aggression. There are many other possible examples that could be given.

12. Defensive aggression: medial nucleus of amygdala → medial hypothalamus → dorsal periaqueductal gray. Predatory aggression: lateral and central nuclei of amygdala → lateral hypothalamus → ventral periaqueductal gray.

13. People with antisocial personality disorder tend to display impulsive behavior, and generally have difficulty getting along with others because they do not follow the "rules" of social conduct. Furthermore, they apparently lack the capacity for remorse or guilt over their disruptive and destructive behavior.

14. In this study, one group of men drank a mixture which reduced tryptophan, and it was assumed would also reduce serotonin, because tryptophan is a precursor for this neurotransmitter. The control group drank another mixture that had no effect. The men in the first group displayed more aggression by subtracting more points from a competitor's score. The first limitation of this study is that no mention is made of whether 5-HIAA was measured; it is assumed that lowered tryptophan would reduce serotonin. Another problem is the nature of the aggression measure. This is not physical aggression, so even if the men deprived of tryptophan indeed had lower serotonin levels, all we can say from this study is that they displayed one form of aggression more than the control subjects, but it is not clear if this would occur with other forms of aggression.

15. Both alcohol and low levels of serotonin are associated with increased aggression. Furthermore, alcohol reduces serotonin. Therefore, alcohol probably enhances aggression through its reduction of serotonin.

Post-Test

All page references in this section pertain to the textbook.

1. a. Wrong; their SCRs do not change after repeatedly choosing from the risky piles.
    b. Wrong; they do not learn to avoid choosing from the risky piles.
    c. Correct; see p. 189.
    d. Wrong

2. a. Wrong; this occurs during sympathetic arousal.
    b. Wrong; this occurs during sympathetic arousal.
    c. Wrong; this occurs during sympathetic arousal.
    d. Correct; this is inhibited by sympathetic activity, and increases when parasympathetic activity takes place.

3. **a. Correct**; see Figure 7.3 on p. 192.
    b. Wrong; this is discussed as being the common-sense notion of emotion, but no evidence is provided to support it.
    c. Wrong; appraisal is part of the cognitive theory – the James-Lange theory did not address this.
    d. Wrong; this summarizes the cognitive theory.

4. **a. Correct**; see p. 193.
    b. Wrong; the men interviewed on the bridge included more sexual content in their stories.
    c. Wrong; although such a result would have supported the hypothesis, there is no mention of SCR being measured.
    d. Wrong; whether or not the men asked the woman on a date is not mentioned, but because the men interviewed while on the bridge were more likely to call her later, it was assumed that sexual attraction was a motivating factor.

5. a. Wrong; there are several differences.
   b. Correct; see p. 194.
   c. Wrong; the text states that heart rate increases during both of these, but does not indicate which, if either, increases more.
   d. Wrong; there is more motor activation during fear than sadness.

6. a. Wrong; the text states that they may be more important.
   b. Wrong; the text states that there is evidence that some facial expressions are innate, since they occur in many cultures, and are displayed by the congenitally blind.
   c. Correct; in one study discussed, facial expressions were manipulated by holding a pencil either between the teeth (producing a smile) or the lips (interfering with smiling). In another study, participants were given verbal instructions to produce a particular expression, and were not aware of what emotion was being expressed.
   d. Wrong

7. a. Wrong
   b. Wrong
   c. Wrong
   d. Correct; the medulla is not part of the limbic system (see Figure 7.6 on p. 197).

8. **a. Correct**; in particular, sexual pleasure seems to be associated with this area.
   b. Wrong
   c. Wrong
   d. Wrong

9. a. Wrong
   b. Correct; fear and anxiety are the emotions it is most strongly related to. Activity in the amygdala is associated with fear and anxiety, while damage to it (or inhibition via drugs) is associated with lack of fear.
   c. Wrong
   d. Wrong

10. a. Wrong; the text states that even people with damage to both amygdalas will show fear to simple stimuli like loud sounds.
    b. Wrong; this is not stated in the text.
    c. Correct; this is particularly true of those with damage to both sides of the brain. The text states that they fail to associate stimuli with loud sounds, and don't seem to experience emotional responses to rewards and punishments, which would make it very difficult for them to learn to avoid harmful situations.
    d. Wrong; people with APD may have prefrontal damage, but the amygdala was not mentioned.

11. a. Wrong
    b. Wrong; the text states that they can learn to avoid situations that are immediately harmful to themselves or others.
    c. Wrong
    d. Correct; this would be most likely to result in long-term harmful consequences, which is what they have the most trouble with.

12. a. Wrong
    b. Wrong
    c. Correct; they are able to do this (see p. 199).
    d. Wrong

13. a. Wrong
    b. Wrong
    c. Correct; see p. 201.
    d. Wrong

14. **a. Correct**; this is not mentioned as a function of cortisol (see p. 201).
    b. Wrong
    c. Wrong
    d. Wrong

15. a. Wrong; these cells are attracted by macrophages and attack invaders with specific antigens.
    b. Wrong; these cells produce antibodies against specific invaders.
    c. Correct; see p. 202.
    d. Wrong; these cells target cells infected with viruses.

16. a. Wrong; these cells identify their targets by antigens.
    b. Correct; see p. 202.
    c. Wrong; these cells will ingest any foreign substance.
    d. Wrong

17. a. Wrong; c is also correct.
    b. Wrong; this was not measured.
    c. Wrong; a is also correct.
    d. Correct; see p. 202.
    e. Wrong

18. **a. Correct**; according to the text, viral infections were associated with stress that lasted longer than 1 month.
    b. Wrong
    c. Wrong
    d. Wrong

19. a. Wrong
    b. Wrong
    c. Wrong
    d. Correct; children who were excessive reactors were more likely to have high blood pressure later in life.

20. a. Wrong; b and c are also correct.
    b. Wrong
    c. Wrong
    d. Wrong
    e. Correct; the text mentions that all of these may trigger sudden cardiac death.

21. a. Wrong
    b. Wrong
    c. Correct; see p. 203.
    d. Wrong

22. **a. Correct**; monkeys with cortisol pellets implanted in their brains showed brain damage.
    b. Wrong; although this is a stress hormone, the text does not mention its involvement in brain damage.
    c. Wrong; although this is a stress hormone, the text does not mention its involvement in brain damage.
    d. Wrong

23. **a. Correct**; see p. 204.
    b. Wrong
    c. Wrong
    d. Wrong

24. a. Wrong
    b. Correct; see p. 204.
    c. Wrong
    d. Wrong

25. a. Wrong; b is also correct.
    b. Wrong
    c. Wrong; this was not mentioned as being related.
    d. Correct; see p. 204.
    e. Wrong

26. a. Wrong
    b. Wrong
    c. Correct; this is false. People who are insensitive to pain often die prematurely.
    d. Wrong

27. a. Wrong
    b. Correct; pain activates this area, which connects to many other limbic system structures.
    c. Wrong
    d. Wrong

28. a. Wrong
    b. Correct; they seemed to feel pain, but did not suffer from it.
    c. Wrong
    d. Wrong

29. **a. Correct**; competitive male-male aggression is a form of offensive aggression.
    b. Wrong; this is predatory aggression.
    c. Wrong; this is defensive aggression.
    d. Wrong; this is predatory aggression.

30. **a.** **Correct**; according to Figure 7.15 on p. 207, most individuals convicted of drug offenses showed low testosterone levels.
   b. Wrong; more than half of the rapists had high testosterone.
   c. Wrong; nearly half of the murderers had high testosterone.
   d. Wrong; more men in this category had high testosterone than those in the drug offenses category, and fewer had low testosterone.

31. a. Wrong
   b. Wrong
   c. **Correct**; the text states that aggressive dominance is linked to testosterone in women prisoners.
   d. Wrong

32. a. Wrong
   b. Wrong
   c. **Correct**; see figure 7.16 on p. 208.
   d. Wrong

33. a. Wrong; it may be related to reduced prefrontal activity.
   b. Wrong; c is also correct.
   c. Wrong
   d. **Correct**
   e. Wrong

34. **a.** **Correct**
   b. Wrong; although there is a link between hypothalamic tumors and aggression, such tumors are not specifically linked to affective murder.
   c. Wrong; although there is a link between seizures in the amygdala and aggression, such seizures are not specifically linked to affective murder.
   d. Wrong; although there is a link between septal tumors and aggression, such tumors are not specifically linked to affective murder.

35. a. Wrong
   b. **Correct**; the book indicates that "people with APD are more likely to have reduced prefrontal gray matter" (p. 209).
   c. Wrong
   d. Wrong

36. a. Wrong; a precursor is a substance that is used to make serotonin.
   b. Wrong; an antagonist is a substance that prevents serotonin from working.
   c. **Correct**; 5-HIAA is a product of the metabolic breakdown of serotonin.
   d. Wrong; an agonist is a substance that enhances serotonin.

37. a. Wrong; the opponents didn't really exist, so physical attack was impossible.
   b. Wrong; it is inferred that all of the participants lost the same amount of points. Because this was something the experimenters controlled, it would have represented a confounding variable if the experimental group had lost more points than men in the control group.
   c. **Correct**
   d. Wrong; although such a result would have supported the hypothesis, this was not measured.

38. a. Wrong
    b. **Correct**; a serotonin reuptake inhibitor increases serotonin levels.
    c. Wrong
    d. Wrong

39. a. Wrong; this was true of the monkeys with low serotonin.
    b. Wrong; overall, these monkeys were less aggressive.
    c. **Correct**
    d. Wrong; they did display some aggression, but only for short bouts, and it was usually limited to dominance disputes.

40. **a.** **Correct**; see p. 210.
    b. Wrong
    c. Wrong
    d. Wrong

Chapter 8: Hearing and Language

Chapter Outline and Learning Objectives

As you read the chapter, use these learning objectives to guide your studying. You should be able to define the key terms from the text, which are shown in boldface type below.

- Define the following terms: **receptor**, **transducer**, **adequate stimulus**, **sensation**, and **perception**.

1) Hearing
- Describe the structure of the auditory system.

a) The Stimulus for Hearing
- What is the adequate stimulus for audition? Give some examples.

- How do **pure tones** and **complex sounds** differ?

- Distinguish between **amplitude** and **loudness**.

- What range of frequencies are humans able to detect? What frequencies are we most sensitive to?

b) The Auditory Mechanism
    i) The Outer and Middle Ear
- Locate and describe the functions of the **pinna**, **tympanic membrane**, and **ossicles**.

    ii) The Inner Ear
- Locate and describe the functions of the **oval window**, **vestibular canal**, **tympanic canal**, and **round window**.

- How does transduction occur in the **hair cells** of the **organ of Corti**?

    iii) The Auditory Cortex
- What is the neural pathway from the cochlea to the cortex?

- Describe the **topographical organization** of the **auditory cortex**.

c) Frequency Analysis
- How is the intensity of sound stimuli coded?

    i) Frequency Theories
- How did Rutherford's **frequency theory** account for frequency coding? Why is it incorrect?

- Describe Wever and Bray's test of the **telephone theory**.

- How does the **volley theory** explain frequency coding? What is the frequency limit of this mechanism?

    ii) Place Theory
- Define resonance. How is resonance incorporated into Helmholtz's **place theory** of frequency coding?

- What did Bekesy discover about the structure and function of the basilar membrane? How does the structure of the basilar membrane contribute to the **tonotopic map** of the auditory cortex?

- How does the **frequency-place theory** account for our ability to distinguish different frequency tones?

- How does a **cochlear implant** work? How successful are these devices?

    iii) Analyzing Complex Sounds
- How is the brain able to analyze the multiple frequencies of a complex sound?

- How may the outer hair cells of the cochlea be involved in the **cocktail party effect**?

- What is an **auditory object**?

d) Locating Sounds
- What are the three **binaural cues** that allow animals to determine the location of sounds? What effect does head size (or inter-ear distance) have on this ability?

i) Binaural Cues
- Explain how **phase difference** and **difference in intensity** cues occur. Where in the brain are these cues processed? In what frequency range does each sound-location mechanism work?

- Explain the **difference in time of arrival** cue.

ii) Brain Circuits for Locating Sounds
- What are **coincidence detectors**, and how do they account for the ability to localize sound?

2) Language
- Why is language so significant for humans?

a) The Brain Structures of Language
- Define **aphasia**.

i) Broca's Area
- Where is Broca's area located? How was it discovered?

- What are the characteristics of **Broca's aphasia**?

ii) Wernicke's Area
- Where is Wernicke's area located?

- What are the characteristics of **Wernicke's aphasia**?

iii) Structures Involved in Reading and Writing
- Define **alexia** and **agraphia**.

- What is the role of the **angular gyrus** in reading and writing?

- What are the characteristics of the visual-perceptual form of **dyslexia**? What brain pathway may be involved?

- What are the characteristics of the phonological form of dyslexia? What brain areas may be involved?

iv) The Wernicke-Geschwind Model
- How does the Wernecke-Geschwind model explain speech? Writing?

- What evidence is there that areas beyond those identified in the model are involved in language?

v) Recovery from Aphasia
- How may the brain compensate for damage to left hemisphere language centers?

b) A Language Generating Mechanism?
- What is a **language acquisition device**? What evidence is there for it (or at least for a biological mechanism underlying language acquisition)?

i) Innate Brain Specializations
- What are the structural differences between the hemispheres regarding language? How early in development are these differences observed?

ii) Location of Other Languages
- How do native and non-native ASL users compare to English speakers in terms of brain areas involved?

- How does the brain apparently handle multiple languages? What role does age at which a language is acquired play?

- How might the brain have evolved to support language?

c) Language in Non-Humans
- Why are language abilities in other species of interest to researchers?

i) Chimpanzee Language Research
- Why did the Gardners use a gestural language in their chimpanzee language project? What were the successes and criticisms of this project?

- What method did Rumbaugh and Savage-Rumbaugh use in their chimpanzee language project? What were the successes of this project?

- What are the apparent language capacities of Pepperberg's parrot Alex?

ii) Lateralization in Animal Brains
- How are the brains of some animal species similar to humans in terms of lateralized functions related to language?

Hearing

Summary and Guided Review

After studying this section in the text, fill in the blanks of the following summary. The answers are found on p. 192.

_____ (1) is the first step in information processing that allows us to interact with the external environment. When we encounter environmental stimuli, our _____ (2), specialized neurons that respond to specific types of stimuli, convert sensory information such as light or sound into neural signals through the process of _____ (3). Once the information is encoded into the nervous system, it undergoes further processing by the brain through _____ (4), and the information is then used in meaningful ways.

Our sense of hearing is highly complex. The auditory stimulus is the vibration of molecules in a conducting medium, which may be air, _____ (5), and even the skull. These vibrations can be represented graphically as _____ (6) with varying frequencies, and the range of frequencies that humans can detect is _____-_____ (7) Hz, although we are most sensitive to sounds between _____ (8) and _____ (9) Hz. A sound with a single frequency wave is a _____ _____ (10). Most sounds are complex because they contain many frequencies. _____ (11) refers to our experience of frequency, and _____ (12) is our experience of a sound's amplitude.

The components of the ear are designed to capture, _____ (13), and transduce sound waves. The _____ (14), or outer ear, captures sound waves and amplifies them by directing them inside the head. When the sound waves reach the _____ _____ (15), it vibrates, transmitting the waves to the ossicles, where the sound is further amplified. The next structure involved is the _____ (16), which is a small coiled object about 35 mm long containing three fluid-filled canals. The _____ (17), or stirrup, rests against the oval window of the cochlea, and it transmits vibrations to the fluid inside the _____ (18), tympanic, and cochlear canals. Transduction occurs when vibrations reach the organ of Corti within the _____ (19) canal. Here, vibration of the _____ _____ (20) bends the hair cells, which opens potassium channels, depolarizing the cells. The inner hair cells, which are less numerous than the _____ (21) hair cells, are apparently responsible for most of what we hear, since mice lacking inner hair cells are deaf.

Cochlear neurons project to the auditory cortex in the _____ _____ (22) via the auditory nerves, passing through the brain stem, inferior colliculi, and _____ _____ _____ (23) of the thalamus. Most, but not all, of the fibers from the auditory nerves cross to the opposite hemisphere. Some of the functions of the auditory cortex of each hemisphere are specialized: _____ (24) in the left, some aspects of music in the right. The auditory cortex is also _____ (25) organized, as neurons from adjacent sites on the basilar membrane project to adjacent sites on the cortex.

In transducing sound waves into neural impulses, the auditory system codes for the intensity and frequency of stimuli. _____ (26) is coded by the number of neurons stimulated by a particular sound: the more intense the sound, the more neurons fire. Frequency coding is more complex, and is not completely understood. A 19th century theory of frequency coding advanced by _____ (27) postulated that auditory neurons fire at the same rate as the frequency of sound that stimulates them. This so-called _____ (28) theory was tested by Wever and Bray in 1930, who found evidence to support it. They recorded from a _____ (29) rather than a single neuron, so they hypothesized that several neurons cooperatively produced volleys of signals, thus following the original stimulus. However, volleying can only reproduce frequencies below about _____ (30) Hz; some other mechanism must be responsible for coding higher frequencies.

The 19th century scientist Helmholtz proposed a _____ _____ (31) of frequency coding which suggested that the _____ _____ (32) was capable of resonating at different frequencies in different locations, much like the strings of a piano. This theory is still widely accepted. Through his studies of the hearing apparatuses of different species, Bekesy has shown that the basilar membrane varies in elasticity along its length. This helps explain why the auditory cortex contains a tonotopic map corresponding with different points along the basilar membrane, and also allows for hearing through _____ (33) conduction. However, the place theory does not account for low frequency sounds (those below about _____ (34) Hz). Currently, most researchers believe that the _____- _____ (35) theory is the most comprehensive account of auditory frequency processing.

Most of the sounds that we hear are complex, containing several frequencies. Research suggests that the ear performs a Fourier analysis of complex sounds, in which the sound is analyzed into several frequencies. Often this includes a single _____ (36) frequency plus one or more overtones, which give a sound its unique quality (and thus explains why a clarinet sounds different from a violin). But we must also explain why we are capable of picking out a target sound among several competing sound sources, such as when we attend to a particular conversation among many different conversations at a party (known as the _____ _____ (37) effect). Such attention may be mediated by the _____ _____ (38) nucleus, which leads to suppression of the inner hair cells. This suppression may involve changes in the _____ (39) hair cells, which in turn would cause changes in the rigidity of the organ of Corti. It is as if the brain is capable of producing an _____ _____ (40), a representation of a target sound source, which helps us track that source amongst competing noises. Sound localization is critical for this.

Much of our ability to locate sounds involves automatic processing of sounds within the nervous system. Animals with two ears use three different binaural cues to locate sounds: phase differences, _____ (41) differences, and time of arrival differences. The farther apart the ears are, the easier it is to locate sounds. Phase differences, which help us locate sounds below _____ (42) Hz, and intensity differences, which help us locate sounds above _____- _____ (43) Hz, are detected by cells in the _____ _____ _____ (44). Time-of- arrival cues have been studied extensively in the barn owl. Neurons called _____ _____ (45), which are located in the nucleus laminaris (a structure analogous to the superior olivary nucleus), fire most when they receive input from both ears at the same time.

Short Answer & Essay Questions

Answer the following questions. See pp. 193-194 for sample answers.

1. What is an adequate stimulus? Define and give an example of an inadequate stimulus.

2. Why is it said that our experiences of sound (pitch and loudness) do not correspond exactly to the physical properties of sound (frequency and amplitude/intensity)?

3. Describe Rutherford's telephone theory of frequency analysis. How did Wever and Bray test this theory? What is the major flaw of the telephone theory?

4. How do frequency theory and place theory account for our ability to process low frequency and high frequency sounds, respectively? Why is neither theory sufficient to explain all frequency analysis?

5. What is the possible role of the outer hair cells in selective attention?

6. Explain phase and intensity difference cues.

7. How does the organization of neural input from auditory neurons to coincidence detectors account for the ability to locate sounds based on time of arrival cues?

_____

Language

Summary and Guided Review

After studying this section in the text, fill in the blanks of the following summary. The answers are found on pp. 192-193.

Language, which includes spoken, _____ (46), and gestural communication, is of central importance in human behavior. There are many brain areas involved in language. When these are damaged, language impairment results. For example, in the 19th century Broca and Wernicke identified different forms of _____ (47), or language impairment, resulting from damage to different brain areas of the _____ (48) hemisphere.

Broca's, or _____ (49), aphasia is the result of damage to Broca's area, located on the _____ _____ (50) anterior to the motor cortex. People with Broca's aphasia have difficulty expressing themselves. They often display _____

_____ (51) (halting) speech, _____ (52) (difficulty finding the right word), difficulty with articulation, and _____ (53) speech (lacking function words). They also have problems with reading and writing; _____ (54) is impaired for grammatically complex sentences.

Wernicke's aphasia, sometimes referred to as _____

_____ (55), is the result of damage to Wernicke's area, located on the posterior _____ _____ (56). People with Wernicke's aphasia can articulate words, but their utterances, described as _____ _____ (57), have little meaning. As the term receptive aphasia implies, they also have difficulty understanding language.

Damage to the _____ _____ (58), which connects the visual projection area with auditory and visual association areas, can result in _____ (59) (the inability to read) and _____ (60) (the inability to write). _____ (61), the most common type of learning disorder, also involves reading and writing difficulties. In many cases dyslexia seems to have a developmental-genetic basis. In _____-

_____ (62) dyslexia, words are read backwards, letters are confused, and words seem to move around on the page. These problems are thought to be the result of the

_____ (63) visual pathway's slowed response to rapidly changing stimuli and decreased ability to correct for _____ _____ (64). People with this form of dyslexia have difficulty learning to read. In _____ (65) dyslexia, people have difficulty translating between _____ (66) words and sounds of words. As a result, they learn to read by visual _____ (67) rather than sounding them out. One physical abnormality in dyslexics is that the left _____

_____ (68), which contains Wernicke's area and is normally larger on the left hemisphere, is smaller and less organized, probably reflecting a prenatal disruption of development.

According to the _____-_____ (69) model, language processing (such as responding to a question or reading out loud) occurs along a pathway involving the auditory cortex, Wernicke's area, _____ _____ (70), and the angular gyrus. However, damage to areas outside this pathway, including other areas of the cortex as well as subcortical structures such as the basal ganglia and _____ (71), also result in language impairment, suggesting that many parts of the brain are involved in language processing. Specific types of words and the objects and actions they represent are stored in specific areas of the brain; for example, naming tools and imagining hand movements activates brain areas adjacent to the

_____ _____ (72) responsible for producing the actions needed to use tools. However, Broca's area and Wernicke's area are essential for the more general language functions of _____ (73) and comprehension, respectively.

Recovery from aphasia, which is more pronounced for Broca's than for Wernicke's aphasia, results in part from a decrease in the _____ (74) that occurs along with brain damage. Reorganization of the brain is also involved. For example, if the left hemisphere is damaged before age _____ (75), there is evidence that the right hemisphere takes over of the language functions. For damage occurring later, other areas on the left hemisphere may become involved in language processing.

Because language is readily learned by almost all children, including those born deaf who are exposed to sign language, some theorists believe that the brain contains a _____

_____ _____ (76), or a structure, that is dedicated to language. Regardless of the form of language children learn, they all show the same stages of language development, including early _____ (77) through speech or gestures. Most people show left hemisphere dominance for language, and several left hemisphere structures, including Broca's area, the _____ (78) fissure, and the planum temporale, are larger than their counterparts on the right hemisphere. Prenatal and early postnatal differences in structure and function of the left hemisphere have been observed, suggesting that the left hemisphere in most people is designed to support language. Furthermore, _____ (79) seems to use the same left hemisphere structures as spoken language, although it also involves right hemisphere areas, probably because of

_____-_____ (80) qualities. People exposed to two

languages from birth show activation of the same areas for both languages, while those who acquired a

_____ (81) language in adulthood show some activation of different areas, but

still within Broca's area. Although it is clear that language involves specific structures, it is not clear if

these structures evolved specifically for language, or if they originally served a more general purpose and

were later taken over by language.

Studying language abilities in other species allows us to speculate on the evolutionary basis of

language in humans, although the results of such studies must be interpreted with caution because it is often

difficult to determine if an animal who uses a language symbol truly understands the meaning of that

symbol. Language abilities in _____ (82) have been studied the most

intensively, although because of limitations to the vocal apparatus they are unable to speak. The Gardners,

and later Fouts, exposed chimpanzees to _____ (83) from an early age. The first chimp in this

project, Washoe, learned _____ (84) signs. She and the others then taught some of these signs to

her adopted son Loulis without human intervention. The Rumbaughs used a different approach involving

symbols printed on the keys of a computer keyboard. The _____ (85) chimpanzee

Kanzi first began using the keyboard as an infant when his mother was being trained on it, and learned

_____ (86) symbols by the age of six. Savage-Rumbaugh claims that Kanzi's use of symbols is

about as sophisticated as a _____-_____-_____ (87) child.

Remarkable language abilities have also been demonstrated by Alex, an _____

_____ _____ (88). Many birds are capable of imitating human speech.

However, Alex is able to give the _____ (89), composition, color, and quantity of

objects, and to compare objects using the same words a human would to perform the same tasks.

There is also evidence that the brains of some species are lateralized in ways similar to humans.

The _____ _____ (90) and planum temporale are larger

on the left hemisphere in chimpanzees. Japanese macaques show a _____ (91) hemisphere

dominance for responding to the calls of other Japanese macaques, but not to those of other monkey

species. _____ (92) and chimpanzees demonstrate faster learning of symbols

when they are presented to the left hemisphere. Canaries with left hemisphere lesions are unable to sing

normally. All of these results indicate that at least some other species possess language-like capacities, and

that these capacities may involve brain areas similar to those involved in human language.

Short Answer & Essay Questions

Answer the following questions. See p. 194 for sample answers.

8. Compare the language limitations observed in people with Broca's and Wernicke's aphasias.

9. How does the Wernicke-Geschwind model account for your ability to write a response to an oral question? To read aloud?

10. What is the Wada technique, and what is it used for?

11. In terms of acquisition and brain mechanisms, how are ASL and spoken language similar? How are they different?

12. What were Terrace's criticisms of the claims made by the Gardners that Washoe was using language? How did the Rumbaughs' work with Kanzi address these criticisms?

Post-Test

Use these multiple-choice questions to check your understanding of the chapter. The answers, along with explanations, are found beginning on p. 194.

1. _____ is defined as the acquisition of sensory information.
   a. perception
   b. sensation
   c. transduction
   d. translation

2. The range of human hearing is
   a. 20 to 200,000 Hz.
   b. 2 to 20,000 Hz.
   c. 20 to 20,000 Hz.
   d. 200 to 2,000 Hz.

3. Sound may be conducted through
   a. air.
   b. water.
   c. bone.
   d. a and c
   e. a, b, and c.

4. We experience the frequency of a sound as
   a. pitch.
   b. loudness.
   c. amplitude.
   d. intensity.

5. A pure tone is most likely to be produced by a(n)
   a. clarinet.
   b. tuning fork.
   c. air conditioner.
   d. flute.

6. Humans are most sensitive to sounds with frequencies in the range of
   a. 1,000-3,000 Hz.
   b. 200-400 Hz.
   c. 2,000-20,000 Hz.
   d. 2,000-4,000 Hz.

7. Which of the following causes the eardrum to stretch or relax in response to different levels of sound?
   a. tensor tympani
   b. incus
   c. pinna
   d. tympanic membrane

8. Which of the following DOES NOT contribute to amplification of sound waves in the ear?
   a. outer ear
   b. eardrum
   c. stapes
   d. malleus

9. Which of the following structures is/are NOT part of the auditory system?
   a. cochlea
   b. ossicles
   c. pinna
   d. semicircular canals

10. Vibrations are initiated in the cochlea by movement of the _____ against the oval window.
    a. stapes
    b. malleus
    c. incus
    d. helicotrema

11. The organ of Corti is located in the _____ canal.
    a. vestibular
    b. tympanic
    c. cochlear
    d. auditory

12. Hair cells rest on top of the
    a. helicotrema.
    b. tectorial membrane.
    c. basilar membrane.
    d. tympanic membrane.

13. When hair cells bend, _____ channels open, causing depolarization.
    a. sodium
    b. potassium
    c. calcium
    d. chloride

14. The auditory cortex is located on the _____ lobe.
    a. temporal
    b. frontal
    c. parietal
    d. occipital

15. Neurons from the left ear project
    a. exclusively to the right hemisphere.
    b. exclusively to the left hemisphere.
    c. mostly to the right hemisphere.
    d. mostly to the left hemisphere.

16. Sound intensity is coded by
    a. the number of receptors responding.
    b. the volley pattern of receptors.
    c. the point on the basilar membrane responding.
    d. none of the above.

17. The volley theory was proposed by
    a. Rutherford.
    b. Helmholtz.
    c. Bekesy.
    d. Wever and Bray.

18. _____ discovered that the basilar membrane is stiffer at one end than at the other.
    a. Rutherford.
    b. Helmholtz.
    c. Bekesy.
    d. Wever and Bray.

19. A 15,000 Hz tone will produce the greatest vibrations at which point along the basilar membrane?
    a. near the base
    b. at the apex
    c. near the apex
    d. in the middle

20. Which sound frequency does not seem to produce maximal vibration at a specific point on the basilar membrane?
    a. 20,000 Hz
    b. 2,400 Hz
    c. 1,200 Hz
    d. 20 Hz

21. The outer hair cells may be involved in
    a. suppressing background noise.
    b. processing high, but not low, frequency sounds.
    c. processing sounds related to language, but not music.
    d. all of the above.

22. Which of the following animals probably has the most difficulty locating sounds?
    a. Elephant
    b. Alligator
    c. Mouse
    d. Owl

23. A sound with a frequency of 50 Hz is located by which of the following cues?
    a. Phase difference
    b. Intensity difference
    c. Time of arrival difference
    d. a and c
    e. a, b, and c

24. In humans, binaural cues for localizing sound are processed by cells in the
    a. planum temporale.
    b. nucleus laminaris.
    c. superior olivary nucleus.
    d. medial geniculate nucleus.

25. Broca's area lies anterior and adjacent to the
    a. motor cortex.
    b. auditory cortex.
    c. somatosensory cortex.
    d. visual cortex.

26. In most people, Wernicke's area is found on the _____ lobe.
    a. left frontal
    b. right frontal
    c. left temporal
    d. right temporal

27. Which of the following is NOT a characteristic of Broca's aphasia?
    a. impairment in writing
    b. word salad
    c. agrammatic speech
    d. difficulty with articulation

28. People with Wernicke's aphasia
    a. have difficulty saying words.
    b. have difficulty understanding others.
    c. produce utterances that have no meaning.
    d. a, b, and c.
    e. b and c.

29. The inability to write is called
    a. agraphia.
    b. alexia.
    c. anomia.
    d. aphasia.

30. The angular gyrus connects the visual projection area with the
    a. auditory association areas.
    b. visual association areas.
    c. motor cortex.
    d. a and b.
    e. a, b, and c.

31. Abnormalities in the magnocellular visual pathway are implicated in
    a. visual-perceptual dyslexia.
    b. phonological dyslexia.
    c. dyscalculia.
    d. all of the above.

32. A characteristic of phonological dyslexia is
    a. difficulty translating letters into sounds.
    b. confusing mirror-image letters like "b" and "d."
    c. reading words backward.
    d. difficulty tracking words on a page.

33. According to the Wernicke-Geschwind model, when we give a spoken response to a question, what is the sequence of brain activation?
    a. auditory cortex → Broca's area → Wernicke's area
    b. Broca's area → Wernicke's area → auditory cortex
    c. auditory cortex → Wernicke's area → Broca's area
    d. Wernicke's area → Broca's area → auditory cortex

34. Someone with damage to the premotor cortex would most likely have difficulty
    a. producing articulate speech.
    b. using verbs.
    c. using nouns.
    d. reading out loud.

35. There is evidence that the right hemisphere may assume left-hemisphere language functions
    a. in adults who have suffered strokes or other brain injuries.
    b. in adults who learn a second language.
    c. in children under five who suffer brain injury.
    d. in children who acquire two languages simultaneously.

36. Babies exposed to ASL
    a. will babble in gestures, but only if they are deaf.
    b. babble in gestures, but later than babies exposed to spoken language begin babbling in sounds.
    c. babble in gestures at about the same time that babies exposed to spoken language babble in sounds.
    d. are at a disadvantage for language learning because ASL is not a true language.

37. Which of the following statements regarding handedness and brain lateralization for language is TRUE?
    a. Left-handed people are more likely to show left-hemisphere dominance for language than right-hemisphere dominance for language.
    b. All right-handed people show left-hemisphere dominance for language.
    c. Left and right-handed people are equally likely to show left-hemisphere dominance for language.
    d. People are either right or left-hemisphere dominant for language; no one shows mixed dominance.

38. The right hemisphere appears to play a more important role in
    a. spoken language than in sign language.
    b. sign language than in spoken language.
    c. one's native language than in a second language.
    d. a second language than in one's native language.

39. Concerning language-trained chimpanzees, which ability is most controversial?
    a. using signs and symbols to communicate with humans
    b. using signs and symbols to communicate with each other
    c. producing grammatically correct sentences
    d. teaching their offspring signs and symbols

40. Which of the following species has NOT demonstrated a possible capacity for language?
    a. Gorilla
    b. African gray parrot
    c. Japanese macaque
    d. Dolphin

Answers and Explanations

Guided Review

1. Sensation
2. receptors
3. transduction
4. perception
5. water
6. waves
7. 20-20,000
8. 2,000
9. 4,000
10. pure tone
11. Pitch
12. loudness
13. amplify
14. pinna
15. tympanic membrane
16. cochlea

17. stapes
18. vestibular
19. cochlear
20. basilar membrane
21. outer
22. temporal lobe
23. medial geniculate nucleus
24. language
25. topographically
26. Intensity
27. Rutherford
28. telephone
29. nerve
30. 5,200
31. place theory
32. basilar membrane

33. bone
34. 200
35. frequency-place
36. fundamental
37. cocktail party
38. superior olivary
39. outer
40. auditory object
41. intensity
42. 1,500
43. 2,000-3,000
44. superior olivary nucleus
45. coincidence detectors
46. written
47. aphasia
48. left
49. expressive

50. frontal lobe
51. non fluent
52. anomia
53. agrammatic
54. comprehension
55. receptive aphasia
56. temporal lobe
57. word salad
58. angular gyrus
59. alexia
60. agraphia
61. Dyslexia
62. visual-perceptual
63. magnocellular
64. eye movements
65. phonological
66. written
67. memory
68. planum temporale
69. Wernicke-Geschwind
70. Broca's area
71. thalamus
72. motor cortex
73. articulation
74. swelling
75. five
76. language acquisition device
77. babbling
78. lateral
79. ASL
80. visual-spatial
81. second
82. chimpanzees
83. ASL
84. 132
85. pygmy
86. 150
87. two-year-old
88. African gray parrot
89. name
90. lateral fissure
91. left
92. Dolphins

Short Answer & Essay

1. An adequate stimulus is the form of energy (light, sound, etc.) for which a sensory receptor is specialized. An inadequate stimulus is a form of energy that triggers the receptor, although it is not of the form that the receptor is specialized for. There are several examples of inadequate stimuli in the book, including pressing on your eyeball to produce the sensation of white light.

2. One reason is that there are often physical differences between two sounds that we cannot detect. For example, we may not be able to detect the difference between tones of 500 and 501 Hz. Another reason is that we are more sensitive to certain sounds, especially those in the 2,000-4,000 Hz range; changes in amplitude of sounds in this range are more easily detected than changes in amplitude of sounds outside of this range.

3. Rutherford proposed that auditory neurons fire at the same frequency as sounds that stimulate them, so that the brain received signals that matched or followed the frequency of sounds in the environment. Wever and Bray tested this theory by recording from the auditory nerve of a cat while it was exposed to sounds and amplifying the signal so that it could be heard. This seemed to work for sounds up to 5,200 Hz. Rutherford's theory is flawed because it is now known that a neuron cannot fire more than several hundred times per second, so while it may be able to follow low frequency sounds, a neuron cannot follow all sounds.

4. Frequency theory accounts for low frequency sounds, as some neurons seem to fire at the same rate as the sounds that stimulate them. Place theory accounts for higher frequency sounds, as different points along the basilar membrane are most responsive to particular frequencies. However, neither theory alone is sufficient to account for all frequency analysis. Frequency theory is limited by the physical property of neurons which prevents them from firing more than a few hundred times per second, and place theory cannot account for processing low frequency sounds, because sounds below 200 Hz cause the entire basilar membrane to vibrate equally.

5. The outer hair cells may be involved in a mechanism for selective attention. Messages from the superior olivary nucleus seem to suppress the inner hair cells, but this may occur via the outer hair cells. When the length of the outer hair cells changes, the tension of the organ of Corti changes. This may allow the organ of Corti to zero in on a particular sound source (with a particular frequency) and tune out others with different frequencies.

6. Phase difference cues involve the point at which a wave of a particular frequency stimulates the ear. If a sound is coming from any direction such that it reaches the ears at different points in the wave. Intensity difference cues work because the head produces a sound shadow for sounds that reach the ears at different times. The ear closest to the source of sound will receive a more intense sound than the other ear, which is detected by specialized neurons.

7. Coincidence detectors receive input from neurons from both ears. However, the length of the input neurons connected to a specific coincidence detector from each ear differs. Therefore, when a sound occurs, it will reach the closer ear first and the farther ear later, but the two signals will arrive at the coincidence detector at the same time because the closer input neuron is longer than the one further away from the source of the sound.

8. In Broca's aphasia, people seem to be able to understand much of what is said to them, and may be able to communicate meaningfully, although in a limited fashion. They have difficulty remembering words, and their speech is halting and lacks many function words. They also have difficulty pronouncing words. Reading and writing are disrupted as well. People with Wernicke's aphasia, on the other hand, often speak fluently, but their utterances make little sense, and they do not seem to understand what others are saying to them.

9. According to this model, when you write an answer to an oral question, the pattern of activation begins in the auditory cortex, then moves to Wernicke's area, and then to the angular gyrus. When reading out loud, the visual system sends input to the angular gyrus, then to Wernicke's area, and then to Broca's area.

10. The Wada technique involves administering an anesthetic to one hemisphere of the brain to suppress its activity, and then giving the person tasks to perform. This allows researchers and clinicians to determine which hemisphere is dominant for different functions (such as language).

11. Babies exposed to sign language seem to progress in language development along the same lines as babies exposed to speech. Both babble at about the same time, and the babbling seems to have the same function in each case (although it is of a very different form). Furthermore, the same areas of the left hemisphere seem to be involved in both spoken language and sign language. One difference between the two forms is that sign language seems to involve more right hemisphere activity, perhaps as a result of its visual-spatial nature (something that the right hemisphere is more specialized for).

12. Terrace claimed that chimpanzees do not form sentences, that the utterances lacked grammatical structure and were simply strings of words. The Rumbaugh's work with Kanzi indicates that chimpanzees are capable of spontaneously making complex utterances and understanding complex directions, including sentences not involving the chimpanzee at all.

Post-Test

All page references in this section pertain to the textbook.

1. a. Wrong; perception is the processing of sensory information.
    b. Correct; see p. 218.
    c. Wrong; although it is part of sensation, transduction is specifically the process of converting environmental energy into neural energy.
    d. Wrong

2. a. Wrong
    b. Wrong
    c. Correct; see p. 218.
    d. Wrong

3. a. Wrong; b and c are also correct.
    b. Wrong
    c. Wrong
    d. Wrong; b is also correct.
    e. Correct; see p. 218.

4. **a. Correct**; see p. 219.
    b. Wrong; this is the name for our experience of amplitude or intensity of a sound.
    c. Wrong
    d. Wrong

5. a. Wrong; the clarinet produces a fundamental frequency and several overtones.
    b. Correct; a tuning fork produces a sound with a single frequency.
    c. Wrong; this produces "noise," which consists of many frequencies.
    d. Wrong; this instrument is similar to a clarinet in the sound it makes.

6. a. Wrong
    b. Wrong
    c. Wrong
    d. Correct; see p. 219.

7. **a. Correct**; see p. 220.
    b. Wrong; this is one of the ossicles in the middle ear.
    c. Wrong; this is the flap of skin making up the outer ear.
    d. Wrong; this is the eardrum itself.

8. a. Wrong
    b. Correct; the eardrum vibrates, but does not amplify sound. All of the other choices are involved in sound amplification.
    c. Wrong
    d. Wrong

9. a. Wrong
    b. Wrong
    c. Wrong
    d. Correct; this is part of the vestibular system. All of the other choices are part of the auditory system.

10. **a. Correct**; see p. 221.
    b. Wrong
    c. Wrong
    d. Wrong

11. a. Wrong
    b. Wrong
    c. Correct; see pp. 221-222
    d. Wrong

12. a. Wrong; this is a small opening between the vestibular and tympanic canals.
    b. Wrong; the tectorial membrane is situated above the hair cells.
    c. Correct; see p. 222.
    d. Wrong; this is not part of the cochlea.

13. a. Wrong
    b. Correct; see p. 222.
    c. Wrong
    d. Wrong

14. **a. Correct**; see p. 222.
    b. Wrong
    c. Wrong
    d. Wrong

15. a. Wrong
    b. Wrong
    c. Correct; most of the fibers cross over to the other hemisphere, but some project to the same side of the brain.
    d. Wrong

16. **a. Correct**; hair cells have different intensity thresholds for firing, so the more intense a sound is, the more hair cells respond.
    b. Wrong; volleying may be involved in frequency coding.
    c. Wrong; this is part of frequency coding.
    d. Wrong

17. a. Wrong; he proposed a frequency theory that did not include volleying.
    b. Wrong; he proposed a place theory.
    c. Wrong; he did work which supported the place theory.
    d. Correct; see p. 224.

18. a. Wrong; he proposed a frequency theory.
    b. Wrong; his version of place theory suggested that the basilar membrane was like the strings of a piano.
    c. Correct; see p. 225.
    d. Wrong; their work involved frequency theory.

19. **a. Correct**; according to Figure 8.9 on p. 225, the "place" for this frequency would fall somewhere near the base end of the membrane.
    b. Wrong; only the lower frequency sounds are coded here.
    c. Wrong; low frequency sounds are coded here.
    d. Wrong; sounds of medium frequency are coded here.

20. a. Wrong
    b. Wrong
    c. Wrong
    d. Correct; the entire basilar membrane vibrates equally when the frequency is this far below 200 Hz.

21. **a. Correct**; see p. 229.
    b. Wrong; the outer hair cells do not seem to contribute much to the actual coding of sound.
    c. Wrong
    d. Wrong

22. a. Wrong; elephants have large heads, so they would not be limited in sound localization.
    b. Wrong; alligator heads are much larger than mouse heads.
    c. Correct; these animals have the smallest heads of those listed, and therefore would have the most difficulty locating sounds.
    d. Wrong; in fact, some owls are exceptional at locating sounds (they also have larger heads than mice).

23. a. Wrong; c is also correct
    b. Wrong; this only works for sounds above 2,000-3,000 Hz.
    c. Wrong; a is also correct.
    d. Correct
    e. Wrong

24. a. Wrong; this is involved in language.
    b. Wrong; this is the bird equivalent of the superior olivary nucleus.
    c. Correct; see p. 230.
    d. Wrong; this is a part of the thalamus that receives auditory information after it has passed through the medulla.

25. **a. Correct**; see p. 232.
    b. Wrong; Broca's area is superior to the auditory cortex.
    c. Wrong; this is posterior to the motor cortex, so it cannot be adjacent to Broca's area.
    d. Wrong; this is located in the occipital lobe, which is far away from Broca's area.

26. a. Wrong
    b. Wrong
    c. Correct; see p. 232.
    d. Wrong; although a few people may have Wernicke's on the right, most have it on the left.

27. a. Wrong
    b. Correct; this is a characteristic of Wernicke's. All of the other choices are characteristic of Broca's aphasia.
    c. Wrong
    d. Wrong

28. a. Wrong; they are actually quite good at pronouncing words; their sentences have little meaning.
    b. Wrong; c is also correct.
    c. Wrong; b is also correct.
    d. Wrong
    e. Correct; see p. 234.

29. **a.** **Correct**; see p. 234.
    b. Wrong; this is the inability to read.
    c. Wrong; this is the inability to remember words.
    d. Wrong; this is a general term for language impairment.

30. a. Wrong; b is also correct.
    b. Wrong; a is also correct.
    c. Wrong
    d. **Correct**; see p. 234.
    e. Wrong

31. **a.** **Correct**; see p. 235.
    b. Wrong; this is not mentioned as being a problem in phonological dyslexia (where the planum temporale may be implicated).
    c. Wrong
    d. Wrong

32. **a.** **Correct**; see p. 235. All of the other choices are characteristics of visual-perceptual dyslexia.
    b. Wrong
    c. Wrong
    d. Wrong

33. a. Wrong
    b. Wrong
    c. **Correct**; see pp. 236-237.
    d. Wrong

34. a. Wrong; this is not mentioned as being related to premotor damage.
    b. **Correct**; see p. 236.
    c. Wrong; while specific types of objects, such as tools, may involve this area, nouns in general do not. The book mentions nouns involving areas below the auditory cortex and Wernicke's area.
    d. Wrong; this is not mentioned as being related to premotor damage.

35. a. Wrong; in such cases, other parts of the left hemisphere may compensate for damage.
    b. Wrong; second language learning seems to involve left hemisphere areas very near those involved in the native language.
    c. **Correct**; Wada studies indicate that people who suffered left hemisphere damage as young children were more likely to show right hemisphere dominance for language.
    d. Wrong; these people seem to use the same brain areas for both languages.

36. a. Wrong; both hearing and deaf babies will babble if their parents use ASL.
    b. Wrong; both babble at about the same time.
    c. **Correct**
    d. Wrong; ASL is a separate language, and while deaf signers may be somewhat isolated from the rest of the world, their language skills do not necessarily suffer.

37. **a.** **Correct**; about 2/3 of left-handed people show left-hemisphere dominance for language.
    b. Wrong; about 90% of right-handers show left-hemisphere dominance.
    c. Wrong
    d. Wrong; some of the left-handers show mixed dominance.

38. a.　Wrong; although it is involved in the emotional component of language (see Ch. 7), it plays a greater role in sign language than in spoken language.
　　b.　Correct; see p. 240.
　　c.　Wrong; both use mainly the left-hemisphere.
　　d.　Wrong

39. a.　Wrong
　　b.　Wrong
　　c.　Correct; this is not mentioned in the text as having been convincingly shown. Chimpanzees have shown all of the other capacities.
　　d.　Wrong

40. a.　Wrong
　　b.　Wrong
　　c.　Correct; although they show some hemispheric specializations for functions related to language (such as processing different calls of their own species), they do not seem to have any capacity for language itself.
　　d.　Wrong

Chapter 9: Vision and Visual Perception

Chapter Outline and Learning Objectives

As you read the chapter, use these learning objectives to guide your studying. You should be able to define the key terms from the text, which are shown in boldface type below.

1) Light and the Visual Apparatus
   a) The Visible Spectrum
      - What is the adequate stimulus for vision? What other forms of this type of energy exist?

      - How is light energy measured? What range are humans capable of detecting?

   b) The Eye and its Receptors
      - Be able to locate and identify of the following components of the eye: vitreous humor, cornea, lens, iris.

      - Describe the events occurring in the **retina** when the photoreceptors are stimulated by light.

      - What are the components of the **photopigments**? What happens to these molecules during transduction? How do the different types of photopigments contribute to the differences between **rods** and **cones**, and between the different types of cones?

      - Discuss the differences between rods and cones in terms of distribution in the retina and **receptive fields**.

      - Outline the pathway that visual information takes from the retina to the occipital lobe. How does the organization of the visual system account for the fact that information appearing in the left visual field gets sent to the right hemisphere?

      - What is retinal disparity, and how does it contribute to our ability to perceive objects in three- dimensional space?

      - What is the importance of the following concepts for understanding how the visual system works: inhibition, **hierarchical processing**, and **modular processing**?

      - What techniques may be used to treat blindness?

2) Color Vision
- Why does color not exactly correspond to wavelength of light?

a) Trichromatic Theory
- How does the **trichromatic theory** explain color vision?

b) Opponent Process Theory
- How does the **opponent process theory** explain color vision?

- What are complementary colors? How do they explain the **negative color aftereffect**?

- Distinguish between pigment mixing and light mixing to produce colors.

c) A Combined Theory
- How are the trichromatic and opponent process theories reconciled? How does this combined theory explain our ability to see red, green, yellow, and blue?

- How does the combined theory account for complementary colors and negative afterimages?

- How were researchers able to demonstrate that the human retina contains three types of color receptors? How specific is each receptor type for its respective color?

- What evidence is there that opponent-process cells exist in the visual system? What is the significance of the concentric-circle receptive fields of some of these cells?

d) Color Blindness
- What are the different forms of colorblindness? What are the causes of color blindness?

3) Form Vision
- How did De Valois show that the visual cortex appears to act like a map of the visual field?

a) Contrast Enhancement and Edge Detection
- What is the Mach band illusion? How does **lateral inhibition** explain this illusion?

- How do on-off ganglion cells work? How does this account for our ability to detect contrast?

b) Hubel and Wiesel's Theory
- How did Hubel and Wiesel discover the shape of cortical **simple cell** receptive fields? How are the ganglion cells that make up a simple cell's receptive field arranged?

- What type of stimulus does a **complex cell** respond to? What inputs make up the complex cell's receptive field?

c) Spatial Frequency Theory
- How does spatial frequency theory account for our ability to detect different levels of contrast on an object?

4) The Perception of Objects, Color, and Movement
- What evidence is there that some visual functions of the cortex are **distributed** rather than modular?

a) The Two Pathways of Visual Analysis
- How are the **parvocellular** and **magnocellular systems** distinguished? What type of visual processing is each responsible for?

- What brain areas and visual functions are the **ventral** and **dorsal streams** associated with?

b) Disorders of Visual Perception
  i) Object Agnosia
- What are the characteristics of **object agnosia**? **Prosopagnosia**? What brain areas are implicated in these disorders?

- What is the significance of **blindsight** for understanding the difference between identification and recognition?

- What are the functions of cells in the inferior temporal cortex and fusiform face area?

  ii) Color Agnosia
- What is **color constancy**? How does color coding in V4 account for color constancy?

iii) Movement Agnosia
- What is **movement agnosia**? What area of the brain is involved in this disorder?

iv) Neglect
- What is the function of the posterior parietal cortex? Why does damage to this area lead to **neglect**?

c) The Problem of Final Integration
- What are the possible explanations for how we are able to perceive visual scenes holistically, even though information about them has been processed in several areas?

Light and the Visual Apparatus

Summary and Guided Review

After studying this section in the text, fill in the blanks of the following summary. The answers are found on p. 215.

The adequate stimulus for the visual system is visible light, a form of

_____ (1) energy that makes up a very small portion of the electromagnetic

spectrum. Other forms of electromagnetic energy that humans cannot detect without special devices are X-

rays, _____ _____ (2) (which some animal species can detect), and radio and

television waves. Light is measured in terms of the distance energy travels before reversing directions; the

portion of the electromagnetic spectrum humans are capable of detecting is _____ - _____ (3)

nanometers (a nanometer is 1 _____ (4) of a meter). Within this range, light rays of

different wavelengths are perceived as different _____ (5).

The _____ (6) is filled with vitreous humor, and with the exception of the

transparent _____ (7), its outer covering is opaque. Behind the cornea, the flexible

_____ (8) allows us to focus on objects at different distances. The circular _____ (9) is a

muscle that partially covers the lens, and the opening in its center is the _____ (10), which

changes its shape to accommodate different levels of light. The visual receptors are located in the

_____ (11) at the back of the eye; these cells contain _____ (12),

which, when stimulated by light, cause _____ (13) channels to close, thus

_____ (14) the cell and disinhibiting the bipolar cells and ganglion cells they

are connected to. Horizontal cells and _____ (15) cells interconnect the bipolar cells

and ganglion cells, respectively, producing a complex web of information processing.

The different types of receptors, _____ (16) and _____ (17), are specialized for different aspects of vision due to the fact that they contain different types of photopigments and have different neural connections. Rods, which are more numerous, contain _____ (18), which is highly sensitive to light; this accounts for our ability to see under low light conditions. Cones, which contain _____ (19), function best in bright light. There are different types of this photopigment, each responding most to different ranges of wavelengths; this is what allows us to see color. In the retina, cones are concentrated in the _____ (20), whereas rods are more numerous in the periphery. Foveal cones show less convergence on the ganglion cells than cones outside the fovea, which accounts for better _____ _____ (21) for images falling on the fovea. Many rods converge on a single ganglion cell, which contributes to _____ (22) to light but not acuity.

The ganglion cells' _____ (23) form the optic nerve, and exit the retina at the _____ _____ (24); the optic nerves join at the _____ _____ (25), where some information crosses over to the opposite side of the brain. The nerves next project to the _____ _____ _____ (26) of the thalamus, and then to the cortex. The partial crossover of information is organized such that stimuli detected by the _____ (27) half of each retina (left visual field) is projected to the _____ (28) hemisphere, and stimuli detected by the _____ (29) half of each retina (right visual field) is projected to the _____ (30) hemisphere.

We are able to perceive objects in three-dimensional space due in part to _____ _____ (31). The degree of disparity triggers activity in different cells in the cortex.

Three principles are helpful in understanding how the visual system works: _____ (32), which allows for more detailed information processing than excitation alone; _____ _____ (33), which means that more basic elements of visual stimuli are processed in lower areas of the nervous system and this information is then analyzed by higher areas of the cortex; and _____ _____ (34), which reflects the fact that much of visual information is physically segregated during processing.

Short Answer & Essay Questions

Answer the following questions. See p. 216 for sample answers.

1. Why is the retina considered by some scientists to be part of the brain rather than the peripheral nervous system?

2. How are the receptive fields of ganglion cells receiving input from cones in the fovea different from those receiving input from rods? How do these differences contribute to the visual specializations of each system?

3. What is the blind spot? Why don't we notice it (most of the time)?

4. How are researchers able to present a visual image to only one hemisphere in people whose brains are intact?

5. How are Viewmaster slides able to produce their vivid three-dimensional effects?

Color Vision

Summary and Guided Review

After studying this section in the text, fill in the blanks of the following summary. The answers are found on pp. 215-216.

Just as _____ (35) refers to our perceptual experience of the frequency of a sound, color refers to our perceptual experience of _____ (36), but does not correspond perfectly with it. The _____ (37) theory of color vision, proposed by Young and _____ (38), explained that our ability to see color is due to three different receptor types that are sensitive to red, green, and _____ (39) light. All colors are the result of mixing different combinations of these colors of light. The competing

_____ _____ (40) theory, proposed by Hering, explained color vision as the result of receptors whose _____ (41) are broken down by one type of light and regenerated by another. This theory is based on the observation of complementary colors, that when mixed in equal amounts produce _____ (42) or white. Presenting complementary colors such as red and green or blue and yellow together enhances the appearance of each. This theory also explains the phenomenon of _____ _____ _____ (43). When you stare at a green object, and then look at a blank piece of paper, you will experience the same image in _____ (44). However, Hering's theory was not well accepted because of the notion that a single photochemical could be affected in opposite ways by different wavelengths of light.

In 1957, _____ _____ _____ (45) proposed a theory of color vision that included elements of both the trichromatic and opponent process theories. This theory suggests that our ability to see color depends on two different levels of processing in the cells of the retina. The first level of color processing occurs in the _____ (46), which contain one of three different photopigments, each of which is maximally sensitive to different wavelengths of light. These red, green, and blue cones are interconnected to _____ (47) cells in such a way as to produce opponent-process effects. For example, long wavelength light stimulates the _____ (48) cones and _____ (49) ganglion cells, whereas medium wavelength light stimulates the green cones and _____ (50) the R-G ganglion cells. Staring at a red stimulus eventually _____ (51) the R-G ganglion cells, resulting in inhibition and the experience of green. Physical evidence for this theory was produced by studies involving shining different wavelengths of light onto the retinas of human eyes, and measuring which wavelengths were absorbed. Each type of cone is _____ (52) responsive to a narrow range of wavelengths. In addition, opponent process cells have been located in the _____ (53) and _____ (54) of monkeys. For each type of cell (R-G and Y-B), two forms exist, so that for example in one form of R-G, red light excites the cell and green light inhibits it, while in the other form green light _____ (55) and red light _____ (56). Some of these cells also have receptive fields that are concentric _____ (57) that are maximally responsive to red/green or yellow/blue light, which allows for greater wavelength discrimination as well as enhanced perception of color contrast. In general, this combined theory of color _____ (58) has been successful because it is _____ (59) with known facts about color, it explains those facts, and it has been used to make valid predictions about the way the visual system works.

The study of color blindness can reveal information about how the visual system works. People who are completely color blind, those who lack functional cones and are limited to vision from _____ (60), are rare. Such people see in shades of _____ (61), are very sensitive to light, and have _____ (62) visual acuity. More common forms of color blindness involve deficiencies of the red or green cones, while some people have a deficiency of _____ (63) cones. Those with red-green color blindness have difficulty distinguishing between these two colors, although they may have no idea that their vision is impaired in any way.

Short Answer & Essay Questions
Answer the following questions. See pp. 216-217 for sample answers.

6. How does Figure 9.6 demonstrate that our perception of color does not perfectly correspond to the wavelength of light we sense?

7. Why is it that when yellow and blue paints are mixed, green is produced, whereas when yellow and blue lights are mixed, they produce gray?

8. How does Hurvich and Jameson's theory of color vision account for our ability to see yellow? In your answer, be sure to include the activity occurring at the receptors as well as in the ganglion cells.

9. What three aspects of the combination theory of color vision make it a successful theory? Give an example of how each aspect is successfully addressed by the theory.

10. What can we conclude about the color receptors in a person who cannot distinguish red, but is especially sensitive to green light?

Form Vision

Summary and Guided Review

After studying this section in the text, fill in the blanks of the following summary. The answers are found on p. 216.

Form vision allows us to detect the boundaries of objects, and is the first step in _____ _____ (64). Form vision involves cells in several areas of the nervous system, including the retina, _____ (65), and cortex.

In order to perceive a form or object, we must first be able to detect its boundaries. The visual system is designed to respond to boundaries so that they stand out from the rest of the visual field. This fact is demonstrated by the _____ _____ _____ (66), in which adjacent areas of contrast appear more distinct from one another than areas of contrast that are not contiguous. This illusion, and the visual system's ability to detect contrast in general, is explained by _____ _____ (67) of ganglion cells within the retina. In mammals, the ganglion cells have concentric circular receptive fields. _____ _____ (68) cells respond by increasing the rate of firing when light stimulates the receptors serving the central portion of the receptive field and _____ (69) the rate of firing when light stimulates the surround portion. Such cells are particularly responsive to the _____ (70) and contours of objects, as these areas typically display high contrast in lighting.

While cells in the LGN also have circular receptive fields, those in the cortex have _____ - _____ (71) receptive fields, a fact discovered by Nobel laureates _____ and _____ (72). They also identified different types of cells in the cortex that respond to different bars of light. _____ _____ (73) respond to lines of a specific orientation in a specific portion of the visual field. The receptive field of a simple cell is composed of several _____ (74) cells with adjacent receptive fields in a line. The receptive fields of complex cells are composed of several _____ _____ (75) with adjacent fields; these complex cells are responsive to lines in a particular orientation over a larger area of the retina, and also can detect _____ (76) (because they continue to respond when a stimulus moves, as long as its orientation remains the same).

Hubel and Wiesel's theory accounts for the detection of edges, but cannot account for other surface details by which we identify objects. Edges represent _____ - _____ (77) changes in light, whereas _____ (78) and subtle shading represent low-frequency changes, to which De Valois suggests that some complex cells are responsive. This _____ _____ (79) theory suggests that different cortical cells have different levels of sensitivity to contrast, which accounts for our ability to make out the subtle details of a visual stimulus.

Short Answer & Essay Questions

Answer the following questions. See p. 217 for sample answers.

11. What is lateral inhibition, and how does it explain the Mach band illusion?

12. What will happen to an on center, off surround ganglion cell when light stimulates the entire receptive field? Only the surround? The center and only part of the surround?

13. Compare the receptive fields of simple and complex cells. How does the difference in receptive fields account for the complex cell's ability to detect movement?

14. What would our vision be like if we were only able to detect only high-frequency visual information, such as from edges?

The Perception of Objects, Color, and Movement

Summary and Guided Review

After studying this section in the text, fill in the blanks of the following summary. The answers are found on p. 216.

Visual perception involves the _____ (80) of visual stimuli, which is dependent upon the analysis of several components of stimuli in different parts of the brain. Most vision researchers believe that visual perception is a highly _____ (81) process, although some of the processing may be distributed across different areas.

Beginning in the _____ (82), visual information is divided into two systems. The _____ (83) system includes cells whose receptive fields are composed of foveal cells, are circular, small, and are color opponent, all of which make them sensitive to the _____ (84) and fine detail of objects. The _____ (85) system includes cells whose receptive fields are large, circular, and brightness opponent, and this system is involved in our perception of contrast, movement and _____ (86). Under poor lighting conditions, the _____ (87) system is most active, and we are particular sensitive to movement in our _____ (88) visual field. Reading and determining the color of objects, functions of the _____ (89) system, become difficult or impossible. The first cortical area for vision is the primary visual cortex (_____ (90)), located in the _____ _____ (91). In the cortex, the parvocellular system forms the majority of the _____ (92) stream of information that projects to the _____ (93) lobes; along this route, color perception and object recognition occur. The magnocellular system forms the majority of the _____ (94) stream that projects to the _____ (95) lobes; along this route, spatial information about visual stimuli is processed. The two streams then converge on the _____ _____ (96), where the information is used, for example, in planning movement.

Damage to one or more areas of the cortex involved in vision can lead to a specific type of _____ (97), or impairment of some type of visual perception. For example, people with object agnosia have difficulty recognizing objects, including faces of familiar people (a condition called _____ (98)). However, evidence that propoagnosics respond to familiar faces emotionally suggests that there are separate pathways for _____ (99) and recognition in the brain. The brain area implicated in these disorders is the _____ _____ _____ (100), which contains specific cells that respond to specific types of objects, including geometric forms, animals, and faces. In addition, there is evidence that the _____ (101) gyrus within the inferior temporal cortex is especially important for recognition of faces.

Another impairment is color agnosia, as characterized by the description of Jonathan I in the introduction to the chapter. Our experience of color depends in part on _____ _____ (102), the perceptual process that allows us to perceive the color of an object in the same way despite different lighting conditions. This ability seems to depend on cells in area _____ (103). Movement agnosia, the inability to detect movement, may be a result of damage to area _____/_____ (104). Individuals with damage to the posterior parietal cortex often display characteristics of _____ (105), such as failing to notice or attend to objects or parts of the body opposite the damage.

How are we able to make sense of all of the visual information we take in? So far, there is no evidence that a single _____ (106) area for incorporating visual information into conscious experience exists. The most likely answer is that our awareness of visual stimuli is the result of _____ (107) activity throughout the brain.

Short Answer & Essay Questions

Answer the following questions. See pp. 217-218 for sample answers.

15. What aspects of vision are the parvocellular and magnocellular systems specialized for? Give an example of each.

16. How does the modular nature of the visual system account for specific agnosias (such as object or movement agnosia)?

17. What is blindsight? What is the possible anatomical basis for it?

18. Describe the procedure used in the "greeble" study. What do the results of this study suggest about the function of the fusiform face area?

19. According to the text, why is it unlikely that there is a single brain area devoted to integrating visual information into a unitary experience?

Post-Test

Use these multiple-choice questions to check your understanding of the chapter. The answers, along with explanations, are found beginning on p. 218.

1. Electromagnetic energy includes
   a. visible light rays.
   b. gamma rays.
   c. infrared rays.
   d. all of the above.
   e. a and c.

2. The range of visible light for humans is
   a. 40-80 nm.
   b. 4,000-8,000 nm.
   c. 400-800 nm.
   d. 40,000-80,000 nm.

3. The _____ is a flexible tissue that allows us to focus on objects at different distances.
   a. cornea
   b. lens
   c. pupil
   d. iris

4. The _____ is actually muscle tissue that responds to different levels of light.
   a. cornea
   b. lens
   c. pupil
   d. iris

5. The transduction of light energy into neural energy occurs in the
   a. receptors.
   b. bipolar cells.
   c. ganglion cells.
   d. a and b.
   e. a, b, and c.

6. When photopigment molecules break down,
   a. the receptor cell is disinhibited.
   b. the receptor cell is inhibited.
   c. the bipolar cell is inhibited.
   d. a and c.
   e. b and c.

7. All of the following types of cells are found in the retina EXCEPT _____ cells.
   a. bipolar
   b. horizontal
   c. amacrine
   d. complex

8. A ganglion cell receiving input from _____ has the smallest receptive field.
   a. rods in the periphery of the retina
   b. rods 20 degrees from the fovea
   c. cones in the fovea
   d. cones outside the fovea

9. The blind spot contains
   a. rods only.
   b. cones only.
   c. both rods and cones.
   d. neither rods nor cones.

10. Visual information from the _____ side of each retina crosses to the other hemisphere at the
    _____.
    a. right; optic chiasm
    b. nasal; optic chiasm
    c. right; lateral geniculate nucleus
    d. nasal; lateral geniculate nucleus

11. _____ refers to the fact that different components of visual stimuli are processed in different areas of the brain.
    a. Hierarchical processing
    b. Modular processing
    c. Neural inhibition
    d. Retinal disparity

12. Light with a wavelength on the lower end of the spectrum (e.g. 450 nm) is normally perceived as
    a. blue.
    b. green.
    c. yellow.
    d. red.

13. Color televisions produce color in accordance with the principles of
    a. the opponent-process theory of color vision.
    b. the trichromatic theory of color vision.
    c. the combined theory of color vision.
    d. none of the above.

14. If you stare at a yellow object for a long time, and then look at a piece of white paper, you will see
    a. the image in blue.
    b. the image in green.
    c. the image in red.
    d. the image in yellow.

15. Which of the following is NOT TRUE of Hering's original opponent-process theory?
    a. It is consistent with principles of mixing light.
    b. It is consistent with the negative color aftereffect.
    c. It proposed four types of color receptors.
    d. It proposed four primary colors.

16. With respect to the cones, yellow light produces
    a. more response in the red than the green cones.
    b. more response in the green than the red cones.
    c. about the same response in the red and green cones.
    d. more response in the blue cones and little response in the green and red cones.

17. Based on Hurvich and Jameson's combined theory of color vision, light with a wavelength somewhere between red and green should have an excitatory effect on _____ ganglion cells.
    a. +Y-B
    b. +B-Y
    c. +R-G
    d. +G-R

18. Which of the following statements regarding people who lack cones is NOT true?
    a. They have poor visual acuity.
    b. They can distinguish only very bright colors.
    c. They are very sensitive to light.
    d. They inherit this condition.

19. People with red-green color blindness
    a. have poor visual acuity.
    b. can see neither red nor green.
    c. may have red photopigment in their green cones.
    d. are less common than those with complete colorblindness.

20. The Mach band illusion is a result of
    a. object recognition.
    b. lateral inhibition.
    c. retinal disparity.
    d. modular processing.

21. A light that stimulates receptors in the _____ of an off-center on-surround cell's receptive field will result in _____ .
    a. center; excitation
    b. surround; excitation
    c. surround; inhibition
    d. center and entire surround; inhibition

22. Which of the following types of cells has (or have) bar-shaped receptive fields?
    a. retinal ganglion cells
    b. LGN cells
    c. simple cells
    d. b and c
    e. a, b, and c

23. Which of the following cells has the largest receptive field?
    a. Retinal ganglion cells
    b. LGN cells
    c. Simple cells
    d. Complex cells

24. Movement is detected in
    a. simple cells.
    b. complex cells.
    c. both simple and complex cells.
    d. neither simple nor complex cells.

25. Hubel and Wiesel's theory accounts for the ability to detect
    a. texture.
    b. edges.
    c. movement.
    d. a and c.
    e. b and c.

26. According to spatial frequency theory,
    a. low-frequency contrast in objects is detected by different cells than high-frequency contrast.
    b. the visual system is only capable of detecting medium- to high-frequency contrast.
    c. the visual system is only capable of detecting low- to medium-frequency contrast.
    d. the brightness of an object is irrelevant.

27. The best explanation of visual processing is that it is
    a. modular.
    b. distributed.
    c. both modular and distributed.
    d. neither modular nor distributed.

28. Which of the following is a characteristic of cells in the parvocellular system?
    a. They have small receptive fields.
    b. They are brightness opponent.
    c. They are responsive to movement.
    d. Their input comes mainly from rods.

29. The magnocellular system dominates the _____ stream, which flows into the _____ lobes.
    a. ventral; temporal
    b. ventral; parietal
    c. dorsal; temporal
    d. dorsal; parietal

30. Magnocellular cells in area V1 are responsive to all of the following EXCEPT
    a. orientation.
    b. movement.
    c. retinal disparity.
    d. color.

31. Movement perception is a function of
    a. V2.
    b. V4.
    c. V5.
    d. V8.

32. The ventral and dorsal streams both converge on the _____ cortex.
    a. posterior parietal
    b. prefrontal
    c. anterior occipital
    d. inferior temporal

33. Object agnosia is often a result of damage to the _____ cortex.
    a. inferior temporal.
    b. prefrontal.
    c. posterior parietal.
    d. posterior occipital.

34. People with prosopagnosia
    a. fail to recognize familiar faces.
    b. fail to recognize familiar voices.
    c. fail to respond emotionally to familiar faces.
    d. all of the above.
    e. a and c.

35. Specialized face-recognition cells have been located in the
    a. dorsal stream.
    b. fusiform gyrus.
    c. V1 area.
    d. parietal lobe.

36. The ability to perceive that an object is the same color despite different lighting conditions is known as
    a. visual constancy.
    b. color agnosia.
    c. retinal disparity.
    d. color constancy.

37. Wavelength is coded in _____ , and color is coded in _____ .
    a.   V4; V1
    b.   V4; V4
    c.   V1; V1
    d.   V1; V4

38. Someone with damage to the right posterior parietal cortex would probably exhibit
    a.   right side neglect.
    b.   left side neglect.
    c.   movement agnosia.
    d.   color agnosia.

39. Neglect probably occurs because of
    a.   a lack of attention to the space on one side of the body.
    b.   an inability to perceive objects on one side of the body.
    c.   both a and b.
    d.   neither a nor b.

40. According to the text, visual awareness is probably due to
    a.   master visual cells in the superior temporal gyrus.
    b.   master visual cells in the parietal cortex.
    c.   distributed processes across the brain.
    d.   master cells in some part of the cortex that has not yet been identified.

Answers & Explanations

Guided Review

1. electromagnetic
2. infrared rays
3. 400-800
4. billionth
5. colors
6. eye
7. cornea
8. lens
9. iris
10. pupil
11. retina
12. photopigments or photo-chemicals
13. Na^+
14. hyperpolarizing
15. amacrine
16. rods or cones
17. cones or rods
18. rhodopsin
19. iodopsin
20. fovea
21. visual acuity
22. sensitivity
23. axons
24. blind spot
25. optic chiasm
26. lateral geniculate nucleus
27. left
28. right
29. right
30. left
31. retinal disparity
32. inhibition
33. hierarchical processing
34. modular processing
35. pitch
36. wavelength
37. trichromatic
38. Helmholtz
39. blue
40. opponent processing
41. photopigments or photochemicals
42. gray
43. negative color aftereffects
44. red
45. Hurvich and Jameson
46. cones or receptors
47. ganglion
48. red
49. R-G
50. inhibits
51. fatigues
52. maximally
53. retina
54. LGN
55. excites
56. inhibits

57. circles	72. Hubel and Wiesel	90. V1
58. vision	73. Simple cells	91. occipital lobe
59. consistent	74. ganglion	92. ventral
60. rods	75. simple cells	93. temporal
61. gray	76. movement	94. dorsal
62. poor	77. high-frequency	95. parietal
63. blue	78. texture	96. prefrontal cortex
64. object perception	79. spatial frequency	97. agnosia
	80. recognition	98. prosopagnosia
65. thalamus	81. modular	99. identification
66. Mach band illusion	82. retina	100. inferior temporal cortex
	83. parvocellular	101. fusiform
67. lateral inhibition	84. color	102. color constancy
	85. magnocellular	103. V4
68. On center	86. depth	104. V5/MT
69. decreasing	87. magnocellular	105. neglect
70. edges	88. peripheral	106. master
71. bar-shaped	89. parvocellular	107. distributed

Short Answer & Essay

1. The retina is highly complex, containing several different cell types with specific functions. Furthermore, these cells are interconnected in such a way that some of the processing of visual information begins in the retina rather than in the brain.

2. Ganglion cells receiving input from foveal cones have smaller receptive fields than those receiving input from rods. Some cones in the fovea have a one-to-one correspondence with ganglion cells (meaning that the ganglion cells receive input only from single cones). This arrangement allows us to make fine discriminations of the details of objects in our visual field. Ganglion cells receiving input from rods have large receptive fields, since they receive input from several rods. They are highly sensitive to light and movement, but are not useful for making out fine details.

3. The blind spot is the portion of the retina where the ganglion cell axons forming the optic nerve exit the retina, and there are no receptors on this area. We don't notice it because when we see with both eyes, the portion of the visual field that falls on the blind spot in the left eye is different than that portion that falls on the blind spot in the right eye. This way, one eye gets the information that the other one misses.

4. An object that is presented very briefly to one side of the visual field (left or right) is typically only processed in one hemisphere. This is because the image only falls on the left or right visual field, and is gone before the person can reorient the eyes toward the object.

5. They take advantage of retinal disparity. The slides project a slightly different image to each eye, reproducing what normally happens when we look at a scene with both eyes. The disparity, or difference, between the two images produces the sensation of depth, giving the scene 3 dimensions rather than 2.

6. In this figure, the Xs reflect the same wavelengths of light, but the background color of each leads to the perception that they are different colors.

7. Yellow and blue paints contain pigments. The principle of color subtracting applies here: pigments absorb some wavelengths of light and reflect others. Mixing yellow and blue paint produces green because these pigments absorb all of the light spectrum except for that corresponding to green. When yellow and blue lights are mixed, the effect is additive. Gray or white is produce because these two wavelengths cancel each other out (in their effects on the Y-B cells).

8. According to the combined theory, we perceive yellow because medium wavelength (yellow) light stimulates both the red and green cones, which lead to zero net effect on the R-G ganglion cells, but an excitatory effect on the Y-B ganglion cells. The Y-B cones receive excitatory messages from the R and/or G cones, with little input from the B cones, so the net effect is excitatory.

9. The combined theory is consistent with what was previously known about color, including the principles of light mixing as well as complementary colors. The theory also explains these facts, whereas the trichromatic theory could not explain the complementary colors phenomenon or negative color afterimages. Finally, the theory was used to predict the different cone types and the connections between the ganglion cells before there was physical evidence for them, and their predictions have been confirmed.

10. If someone cannot distinguish red from green, but is highly sensitive to green, then it is possible that s/he has the photopigment for green in the red cones.

11. Lateral inhibition is the result of the way in which receptors and ganglion cells are interconnected. A receptor will have an excitatory effect on one ganglion cell while it inhibits those ganglion cells adjacent to the excitatory target. This produces the Mach band illusion, which is the perception that at areas of contrast, dark edges are darker and light edges are lighter. This occurs because at the border between light and dark, ganglion cells at the edge of the dark region are receiving more inhibition than those further from the border, and ganglion cells immediately adjacent in the light region are receiving less inhibition than those further from the border.

12. In an on center, off surround cell, light falling on the entire receptive field will produce no change in the rate of firing, because the effects of light on the two areas cancel each other out. When the surround is illuminated, the cell will be inhibited, whereas when the center and a portion of the surround are illuminated, the net effect will be excitation.

13. A simple cell receives input from several adjacent retinal ganglion cells, a complex cell receives input from several simple cells. The complex cell responds to movement because its receptive field is larger, and is composed of sub-units of simple cells that respond to stimuli of the same orientation. Therefore, the cell will continue to respond to a stimulus that moves across its receptive field, as long as it maintains the same orientation.

14. Objects would either appear very simple, like line drawings, or somewhat disconnected, as in Figure 9.22. We would not be able to make out subtle gradations of shading and texture.

15. The parvocellular system is specialized for seeing in color and contrast; reading is dependent on this system. The magnocellular system is specialized for perceiving movement and depth; detecting movement in the periphery of the visual field is dependent on this system.

16. The different agnosias (object, color, movement) exist because different parts of the brain are responsible for processing these aspects of visual stimuli. When a specific area is damaged, such as the inferior temporal cortex, the person may experience object agnosia, but will probably not suffer from

the other types. Because these functions are handled in distinct areas of the brain, they are disrupted only by damage to specific areas.

17. Blindsight is a phenomenon in which people with damage to the primary visual area act as if they can see objects, even though they have no awareness of them. This may occur because of other connections between the optic tract and parts of the cortex not involved in conscious awareness.

18. In the greeble study, people were presented with different novel facial stimuli. At first, the participants could not discriminate between the different examples of greebles, but after several trials, they could tell them apart. The "experts," those who could distinguish between greebles, showed activity in the fusiform face area, whereas the novices did not. This suggests that this area is used in recognizing familiar people (or members of another species), and that it is affected by our experiences.

19. So far, there have been no cases in which damage to a specific part of the brain leads to complete lack of visual awareness, which suggests that there is no such "master" area that integrates all visual information into a unitary experience.

Post-Test

All page references in this section pertain to the textbook.

1. a. Wrong; b and c are also correct.
   b. Wrong
   c. Wrong
   d. Correct; see p. 252.
   e. Wrong

2. a. Wrong
   b. Wrong
   c. Correct; see p. 252.
   d. Wrong

3. a. Wrong; this is the outer layer of tissue.
   b. Correct; see p. 253.
   c. Wrong; this is really a gap in the iris where the lens shows through.
   d. Wrong; this is the muscle that controls the level of light entering the eye.

4. a. Wrong; this is the outer layer of tissue.
   b. Wrong; this responds to objects at different distances.
   c. Wrong; this is the gap within the iris (that appears to constrict or dilate when the iris changes shape)
   d. Correct; see p. 253.

5. **a. Correct**; the other cells do not respond directly to light energy.
   b. Wrong
   c. Wrong
   d. Wrong
   e. Wrong

6. a. Wrong
    b. Correct; light causes Na+ channels to close, which hyperpolarizes the cell.
    c. Wrong; inhibition of the receptors leads to disinhibition of the bipolar cells.
    d. Wrong
    e. Wrong

7. a. Wrong
    b. Wrong
    c. Wrong
    d. Correct; all of the other types of cells are found in the retina.

8. a. Wrong; this would have a very large receptive field, composed of many rods.
    b. Wrong; this is where the rods are most concentrated, but the receptive field of ganglion cells receiving input from this area would still be larger than those receiving input from foveal cones.
    c. Correct
    d. Wrong; more cones converge on a single ganglion cell outside the fovea than within it.

9. a. Wrong
    b. Wrong
    c. Wrong
    d. Correct; there are no receptors in the blind spot.

10. a. Wrong; this information makes up the right visual field; only in the left eye would this information cross over at the optic chiasm.
    b. Correct; see p. 255.
    c. Wrong
    d. Wrong; the information does not cross over in the LGN.

11. a. Wrong; this refers to the fact that basic processing occurs lower in the nervous system than more complex processing.
    b. Correct; see p. 256.
    c. Wrong; this principle asserts that inhibition is an important part of visual processing.
    d. Wrong; this refers to the difference between images in each eye.

12. **a. Correct**; see p. 257.
    b. Wrong; this corresponds to medium wavelengths.
    c. Wrong; this corresponds to medium-long wavelengths.
    d. Wrong; this corresponds to long wavelengths.

13. a. Wrong
    b. Correct; see p. 257.
    c. Wrong
    d. Wrong

14. **a. Correct**; this occurs because staring at something reflecting yellow light fatigues Y-B ganglion cells, and after a while they will give the opposite response.
    b. Wrong; blue is the complementary color for yellow.
    c. Wrong; blue is the complementary color for yellow.
    d. Wrong; blue is the complementary color for yellow.

15. a.   Wrong
    b.   Wrong
    c.   Correct; Hering proposed only 2 receptor types, each of which contained a photochemical that could be broken down by one type of light and regenerated by another. All of the other choices are true of his theory.
    d.   Wrong

16. a.   Wrong
    b.   Wrong
    c.   Correct; see figure 9.11 on p. 262.
    d.   Wrong

17. **a.   Correct**; these are on-yellow, off-blue cells, which means they are excited by yellow and inhibited by blue.
    b.   Wrong; these cells are excited by blue and inhibited by yellow.
    c.   Wrong; yellow light would have zero net effect on these cells.
    d.   Wrong; yellow light would have zero net effect on these cells.

18. a.   Wrong
    b.   Correct; people with only rods discriminate no colors at all. All of the other choices are true of people with this condition.
    c.   Wrong
    d.   Wrong

19. a.   Wrong; their acuity is usually not affected (because they have the same number of cones as those without color blindness).
    b.   Wrong; they may have difficulty distinguishing these colors, but they usually see red and green light..
    c.   Correct; see p. 263.
    d.   Wrong; it is implied that partial color blindness is more common than complete color blindness.

20. a.   Wrong; this is unrelated.
    b.   Correct; see p. 265.
    c.   Wrong; this is unrelated.
    d.   Wrong; this is not directly related.

21. a.   Wrong; a light in the center would lead to inhibition.
    b.   Correct; this cell is excited by light in its surround.
    c.   Wrong
    d.   Wrong; this would lead to no net effect on the cell.

22. a.   Wrong; these cells have circular receptive fields.
    b.   Wrong; these cells have circular receptive fields.
    c.   Correct; see p. 267.
    d.   Wrong
    e.   Wrong

23. a. Wrong
    b. Wrong
    c. Wrong
    d. **Correct**; because these cells have receptive fields composed of the fields of several of the lower types of cells, theirs are the largest.

24. a. Wrong
    b. **Correct**; complex cells respond to stimuli that change position.
    c. Wrong
    d. Wrong

25. a. Wrong; Hubel and Wiesel's theory does not account for detection of the subtle differences in texture of objects.
    b. Wrong; c is also correct.
    c. Wrong
    d. Wrong
    e. **Correct**; simple cells detect edges, and complex cells detect edges and movement.

26. **a.** **Correct**; see pp. 268-269.
    b. Wrong; it can also detect low-frequency contrast (such as texture and shading).
    c. Wrong
    d. Wrong; brightness is important in determining the degree of contrast of edges, contours, and texture.

27. a. Wrong; b is also correct.
    b. Wrong; a is also correct.
    c. **Correct**; specific areas of the brain handle specific components of vision, and this processing occurs simultaneously.
    d. Wrong

28. **a.** **Correct**; they typically receive input from one or a few cones.
    b. Wrong; they are sensitive to color.
    c. Wrong; this is true of magnocellular cells.
    d. Wrong; this is true of magnocellular cells.

29. a. Wrong; this is true of the parvocellular system.
    b. Wrong; although it projects to the parietal lobes, the magnocellular system dominates the dorsal stream.
    c. Wrong; although it dominates the dorsal stream, it projects to the parietal lobes.
    d. **Correct**; see p. 271.

30. a. Wrong
    b. Wrong
    c. Wrong
    d. **Correct**; the magnocellular system does not process color. All of the other choices are true of cells in this area.

31. a.   Wrong; although information about movement passes through here, the book does not mention that damage to this area leads to movement agnosia.
    b.   Wrong; this area is involved in color.
    c.   Correct; see pp. 274-275.
    d.   Wrong; this area is not mentioned in the text.

32. a.   Wrong; the dorsal stream projects here.
    b.   Correct; see p. 271.
    c.   Wrong; this area is not mentioned.
    d.   Wrong; the ventral stream projects here.

33. **a.   Correct**; see p. 272.
    b.   Wrong; this area is involved in planning of movements.
    c.   Wrong; this area is not involved in object recognition.
    d.   Wrong; this area is not mentioned in the text.

34. **a.   Correct**; see p. 272.
    b.   Wrong; the book states that although they do not recognize faces, they can recognize people by their voices.
    c.   Wrong; the book states that they show emotional responses to familiar faces, even if they can't identify the faces.
    d.   Wrong
    e.   Wrong

35. a.   Wrong; this area is in the temporal lobe, which is part of the ventral stream.
    b.   Correct; see p. 272.
    c.   Wrong; only very simple shapes may be recognized at this level.
    d.   Wrong; this area is not involved in object recognition.

36. a.   Wrong; this term is not mentioned.
    b.   Wrong; people with color agnosia have difficulty perceiving color at all.
    c.   Wrong; this is unrelated.
    d.   Correct; see p. 274.

37. a.   Wrong
    b.   Wrong
    c.   Wrong
    d.   Correct; see p. 274.

38. a.   Wrong; the book does not mention right-side neglect.
    b.   Wrong; see p. 275..
    c.   Wrong; this is related to damage in V5.
    d.   Wrong; this is probably related to damage in V4.

39. **a.   Correct**; studies indicate that people with neglect can see things on the neglected side, but that they do not always attend to them or have awareness of them.
    b.   Wrong
    c.   Wrong
    d.   Wrong

40. a. Wrong; the book states that this is inconclusive.
    b. Wrong; the book states that this is inconclusive.
    c. **Correct**; see p. 276.
    d. Wrong; the fact that no such cases have been reported strongly suggests that no such area exists.

Chapter 10: The Body Senses and Movement

Chapter Outline and Learning Objectives

As you read the chapter, use these learning objectives to guide your studying. You should be able to define the key terms from the text, which are shown in boldface type below.

1) The Body Senses
   a) Proprioception
      - What is **proprioception**? What information is derived from it?

      - Describe what happens when proprioception is disrupted or damaged, as illustrated by the case of Christina.

   b) The Vestibular Sense
      - What are the organs of the **vestibular sense**? How does each help us to maintain balance?

      - Describe what happens when the vestibular sense is disrupted, as illustrated by the case of Mr. MacGregor.

      - How do we use proprioception and the vestibular sense together?

   c) The Skin Senses
      - What are the **skin senses**? What types of receptors contribute to these senses?

      - Distinguish between the forms of touch detected by each type of receptor.

      - How is the variability in the density of skin receptors related to sensitivity of different areas of the body?

      - Describe how the skin senses are functionally and anatomically distinct from one another.

   d) The Somatosensory Cortex and Posterior Parietal Cortex
      - What is a **dermatome**? How distinct are the divisions between dermatomes?

      - Trace the path of somatosensory information to the cortex.

- What are the organizational and functional similarities of the **somatosensory cortex** and the visual cortex?

- How is the **primary somatosensory cortex** organized? Discuss the feature detectors and receptive fields of cells in this area.

- What is the function of the **secondary somatosensory cortex**, and to what other brain areas do its cells project?

- What are the functions of the **posterior parietal cortex**?

e) The Sensation of Pain
  i) Detecting Pain
  - What stimulates pain? What types of receptors are involved?

  - What are the anatomical bases of sharp and dull pain?

  - What transmitters are involved in pain signals in the spinal cord?

  - How do drugs that relieve pain work?

  ii) Internal mechanisms of Pain Relief
  - What, according to the **gate control theory**, are the mechanisms of pain relief? How has this theory been applied to help relieve pain?

  - How did Pert and Snyder discover opiate receptors?

  - What is the function of endorphins, with respect to pain relief? Under what conditions are they most likely to be released?

  - What external forms of pain relief seem to trigger endorphins?

  - How is the **periaqueductal gray** thought to be involved in pain relief? How has this knowledge been used to treat chronic pain?

- What non-opioid mechanisms for pain relief exist?

   iii) Phantom Pain
- How do people with amputated limbs describe the phantom limb experience?

- What evidence suggests that **phantom pain** is a result of brain activity, and in particular, neural reorganization?

2) Movement
- Why is the study of movement important for biological psychology?

  a) The Muscles
- Distinguish between **skeletal, smooth, and cardiac muscles**.

- Describe the components of the **neuromuscular junction**. How is precision of movement related to the degree of neural input to muscles?

- How do skeletal muscles work to produce movement? What is the importance of the **antagonistic** arrangement of muscles controlling the limbs?

  b) The Spinal Cord
- What role does the spinal cord play in maintaining posture and balance?

- What is the anatomical basis of the patellar reflex? What is the functional significance of this reflex?

- How do **muscle spindles** and **Golgi tendon organs** function?

- What are **central pattern generators**? What types of movement do they produce? Under what conditions can they be observed?

  c) The Brain and Movement
- What brain areas are involved in movement?

   i) The Prefrontal Cortex
- What role does the **prefrontal cortex** play in movement?

- Describe the delayed match-to-sample procedure. How does cell activity in the PFC correspond to different parts of the procedure?

ii) The Secondary Motor Areas
- What are the functions of cells in the **premotor cortex**? What is the result of damage in this area?

- What is the function of cells in the **supplementary motor area**? What is the result of damage to this area?

iii) The Primary Motor Cortex
- What are the functions of the **primary motor cortex**?

- How does this area coordinate information from other brain areas?

iv) The Basal Ganglia and Cerebellum
- What general aspects of movement do the basal ganglia and cerebellum contribute to?

- What structures make up the basal ganglia? How are they thought to smooth out movements? What is their role in learning?

- What are the functions of the cerebellum? What are the results of damage to this structure?

d) Disorders of Movement
  i) Parkinson's Disease
  - What are the characteristics of **Parkinson's disease**? Damage to what brain areas is involved?

  - What evidence is there that PD is in some cases **familial**? What gene mutations (and what proteins) may be involved?

  - What role may toxins play in the development of PD?

  - What evidence is there that caffeine and nicotine reduce the risk of PD?

  - What are the drugs used to treat PD? What other treatments are available?

ii) Huntington's Disease
- What are the characteristics of **Huntington's disease**? Describe the typical progression of the disease.

- Discuss the genetic basis of HD.

- What form of treatment is potentially effective for treating HD?

iii) Autoimmune Diseases
- What causes **myasthenia gravis**? How is it treated?

- What are the characteristics of **multiple sclerosis**? Why is it considered an autoimmune disease?

The Body Senses

Summary and Guided Review

After studying this section in the text, fill in the blanks of the following summary. The answers are found on pp. 239-240.

Unlike vision and _____ (1), which tell us about things and conditions external to ourselves, the body senses convey information about things we are directly in contact with as well as our own internal conditions. Because the body senses provide information about spatial position, posture, and balance, they are intimately tied in with _____ (2), those behaviors which allow us to interact with the environment.

_____ (3) refers to our sense of position and bodily movement. These messages originate in the muscles. The _____ (4) system, whose receptors are located in the vestibular organs, is involved in maintaining balance as well as providing information about head position and movement. The three _____ _____ (5), located near the cochlea, each project in a different dimension in space. When we accelerate, this forces the gelatinous mass inside the canals to move, which in turn causes changes in the firing rate of _____ (6) cells. The _____ (7) and saccule contain _____ (8) embedded in a jelly-like substance, as well as patches of hair cells (in horizontal and vertical patches, respectively). When the head is tilted or acceleration occurs, the otoliths and jelly bend the hair cells. Once we reach a stable speed when moving, the vestibular organs return to their resting state. Without the vestibular sense, we would have difficulty sensing when we are out of balance. In general, proprioception and the vestibular sense provide coordinated information about the _____ (9) and movement of our bodies.

      The skin senses include touch, _____ (10), cold, and _____ (11), and as such they provide information about both internal and external events. There are several types of encapsulated receptors, each of which is sensitive to different aspects of _____ (12). Free nerve endings, which are distributed variably throughout the body, are sensitive to _____ (13) and pain. Although the same types of receptors respond to cold, warmth and pain, they display maximal firing when stimulated by different temperatures. They also originate in different areas of the skin; for example, the _____ (14) receptors are near the surface, and the warmth receptors are deeper. In the spinal cord and brain, information about cold, warmth, and pain remain in distinct pathways.

      Each spinal nerve receives sensory information from a different _____ (15), although the body areas served by these are not completely distinct, thus allowing for compensation if one nerve is injured. Body sensory information is carried to the _____ (16), and then to the somatosensory cortex, mostly on the _____ (17) side of the brain. There are many similarities in the organization and function of the visual and somatosensory systems: the somatosensory cortex contains a map of the body, with more neural input from areas of greater _____ (18); cells in the same _____ (19) have the same function; some cells have center-surround _____ _____ (20); somatosensory processing is _____ (21), controlled by two of the four subareas of S-I; and some _____ (22) cells respond to specific features of objects. S-I sends information to the _____ _____ (23) cortex, which integrates information from S-I of both hemispheres, and is particularly responsive to stimuli that have meaning, suggesting a role in learning and memory. Another S-I target area is the _____ _____ (24) cortex, where information from several sensory modalities is integrated, and output allowing for coordinated movements is sent to the _____ (25) areas of the brain.

      Painful stimuli are detected by _____ (26) receptors which respond to extreme heat and cold; _____ (27) receptors which respond to intense pressure; and _____ (28) receptors, which respond to temperature, pressure, and certain chemicals released during tissue injury. Pain information first travels to the spinal cord. The immediate sharp pain sensed following an injury is a result of stimulation of large, myelinated ___-_____ (29) neurons, whereas the more persistent _____ (30) pain experienced is the result of stimulation of smaller C fibers. In the spinal cord, _____ ____ (31) and glutamate send pain signals to others neurons, and the message is carried to the brain.

Although there are many artificial forms of pain relief, many of them are problematic. It turns out that the body has its own mechanisms for countering pain, and understanding them may provide clues to more effective relief of pain. For example, the _____ _____ (32) theory of pain, which suggested that pressure signals occurring simultaneously with pain signals could result in inhibition of pain in the spinal cord, led to the development of transcutaneous

_____ _____ _____ (33), whereby electrical stimulation of the skin produces inhibition of pain neurons.

Under certain conditions, people suffering massive injury or trauma report experiencing little or no pain. Also, it has long been known that _____ (34) drugs are effective pain relievers. However, it was not until 1973 that _____ _____ _____ (35) provided evidence for opiate receptors in the brain. Later, _____ (36) were identified, and it was discovered that pain, particularly if it is unavoidable, causes their release, as does stress. Other forms of pain relief appear to be opiate-based, including acupuncture,

_____ (37) effects, and vaginal stimulation, which may be involved in childbirth. The pain-relief mechanism for endorphins may involve something akin to the gate control theory. Painful stimuli result in release of endorphins in the _____ _____ (38) of the brainstem; the PAG neurons send messages down the spinal cord, where they presynaptically inhibit the release of _____ _____ (39).

Internal, non-endorphin pain relief mechanisms also exist, but less is known about them. Some substances implicated in these mechanisms are substance P, NMDA, and ABT-594 (a

_____ (40)-like stimulant).

Sensations from _____ (41) limbs are real for many amputees. Despite the fact that signals are no longer being sent to the brain from the amputated limb, about _____(42)% of amputees report feeling pain that seems to be located in the missing limb. Early attempts to control pain through lesions to pain pathways in the spinal cord and _____ (43) were unsuccessful, and evidence from spinal cord injury patients suggested that phantom pain was a result of brain activation. In the 1990's, German researchers discovered that in some people with amputated arms, neurons receiving information from _____ (44) areas invaded parts of the somatosensory cortex that formerly received input from the hands, and the extent of invasion was related to the presence of phantom pain.

Short Answer & Essay Questions

Answer the following questions. See pp. 240-241 for sample answers.

1. Melanie is driving along the interstate at 55 mph. She crosses into a 70 mph zone, and accelerates up to 70. She can feel the difference in speed as she accelerates, but once she reaches 70 and sets the cruise control, she no longer notices that she is moving. How does the activity in the vestibular system explain her sense of acceleration? How does it explain her sense of no movement once her speed has stabilized?

2. List the different forms of encapsulated nerve endings and the types of touch to which they are sensitive.

3. Describe five similarities that somatosensation and vision share.

4. Anatomically, what are the bases of sharp and dull pain? How is each adaptive?

5. Describe the procedure Pert and Snyder used in discovering opiate receptors.

6. Describe the mechanism by which endorphins are thought to control pain.

7. What is the possible anatomical basis of phantom pain?

Movement

Summary and Guided Review

After studying this section in the text, fill in the blanks of the following summary. The answers are found on p. 240.

Studying the biological basis of movement is important for obtaining a more complete picture of brain functions underlying many of our behaviors. Historically, this area of study has contributed much to our understanding of the brain.

Movement involves _____ (45), or striated, muscles, which are composed of individual cells; these cells are controlled by motor neurons at the _____ (46) junction via the neurotransmitter _____ (47). A single neuron may control a few or many muscle cells. _____ (48) connect muscles to bone, and movement occurs when muscles contract, pulling against the bone. On the limbs, muscles are paired _____ (49) so that they produce opposing movements. Most muscle tension adjustments occur due to _____ (50) reflexes.

An example of a spinal reflex occurs when the _____ (51) tendon is tapped; this stretches the quadriceps muscle, whose _____ (52) receptors send a

231

signal up the sensory nerve into the spinal cord. The sensory neurons form synapses with

_____ (53) neurons, and a message is sent back to the quadriceps, causing it to

_____ (54). This allows for quick, automatic postural adjustments. Muscle

contractions are detected by _____ _____ _____ (55),

which respond by inhibiting further contraction. The spinal cord also contains networks responsible for

generating patterns of _____ (56), such as walking, flying, and swimming, so

that conscious effort is not required to produce these rhythmic movements.

     There are several cortical and subcortical brain areas involved in movement. The

_____ (57) cortex is an important center in the planning of movement, because

it receives, integrates, and briefly stores information about the body and the environment. Studies of brain

activity in monkeys during different stages of a _____ _____ -

_____ - _____ (58) task indicate that certain cells become active when a stimulus is

presented and remain active following its removal, while other cells become active once reinforcement for

responding becomes available. Output is sent to the _____ (59) cortex, where

movement is then programmed. Different cells in this region are involved in different movements toward

different targets, and some cells use sensory information about objects when adjusting movement.

Sequences of movement are coordinated by the _____

_____ _____ (60); activity of different cells in this area produce different

types of movements.

     The _____ _____ (61) cortex receives input from the

other cortical motor areas, the somatosensory cortex, and the posterior parietal area; movements are

executed in this area. Cells in this area show less specificity than cells in the other cortical motor areas:

each cell may contribute to different types of movement. However, cells within a _____ (62)

contribute to movement in the same direction, and groups of columns control specific movements.

     The basal ganglia and _____ (63) are involved in modulating

movement, although they do not directly control it. The basal ganglia include the caudate nucleus,

_____ (64), and globus pallidus, which fine-tune movements, making them smooth.

They are also involved in the learning of sequences of movement. The cerebellum receives input from the

vestibular system, and is involved in several functions related to balance and the control of eye movements

in compensation for head movements. It coordinates the different components of complex movements and

provides corrections as movements are being executed. It is also involved in motor and _____ -

_____ (65) learning, as well as attention.

     There are several neurologically based movement disorders. Parkinson's disease, which affects

about 2% of the population, results from damage to the _____ _____ (66), the source of dopaminergic neurons projecting to the striatum. Symptoms of PD include tremor, rigidity, and problems with balance, coordination, and the initiation of movement. The cause of PD appears to be familial in about _____ - _____ (67) % of cases; genes involved in the production of the protein α-synuclein, which accumulate in the brains of PD patients and form _____ _____ (68), and other proteins, appear to be implicated in the development of PD. In the remainder of cases, environmental _____ (69) may be the cause of brain damage, and some people may inherit a reduced ability to metabolize toxins. The risk of PD is reduced by _____ (70) % in coffee drinkers, and _____ (71) % in smokers. _____ (72) is believed to reduce the effects of toxins by blocking adenosine receptors, while cigarette smoke is thought to prevent the accumulation of toxins. Although treatment of PD has traditionally involved administration of the dopamine precursor _____ (73), the use of embryonic stem cells is being tested. Another alternative to drug treatment is stimulation of the _____ _____ (74) and subthalamic nuclei, and although current studies suggest this is effective, it is not known if this treatment will prove effective in the long-term.

Huntington's disease occurs as a result of progressive cell loss in the _____ (75), producing movement impairments that become more pronounced with time, as well as psychological changes. The disease is fatal. Cell death is thought to result from a build up of the protein _____ (76); the gene responsible for this protein has been located, and a person inheriting a single copy of the defective gene will develop HD. Fetal cell transplant may work to counter the disease, although this treatment has not been thoroughly studied.

Several autoimmune disorders also involve the disruption of movement. Myasthenia gravis occurs as a result of changes in number or sensitivity of _____ (77) receptors, and is characterized by muscular weakness that, if untreated, may cause death. A study using snake venom that blocks ACh receptors revealed that people with MG have significantly fewer of these receptors. MG can be treated with _____ (78) inhibitors, but a more permanent treatment involves removal of the _____ (79) gland, an endocrine gland that contains tumors in many people with MG. _____ _____ (80) involves the loss of myelin in CNS cells, producing scarring and reducing or eliminating the functioning of affected cells. Weakness, tremor, and impaired coordination result. Evidence suggests that myelin is destroyed by the _____ _____ (81), perhaps as a result of exposure to a virus such as measles, mumps, or Epstein-Barr.

Short Answer & Essay Questions

Answer the following questions. See p. 241 for sample answers.

8. In terms of precision of movement, what are the consequences of the fact that a single motor neuron projecting to the biceps muscle serves 100 muscle cells, whereas a single motor neuron projecting to the eye muscles serves only three cells?

9. How might spinal reflexes and central pattern generators be useful in treating spinal cord injuries?

10. Explain the delayed match-to-sample task. How does activity in the prefrontal cortex correspond with different components of this task?

11. How do researchers know that the primary motor cortex, and not other motor areas, is responsible for the execution of movement?

12. Compare Parkinson's and Huntington's diseases in terms of what is known about the genetic basis of each. For which disease does the environment seem to play a more important role? Why?

13. Why is myasthenia gravis considered to be an autoimmune disease?

Post-Test

Use these multiple-choice questions to check your understanding of the chapter. The answers, along with explanations, are found beginning on p. 241.

1. The receptors in the body that convey information about muscle tension and limb position are part of which sensory system?
    a. vestibular sense
    b. somatosensation
    c. proprioception
    d. none of the above.

2. Otoliths are found in the
    a. utricle
    b. saccule
    c. semicircular canals
    d. a and b.
    e. a, b, and c.

3. Hair cells are found in the
    a. utricle
    b. saccule
    c. semicircular canals
    d. a and b.
    e. a, b, and c.

4. Which of the body senses is/are stimulated by both external (environmental) and internal stimuli?
   a. proprioception
   b. vestibular sense
   c. skin senses
   d. all of the above
   e. a and b

5. Pacinian corpuscles are found _____ the surface of the skin and detect _____ .
   a. near; touch
   b. far from; touch
   c. near; warmth
   d. far from; warmth

6. Which of the following areas of the body probably contains the FEWEST skin receptors?
   a. tongue
   b. upper arm
   c. thumb
   d. foot

7. Which of the following statements regarding warmth receptors is FALSE?
   a. They are located away from the surface of the skin.
   b. They have a peak firing rate at 45 degrees C.
   c. They respond to temperatures above 50 degrees C.
   d. They are free nerve endings.

8. The body segment served by a specific spinal nerve is called a(n)
   a. dermatome.
   b. spinal area.
   c. cupula.
   d. Ruffini area.

9. Information about touch from the right side of the body projects
   a. only to the left hemisphere.
   b. only to the right hemisphere.
   c. to the left and right hemispheres equally.
   d. mostly to the left hemisphere.

10. The primary somatosensory cortex is located in the
    a. anterior parietal lobe.
    b. posterior frontal lobe.
    c. central sulcus.
    d. superior temporal lobe.

11. Chemicals such as histamine and bradykinin that are released when tissue is injured result in activation of which type of pain receptor?
    a. thermal
    b. mechanical
    c. polymodal
    d. b and c
    e. a, b, and c

12. A-delta fibers are _____ and are responsible for our experience of
_____ pain.
    a. myelinated; sharp
    b. myelinated; dull
    c. unmyelinated; sharp
    d. unmyelinated; dull

13. Mice that lack receptors for substance P appear to experience
    a. no pain.
    b. only mild pain.
    c. only intense pain.
    d. moderate pain all of the time.

14. Transcutaneous electrical nerve stimulation relieves pain because
    a. it destroys the pain neurons in a particular area.
    b. it activates dull pain neurons rather than sharp pain neurons.
    c. it stimulates large diameter sensory neurons that inhibit pain neurons.
    d. none of the above.

15. Naloxone is an antagonist for
    a. endorphins.
    b. morphine.
    c. both endorphins and morphine.
    d. neither endorphin nor morphine.

16. Endorphins are LEAST likely to be released in response to which of the following?
    a. acupuncture
    b. vaginal stimulation
    c. placebo
    d. escapable shock

17. A mechanism by which endorphins are thought to relieve pain is through the _____
inhibition of substance P in the _____.
    a. presynaptic; spinal cord
    b. postsynaptic; spinal cord
    c. presynaptic; periaqueductal gray
    d. postsynaptic; periaqueductal gray

18. Which of the following statements regarding pain relief is FALSE?
    a. The analgesia experienced from acupuncture needles placed near the source of pain is not
       opiate based.
    b. Hypnotic analgesia is blocked by naloxone.
    c. An analgesic drug derived from frogs is as effective as morphine.
    d. Stimulation of some areas of the PAG produce non-opiate analgesic effects.

19. Phantom pain
    a. occurs only in limbs that have been amputated.
    b. appears to be a result of damage to the peripheral nerves.
    c. is probably the result of neural reorganization in the cortex.
    d. has no physiological basis.

20. The stomach and intestines are controlled by
    a. smooth muscle.
    b. skeletal muscle.
    c. striated muscle.
    d. cardiac muscle.

21. Which of the following muscles probably has the MOST individual muscles cells controlled by a single motor neuron?
    a. Triceps muscle
    b. Eye muscle
    c. Index finger muscle
    d. Tongue muscle

22. Which of the following statements regarding antagonistic muscle pairs is FALSE?
    a. Each muscle has opposing effects on a limb.
    b. Both muscles may be contracted simultaneously.
    c. All skeletal muscles are antagonistically paired.
    d. Coordination of antagonistic muscles is controlled by the spinal cord.

23. Muscle tension (extent of contraction) is detected by
    a. Golgi tendon organs.
    b. muscle spindles.
    c. Lewi bodies.
    d. a and b.
    e. a, b, and c.

24. Central pattern generators
    a. are found in lower animals, but not in humans.
    b. are present in young infants, but adults have outgrown them.
    c. work even when the spinal cord is severed.
    d. none of the above.

25. In producing movement, the last cortical area to be activated is the
    a. premotor area.
    b. association cortex.
    c. supplementary motor cortex.
    d. primary motor cortex.

26. The "memory" of a stimulus used in the delayed match-to-sample task seems to be held in the
    a. primary motor cortex.
    b. supplementary motor cortex.
    c. premotor cortex.
    d. prefrontal cortex.

27. Selection of arm movement needed for reaching a specific target seems to occur in the
    a. primary motor cortex.
    b. supplementary motor cortex.
    c. premotor cortex.
    d. prefrontal cortex.

28. Sequences of movements, such as those involved in typing on a computer keyboard, are coordinated by cells in the
    a. primary motor cortex.
    b. supplementary motor cortex.
    c. premotor cortex.
    d. prefrontal cortex.

29. The actual execution of a movement is triggered by activity in the
    a. primary motor cortex.
    b. supplementary motor cortex.
    c. premotor cortex.
    d. prefrontal cortex.

30. Which brain areas contribute to the smoothness of movement?
    a. cerebellum and premotor cortex
    b. supplementary motor cortex and basal ganglia
    c. prefrontal cortex and premotor cortex
    d. cerebellum and basal ganglia

31. Which of the following structures is NOT part of the basal ganglia?
    a. caudate nucleus
    b. globus pallidus
    c. thalamus
    d. putamen

32. The cerebellum is involved in
    a. the order and timing of complex movements.
    b. the learning of motor skills.
    c. judging the speed of objects.
    d. a and b.
    e. a, b, and c.

33. Parkinson's disease results from a loss of _____ neurons originating in the
    _____.
    a. dopaminergic; striatum
    b. dopaminergic; substantia nigra
    c. cholinergic; striatum
    d. cholinergic; substantia nigra

34. Which of the following proteins forms Lewy bodies?
    a. huntingtin
    b. acetylcholinesterase
    c. α-synuclein
    d. all of the above

35. Currently, which of the following treatments for Parkinson's disease has been shown to have the fewest side effects?
    a. brain stimulation
    b. brain lesions
    c. l-dopa
    d. fetal tissue transplant

36. Which of the following statements is/are true of Huntington's disease but not Parkinson's disease?
    a. It is a degenerative disease, becoming progressively worse over time.
    b. Cognitive and emotional deficits always occur.
    c. Researchers know which genes are involved and how they work.
    d. a and b
    e. b and c

37. What form of treatment holds promise for Huntington's disease?
    a. fetal tissue transplant
    b. drug therapy
    c. brain stimulation
    d. brain lesion

38. People with myasthenia gravis have fewer _____ receptors.
    a. dopamine
    b. serotonin
    c. endorphin
    d. acetylcholine

39. Myasthenia gravis is MOST EFFECTIVELY treated by
    a. acetylcholinesterase inhibitors.
    b. thymectomy.
    c. fetal tissue transplant.
    d. brain stimulation.

40. Multiple sclerosis involves
    a. loss of myelin in the central nervous system.
    b. loss of myelin in the peripheral nervous system.
    c. loss of myelin in both the central and peripheral nervous systems.
    d. none of the above.

Answers & Explanations

Guided Review

1. hearing
2. movement
3. Proprioception
4. vestibular
5. semicircular canals
6. hair
7. utricle
8. otoliths
9. position or orientation
10. warmth
11. pain
12. touch
13. temperature
14. cold
15. dermatome
16. thalamus
17. opposite
18. sensitivity
19. column
20. receptive fields
21. hierarchical
22. S-I
23. secondary somatosensory
24. posterior parietal
25. frontal
26. thermal
27. mechanical
28. polymodal
29. A-delta
30. dull
31. substance P
32. gate control
33. electrical nerve stimulation
34. opiate
35. Pert and Snyder

36. endorphins
37. placebo
38. periaqueductal gray
39. substance P
40. nicotine
41. phantom
42. 70
43. thalamus
44. facial
45. skeletal
46. neuromuscular
47. acetylcholine
48. Tendons
49. antagonistically
50. spinal
51. patellar
52. stretch
53. motor
54. contract
55. Golgi tendon organs
56. movement
57. prefrontal
58. delayed match-to-sample
59. premotor
60. supplementary motor area
61. primary motor
62. column
63. cerebellum
64. putamen
65. non-motor
66. substantia nigra
67. 5-10
68. Lewy bodies
69. toxins
70. 80
71. 50
72. Caffeine
73. levadopa
74. globus pallidus
75. striatum
76. huntingtin
77. acetylcholine
78. acetylcholinesterase
79. thymus
80. Multiple sclerosis
81. immune system

Short Answer & Essay

1. When we accelerate, the increase in speed displaces the gelatinous masses inside the vestibular organs, causing the hair cells to bend and change their rate of firing. Once we reach a stable speed, the jelly returns to normal, and the hair cells are no longer affected by its displacement, so we do not notice movement.

2. Meissner's corpuscles and Merkel's disks are located near the surface of the skin, and they can detect texture, fine detail, and movement of objects. Pacinian corpuscles and Ruffini endings are located deeper, and because they detect stretching of the skin, they can detect the shape of objects that are grasped.

3. The primary visual and somatosensory areas are similar in the following ways: they contain a map of their respective receptive fields (the body and the retina, respectively); their cells are organized into columns, within which cells respond to the same stimuli and have the same receptive fields; the receptive fields of some of the cells are arranged with an excitatory center and inhibitory surround; processing is hierarchical, with certain subareas of the somatosensory cortex passing information along to other areas (similar to the simple → complex cell arrangement in the visual cortex); and both systems contain cells which are feature detectors.

4. Sharp pain is encoded along large diameter A-delta fibers; as a result, these pain messages travel to the brain quickly. They signal the onset of a painful stimulus, and probably are instrumental in triggering a withdrawal or avoidance response (such as pulling your hand away from a hot burner). Dull pain is encoded along smaller diameter C fibers, and this message travels more slowly, but the pain is more persistent. Dull pain probably reminds us that we have been injured, and may prevent further injury and also motivate us to seek treatment.

5. They discovered the receptors by using naloxone, an opiate antagonist. They hypothesized that this chemical works by binding to opiate receptors. In order to provide evidence for such receptors, they used radioactive naloxone. After administering it to tissue samples, they were able to measure the presence of the radioactive material because the naloxone was bound to the receptors.

6. It is believed that when pain messages are received in the PAG, endorphins are released onto neurons which project down the spinal cord and subsequently inhibit the neurons responsible for releasing substance P.

7. When a limb is amputated or no longer sends sensory input to the brain because of a spinal cord injury, the area of the somatosensory cortex served by that limb may be "taken over" by neurons from adjacent areas.

8. When the ratio of motor neurons to muscles cells is low, as in the case of eye muscles, it allows for a great deal more precision of movement than when the ration is high, as in the biceps muscle.

9. These networks contain "instructions" for producing rhythmic movements such as walking. When the spinal cord is severed, no cortical control of the pattern generators exists. There is some evidence that they can be stimulated without cortical control, so it might be possible to artificially stimulate them, thus allowing people to walk.

10. In this task, the subject is shown a stimulus, and then the stimulus is removed. After a delay, two stimuli are shown, the original and another one. At this point, the subject must select the original in order to receive reinforcement. This requires remembering the original stimulus. It turns out that during the initial presentation and the delay period, specific cells in the prefrontal cortex become active, suggesting that they are encoding and "holding" the stimulus in memory. When the opportunity for reinforcement occurs, additional cells become active, which may signal the premotor areas about which stimulus to select.

11. Activity in the prefrontal and premotor cortex occurs prior to the onset of movement, whereas activity in the primary motor cortex corresponds with movement. This suggests that although the prefrontal and premotor areas are involved in planning movements, the primary motor cortex initiates signals to the motor neurons themselves.

12. The genetic basis of Huntington's disease is much clearer. There seems to be a single gene involved, and anyone with that gene will develop the disease (although the timing of onset depends on the number of extra repetitions of base pairs). The genetic basis of Parkinson's is not well understood. It seems to be familial (inherited) in only a minority of cases. In familial PD, at least three different genes may be involved. In some PD cases, individuals may inherit a reduced capacity for metabolizing toxins that may cause PD. In these cases, exposure to the toxins is probably necessary in order for the disease to develop, so both environment and genetics are important.

13. Myasthenia gravis is often the result of tumors of the thymus gland, which produces the antibodies that are believed to affect ACh receptors. In most cases, removal of the thymus provides near-complete recovery.

Post-Test

All page references in this section pertain to the textbook.

1. a. Wrong; because its receptors are located only in the head, this receives information about what is happening to the head.
    b. Wrong; this system receives information about touch, warmth, cold, and pain.
    c. **Correct**; see p. 283.
    d. Wrong

2. a.   Wrong; b is also correct.
    b.   Wrong; a is also correct.
    c.   Wrong; there are no otoliths in the semicircular canals.
    d.   Correct; see p. 284.
    e.   Wrong

3. a.   Wrong; b and c are also correct.
    b.   Wrong; a and c are also correct.
    c.   Wrong; a and b are also correct.
    d.   Wrong
    e.   Correct; hair cells are the receptors for all of the vestibular organs.

4. a.   Wrong; this sense receives information about position of the limbs and muscle tension, which are internal stimuli.
    b.   Wrong; this sense receives information about the position and acceleration of the head.
    c.   Correct; this sense receives information about objects, as well as internal events (such as skin temperature).
    d.   Wrong
    e.   Wrong

5. a.   Wrong; although they are sensitive to touch, they are located deep under the skin surface. Meissner's corpuscles and Merkel's disks are located near the skin surface.
    b.   Correct; see p. 285.
    c.   Wrong; although they are near the surface, they are not sensitive to temperature.
    d.   Wrong

6. a.   Wrong; this area is very sensitive, as can be seen from Figure 10.5 on p. 287.
    b.   Correct; of all the areas listed, this one contains the fewest skin receptors.
    c.   Wrong; see Figure 10.5
    d.   Wrong; see Figure 10.5

7. a.   Wrong
    b.   Wrong
    c.   Correct; warmth receptors do not respond to temperatures above 50 degrees C. All of the other statements are true.
    d.   Wrong

8. **a.   Correct**; see p. 286.
    b.   Wrong; this is not a term used in the textbook.
    c.   Wrong; a cupula is a gelatinous mass found in the semicircular canals.
    d.   Wrong; Ruffini endings are touch receptors, and there is no mention of a "Ruffini area."

9. a.   Wrong; although most of it projects to the left hemisphere, a small amount goes to the right.
    b.   Wrong
    c.   Wrong
    d.   Correct; see p. 286.

10. **a.   Correct**; see Figure 10.4 on p. 287.
    b.   Wrong; this is where the primary motor cortex is located.
    c.   Wrong; this separates the motor and somatosensory cortices.
    d.   Wrong; this area is not involved in somatosensation.

242

11. a. Wrong; these receptors only respond to extreme temperatures.
    b. Wrong; these receptors only respond to pressure.
    c. **Correct**; these receptors respond to temperature, pressure, and injury-related chemicals.
    d. Wrong
    e. Wrong

12. **a.** **Correct**; see p. 289.
    b. Wrong; while they are myelinated, they are not associated with dull pain. C fibers are associated with dull pain.
    c. Wrong
    d. Wrong

13. a. Wrong
    b. **Correct**; see p. 289.
    c. Wrong
    d. Wrong

14. a. Wrong; this is not mentioned in the text.
    b. Wrong; this is not mentioned in the text.
    c. **Correct**; see p. 290.
    d. Wrong

15. a. Wrong; b is also correct.
    b. Wrong; a is also correct.
    c. **Correct**; morphine is an endorphin agonist, and naloxone will block the receptor.
    d. Wrong

16. a. Wrong
    b. Wrong
    c. Wrong
    d. **Correct**; rats exposed to escapable shock were less pain tolerant than those exposed to unavoidable shock, suggesting that endorphins were less likely to be released when the pain could motivate an escape response. All of the other choices seem to involve an increase in the release of endorphins.

17. **a.** **Correct**; see p. 291.
    b. Wrong; although inhibition occurs in the spinal cord, the inhibition is presynaptic.
    c. Wrong; although endorphins inhibit substance P presynaptically, this occurs in the spinal cord (although endorphins are released in the PAG, triggering the pain-inhibition response).
    d. Wrong

18. a. Wrong; naloxone does not block analgesia from acupuncture needles placed near the site of pain, indicating that this is not an endorphin response.
    b. **Correct**; see p. 292. All of the other choices are true.
    c. Wrong; ABT-594 does seem to be as effective as morphine, although it is not related at all.
    d. Wrong; this is true.

19. a.   Wrong; people with severed spinal cords who cannot otherwise feel sensations from the limbs may experience phantom pain.
    b.   Wrong; this has not been supported.
    c.   Correct; based on the German study discussed in the book, this is the most likely explanation.
    d.   Wrong

20. **a.   Correct**; see p. 295.
    b.   Wrong; these move the limbs and other body parts, and are under voluntary control.
    c.   Wrong; this is another term for "skeletal" muscles.
    d.   Wrong; this muscle is specific to the heart.

21. **a.   Correct**; the text states that a single motor neuron controls about 100 biceps muscle cells. Because the biceps and triceps muscles are antagonistically paired, it is logical to conclude that the triceps muscles receives about the same amount of neural control.
    b.   Wrong; the text states that a single motor neuron controls only about 3 eye muscle cells.
    c.   Wrong; based on the degree of precision of movement that the index finger displays, as well as the size of area of representation in the primary motor cortex (see Figure 10.18 on p. 298), it is logical to assume that there is greater enervation of muscles for the index finger than the triceps muscle.
    d.   Wrong; the reasoning is similar to choice c; see Figure 10.18.

22. a.   Wrong; this is true.
    b.   Wrong; this is true.
    c.   Correct; this is not stated or implied in the text, because skeletal muscles are also found on areas of the body other than limbs.
    d.   Wrong; this is true.

23. **a.   Correct**; see p. 296.
    b.   Wrong; these determine the amount of stretching a muscle is undergoing.
    c.   Wrong; these are deposits found in the brains of people with Parkinson's disease.
    d.   Wrong
    e.   Wrong

24. a.   Wrong; the text states that humans have them (as well as other animals).
    b.   Wrong; they are present, and can be elicited in people with spinal cord injury who cannot otherwise control their legs.
    c.   Correct; given the right stimulation (such as being placed on a treadmill), they appear to work in cats whose spinal cords have been severed, and in human adults with spinal cord injuries.
    d.   Wrong

25. a.   Wrong; activity in this area precedes activity in the primary motor cortex.
    b.   Wrong; activity in this area precedes activity in the primary motor cortex.
    c.   Wrong; activity in this area precedes activity in the primary motor cortex.
    d.   Correct; see p. 299.

26. a.   Wrong
    b.   Wrong
    c.   Wrong
    d.   Correct; see p. 297.

27. a. Wrong
    b. Wrong
    c. Correct; see p. 298.
    d. Wrong

28. a. Wrong
    b. Correct; see pp. 298-299.
    c. Wrong
    d. Wrong

29. **a. Correct**; see p. 299.
    b. Wrong; this area is active prior to movement.
    c. Wrong; this area is active prior to movement.
    d. Wrong; this area is active prior to movement.

30. a. Wrong; the cerebellum, but not the premotor cortex, is involved.
    b. Wrong; the basal ganglia, but not the supplementary motor cortex, is involved.
    c. Wrong
    d. Correct; see p. 299.

31. a. Wrong; this is part of the basal ganglia.
    b. Wrong; this is part of the basal ganglia.
    c. Correct; see Figure 10.20 on p. 300.
    d. Wrong; this is part of the basal ganglia.

32. a. Wrong; b and c area also correct.
    b. Wrong; a and c are also correct.
    c. Wrong; a and b are also correct.
    d. Wrong
    e. Correct; see pp. 300-301.

33. a. Wrong; although dopaminergic neurons are involved, these originate in the substantia nigra and project to the striatum.
    b. Correct; see p. 301.
    c. Wrong
    d. Wrong; cholinergic neurons are not mentioned as being involved.

34. a. Wrong; this is the protein implicated in Huntington's disease, which is not mentioned as being associated with Lewy bodies.
    b. Wrong; this is an enzyme that breaks down acetylcholine, and drugs that inhibit are sometimes given for temporary relief of myasthenia gravis.
    c. Correct; this is one of the proteins implicated in Parkinson's disease, in which Lewy bodies are involved.
    d. Wrong

35. **a. Correct**; however, it is not yet known if there are any long-term problems with this treatment.
    b. Wrong; the text indicates that there are problems with this form of treatment (see p. 302).
    c. Wrong; this has side effects, and because more of it is required over time, the longer a person takes it, the worse they become.
    d. Wrong; not only is it less effective, it also has been associated with some of the same side effects as the drugs; however, only a very small number of people have undergone this procedure.

36. a.   Wrong; this is true of both Huntington's and Parkinson's.
    b.   Wrong; c is also true.
    c.   Wrong; b is also true.
    d.   Wrong
    e.   Correct; although cognitive and emotional deficits occur sometimes with PD, they always do with HD. Furthermore, the gene responsible for HD has been identified, whereas researchers are not sure what the genetic basis of PD is (there may be more than one gene involved, and "inheritance" of the disease is not straightforward, whereas in HD if someone gets the gene, they will develop the disease).

37. **a.   Correct**; this is the only form of therapy for HD mentioned in the book, and preliminary results suggest it may work.
    b.   Wrong
    c.   Wrong
    d.   Wrong

38. a.   Wrong
    b.   Wrong
    c.   Wrong
    d.   Correct; see p. 304.

39. a.   Wrong; these produce temporary results, but thymectomy is a more permanent solution.
    b.   Correct; see p. 304.
    c.   Wrong; this is not mentioned as a treatment for MG.
    d.   Wrong; this is not mentioned as a treatment for MG.

40. **a.   Correct**; see p. 304.
    b.   Wrong; loss of PNS myelin is not mentioned in the text. Furthermore, because damage to the PNS can often be repaired, it is likely that loss of PNS myelin would not be permanent.
    c.   Wrong
    d.   Wrong

Chapter 11: Learning and Memory

Chapter Outline and Learning Objectives

As you read the chapter, use these learning objectives to guide your studying. You should be able to define the key terms from the text, which are shown in boldface type below.

1) Learning as the Storage of Memories
   - What is the importance of long-term storage of information?

   a) Amnesia: The Failure of Storage or Retrieval
      - Distinguish between **anterograde** and **retrograde amnesia**.

      - What structures in the medial temporal lobe seem to be involved in memory? What types of memory deficits does damage to them produce?

   b) Mechanisms of Consolidation and Retrieval
      - Define **consolidation** and **retrieval**. What events can disrupt consolidation?

      - Describe the evidence from human EEG and PET studies that indicate the hippocampus plays a role in memory consolidation and retrieval.

      - Describe the evidence from animal studies that the hippocampus plays a role in memory consolidation and retrieval.

      - How does the role of the hippocampus in memory retrieval change over time?

      - What role does the prefrontal area seem to play in memory retrieval?

   c) Where Memories are Stored
      - Does the hippocampus hold stored memories? If not, what is its role in memory?

      - Where are memories stored?

   d) Two Kinds of Learning
      - Distinguish between **declarative** and **non-declarative memory**. How does HM's case differentiate between the two?

- What is the evidence from animal studies that declarative and non-declarative memory involve different brain areas?

- Which type of learning is disrupted in Parkinson's and Huntington's disease, and why?

- What role does the amygdala appear to play in memory, particularly memory related to emotion? How does stimulation of the amygdala affect non-emotional learning?

e) Working Memory
  - What is the function of **working memory**?

  - What brain areas are involved in working memory? Why is the prefrontal cortex considered to be the most important?

  - Why is the prefrontal cortex considered to be a "central executive" with respect to learning tasks?

2) Brain Changes in Learning
  - Why is learning considered to be a form of neural plasticity?

a) Long-Term Potentiation
  - What is **long-term potentiation**? How is it produced experimentally?

  - How do LTP, **ALTP**, **LTD**, and **ALTD** supposedly account for different elements of learning (e.g. classical conditioning and extinction)?

  - Why do researchers believe that LTD can block LTP? What are the potential advantages of this mechanism?

  - What are theta rhythms? Why are they believed to be important in learning?

b) Synaptic Changes
  - How do AMPA and NMDA receptors respond to glutamate released during LTP stimulation? What postsynaptic changes occur as a result of NMDA receptor activity?

  - What role does NO play in LTP?

- What structural changes occur as a result of LTP stimulation?

- What evidence is there that in humans, learning to navigate a complex environment changes the gross structure of the brain?

c) The Role of LTP in Learning
- What evidence exists that reducing LTP impairs learning? That enhancing LTP facilitates learning?

- How are LTP and LTD compatible with neural network models of memory?

- What are the problems with the LTP model of learning?

d) Consolidation Revisited
- What is the relationship between α-CaMKII and learning? How do mice with different genes for this enzyme differ in terms of their ability to learn, particularly with respect to hippocampal versus cortical learning?

- What evidence is there that sleep contributes to memory consolidation? What is the role of the hippocampus in this process?

- What is meant by "reconstructed" memory? What evidence is there that reconsolidation occurs after a memory has been retrieved?

3) Disorders of Learning
a) Aging
- What are some possible reasons why people who remain mentally active throughout adulthood are less likely to suffer from losses of cognitive abilities in late adulthood?

- What mechanisms are currently believed to be responsible for loss of cognitive abilities in the elderly?

- What is the significance of cell loss in the basal forebrain region?

- How do the elderly perform on the safe/risky gambling task?

b) Alzheimer's Disease
- What are the characteristics of Alzheimer's disease? How prevalent is it in older adults?

i) The Diseased Brain: Plaques and Tangles
- How are **plaques** and **neurofibrillary tangles** thought to contribute to AD?

- What specific brain areas are damaged in AD? How may these damaged areas account for the behavioral symptoms of AD?

ii) Alzheimer's and Heredity
- What do AD and Down syndrome have in common?

- Discuss the genetic basis of AD.

iii) Treatment of Alzheimer's Disease
- What is the role of acetylcholine in AD? What types of drugs may improve cholinergic functioning?

- What other types of drugs may be useful for treating AD?

- What are the social and financial implications of our aging population?

- Discuss immunization against AD and genetic treatment.

- Why is it important to detect AD early on? How might this be done?

c) Korsakoff's Syndrome
- What causes Korsakoff's syndrome? Which brain areas are affected?

- What types of memory loss do people with Korsakoff's exhibit?

- What is **confabulation**? What type of abnormal brain activity is it related to? What does it suggest about our experiences of current reality versus memories?

Learning as the Storage of Memories

Summary and Guided Review

After studying this section in the text, fill in the blanks of the following summary. The answers are found on p. 263.

In order to be useful for future behavior, experiences must be somehow stored within the nervous system; without _____ (1), we would be capable of only very simple forms of behavior. This point is demonstrated by the case of HM described in the introduction to the chapter. HM, who underwent surgery on his _____ (2) lobes to reduce his debilitating seizures, suffered from both anterograde and retrograde _____ (3). Consequently, he had great difficulty forming new memories, as well as remembering past events. Because of the extent of damage to HM's brain, it is not known exactly which structures were responsible for his amnesia, although the _____ (4) and associated areas were certainly involved. Studies of other individuals with temporal lobe damage suggest that bilateral damage to hippocampal area _____ (5) produces moderate anterograde amnesia and minimal retrograde amnesia. Severe _____ (6) amnesia results from damage to the entire hippocampus, and severe retrograde amnesia occurs if the hippocampal _____ (7) is damaged as well.

Until information stored in memory undergoes _____ (8), which is the process of forming a permanent physical representation, it is subject to disruption. New memories are easily disrupted, and even old memories may be lost as a result of physiological trauma. Evidence from studies using EEG evoked potential measurements suggests that consolidation involves heightened activity in the hippocampus and _____ (9) gyrus. _____ (10), the process by which stored memories are accessed, also appears to involve the hippocampus. In rats, when a _____ (11)-blocking drug, which disables the hippocampus, is administered during or a few days after training, consolidation is disrupted; if the drug is administered during testing, retrieval is disrupted as well. However, because very old memories are not affected by hippocampal damage, there must be some other mechanism responsible for maintaining and retrieving them; some research suggests that the _____ (12) is involved in this.

The hippocampus is not the actual storage site of memories. Researchers believe that the hippocampus, through its connections with various cortical areas, controls the consolidation process, but that memories themselves are stored in the areas of the _____ (13) where specific types of information are processed.

The fact that HM displayed some forms of _____ (14) without being consciously aware of his newly acquired skills suggests that there are at least two different forms of memory within the brain. _____ (15) memory refers to information about which we can verbalize, whereas non-declarative memory refers to _____ (16), skills, _____ (17) learning, and simple conditioning, which are not verbalized. Studies with rats demonstrate that different brain areas are involved in each form of memory; declarative memory is disrupted by damage to the _____ (18), whereas non-declarative or _____ (19) memory is disrupted by damage to the _____ (20). In humans, this latter form of learning is disrupted in people with _____ (21) and Huntington's diseases. The _____ (22) seems to be involved in conditioning of emotional responses; a subject with bilateral amygdala damage failed to show a conditioned response when a loud noise was paired with a blue slide. The amygdala's role in learning may explain why a strong _____ (23) experience affects our later behavior, even if we don't explicitly recall the experience. Furthermore, activity in the amygdala may enhance _____ (24) learning, through its connections with the hippocampus.

Both new and old information are held temporarily in _____ _____ (25) while processing occurs; this is somewhat similar to a computer's RAM, although the capacity of working memory is very small. The neurological basis of working memory can be studied using the delayed _____-_____-_____ (26) task. Following presentation and removal of a stimulus, specific cells in the _____ _____ (27) cortex increase their rate of firing; the exact location of cells depends on the color or shape of the target stimulus. However, activity in the _____ (28) cortex seems to be more important. In this area, specific cells respond to target stimuli, and distracting stimuli do not disrupt activity. Damage to this area results in _____ (29) of the delayed match-to-sample task. The prefrontal cortex seems to be responsible for managing information in working memory in executing decisions and actions, rather than merely serving as a storage facility for _____ (30).

Short Answer & Essay Questions

Answer the following questions. See pp. 263-264 for sample answers.

1. Distinguish between anterograde and retrograde amnesia. Using HM's case, give one example of each form.

2. Riedel and colleagues studied the role of the hippocampus in learning in rats by placing them in a water maze. The rats could escape from the water by learning the location of a platform. How were the researchers able to show that impairment of the hippocampus can disrupt both consolidation and retrieval?

3. Distinguish between declarative and non-declarative memory.

4. What did Bechara and colleagues discover about the different roles of the hippocampus and the amygdala in learning?

Brain Changes in Learning

Summary & Guided Review

After studying this section in the text, fill in the blanks of the following summary. The answers are found on p. 263.

Many researchers believe that the physiological mechanism that underlies learning is an increase in synapse strength that occurs as a result of repeated _____ (31) of postsynaptic neurons by presynaptic neurons. This mechanism, known as _____ -

_____ _____ (32), is similar to the neural plasticity exhibited by neurons early in development as synapses are being formed, and has been observed in the

_____ (33) as well as the visual, auditory, and motor cortex. Compared to baseline rates of firing, after repeated presynaptic stimulation, _____ (34) neurons will show a stronger response when stimulated. This change may last briefly or for several months. LTP and several related mechanisms appear to explain forms of learning such as classical conditioning and

_____ (35). Furthermore, long-term depression, the result of _____ -

_____ (36) stimulation from a presynaptic neuron, can inhibit LTP, and may be an important mechanism for regulating memory. LTP is enhanced when presynaptic stimulation coincides with hippocampal _____ _____ (37) activity, EEG activity that occurs when an animal encounters _____ (38) stimuli. When hippocampal theta rhythms were suppressed in rats, performance on a choice task was impaired. This suggests that the hippocampus plays an _____ (39) role in managing working memory.

The precise changes that account for LTP are beginning to be understood. For example, when presynaptic neurons release _____ (40), at first only the AMPA receptors are activated; this partially depolarizes the postsynaptic membrane, which results in activation of the

_____ (41) receptors, further depolarizing the membrane and increasing the likelihood of the cell firing. Additionally, the postsynaptic neuron seems to facilitate presynaptic stimulation via the release of _____ _____ (42). Changes in gene activity also produce dendritic structural changes, such as an increase in the number of _____ (43) receptors and proliferation of dendritic _____ (44). These changes are long term, and they may explain why London cabbies who memorize the layout of the city exhibit greater brain _____ (45) in part of the hippocampus.

The artificial methods used to produce LTP only provide indirect evidence of LTP's role in learning. More direct evidence comes from a study in which mice with fewer _____ (46) receptors showed reduced hippocampal LTP and impaired _____ (47). In another study, _____ (48), drugs that enhance the response of AMPA receptors, were shown to facilitate learning. However, it should not be assumed that a memory is _____ (49) in the connection between two neurons. It is more likely that a _____ (50) of neurons is involved, much like the neural net model discussed in Chapter 2. A major problem with the assumption that LTP represents learning is that experimentally produced LTP is not _____ (51), whereas learning often is. Clearly there is more to learning than just LTP in the hippocampus.

Although there is ample evidence that memory consolidation depends on the hippocampus, long-term and permanent storage of information involves the _____ (52). The enzyme _____ (53) appears to be involved in transferring information from the hippocampus to the cortex. Mice with very low levels of this enzyme show no _____ (54) LTP and no learning, whereas mice with moderate amounts show hippocampal, but not _____ (55), LTP. Mice in this group quickly forget tasks that they have learned. There is evidence that some transfer of information occurs during _____ (56). In both humans and other animals, certain types of learning are enhanced by sleep; and in rats, during sleep the _____ (57) repeats neural firing sequences that occurred while they were actively exploring.

Finally, it is important to understand that although memories may be long-lasting, they are subject to change. Retrieved memories may be _____ (58) (for example by being blended with other memories). In rats, it has been shown that _____ (59), may be disrupted by giving an antibiotic that interferes with protein synthesis.

Short Answer & Essay Questions

Answer the following questions. See p. 264 for sample answers.

5. How does LTP resemble the prenatal and postnatal mechanism for establishing synapses?

6. What is LTD? Why is it thought to be important for learning?

7. What role does NO play in LTP?

8. What is the problem with LTP as an explanation for learning?

9. It is 7:00 pm on Tuesday, and your roommate has an exam in her first class tomorrow at 8:00 am. She is not sure if it would be better to spend the next three hours studying for the exam and go to bed around 10:30 pm, or not study tonight, go to bed at 9:00 pm, and then get up around 5:00 am to study. Based on what the book says about the role of sleep in learning, what advice would you offer your roommate?

10. At the age of 18, Winona witnessed a bank robbery involving two gunmen wearing masks. Two years later, she is asked to testify at a trial of two people suspected of committing the crime. Immediately following the event, she had been extensively interviewed by the police, and has thought about it frequently since then. Now, while on the witness stand, she recalls information about the suspects that she did not include in her earlier report. For example, she now claims that she saw the hair color of one of the defendants because the mask did not completely cover his head, whereas in her initial statement, she could not recall having seen either robber's hair. The defense attorney questions the accuracy of her memory for these details, but she insists that she vividly remembers them. Based on what the book says about reconstructive memory, should the jury take her statements at face value? Why or why not?

Disorders of Learning

Summary and Guided Review

After studying this section in the text, fill in the blanks of the following summary. The answers are found on p. 263.

Because the physiological mechanisms behind learning and memory are so complex, they are especially vulnerable to damage, through injury, _____ (60), and even aging, which affects other bodily organs and systems as well. Until recently, it was believed that loss of memory and cognitive skills were a natural consequence of _____ (61); however, some studies indicate that older adults who maintain an active mental life are less likely to show such deficits. Another misconception is that when memory loss does occur, it results from cell loss, particularly in the cortex and the _____ (62). What does seem to happen is that as animals age the hippocampus loses synapses and _____ (63) receptors, which probably leads to a reduced capacity for _____ (64) and therefore learning. In addition, reduced activity in the _____ (65) cortex, which is linked to the hippocampus, and loss of _____ (66) are also thought to be involved. Cell loss in the _____ _____ (67) region may contribute to memory deficits in both _____ (68) disease and normal aging, and _____ (69) lobe deficits may be present in many elderly as well.

_____ (70) refers to the loss of memory and cognitive abilities in the elderly. Alzheimer's disease (AD), in which the brain progressively deteriorates, is a form of dementia. In the early stages, _____ (71) memory is impaired, a symptom that becomes worse over time. Other cognitive deficits, such as loss of reasoning, occur; behavioral problems may occur as well. AD is strongly associated with aging; whereas _____ (72) % of 65-year-olds have it, nearly half of those over _____ (73) have it.

The brains of people with AD contain _____ _____ (74), which interfere with neuron functioning, and _____ (75) tangles; both are associated with cell death. Over time, large deficits in brain tissue can be observed in the temporal lobes, where they disrupt _____ (76) connections, in the frontal lobes, and sometimes in the visual areas of the brain. Damage to these areas are implicated in the cognitive and behavioral symptoms of AD.

Another disorder involving plaques and tangles is _____ _____ (77), which as caused by an extra chromosome 21. This chromosome contains a gene that contributes to _____ (78) protein, and mice with mutations of this gene develop deficits similar to those observed in AD. _____ (79) other genes involved in AD have been identified, and there are probably more. The environment seems to have little effect on the development of AD.

There are several different forms of drugs that are used to treat AD, although none of them provides a cure. _____ (80) is an important CNS neurotransmitter for learning and memory, and loss of cholinergic neurons is implicated in AD.

_____ (81) inhibiting drugs such as tacrine and donepezil are currently used to relieve cognitive and behavioral symptoms in mild and _____ (82) cases of AD. _____ (83), anticholesterol drugs, nonsteroidal anti-inflammatory drugs, and _____ _____ (84) hold some promise for treating AD. Estrogen therapy may protect some _____ (85) from developing AD. Because of the prevalence of AD among the elderly, and because this segment of the population will _____ (86), delaying or preventing AD is an important social issue. _____ (87) that reduce or reverse the accumulation of plaques are being tested in animals. Manipulating the genes responsible for nerve growth _____ (88) restores cholinergic functioning in aged monkeys. If AD can be detected early, even prior to the onset of symptoms, for example by using _____ _____ (89) techniques, then treatment efforts may be more successful.

Thiamine deficiency, a result of the _____ (90) associated with alcohol abuse, is the cause of _____ _____ (91); this degenerative disorder results in anterograde and retrograde amnesia due to damage to the _____ (92) bodies, medial thalamic area, and the _____ (93) lobes. In the early stages, _____ (94) can relieve the symptoms, but not reverse the damage. Korsakoff's patients often exhibit _____ (95), or the fabrication of stories, probably as an attempt to fill in information they can no longer recall. Confabulation seems to be related to impaired _____ (96) lobe activity, rendering patients unable to distinguish current reality and memories of prior events.

Short Answer & Essay Questions

Answer the following questions. See pp. 264-265 for sample answers.

11. Why is memory loss in the elderly no longer considered to be an inevitable consequence of the aging process?

12. Briefly describe five possible reasons for age-related memory loss (not including Alzheimer's).

13. In their search for a genetic basis of Alzheimer's disease, why did researchers focus on Chromosome 21?

14. What treatments for AD are most commonly used? What treatments may be widely available in the future?

15. What is confabulation? Give an example.

Post-Test

Use these multiple-choice questions to check your understanding of the chapter. The answers, along with explanations, are found beginning on p. 265.

1. Which of the following was NOT a result of HM's surgery?
    a. lowered IQ
    b. anterograde amnesia
    c. retrograde amnesia
    d. relief from seizures

2. Which of the following deficits is an example of anterograde amnesia?
    a. being unable to recall events just prior to brain injury
    b. being unable to recall events following brain injury
    c. being unable to recall events many years prior to brain injury
    d. none of the above

3. Brain damage that is limited to hippocampal area CA1 results in
    a. moderate anterograde amnesia and profound retrograde amnesia.
    b. moderate anterograde amnesia and minimal retrograde amnesia.
    c. profound anterograde amnesia and profound retrograde amnesia.
    d. profound anterograde amnesia and minimal retrograde amnesia.

4. Consolidation is the process of
    a. accessing stored information.
    b. altering memories during retrieval.
    c. fabricating information missing from memory.
    d. making memories long-lasting or permanent.

5. The hippocampus plays a role in
    a. consolidation.
    b. retrieval
    c. both consolidation and retrieval.
    d. neither consolidation nor retrieval.

6. Over 25 days of being tested for retention of a spatial discrimination task, researchers found that mice showed
    a. increased activity in the hippocampus and increased activity in the cortex.
    b. increased activity in the hippocampus and decreased activity in the cortex.
    c. decreased activity in the hippocampus and increased activity in the cortex.
    d. decreased activity in the hippocampus and decreased activity in the cortex.

7. Effortful attempts at retrieval are associated with increased activity in
    a. the prefrontal area.
    b. the hippocampus.
    c. both the prefrontal area and the hippocampus.
    d. neither the prefrontal area nor the hippocampus.

8. Researchers believe that memories are stored
    a. in the hippocampus.
    b. in a single storage area of the cortex.
    c. evenly throughout the cortex.
    d. none of the above.

9. People with damage to the striatum (as in Parkinson's and Huntington's diseases) have difficulty with
    a. procedural memory.
    b. declarative memory.
    c. relational memory.
    d. b and c.

10. Incorporating emotional information into memory probably depends on the
    a.   amygdala.
    b.   cingulate gyrus.
    c.   basal ganglia.
    d.   cerebellum.

11. Which of the following statements regarding working memory is FALSE?
    a.   It holds information temporarily.
    b.   It has an unlimited capacity.
    c.   It provides the basis for problem solving and decision making.
    d.   It can hold new information as well as memories already stored.

12. The brain area that seems to be MOST important for working memory is the
    a.   inferior temporal cortex.
    b.   parietal cortex.
    c.   prefrontal cortex.
    d.   superior frontal cortex.

13. Following high frequency impulses of presynaptic neurons, postsynaptic neurons will
    a.   decrease their firing rate.
    b.   produce larger EPSPs.
    c.   produce smaller EPSPs.
    d.   produce larger IPSPs.

14. LTP occurs
    a.   only in the hippocampus.
    b.   only in the visual cortex.
    c.   only in the motor cortex.
    d.   none of the above is correct.

15. Extinction is similar to
    a.   LTP.
    b.   ALTP.
    c.   LTD.
    d.   ALTD.

16. Low frequency stimulation of presynaptic neurons results in
    a.   LTP.
    b.   LTD.
    c.   more EPSPs.
    d.   more postsynaptic action potentials.

17. Suppression of _____ rhythms in the _____ inhibits some forms of
    learning.
    a.   theta; hippocampus
    b.   theta; cortex
    c.   beta; hippocampus
    d.   beta; cortex

18. Which of the following is/are thought to be a mechanism of LTP?
    a.   Increased receptor sensitivity
    b.   Increased neurotransmitter release
    c.   Structural changes in the synapse
    d.   b and c
    e.   all of the above

19. In order for NMDA receptors to be activated, _____ must be dislodged.
    a.   glutamate
    b.   magnesium
    c.   sodium
    d.   nitric oxide

20. Presynaptic neurons may increase their release of glutamate when the postsynaptic neuron releases
    a.   acetylcholine.
    b.   magnesium.
    c.   sodium.
    d.   nitric oxide.

21. On postsynaptic neurons, LTP results in
    a.   more dendritic spines.
    b.   more AMPA receptors.
    c.   more NMDA receptors.
    d.   a and c.
    e.   all of the above.

22. A study of London taxi cab drivers revealed that
    a.   the entire hippocampus is larger than in other people.
    b.   all of the spatial areas of the brain are larger than in other people.
    c.   the posterior portion of the hippocampus was larger than in other people.
    d.   none of the above.

23. The presence of which of the following substances is/are associated with reduced LTP?
    a.   ampakines
    b.   NO blockers
    c. α-CaMKII
    d.   a and b
    e.   all of the above

24. Which of the following statements regarding LTP is MOST LIKELY true?
    a.   It is only a laboratory (or experimental) phenomenon.
    b.   Hippocampal LTP is permanent.
    c.   Cortical LTP is responsible for long-term memory.
    d.   Only mammals exhibit LTP.

25. α-CaMKII$^{+/-}$ mice
    a.   are better learners than normal mice.
    b.   are incapable of retaining information for more than a few hours.
    c.   show no LTP.
    d.   have more α-CaMKII than α-CaMKII$^{-/-}$ mice.

26. Three groups of people are trained on a visual discrimination task. Group 1 is tested within 4 hours after training ends. Group 2 is tested 24 hours later. Group 3 is tested 48 hours later. Which group will probably show the WORST performance on the test?
    a. Group 1
    b. Group 2
    c. Group 3
    d. There is not enough information given to determine the answer

27. Memories seem to be vulnerable to change during
    a. reconsolidation.
    b. reconstruction.
    c. both a and b.
    d. neither a nor b.

28. Regarding memory and aging,
    a. memory failure is an inevitable, normal consequence of aging.
    b. engaging in mental activity clearly reduces memory loss in older adults.
    c. there is no relationship between aging and memory loss.
    d. remaining mentally active is associated with better cognitive functioning.

29. In older rats,
    a. there are fewer NMDA receptors in the hippocampus.
    b. there are significantly fewer cells in the hippocampus.
    c. there are significantly fewer cells in the cortex.
    d. there is a steady loss of synapses throughout the brain.

30. Loss of cells in the _____ that release acetylcholine is associated with cognitive decline.
    a. hippocampus
    b. basal forebrain region
    c. medial forebrain bundle
    d. entorhinal cortex

31. The most common cause of dementia is
    a. Alzheimer's disease.
    b. Korsakoff's syndrome.
    c. stroke.
    d. amnesia.

32. What percentage of people over the age of 65 have Alzheimer's disease?
    a. 50%
    b. 35%
    c. 20%
    d. 10%

33. In Alzheimer's patients, plaques and tangles found in the _____ lobes disrupt connections between the hippocampus and other structures.
    a. frontal
    b. parietal
    c. temporal
    d. occipital

34. Which of the following statements regarding Alzheimer's disease is FALSE?
    a. There are at least 4 different genes that cause it.
    b. People with Down syndrome will develop it if they live past 50.
    c. The amyloid precursor protein gene is found on Chromosome 21.
    d. Symptoms of Alzheimer's disease never appear before the age of 50.

35. The Alzheimer's drugs tacrine and donepezil
    a. inhibit acetylcholinesterase.
    b. promote the production of acetylcholine.
    c. block acetylcholine receptors.
    d. both a and b.

36. Which of the following is NOT discussed in the book as a potential treatment for Alzheimer's disease?
    a. the nicotine patch
    b. Ginkgo biloba
    c. anticholesterol drugs
    d. thiamine

37. Which of the following statements regarding estrogen and Alzheimer's is TRUE?
    a. Men as well as women benefit from estrogen treatment.
    b. Estrogen treatment reduces the risk of Alzheimer's disease in women by more than 50%.
    c. Men produce small amounts of estrogen throughout the lifespan.
    d. Female rats deprived of estrogen develop Alzheimer's disease.

38. New treatments that may be effective in treating Alzheimer's disease involve
    a. stimulating an immune response against amyloid-β.
    b. injecting brain cells with nerve growth factor.
    c. the use of antibiotics to dissolve plaques.
    d. a and c.
    e. a, b, and c.

39. Which of the following structures is NOT damaged in Korsakoff's syndrome?
    a. hippocampus
    b. mammillary bodies
    c. medial thalamic area
    d. frontal lobes

40. Korsakoff's patients are believed to engage in confabulation because
    a. their sense of right and wrong has deteriorated, and they do not care if they lie to others.
    b. they have difficulty distinguishing between current reality and their memories of the past.
    c. they are completely out of touch with reality.
    d. none of the above.

Answers & Explanations

Guided Review

1. memory
2. temporal
3. amnesia
4. hippocampus
5. CA1
6. anterograde
7. formation
8. consolidation
9. parahippo-campal
10. Retrieval
11. glutamate
12. cortex
13. cortex
14. learning
15. Declarative
16. procedures
17. emotional
18. hippocampus
19. relational
20. striatum
21. Parkinson's
22. amygdala
23. emotional
24. declarative
25. working memory
26. match-to-sample
27. inferior temporal
28. prefrontal
29. impairment
30. memory
31. stimulation
32. long-term potentiation
33. hippocampus
34. postsynaptic
35. extinction
36. low-frequency
37. theta rhythm
38. novel
39. executive
40. glutamate
41. NMDA
42. nitric oxide
43. NMDA
44. spines
45. volume
46. NMDA
47. learning
48. ampakines
49. stored
50. network
51. permanent
52. cortex
53. α-CaMKII
54. hippocampal
55. cortical
56. sleep
57. hippocampus
58. reconstruction
59. reconsolidation
60. disease
61. aging
62. hippocampus
63. NMDA
64. LTP
65. entorhinal
66. myelin
67. basal forebrain
68. Alzheimer's
69. frontal
70. Dementia
71. declarative
72. 10
73. 85
74. amyloid plaques
75. neurofibrillary
76. hippocampal
77. Down syndrome
78. amyloid
79. Three
80. Acetylcholine
81. Acetylcholinesterase
82. moderate
83. Nicotine
84. Ginkgo biloba
85. women
86. increase
87. Vaccines
88. factor
89. brain imaging
90. malnutrition
91. Korsakoff's syndrome
92. mammillary
93. frontal
94. thiamine
95. confabulation
96. frontal

Short Answer & Essay

1. Anterograde amnesia is the failure to form new memories following a brain injury, whereas retrograde amnesia is the failure to retrieve memories for events and information experienced prior to the injury. In the case of HM, there are many examples of anterograde amnesia. For example, he could not find his way home to his parents' new house (they moved after his surgery was done), and he couldn't recall what type of work he was doing. He also experienced retrograde amnesia; he could not recall several significant events from his late teens and early adult years, such as high school graduation and the end of WWII.

2. These researchers injected a glutamate blocker bilaterally into the hippocampus of different groups of rats at different times, including during training, after training, and during testing. When the drug was given during or shortly after training, the rats showed poor performances at testing, suggesting that consolidation was impaired. However, the rats that were not given the drug until testing also failed to perform the task, suggesting that the hippocampus is important in retrieval as well.

3. Declarative memory is information about which we can verbalize, whereas non-declarative memory does not require verbalization in order to be used.

4. These patients underwent a conditioning procedure in which a loud sound (which would normally elicit an emotional response) was paired with a blue slide. Both showed a normal physiological response (SCR) to the sound, but the hippocampal patient showed conditioning and the amygdala patient did not. What this suggests is that the hippocampus is necessary for declarative memory, whereas the amygdala is necessary for emotional learning, a form of procedural learning.

5. During early development, synapses are "selected" for survival based on patterns of firing; the synapses that are most likely to survive are those for which pre- and post-synaptic neurons fire together frequently. LTP operates under a similar mechanism. The postsynaptic changes of LTP seem to occur as a result of high frequency input from the presynaptic neurons; following LTP, the post-synaptic neurons are more likely to fire when stimulated by the presynaptic neurons.

6. Long-term depression is the inhibition or weakening of a synapse between two neurons as a result of the presence of a second presynaptic neuron that stimulates the postsynaptic neuron. It is believed that this is an important mechanism in learning because it would limit the degree of LTP, so that a postsynaptic neuron would be limited in its extent of firing. Also, LTD may be important for working memory, which has a limited capacity. This inhibitory mechanism would allow new information to enter working memory and get rid of old information that was less important.

7. Nitric oxide is a transmitter released by the postsynaptic neuron; it facilitates transmitter release in the presynaptic neuron, which then stimulates the postsynaptic neuron.

8. The major shortcoming of LTP as an explanation for learning is that it seems to be a temporary phenomenon, at least in the hippocampus where it has been most extensively studied. This is problematic because learning is often permanent.

9. There is some evidence suggesting that sleep facilitates consolidation, so I would advise my roommate to study the night before the exam, and maybe even two nights before, to ensure that sleep-dependent consolidation has a chance to occur.

10. The jury should not consider her current statement to be accurate. Because she did not recall the hair color until after multiple chances for reconstruction and reconsolidation of the memory (including actually seeing the defendant's hair), it is likely that her memory for the event has been altered.

11. Not all elderly individuals undergo memory loss or cognitive deficits. For example, the book cites a study in which college professors in their 60s scored about the same as those in their 30s.

12. The hippocampus loses synapses and NMDA receptors, which seems to result in impaired LTP. There is decreased activity in the entorhinal cortex, which provides connections between the hippocampus and other brain areas. Cells in the brain lose myelin, which interferes with their functioning. The basal forebrain region may also undergo neuron loss; this is an important area because its cells connect to the hippocampus, amygdala, and cortex. Finally, there may be frontal lobe damage.

13. This chromosome was targeted because of its role in Down syndrome. People with Down have 3 of the 21st chromosome, rather than the usual 2. They also display the physical brain signs of AD, such as plaques and tangles. Researchers then suspected that one or more genes on this chromosome were responsible for these brain abnormalities.

14. Currently, drugs that inhibit acetylcholinesterase are used to treat AD. Treatments that are in the experimental stages include using nicotine patches, anticholesterol drugs, nonsteroidal anti-inflammatory drugs, Ginkgo biloba, estrogen treatment, vaccines that reduce or eliminate plaques, and genetic manipulation to introduce nerve growth factor into the brain.

15. Confabulation is the tendency of some amnesiacs, especially people with Korsakoff's syndrome, to make up stories about their current lives. Several examples are given in the book about a woman living in a nursing home who at various times seemed confused about where she was and what she should have been doing. For example, she apparently thought she was being held prisoner, and asked the nurse what she had done wrong.

Post-Test

All page references in this section pertain to the textbook.

1. **a. Correct**; his IQ actually increased. All of the other choices occurred as a result of his surgery.
    b. Wrong
    c. Wrong
    d. Wrong

2. a. Wrong; this is retrograde amnesia.
    b. Correct; see p. 314.
    c. Wrong; this is retrograde amnesia.
    d. Wrong

3. a. Wrong; while damage to CA1 results in moderate anterograde amnesia, usually only more extensive damage would result in profound retrograde amnesia.
    b. Correct; see p. 315.
    c. Wrong
    d. Wrong

4. a. Wrong; this is retrieval.
    b. Wrong; this is reconstruction.
    c. Wrong; this is confabulation.
    d. Correct; see p. 315.

5. a. Wrong; the hippocampus also plays a role in retrieval.
    b. Wrong; the hippocampus also plays a role in consolidation.
    c. Correct; there is evidence that the hippocampus is involved in both of these functions. For example, rats whose hippocampi were impaired during consolidation failed to learn, and those whose hippocampi were impaired during testing did very poorly on a previously learned task.
    d. Wrong

6. a. Wrong; the activity in the hippocampus decreases, while the activity in the cortex increases.
    b. Wrong
    c. Correct; see p. 317.
    d. Wrong

7. **a.** **Correct**; see p. 316-317.
    b. Wrong; the hippocampus is active during successful retrieval.
    c. Wrong
    d. Wrong

8. a. Wrong; because hippocampal damage does not affect all memories, they must be stored elsewhere.
    b. Wrong; there is evidence that there are several storage areas.
    c. Wrong; there is no evidence that memories are evenly distributed, but rather seem to be pooled in particular areas.
    d. **Correct**; memories seem to be stored according to where their information is processed (see p. 318).

9. **a.** **Correct**; they have problems with the Tower of Hanoi puzzle and mirror-tracing tasks, both of which require procedural memory.
    b. Wrong; damage to the hippocampus, but not the striatum is implicated in problems with declarative memory.
    c. Wrong; relational memory is a broader term for declarative memory, used to describe some forms of memory in non-human animals (who cannot verbalize).
    d. Wrong

10. **a.** **Correct**; see p. 319.
    b. Wrong
    c. Wrong
    d. Wrong

11. a. Wrong
    b. **Correct**; the capacity of working memory is quite small. All of the other choices are true.
    c. Wrong
    d. Wrong

12. a. Wrong; while this is involved, it ceases activity when a distracting stimulus is presented without impairment to working memory, so it is not the most important brain area.
    b. Wrong; again, this area is involved, but does not seem to be critical.
    c. **Correct**; cells in this area display several characteristics associated with working memory, and a distracting stimulus does not interfere with their activity. Furthermore, when this area is damaged, working memory is impaired.
    d. Wrong; this area is not mentioned in the text.

13. a. Wrong; it is more likely that they will increase their firing rate.
    b. **Correct**; see p. 321.
    c. Wrong
    d. Wrong; although this is not directly discussed in the book, it is unlikely that both EPSPs and IPSPs would increase at the same synapse.

14. a. Wrong; it occurs in both the visual and motor cortex as well.
    b. Wrong
    c. Wrong
    d. **Correct**; see p. 321.

15. a. Wrong; this is probably how learning is acquired.
    b. Wrong; this is similar to the process of classical conditioning in which a neutral stimulus becomes associated with an unconditioned stimulus.
    c. Correct; see p. 322.
    d. Wrong

16. a. Wrong; this is a result of high frequency stimulation.
    b. Correct; see p. 322.
    c. Wrong; it would probably result in fewer EPSPs or more IPSPs.
    d. Wrong; if there are fewer EPSPs, there will be fewer action potentials generated.

17. **a. Correct**; see p. 322.
    b. Wrong; the book does not mention a relationship between cortical theta rhythm activity and learning.
    c. Wrong; there is no mention of beta rhythms being associated with learning.
    d. Wrong

18. a. Wrong; b and c are also correct.
    b. Wrong; a and c are also correct.
    c. Wrong; a and b are also correct.
    d. Wrong; a is also correct.
    e. Correct; see pp. 322-323.

19. a. Wrong; glutamate will occupy the NMDA receptor after magnesium is dislodged (because of depolarization from the AMPA receptor).
    b. Correct; see p. 323.
    c. Wrong; sodium does not block the NMDA receptor, and in fact it enters the cell when the AMPA receptor is activated.
    d. Wrong; this is involved in presynaptic facilitation.

20. a. Wrong; this is not discussed as being directly related to LTP.
    b. Wrong; this ion blocks NMDA receptors.
    c. Wrong; this leads to depolarization of the postsynaptic membrane (and may cause magnesium to be expelled from the NMDA receptor.
    d. Correct; see p. 323.

21. a. Wrong; c is also correct.
    b. Wrong; AMPA receptors migrate from other locations, but new ones are not created.
    c. Wrong; a is also correct.
    d. Correct; see p. 323.
    e. Wrong

22. a. Wrong; only the posterior portion was larger. The anterior portion was smaller.
    b. Wrong; the textbook only mentions the hippocampus.
    c. Correct; see p. 324.
    d. Wrong

23. a. Wrong; ampakines enhance LTP.
 b. Correct; because NO is involved in presynaptic facilitation (it increases the release of glutamate from the presynaptic neuron), blocking it would impair LTP.
 c. Wrong; α-CaMKII is involved in consolidation, and with reduced amounts of it, consolidation is impaired.
 d. Wrong
 e. Wrong

24. a. Wrong; while it has been most extensively studied in the laboratory, the book also provides evidence that it occurs naturally (see p. 324).
 b. Wrong; the book states that hippocampal LTP is temporary (p. 324).
 c. Correct; because consolidation appears to involve moving information from the hippocampus to the cortex, LTP in the cortex is most likely the basis of long-term retention of information.
 d. Wrong; while only mammals are discussed in the book, it is not stated that this phenomenon is limited to mammals. Furthermore, because many other types of animals (including birds, reptiles, and invertebrates) can learn, it is likely that they do so because of the same or a similar mechanism.

25. a. Wrong; while they show hippocampal LTP, they forget things after a few days.
 b. Wrong
 c. Wrong; they do show LTP.
 d. Correct; see pp. 324-325.

26. **a. Correct**; because there is no opportunity for sleep, which may contribute to consolidation, these people are likely to perform most poorly compared to the other two groups.
 b. Wrong; because these people are tested after a period involving sleep, consolidation is more likely to occur.
 c. Wrong; because these people are tested after a period involving sleep, consolidation is more likely to occur.
 d. Wrong

27. a. Wrong; b is also correct.
 b. Wrong; a is also correct.
 c. Correct; there is evidence that memories may be altered during both of these.
 d. Wrong

28. a. Wrong; there is evidence that not all older people experience memory loss and cognitive declines.
 b. Wrong; while there is a connection, it is only correlational at this point.
 c. Wrong; many older adults do experience cognitive problems.
 d. Correct; see p. 326.

29. **a. Correct**; see p. 326.
 b. Wrong; while this was once thought to be true, more recent studies suggest it is not.
 c. Wrong; there is no evidence of this.
 d. Wrong; the book mentions loss of synapses in the hippocampus, but not throughout the brain.

30. a. Wrong; acetylcholine is not mentioned as an important neurotransmitter for the hippocampus.
 b. Correct; see p. 326.
 c. Wrong; this area is not mentioned as being associated with learning.
 d. Wrong; acetylcholine is not mentioned as being important for this area.

31. **a.** **Correct**; see p. 327.
    b. Wrong
    c. Wrong
    d. Wrong

32. a. Wrong
    b. Wrong
    c. Wrong
    d. **Correct**; see p. 327.

33. a. Wrong; although plaques may be found here, those in the temporal lobes are more likely to disrupt connections with the hippocampus.
    b. Wrong
    c. **Correct**; see pp. 327-328.
    d. Wrong

34. a. Wrong
    b. Wrong
    c. Wrong
    d. **Correct**; although it is uncommon, some people do develop the disease before age 50. All of the other choices are true.

35. **a.** **Correct**; see p. 329.
    b. Wrong; this is not mentioned as one of their functions.
    c. Wrong; this would probably have a negative effect on people with Alzheimer's (who lack sufficient ACh.
    d. Wrong

36. a. Wrong
    b. Wrong
    c. Wrong
    d. **Correct**; this is used to treat Korsakoff's syndrome, not AD. All of the other choices are used to treat AD.

37. a. Wrong; because men continue to produce estrogen throughout the lifespan, it is unlikely that they would benefit from any protection estrogen offers.
    b. Wrong; it reduces it by about 33%.
    c. **Correct**; see p. 329.
    d. Wrong; while these rats show impairment in learning, it has not been established that it is the same thing as AD.

38. a. Wrong; c is also correct.
    b. Wrong; nerve growth factor is not injected into the brain, but instead the genes that produce it are activated.
    c. Wrong; a is also correct.
    d. **Correct**; see pp. 330-331.
    e. Wrong

39. **a.** **Correct**; the hippocampus is not affected in Korsakoff's. All of the other brain areas are affected (see p. 331).
   b. Wrong
   c. Wrong
   d. Wrong

40. a. Wrong; confabulation does not seem to be intentional.
   b. **Correct**; see pp. 332-333.
   c. Wrong; the examples in the text indicate that they are aware of their surroundings to a certain extent.
   d. Wrong

Chapter 12: The Biological Bases of Intelligence

Chapter Outline and Learning Objectives

As you read the chapter, use these learning objectives to guide your studying. You should be able to define the key terms from the text, which are shown in boldface type below.

1) The Nature of Intelligence
- What is **intelligence**? What do intelligence tests measure?

a) What Intelligence Tests Measure
- How were **IQ scores** originally calculated? Describe the distribution of IQ scores shown in Figure 12.2.

- Discuss the predictive value of IQ scores for academic success and overall success (including the results of Terman's study).

- What is the rationale behind the Raven Progressive Matrices test?

- What evidence is there that practical intelligence is not perfectly correlated with IQ scores?

- Why does Sternberg refer to intelligence as a "cultural invention?"

b) The Structure of Intelligence
- Compare the perspectives of lumpers and splitters regarding the structure of intelligence.

2) The Origins of Intelligence
a) The Brain and Intelligence
- How does Einstein's brain differ from other brains it was compared to? What, if any, evidence exists that his brain reflects his genius?

- Why do some researchers think that the frontal lobes are involved in general intelligence?

i) Brain Size
- In terms of intelligence, why is the ratio of brain to body size more important than brain size alone?

- Discuss the relationship between brain size and intelligence in humans. What explanations account for the fact that men's brains are on average heavier than women's?

ii) Neural Conduction Speed and Processing Speed
  - Discuss the relationship between reaction time and intelligence. What recent evidence exists for a relationship between nerve conduction velocity and intelligence?

iii) Processing Efficiency
  - How are myelination and intelligence related?

  - How are working memory, NCV, and intelligence related?

  - What evidence is there that more intelligent brains use less fuel?

b) Specific Abilities and the Brain
  - Describe the factor analysis method. How is it used in intelligence testing? What specific types of intelligence have emerged using this method?

  - What evidence is there that linguistic and spatial intelligence rely on different modules in the brain?

  - What brain areas are thought to be involved in mathematical skills?

  - What evidence is there from studies of human infants and nonhuman primates that the brain has areas specialized for processing quantity?

  - Why does it make more sense to look for biological bases of general intelligence and specific mental capabilities, rather than focusing on one or the other?

c) Heredity and Environment
  i) Heritability of Intelligence
    - What evidence is there that intelligence is inheritable? How does the influence of genes on intelligence change over the lifespan?

    - What specific mental functions that contribute to intelligence may be inheritable?

ii) The Genetic Controversy
- What is the controversy surrounding the genetic basis of intelligence?

- Summarize the debate regarding the role of genes and environment in racial differences in intelligence.

iii) Environmental Effects
- Why has it been so difficult to determine what environmental factors influence intelligence?

- What were the outcomes of the Head Start and Abecedarian projects?

- What do adoption studies tell us about the genetic and environmental contributions to intelligence?

3) Disorders of Intelligence
   a) Retardation
- What are the criteria for mental retardation? Why is retardation considered to be a somewhat arbitrary designation?

- Describe the four categories of retardation in terms of IQ range, prevalence, and adaptation.

- Discuss retardation resulting from **Down syndrome, phenylketonuria**, and **hydrocephalus**.

   b) Autism
- What are the characteristics of **autism**?

i) The Autistic Individual
- What specific impairments do autistic individuals exhibit?

- What is **theory of mind**? What role does it seem to play in autism?

- What are **autistic savants**? Give some examples. What may cause an autistic to become a savant?

- Describe the high-functioning autistic Temple Grandin.

ii) Brain Anomalies in Autism
- What brain anomalies have been linked to autism?

- How might thalidomide and rubella be linked to autism?

iii) Biochemical Anomalies
- What roles may serotonin and oxytocin play in autism?

iv) Heredity and Autism
- What evidence is there that autism is hereditary?

- What is a **spectrum disorder**? What does the prevalence of spectrum disorders suggest about the genetic basis of autism?

- What specific chromosomes may be involved in autism?

c) Effects of Aging on Intelligence
- Why have declines associated with aging been overestimated?

- What is the significance of age-related loss of speed of processing?

- What evidence is there that some losses are reversible?

The Nature of Intelligence

Summary and Guided Review

After studying this section in the text, fill in the blanks of the following summary. The answers are found on p. 286.

Intelligence, defined as the capacity for _____ (1), reasoning, and understanding, is challenging to measure. Originally, the intelligence quotient (or IQ) reflected the ratio between a child's mental and _____ _____ (2). Currently, a person's IQ represents her or his performance compared with the general population; the average IQ is _____ (3), and most people's scores fall near this number. Very few people score above 130 or below _____ (4). Intelligence tests, which were first used to identify children with special needs, produce scores that are correlated with both school grades and level of education, as well as job performance, income, and

_____ (5) level. Beginning in 1921 researcher

_____ _____ (6) began a longitudinal study of 1500 children with high IQs, and discovered that as they grew they were generally larger, healthier, better educated, and more _____ (7) in terms of accomplishments and earnings, compared with the general population. The relationship between intelligence and health remains strong even when _____ (8) status is controlled for.

Intelligence tests have been criticized by many for defining intelligence too _____ (9); because of the correlation between IQ and academic success/ socioeconomic status, critics argue that IQ tests are designed to reflect these forms of success. The

_____ _____ _____ (10) test, a culture-free test, attempts to measure knowledge that is not necessarily related to academic performance. Another criticism is that _____ (11) intelligence, knowledge and cognitive skills that people use in their everyday lives, is not measured by standard IQ tests, and so IQ tests are not truly reflective of how intelligent people are. _____ (12) asserts that intelligence is actually a cultural invention. The fact that there is no one accepted definition or means of measuring intelligence makes it difficult to determine what the physiological and anatomical bases of intelligence might be.

There is also controversy over the structure of intelligence. _____ (13) are intelligence theorists who assume that there is a unitary capability underlying intelligence; this argument is supported by the fact that different abilities such as math and verbal skills are often correlated.

_____ (14) argue that mental abilities are distinct from one another; this perspective is supported by the fact that brain damage often impairs one type of skill and not others.

Short Answer & Essay Questions

Answer the following questions. See pp. 286-287 for sample answers.

1. Describe the outcome of Terman's study of intelligent children.

2. What are two criticisms of intelligence tests?

3. How do lumpers and splitters differ on their positions regarding a general factor of intelligence?

The Origins of Intelligence

Summary and Guided Review

After studying this section in the text, fill in the blanks of the following summary. The answers are found on p. 286.

The search for an anatomical basis of intelligence has led some researchers to speculate that people who are more intelligent have bigger brains. However, the brain of the genius _____ _____ (15) is not significantly different from other brains. One exception is that his parietal lobes, which correspond with mathematical skills, were larger; this suggests that at least in Einstein's case, intellectual ability was related to a specific brain area. PET scans reveal that _____ (16) areas of the brain are more active during tasks believed to reflect a general factor of intelligence; some of the functions of this area thought to be related to general intelligence are _____ (17) memory and executive control of problem solving.

If we compare across species, brain size alone is not a good predictor of intelligence. In humans, who have the highest brain-to-body size _____ (18), there is some evidence for a relationship between IQ and brain-to-body size ratio, although this is not clear. There is a gender difference in the ratio, with males' brains being proportionately _____ (19) than females' brains, although men and women do not differ in intelligence. One possible reason for the gender difference is that women's brains, which have more densely packed neurons and more _____ _____ (20), are more efficient. Another possibility is that the difference reflects males' advantage in _____ (21) abilities.

The speed at which people process information may be an indication of general intelligence; in fact, IQ and reaction time are correlated. An even stronger correlation exists between IQ scores and _____ _____ (22) velocity. _____ (23), which speeds neural impulses and prevents inappropriate communication between neurons, is also believed to be related to intelligence. People with relatively more _____ (24) matter also have higher IQs, and the developmental changes of myelination, intelligence and speed of processing information follow the same curvilinear path. _____ (25) memory, which places a limit on how much information we can handle at one time, is probably influenced by NCV. Because the contents of working memory decays quickly, people whose neurons conduct faster are probably able to _____ (26) and retain more information than those whose neurons work more slowly. In fact, IQ is more strongly correlated with _____ _____ (27) memory than reaction time, particularly when tasks are complex. Furthermore, people with higher IQs show less glucose use while playing Tetris, while

_____ _____ (28) individuals exhibit more brain activity than above average individuals while performing a mental task. These results suggest that IQ is related to _____ (29) of neural processing.

Individual components of intelligence may be identified by _____ _____ (30), which involves giving people a variety of mental tests and then looking for correlations among clusters of related tests. Although performance on all mental tests tends to be correlated, _____ (31), logical-mathematical, and _____ (32) components have emerged. One brain-based explanation for these different components is that they evolved separately and consist of different _____ (33) of structures. However, mathematical skills use some of the same areas and functions as the other components. Performing exact calculations corresponds to activity in frontal _____ (34) areas, while estimating calculations involves the visual-spatial association areas of the _____ (35) lobes. Research involving human infants and nonhuman _____ (36) suggests that the brain is "wired" for numbers, language may have emerged in the frontal areas in part because it requires the same type of processing as counting.

Currently, there is neurological evidence to support both the _____ (37) -factor and specific-components positions on the nature of intelligence.

Because intelligence is complex, identifying its genetic and environmental components has proven to be extremely difficult. Family and twin studies show that IQ is _____ (38), with about half of the variability due to heredity. Genes influence the general processes related to intelligence, such as working memory and processing speed. A specific allele on chromosome 6 is more common among people with IQs above _____ (39) than in those with average IQs; however this gene only accounts for a small amount of the _____ (40) in IQ. There are likely hundreds of genes that contribute to intelligence.

The fact that intelligence is heritable does not mean that it cannot be influenced by the _____ (41); rather, genes set a range of potential intelligence levels, and the environment determines where in that range intelligence falls. Furthermore, IQ scoring has been adjusted as people's performance on intelligence tests has steadily _____ (42). Someone with an IQ of 100 today is probably more intelligent than someone with that score 50 years ago. On the other hand, the strong correlation in IQ between identical twins cannot be explained away by shared environmental factors, since identical twins raised _____ (43) are more similar in IQ than fraternal twins raised together, and the degree of correlation is associated with the actual genetic relationship of twins rather than parents' assumptions about whether they are identical or fraternal.

The reasons behind racial differences in IQ scores are hotly debated. Some researchers argue that _____ (44) differences between blacks and whites are the cause of blacks' lower scores, while others suggest that this is not the case. For example, Scarr showed that there were no differences in performance on cognitive tests between blacks with different degrees of _____ _____ (45), and the American Psychological Association has concluded that there is little evidence for a genetic explanation of the racial differences.

Environmental contributions to intelligence are also difficult to identify, in part because environmental and genetic factors are _____ (46). Children share both genes and environment with their parents, and it is difficult to determine which factor is more important in the child's behavior. Also, several environmental factors are only _____ (47) related to intelligence.

Some forms of environmental intervention have been successful in improving achievement in at-risk children. Although the moderate gain in IQ scores attained by children in _____ _____ (48) disappears over time, they have higher educational and career attainments. The _____ (49) project seems to produce longer-lasting IQ improvement.

Children who are adopted show stronger IQ correlations with their biological than their adopted parents, but _____ (50) children from impoverished backgrounds adopted into middle-class homes showed IQ score increases of about 15 points.

Short Answer & Essay Questions

Answer the following questions. See p. 287 for sample answers.

4. What are two possible explanations for the gender difference in brain to body ratio?

5. What is the evidence that the degree of myelination in the brain is an indicator of intelligence?

6. Describe how factor analysis is used to identify components of intelligence. What components have consistently emerged?

7. Why is it incorrect to assume that because intelligence is highly heritable, it is influenced very little by the environment?

8. What have adoption studies revealed about the genetic and environmental contributions to intelligence?

Disorders of Intelligence

Summary and Guided Review

After studying this section in the text, fill in the blanks of the following summary. The answers are found on p. 286.

Mental retardation, as defined by the American Psychiatric Association, is a label assigned to people with an IQ below _____ (51) who have difficulty caring for themselves. Being considered retarded may depend on the situation, as children with low IQ may become adults who are capable of living independently. Most retarded individuals fall into the _____ (52) category, displaying such characteristics as less factual knowledge, fewer strategies for cognition, and slower mental operations. For most individuals In this group, there is no single attributable cause of retardation. About _____ (53) % of all cases of retardation can be traced to a physical cause; prenatal exposure to _____ (54) is the most common of these causes. Down syndrome, which results from an extra 21st chromosome, and _____ _____ (55) syndrome are the most common genetic causes of retardation. _____ (56), another genetic disorder, may not lead to retardation if the affected individual avoids foods with phenylalanine. _____ (57), the build-up of cerebrospinal fluid, may also lead to retardation, but can be treated if caught early. However, many hydrocephalic individuals have normal IQs.

Autism is a disorder characterized by compulsive, ritualistic _____ (58), impaired sociability, and mental retardation. Not all autistics are retarded, but many children in the _____ (59), severe, and moderate categories are autistic. Specific cognitive impairments of this disorder include delayed language development, difficulty or inability to _____ (60), and an inability to understand other's states of mind. Autistic children perform more poorly on _____ _____ _____ (61) tasks than very young normal children and even children with Down syndrome. Some autistics, referred to as _____ (62), are extremely talented in one area, such as music, drawing, painting, computation, or memorizing. The most likely explanation for these skills is that the autistic lacks _____ (63) or integrative functions within the brain, and this gives the savant access to speedy lower levels of processing.. There are also _____ _____ (64) autistics, individuals such as Temple Grandin, who have normal or above normal intelligence, but who still show autistic characteristics such as poorly developed theory of mind.

Although originally thought to be the result of a poor _____ (65) relationship, autism is now considered a brain-based disorder. However, because not all autistics show the same pattern of brain abnormalities, there are probably several ways in which the disorder can develop.

Environmental factors such as prenatal exposure to the drug _____ (66) and viruses such as rubella have been implicated in some cases. Different brain chemicals may be responsible for the different characteristics of autism. Some autistics respond to drugs that alter the activity of serotonin, suggesting that impaired serotonin receptors may be a factor, particularly in _____ (67) behavior. _____ (68), a substance thought to contribute to sociability, is lower in autistic children

Autism has a _____ (69) component, as autistic children have a much higher chance of having an autistic sibling than normal children, and the concordance rate for identical twins is 60%. When _____ _____ (70), milder, autistic-like symptoms, are considered, the concordance rate for identical twins is _____ (71) %. Autism is more common in _____ (72), but the evidence for involvement of genes on the X chromosome is unclear. Genes on chromosome 6 that contribute to the regulation of the _____ (73) system may be involved, as well as genes on other chromosomes. It is likely that the more autism-related genes one inherits, the more likely one is to develop full-blown autism.

Cognitive impairment is often associated with aging, but the degree of loss has been _____ (74). When older adults are given tests on material relevant to their lives, they show much less deterioration than when given lists of words to remember. Also, _____ (75) studies of the same people reveal less decline than cross-sectional studies of different people. Speed of information processing, which is important for _____ (76) memory, does decrease in the elderly. But elderly individuals can regain lost skills through practice and enhancement of _____ _____ (77).

Short Answer & Essay Questions
Answer the following questions. See pp. 287-288 for sample answers.

9. How does phenylketonuria lead to retardation? What, if anything, can be done to prevent retardation from developing?

10. What does it mean to have a theory of mind? Why are autistic individuals thought to have poorly developed theory of mind?

11. What are the possible explanations for autistic savants? Which one seems most likely to be correct? Why?

12. How is serotonin thought to be involved in autism? Which symptoms is it most likely implicated in?

13. Give a reason why the degree of cognitive impairment in the elderly has been overestimated.

Post-Test

Use these multiple-choice questions to check your understanding of the chapter. The answers, along with explanations, are found beginning on p. 288.

1. The intelligence quotient originally represented
   a. a person's intellectual capacity compared to the general population.
   b. a child's mental age divided by his chronological age.
   c. a child's chronological age divided by her mental age.
   d. none of the above.

2. What percent of the population currently has an IQ above 130?
   a. 2%
   b. 12%
   c. 20%
   d. 0.2%

3. IQ scores are correlated with which of the following?
   a. grades earned in school
   b. years of schooling completed
   c. job performance
   d. a and b
   e. a, b, and c

4. The longitudinal study of California children with high IQs was conducted by
   a. Lewis Terman.
   b. Alfred Binet.
   c. Stephen Hawking.
   d. Francis Galton.

5. The Raven Progressive Matrices test is designed to
   a. be culture free.
   b. measure nonverbal abilities.
   c. measure practical intelligence.
   d. a and b.
   e. a, b, and c.

6. Robert Sternberg argues that
   a. intelligence tests measure a general, underlying factor of cognitive ability that contributes to specific mental skills.
   b. intelligence tests are completely useless.
   c. intelligence is how a culture defines people's ability to succeed.
   d. tests that measure practical intelligence are better than traditional intelligence tests.

7. Howard Gardner, who proposes 7 different types of intelligence, is best described as a
   a. lumper.
   b. splitter.
   c. general factor theorist.
   d. reaction time theorist.

8. Which of the following is TRUE regarding Albert Einstein's brain?
   a. It is larger than the average female's brain.
   b. It is larger than the average male's brain.
   c. It contains more neurons that the average brain.
   d. The parietal lobes are larger than the average brain.

9. PET studies reveal that tasks requiring general intelligence produce higher activity in the _____ areas of the brain.
   a. frontal
   b. temporal
   c. parietal
   d. occipital

10. Which of the following statements regarding brain size is FALSE?
    a. Species with the highest brain-body ratio are the most intelligent.
    b. There is no correlation between brain size and intelligence in humans.
    c. Men's brains are proportionately larger than women's brains.
    d. Elephants' brains are larger than humans' brains.

11. Which of the following is probably the BEST predictor of IQ score?
    a. brain size
    b. reaction time
    c. nerve conduction velocity
    d. frontal area activity

12. Which of the following statements about myelination is/are true?
    a. People with more white matter tend to have higher IQs.
    b. Myelination increases across the lifespan.
    c. Myelination prevents cross-talk between neurons.
    d. b and c
    e. a and c

13. People with higher IQs tend to
    a. have faster nerve conduction velocity.
    b. use less energy when processing information.
    c. have more gray matter.
    d. a and b
    e. b and c

14. Which of the following is NOT one of the components of intelligence frequently identified by factor analysis?
    a. practical intelligence
    b. linguistic intelligence
    c. logical-mathematical intelligence
    d. spatial intelligence

15. Which of the following most specifically engages the right parietal lobe?
    a. linguistic intelligence
    b. logical-mathematical intelligence
    c. spatial intelligence
    d. a and c.

282

16. Remembering that 8 x 8 = 64 most likely involves which brain area(s)?
    a. frontal lobe
    b. parietal lobe
    c. temporal lobe
    d. b and c

17. The ability to estimate number has been demonstrated in
    a. human infants.
    b. rhesus monkeys.
    c. chimpanzees.
    d. a and c.
    e. a, b, and c.

18. The proportion of variability in intelligence due to heredity is highest in
    a. infancy.
    b. childhood.
    c. adolescence.
    d. adulthood.

19. A gene associated with genius has been located on Chromosome _____ .
    a. 6
    b. 15
    c. 21
    d. 23

20. IQ scoring standards have been adjusted in the last 50 years to reflect the fact that
    a. people are scoring more poorly on the tests than they have in the past.
    b. the average performance on IQ tests has risen.
    c. fewer people are mentally retarded now.
    d. our genes are making us more intelligent.

21. Studies of identical and fraternal twins reveal that the weakest correlation for IQ scores is between
    a. identical twins correctly identified by their parents as identical.
    b. fraternal twins incorrectly identified by their parents as identical.
    c. identical twins, regardless of whether their parents identified them as identical or fraternal.
    d. identical twins incorrectly identified by their parents as fraternal.

22. Scarr's study of IQ scores among blacks revealed that
    a. there was no relationship between degree of African ancestry and IQ.
    b. Blacks with more African ancestors had lower IQs than those with fewer African ancestors.
    c. there were no differences between blacks and whites.
    d. none of the above.

23. Which of the following statements regarding environmental contributions to intelligence is FALSE?
    a. Environmental factors may be confounded with genetic factors.
    b. The results from projects like Head Start suggest that the environment is not as important as genes when it comes to intelligence.
    c. Many environmental factors may weakly contribute to intelligence.
    d. A study comparing identical twins revealed that those pairs who had different experiences did not differ much in IQ.

24. Which of the following statements regarding Head Start is FALSE?
    a. There are long-term benefits in IQ scores.
    b. There are long-term benefits in career accomplishments.
    c. There are long-term benefits in mathematics.
    d. There are long-term benefits in educational attainment.

25. Adoption studies reveal that adopted children's IQ scores are
    a. relatively unaffected by the adoptive home.
    b. most strongly correlated with one's biological parents in childhood and adulthood.
    c. most strongly correlated with one's adopted parents in childhood and adulthood.
    d. initially more similar to their biological parents', but become more similar to their adopted parents' in adulthood.

26. What percentage of the population falls in the IQ range for mental retardation?
    a. 0.02%
    b. 0.2%
    c. 2%
    d. 5%

27. Most retarded individuals
    a. may achieve only a second-grade level education.
    b. are incapable of caring for themselves.
    c. can become somewhat self-sufficient.
    d. have an IQ below 50.

28. The leading known cause of mental retardation is
    a. fragile X syndrome.
    b. prenatal exposure to alcohol.
    c. Down syndrome.
    d. hydrocephalus.

29. Which of the following statements regarding hydrocephalus is/are TRUE?
    a. It is treatable.
    b. If untreated, it always causes mental retardation.
    c. It results from a build up of cerebrospinal fluid.
    d. a and c
    e. a, b, and c

30. What percentage of children with IQs below 20 are autistic?
    a. 42%
    b. 86%
    c. 50%
    d. 23%

31. Which of the following is NOT a common characteristic of autism?
    a. Locked in a world of fantasy
    b. Delayed language development
    c. Compulsive behaviors
    d. Limited interactions with others

32. Which of the following statements regarding autistic savants is TRUE?
    a. Their skills usually result from a great deal of concentrated practice.
    b. Their skills typically generalize to other related tasks.
    c. Their skills usually require lower levels of cognitive processing.
    d. All autistics are savants.

33. Which of the following is NOT TRUE of Temple Grandin, the high-functioning autistic described in the book?
    a. She has a PhD in animal science.
    b. She gives lectures about her condition.
    c. She had normal language development as a child.
    d. She exhibits a poorly developed theory of mind.

34. Which of following brain areas was NOT listed in the textbook as being implicated in autism?
    a. occipital lobe
    b. temporal lobe
    c. brain stem
    d. cerebellum

35. An early theory about the origins of autism that has been discarded is that
    a. prenatal exposure to thalidomide is responsible for some cases of autism.
    b. unresponsive parenting is responsible for some cases of autism.
    c. prenatal exposure to a virus is responsible for some cases of autism.
    d. the loss of one's primary caregiver in infancy is responsible for some cases of autism.

36. The impairment of sociability in autistics has been linked to
    a. Oxytocin.
    b. serotonin.
    c. endorphins.
    d. a and b.

37. When spectrum disorders are considered along with autism, the concordance rate for identical twins is
    a. 75%.
    b. 60%.
    c. over 90%.
    d. 10%.

38. Which of the following genetic factors seems to be involved in autism?
    a. a single gene on chromosome 6
    b. the X chromosome
    c. genes associated with the major histocompatibility complex
    d. none of the above

39. Longitudinal studies of aging and cognition reveal that
    a. perceptual speed begins declining around age 25.
    b. skills involving numbers begin declining around age 25.
    c. verbal ability remains unchanged until age 60, and then drops.
    d. a and b.
    e. a, b, and c.

40. Which of the following is NOT true regarding age-related cognitive loss?
    a. enhancing self-esteem may improve memory
    b. practicing mental skills may improve them
    c. results of cross-sectional studies have probably exaggerated loss of cognitive skills
    d. inductive reasoning skills actually improve in old age

Answers & Explanations

Guided Review

1. learning
2. chronological age
3. 100
4. 70
5. socioeconomic
6. Lewis Terman
7. successful
8. socioeconomic
9. narrowly
10. Raven Progressive Matrices
11. practical
12. Sternberg
13. Lumpers
14. Splitters
15. Albert Einstein
16. frontal
17. working
18. ratio
19. heavier or larger
20. gray matter
21. spatial
22. nerve conduction
23. Myelination
24. white
25. Working
26. process
27. short-term
28. mildly retarded
29. efficiency
30. factor analysis
31. linguistic
32. spatial
33. modules
34. language
35. parietal
36. primates
37. general
38. heritable
39. 160
40. variability
41. environment
42. improved
43. apart
44. hereditary
45. African ancestry
46. confounded
47. weakly
48. Head Start
49. Abecedarian
50. black
51. 70
52. mild
53. 25
54. alcohol
55. fragile X
56. Phenylketonuria
57. Hydrocephalus
58. behavior
59. profound
60. pretend
61. theory of mind
62. savants
63. executive
64. high-functioning
65. maternal or parental
66. thalidomide
67. compulsive
68. Oxytocin
69. genetic
70. spectrum disorders
71. 92%
72. males
73. immune
74. overestimated
75. longitudinal
76. working
77. self esteem

Short Answer & Essay

1. While growing up, these individuals were healthier, stronger and larger than their peers. As adults, they were 10 times as likely to graduate from college. In their careers they were productive in demonstrating creative work, and they earned about twice as much as the national average.

2. One criticism of intelligence tests is that they are designed to measure or reflect standard forms of academic and socioeconomic success, and thus do not measure important things like practical intelligence. Another criticism is that people who are highly successful (such as George W. Bush) often score in the mediocre range on these tests, suggesting that they are not really useful for predicting success.

3. Lumpers argue that because people's scores on different tasks such as math and verbal skills are often highly correlated, intelligence is a unitary capacity that we apply to many different tasks; a single IQ score is sufficient to represent a person's intelligence. Splitters argue that it is necessary to look at people's scores on different types of tests to get an accurate picture of intelligence, because many people have strengths in some areas and weaknesses in others. Splitters believe that there are actually several types of intelligence.

4. One possibility is that women's brains are more efficient, and another is that the difference reflects males' superiority on spatial tasks.

5. Myelination contributes to nerve conduction velocity (because it insulates neurons and allows them to propagate action potentials more quickly), which in turn is strongly correlated with IQ. Furthermore, the species with the most myelination appear to be more intelligent, and among humans, those with more myelin are more intelligent. Finally, the degree of myelination across the lifespan is correlated with intelligence and speed of processing information.

6. Factor analysis involves giving people several tests related to intelligence, and then looking for clusters of tests that are more strongly correlated with one another than with other tests. Such clusters are assumed to be testing approximately the same types of skills. Researchers have found high degrees of intercorrelations among tests for linguistic, logical-mathematical, and spatial skills..

7. If a particular trait is highly heritable, the environment can still have profound influence over it. For example, although height is even more heritable than intelligence, people's heights have been steadily increasing over the past few generations, as a result of improved environment. A better way of thinking about how genes influence intelligence is that they provide a range of possibilities, and whatever environment a person is exposed to will then determine where within that range her intelligence will fall.

8. Adoption studies have shown that children's IQs are more strongly correlated with their biological parents' than their adoptive parents'. However, they have also shown that disadvantaged children's IQs can be dramatically improved in an adoptive home.

9. People with phenylketonuria are unable to metabolize the amino acid phenylalanine, and so it builds up within the body and destroys myelin, leading to profound mental retardation. These serious effects can be prevented by limiting the amount of phenalynine in the diet.

10. Theory of mind refers to awareness of or knowledge about the mental states of oneself and others. Autistic children perform poorly on theory of mind tests that normal children and even children with Down syndrome with a lower mental age than the autistic children perform well on. Also, many autistics have difficulty "reading" other people, or making inferences about what other people know.

11. One possibility is that they acquire skills through extensive, focused practice; however, often their skills appear without any apparent practice. Another possibility is that they have more brain area devoted to a particular skill, although no evidence is given for this in the text. A third possibility, one that is more likely to be correct, is that because they lack central executive functions (mental processes that allow us to perform several tasks at the same time, for example), their attention may be focused on low level skills. This hypothesis is supported by the fact that often the individual's skill is limited to a very specific task and does not generalize to related tasks. Also, the book discusses a non-autistic individual with damage to his executive areas who became skilled at composing music without much previous training.

12. Drugs that reduce serotonin activity sometimes alleviate the compulsive behaviors associated with this disorder. This suggests that serotonin receptors are involved.

13. One reason is that the tasks given to elderly research participants may not be interesting or relevant to them. They perform much better on tasks involving meaningful material than on simple word memorization tasks. Another reason is that some studies compare people of different ages on the same task, and the older participants may have different experience.

Post-Test

All page references in this section pertain to the textbook.

1. a. Wrong; this is what IQ scores represent now.
    b. Correct; see p. 339.
    c. Wrong
    d. Wrong

2. **a. Correct**; see p. 340.
    b. Wrong
    c. Wrong
    d. Wrong

3. a. Wrong; b and c are also correct.
    b. Wrong
    c. Wrong
    d. Wrong
    e. Correct; see p. 340.

4. **a. Correct**; see p. 340.
    b. Wrong; Binet developed the first IQ tests.
    c. Wrong; Hawking is the scientist with ALS discussed in the beginning of the chapter.
    d. Wrong; Galton attempted to relate reaction time with intelligence.

5. a. Wrong; b is also correct.
    b. Wrong
    c. Wrong; there is no mention of this test measuring practical intelligence.
    d. Correct; see p. 341.
    e. Wrong

6. a. Wrong; the text does not discuss Sternberg's stance on the g factor issue.
    b. Wrong; this is not stated in the text, nor is it logically inferred from the information.
    c. Correct; Sternberg is saying we need to be careful about how we use intelligence tests, but isn't saying that they have no value whatsoever.
    d. Wrong; he does not say this.

7. a. Wrong; theorists in this camp argue that abilities are not distinct, whereas Gardner does make this argument.
    b. Correct; because of his stance on multiple intelligences, he should be placed in this camp.
    c. Wrong; these are lumpers.
    d. Wrong; Galton is the only reaction time theorist mentioned in the book.

8.　a.　Wrong; it is smaller than the average female brain.
　　b.　Wrong; it is smaller than the average male brain.
　　c.　Wrong; this was found to be true at only one of the brain sites sampled.
　　d.　Correct; see p. 342.

9.　**a.　Correct**; see p. 343.
　　b.　Wrong
　　c.　Wrong
　　d.　Wrong

10.　a.　Wrong
　　b.　Correct; there is some correlation between brain size and intelligence, but it is not very strong. All of the other choices are true.
　　c.　Wrong
　　d.　Wrong

11.　a.　Wrong; the book gives several reasons why this is not the best predictor of intelligence, including the fact that Einstein's brain was small, and men's brains are larger than women's, but there is no overall differences between them in intelligence.
　　b.　Wrong; simple reaction time is more weakly correlated with IQ than processing speed.
　　c.　Correct; this represents processing speed, and is highly correlated with IQ.
　　d.　Wrong; this is not discussed as being correlated with IQ per se, but rather with tasks using g factor.

12.　a.　Wrong; c is also true
　　b.　Wrong; it increases until later adulthood, and then it decreases.
　　c.　Wrong
　　d.　Wrong
　　e.　Correct; see pp. 344-345.

13.　a.　Wrong; b is also true.
　　b.　Wrong
　　c.　Wrong; they have more white matter (more myelination).
　　d.　Correct; see pp. 344-345.
　　e.　Wrong

14.　**a.　Correct**; see p. 345. All of the other choices are types of intelligence identified using factor analysis.
　　b.　Wrong
　　c.　Wrong
　　d.　Wrong

15.　a.　Wrong; this is associated with frontal activity.
　　b.　Wrong; both parietal lobes seem to be involved in this type of intelligence.
　　c.　Correct; see p. 346.
　　d.　Wrong

16. **a.** **Correct**; this area is involved in storing information about exact calculations, such as information from multiplication tables.
    b. Wrong; the parietal area for numbers is more involved in estimating quantities.
    c. Wrong; the temporal lobe is not mentioned as being involved in processing numbers.
    d. Wrong

17. a. Wrong; b and c are also correct.
    b. Wrong
    c. Wrong
    d. Wrong
    e. **Correct**; see p. 346.

18. a. Wrong
    b. Wrong
    c. Wrong
    d. **Correct**; genetic contributions to intelligence increase with age.

19. **a.** **Correct**; see p. 347.
    b. Wrong
    c. Wrong
    d. Wrong

20. a. Wrong; people are actually performing better on the tests.
    b. **Correct**; see p. 348.
    c. Wrong; mental retardation is an arbitrary label applied to those whose IQs are below 70.
    d. Wrong; because the increase in intelligence scores has occurred so quickly, it is unlikely to be due to genes.

21. a. Wrong; identical twins showed the strongest correlations, regardless of whether or not parents identified them as identical.
    b. **Correct**; see p. 348.
    c. Wrong
    d. Wrong

22. **a.** **Correct**; see p. 349.
    b. Wrong; if this were true, it would have supported the heriditarian argument for racial differences in intelligence, but in fact Scarr did not find this.
    c. Wrong; whites were not mentioned as being included in the study.
    d. Wrong

23. a. Wrong; this is true, especially when children raised in their biological homes are studied.
    b. **Correct**; this conclusion does not seem logical considering that children involved in Head Start exhibit a number of benefits.
    c. Wrong; this is true.
    d. Wrong; this is true.

24. **a.** **Correct**; early gains in IQ disappear, although other benefits remain.
    b. Wrong
    c. Wrong
    d. Wrong

25. a. Wrong; black children from impoverished backgrounds experienced about a 15 point increase in IQ following adoption.
    b. Correct; see pp. 349-350.
    c. Wrong
    d. Wrong

26. a. Wrong
    b. Wrong
    c. Correct; see p. 351.
    d. Wrong

27. a. Wrong; referring to Table 12.1, you can see that 85% of mentally retarded individuals fall into the mild category, and are typically educable to the 6th grade level.
    b. Wrong
    c. Correct; see Table 12.1 on p. 351.
    d. Wrong; mildly retarded individuals have IQs over 50.

28. a. Wrong
    b. Correct; see p. 351.
    c. Wrong
    d. Wrong

29. a. Wrong; c is also correct.
    b. Wrong; the book states that many hydrocephalics have normal intelligence even without treatment.
    c. Wrong
    d. Correct; see p. 352.
    e. Wrong

30. a. Wrong
    b. Correct; see p. 352.
    c. Wrong
    d. Wrong

31. **a. Correct**; in fact, they have difficulty pretending.
    b. Wrong; this is a common characteristic.
    c. Wrong; this is a common characteristic.
    d. Wrong; this is a common characteristic.

32. a. Wrong; often this is not the case.
    b. Wrong; their skills rarely generalize.
    c. Correct; see p. 354.
    d. Wrong; this is not implied to be true.

33. a. Wrong; this is true.
    b. Wrong; this is true.
    c. Correct; she actually have delayed language development.
    d. Wrong; this is true.

34. **a.** **Correct**; this area is not mentioned in the book; all of the other choices are listed.
    b. Wrong
    c. Wrong
    d. Wrong

35. a. Wrong; this is still a viable theory, although it probably only accounts for a small number of cases.
    b. **Correct**; see p. 355.
    c. Wrong; this is still a viable theory.
    d. Wrong; this is not mentioned as a theory at all.

36. **a.** **Correct**; see p. 356.
    b. Wrong; this is probably involved in the compulsive behaviors associated with autism.
    c. Wrong; this is not mentioned as being related to autism.
    d. Wrong

37. a. Wrong
    b. Wrong; this is the rate when spectrum disorders are not considered.
    c. **Correct**; see p. 357.
    d. Wrong

38. a. Wrong; many genes are probably involved.
    b. Wrong; many chromosomes may be involved.
    c. **Correct**; see p. 357.
    d. Wrong

39. **a.** **Correct**; see p. 357.
    b. Wrong; this drops after age 60.
    c. Wrong; this actually improves until middle age, and then drops slightly.
    d. Wrong
    e. Wrong

40. a. Wrong; this is true.
    b. Wrong; this is true.
    c. Wrong; this is true.
    d. **Correct**; this improves until middle age, and then drops.

Chapter 13: Psychological Disorders

Chapter Outline and Learning Objectives

As you read the chapter, use these learning objectives to guide your studying. You should be able to define the key terms from the text, which are shown in boldface type below.

1) Schizophrenia
   - What is **schizophrenia**? How common is it?

   a) Characteristics of the Disorder
      - What are the characteristics of schizophrenia? To what extent is there agreement over the subtypes of schizophrenia?

      - Distinguish between **acute** and **chronic** symptoms, and the prognosis for recovery.

      - Briefly outline the history of the study of schizophrenia, including suspected causes.

   b) Heredity
      i) Twin and Adoption Studies
         - What are the concordance rates of schizophrenia for different pairs of relatives? What degree of heritability does it have?

      ii) The search for the Schizophrenia Gene
         - Why has the search for a genetic basis of schizophrenia been difficult?

         - What do the results of Gottesman and Bertelsen suggest about the genetic basis of schizophrenia?

      iii) The Vulnerability Model
         - How, according to the **vulnerability model**, does schizophrenia develop?

   c) Two Kinds of Schizophrenia
      - Distinguish between the **positive** and **negative** symptoms of schizophrenia. What evidence is there that these types represent different syndromes (and probably have different causes)?

d) The Dopamine Hypothesis
   - What is the **dopamine hypothesis**, and what evidence supports it?

   - How do neuroleptic drugs alter dopamine activity?

e) Serotonin and Glutamate
   - What are the shortcomings of the dopamine hypothesis?

   - How are atypical antipsychotics thought to work? What advantages do they have over traditional neuroleptics?

   - What evidence supports the **glutamate theory** of schizophrenia?

f) The Neurological Disorder Hypothesis
   i) Ventricular Enlargement and Brain Tissue Deficits
      - What brain areas are typically affected in schizophrenics with enlarged ventricles?

   ii) Hypofrontality
      - How do schizophrenics perform on the **Wisconsin Card Sorting Task**?

      - What role does hypofrontality seem to play in schizophrenia? What specific prefrontal area is involved?

   iii) Disordered Connections
      - What evidence is there that schizophrenic symptoms are the result of disrupted connections in the brain?

      - What is auditory gating, and how is it thought to be involved in schizophrenia?

   iv) Causes of the Brain Deficits
      - What is the evidence that prenatal factors may contribute to schizophrenia?

   v) Schizophrenia as a Developmental Disease
      - What early nervous system anomalies are associated with later development of schizophrenia?

g) An Integrative Theory
- How does Weinberger's integrated theory of frontal lobe dysfunction and dopamine hyperactivity explain the development of schizophrenia? How does it account for both positive and negative symptoms?

- What evidence supports the integrated theory?

2) Affective Disorders
- What are the characteristics of **major depression** and **mania**? Distinguish between **unipolar depression** and **bipolar disorder**.

- What gender differences exist in affective disorders?

a) Heredity
- Discuss the evidence for genetic and environmental explanations for affective disorders.

b) The Monoamine Hypothesis of Depression
- What is the **monoamine hypothesis** of depression? What evidence supports it?

- How do antidepressant drugs produce their therapeutic effect?

c) Bipolar Disorder
- Describe the cycling associated with bipolar disorder.

- What effects does **lithium** have on bipolar disorder?

d) Electroconvulsive Therapy
- What is **electroconvulsive shock therapy**?

- When is ECT used for depression? How effective is it? Why is it thought to have therapeutic effects?

e) Rhythms and Affective Disorders
- How are **circadian rhythms** and **REM** related to depression?

i) Circadian Rhythms and Antidepressant Therapy
- How can circadian rhythms and REM sleep be manipulated to relieve depression?

ii) Seasonal Affective Disorder
- Describe the conditions under which **seasonal affective disorder** occurs. How common is it?

- How is **phototherapy** thought to relieve SAD? How might carbohydrate cravings be related to SAD?

f) Brain Anomalies in Affective Disorder
- What brain anomalies coincide with depression and bipolar disorder?

g) Suicide
- How prevalent is suicide among people with affective disorders?

- How is serotonin thought to be involved in suicide?

- Which psychoactive drugs may reduce the likelihood of suicide? Which may increase it?

3) Anxiety Disorders
- How common are anxiety disorders?

a) Generalized Anxiety, Panic Disorder, and Phobia
- What distinguishes anxiety from fear? What are the characteristics of generalized anxiety, panic disorder, and phobia?

i) Heredity
- Discuss the hereditary nature of anxiety disorders. Which disorders are thought to be genetically related?

- Why is generalized anxiety disorder thought to be more related to depression than to the other anxiety disorders?

ii) Neurotransmitters
- What neurotransmitters are thought to be involved in anxiety? What effects do anxiolytic drugs have on their activity?

iii) Brain Structures
- What brain areas are thought to be involved in these disorders?

b) Obsessive-Compulsive Disorder
- What are the characteristics of obsessive-compulsive disorder?

i) Brain Anomalies
- What brain areas are involved in OCD?

ii) Serotonin
- How is serotonin thought to be involved in OCD? What drugs are used to treat OCD, and how are they thought to work?

iii) Related Disorders
- What is the acral lick syndrome, and how is it similar to OCD?

- What is **Tourette's syndrome**, and how is it similar to OCD?

- What is the prevalence of Tourette's? What evidence is there for a genetic basis?

Schizophrenia

Summary and Guided Review

After studying this section in the text, fill in the blanks of the following summary. The answers are found on p. 309.

Schizophrenia is a mental disorder marked by a number of perceptual, emotional, and

_____ (1) deficits and associated with bizarre behavior. It affects about

_____ (2) % of the population regardless of gender or socioeconomic status, and about 20% of people

hospitalized for psychiatric care suffer from it.

Schizophrenia literally means "split mind," and reflects a split between _____ (3)

and mental experience, as evidenced by symptoms such as hallucinations, delusions, and paranoia. Many

subtypes of schizophrenia are thought to exist, but there is disagreement as to how many. There is some

evidence for schizophrenia-related spectrum disorders such as schizotypal and _____ (4)

personality. The lack of consensus on diagnosis makes it difficult to either predict whether or not a person

will get better, or to pinpoint genetic causes. People exhibiting _____ (5) symptoms

generally respond to treatment better than those who suffer from chronic symptoms; over half of

schizophrenics show some degree of recovery, and 22% show full recovery 20 years after the symptoms first appear. Although in the early 1900s schizophrenia was believed to have a _____ (6) basis, the technology for determining this did not become available until the 1960s.

Twin and adoption studies suggest a strong genetic component to schizophrenia; heritability has been estimated at _____ - _____ (7) %. Furthermore, _____ (8) out of a family with a history of schizophrenia has little impact on the disease's development. Genes on several chromosomes are thought to be involved in schizophrenia, but identifying specific genes is difficult because studies have been inconsistent in classifying, or including schizophrenics' relatives with _____ (9) disorders. Among twins _____ (10) for schizophrenia, children of the "normal" twins were as likely to become schizophrenic as children of the schizophrenic twin. The more schizophrenic relatives one has, the more likely one is to become schizophrenic and the more severe the disorder is likely to be. Some people are probably more genetically vulnerable than others. According to the _____ (11) model, a person will become schizophrenic if the combined genetic and environmental causal factors reach or exceed a threshold.

The symptoms of schizophrenia may be classified as either _____ (12) (including hallucinations and delusions) or negative (including lack of emotion or motivation). While positive symptoms tend to have acute onset and respond to drug treatments, _____ (13) symptoms tend to be chronic and are associated with indications of brain deficits. Research suggests there are different causes of the two types.

The first effective neuroleptic drugs were used in the _____ (14), although researchers did not know why these drugs worked. Later, it was discovered that _____ (15) produce psychotic behavior via increased dopamine activity, suggesting that excess dopaminergic activity was involved in schizophrenia. This was supported by the fact that drugs that _____ (16) dopamine receptors are effective in reducing positive symptoms of schizophrenia. The decrease in symptoms, which takes _____ - _____ (17) weeks, probably occurs as a result of a reduction of DA release following stimulation of presynaptic _____ (18), particularly in the mesolimbic dopamine system.

Not all schizophrenics respond to dopamine-blocking neuroleptics; some, especially those with negative symptoms, are more responsive to atypical antipsychotic drugs that block _____ (19) receptors. Whereas traditional neuroleptics often produce the motor disturbance _____ _____ (20), the atypical drugs produce fewer side-effects. Drugs such as glycine that activate the _____ (21) glutamate receptor also relieve symptoms of schizophrenia, suggesting that reduced glutamate is involved in schizophrenia as well. In fact, the dopamine system is influenced by both serotonin activity and glutamate activity.

Enlarged _____ (22) are commonly associated with schizophrenia, although it is not unique to this condition. It seems to result from the loss of cortical _____ _____ (23) and shrinkage of other brain areas.

The negative symptoms of dopamine have been associated with _____ (24), a condition in which the functioning of working memory in the prefrontal cortex is impaired. This may be due to a _____ (25) deficiency. The behavioral results of hypofrontality include flat affect, social withdrawal, and impaired attention.

Schizophrenia may also involve a _____ (26) in the connections between specific brain areas. For example, hallucinations and delusions may be the result of the individual's failure to recognize her own thoughts, due to a disconnection between the _____ (27) lobes and other brain areas. Impaired _____ _____ (28), which results in the schizophrenic's reduced ability to ignore or correctly interpret sounds, may be the result of impaired inhibition of the auditory system by the hippocampus.

Prenatal factors such as _____ _____ (29), winter birth, and viral infections may be associated with schizophrenia. For example, studies suggest that babies born in winter are at greater risk for prenatal exposure to viruses in the second trimester of pregnancy, and diseases such as _____ (30) have been linked to schizophrenia.

Explaining the biological basis of schizophrenia is challenging. First of all, the fact that damage found in schizophrenics' brains seems to occur _____ (31) the onset of the disorder makes it difficult to understand how brain anomalies contribute to the disorder. Also, the positive and negative symptoms appear to result from different causes. The _____ (32) theory proposed by Weinberger attempts to reconcile the seemingly unrelated clues about the cause of schizophrenia. According to this theory, because of prefrontal abnormalities, tonic DA release is reduced, which results in an increase in the number and sensitivity of _____ (33) dopamine receptors. Then when stress occurs, excessive DA release occurs onto all of these receptors. This mechanism is controlled by the _____ (34) cortex, which completes myelination and connection formation in adolescence and early adulthood. In someone with a predisposition for schizophrenia, the prefrontal area is improperly connected to other brain areas, and cannot control the subcortical _____ (35) activity. This accounts for the positive symptoms. Negative symptoms occur later, as DA activity _____ (36) with age. Although this theory does account for many aspects of schizophrenia, it does not explain how serotonin or _____ (37) are involved. However, remember that these latter two neurotransmitters are implicated in DA activity.

Short Answer & Essay

Answer the following questions. See pp. 310-311 for sample answers.

1. The book describes a study that showed that among identical twins in which one twin was schizophrenic and the other was "normal," the children of both twins were equally likely to develop the disorder. What does this suggest about the contributions of genes and environmental factors to schizophrenia?

2. What is the vulnerability model of schizophrenia? How does it account for schizophrenia developing in an individual with a low genetic predisposition? How does it account for schizophrenia NOT developing in someone with a high genetic predisposition?

3. If DA blockers immediately reduce postsynaptic effects of dopamine, why do schizophrenic symptoms not improve for 2-4 weeks?

4. How has research on recreational drugs such as amphetamine and PCP contributed to our understanding of schizophrenia?

5. What functional and anatomical brain deficits exist in schizophrenics? When do these deficits occur?

6. How does the integrative theory of schizophrenia account for cases involving both positive and negative symptoms?

Affective Disorders

Summary and Guided Review

After studying this section in the text, fill in the blanks of the following summary. The answers are found on pp. 309-310.

Major depression, or _____ (38) affective disorder, is characterized by hopelessness, loss of ability to enjoy many aspects of life, slowed thought, and sleep disturbances. _____ (39) disorder involves cycling between depression and mania, which is characterized by periods of excess energy and confidence, and development of grandiose schemes. Unipolar depression is more common in _____ (40), but bipolar disorder is equally common in men and women.

There is evidence for a genetic basis of affective disorders. The concordance rate is 69% for _____ (41) and 13% for fraternal twins, and adoption has little effect on this rate. Unipolar and bipolar disorders are not believed to be genetically related. The genes involved have not been identified.

Iproniazid was the first drug used to treat depression. Because it has effects on the _____ (42) neurotransmitters, it was assumed that norepinephrine and serotonin are involved in depression, supporting the monoamine hypothesis of depression. Other drugs such as

Prozac that _____ (43) the activity of one or both of these substances have been used to treat depression; their mechanisms of action vary. _____ (44) is involved in mood, activity level, sleep and temperature cycles, eating and sex, and cognition. _____ (45) is related to motivation and responsiveness to the environment. Antidepressants also decrease sensitivity of the ____ - _____ (46) receptor; heightened sensitivity of this receptor type may account for the agitation some depressed people experience. Finally, a component of tobacco smoke serves as a _____ _____ _____ (47), which may explain why so many depressed people smoke, and why they have so much difficulty quitting.

People with _____ (48) disorder exhibit a great deal of variability in their cycling between states of mania and depression. Stress often seems to trigger _____ (49) phases, although over time it has less of an effect. Bipolar disorder is most often treated with _____ (50), which stabilizes both manic and depressive episodes; it is believed that this is accomplished through stabilization of several neurotransmitter and receptor systems.

Electroconvulsive shock therapy is sometimes used to treat depression; this requires generating a brief but strong _____ (51) in the brain under carefully controlled conditions. Patients are unconscious during the procedure and wake up soon afterwards. The procedure is repeated _____ - _____ (52) times over 3-4 weeks. This treatment was first found to be useful with _____ (53), but antipsychotic drugs have replaced its usage for that disorder. For depression, ECT is rarely used, and only as a last resort after drug treatments have failed. It is more effective than drug treatments, and its effects are experienced more quickly; thus it is likely to be used with patients who are _____ (54). The benefits of ECT are short term, and its use is often combined with drug treatment over the longer term. ECT seems to have the same effects on _____ (55) and norepinephrine systems as antidepressant drugs; it also seems to _____ (56) neural firing throughout the brain, which may account for the faster relief it offers.

People with depression often suffer from _____ (57) rhythm disturbances, including feeling tired early in the evening, waking early in the morning, and spending more time in _____ (58) sleep. Readjusting one's circadian rhythm by altering sleep habits may bring relief, as may reducing REM sleep. In many people, antidepressants _____ (59) REM sleep through their moderating effects on serotonin and norepinephrine activity.

People with _____ _____ _____ (60) experience depression, either in the summer or winter, and improve or experience hypomania in the other season. SAD accounts for 10% of all affective disorders, and is much more common in _____ (61).

Depression in SAD is usually characterized by excess sleepiness, increased _____ (62) intake, and weight gain. Amount of natural _____ (63) is associated with winter depression; moving to or visiting a more tropical region often brings some relief. Heat is associated with _____ (64) depression; finding ways to stay cool seems to relieve this form of depression. Winter depression is often treated with _____ (65), which involves exposure to intense light for a few hours each day. The light exposure must mimic bright sunlight, and it seems to work by resetting the _____ _____ (66). In addition, people suffering from winter depression may self-medicate by eating more carbohydrates, which increases brain _____ (67) levels.

Depression is associated with reduced activity in the _____ (68) nucleus and dorsolateral prefrontal cortex, and increased activity in the ventral prefrontal cortex, which is connected to the amygdala. Mania is also characterized by increased brain activity; the _____ (69) prefrontal cortex may control cycling.

People with affective disorders, particularly those with bipolar disorder, are at greater risk for suicide than others in the population. Suicide, even among non-depressed individuals, is associated with low levels of the serotonin metabolite ___ - _____ (70). Selective serotonin reuptake inhibitors may reduce the risk of suicide in non-depressed individuals. However, noradrenergic _____ (71) and sedatives may increase the risk of suicide.

Short Answer & Essay

Answer the following questions. See p. 311 for sample answers.

7. Distinguish between the mechanisms of monoamine oxidase inhibitors, tricyclic antidepressants, and second generation antidepressants.

8. What are two ways in which depressed individuals may self-medicate to relieve depression?

9. What are the procedures that may be used to alter a depressed patient's sleep patterns? How does altering sleep affect their circadian rhythm?

10. What are the ways of alleviating the symptoms of winter-depression SAD?

11. Why does the author of the text suggest that the ventral prefrontal cortex acts as a "depression switch" and the subgenual prefrontal cortex acts as a bipolar "switch?"

12. Why are people with low serotonin levels thought to be the most at risk for suicide?

Anxiety Disorders

Summary and Guided Review

After studying this section in the text, fill in the blanks of the following summary. The answers are found on p. 310.

Anxiety disorders include generalized anxiety disorder, panic disorder, _____ (72), and obsessive-compulsive disorder. Whereas _____ (73) is an adaptive reaction to real objects or events, anxiety involves the anticipation of events and inappropriately fearful reactions to objects and events. While panic disorder and phobia seem to be genetically related, generalized anxiety disorder seems to be more related to _____ _____ (74).

Anxiety disorders may be treated with benzodiazepines, which increase sensitivity to _____ (75). Reduced _____ (76) activity is also implicated in anxiety disorders, and drugs that increase serotonin activity may alleviate anxiety. Anxiety is associated with heightened activity in the amygdala and _____ _____ (77), and in panic disorder the entire brain may be overactive.

_____ - _____ _____ (78) is marked by recurring thoughts (obsessions) and compulsive actions over which the person has no control. These behaviors are often repetitive and _____ (79), such as checking locks or appliances, or engaging in routines that have no purpose. OCD seems to run in families.

OCD is associated with increased activity in the orbital frontal cortex and the caudate nucleus; damage to the _____ _____ (80) is associated with OCD. For example, the millionaire Howard Hughes displayed OCD later in his life, after a series of _____ (81), although his mother was obsessive about germs when he was a child. Both genes and environment may have been involved in his disorder. Serotonin activity is _____ (82) in OCD, and selective serotonin reuptake inhibitors can reduce the symptoms.

OCD is related to _____ _____ _____ (83), a disorder in which non-human animals (usually pets) over-groom themselves. It is also related to _____ _____ (84), which is characterized by motor and phonic _____ (85), including making facial expressions, irrelevant and insulting remarks, and various noises. Although people with Tourette's may be able to control themselves under some circumstances, they cannot do so all the time. The disorder typically emerges in _____ (86) and becomes more pronounced over time; _____ (87) are more likely to have this disorder. Heritability for Tourette's is high, and Tourette's and OCD are thought to have the same _____ (88) basis. Tourette's involves increased dopamine

activity in the _____ _____ (89), and the

_____ (90) blocker Haloperidol is the treatment of choice.

Short Answer & Essay

Answer the following questions. See pp. 311-312 for sample answers.

13. Why is generalized anxiety disorder thought to be more related to major depression than to other anxiety disorders?

14. How are the symptoms of acral lick syndrome similar to OCD? Why are these two disorders thought to be related?

15. How are OCD and Tourette's syndrome similar? Why are they thought to be related?

Post-Test

Use these multiple-choice questions to check your understanding of the chapter. The answers, along with explanations, are found beginning on p. 312.

1. What percentage of the US population can expect to experience a psychological disorder during their lifetime?
   a. 10%
   b. 20%
   c. 30%
   d. 50%

2. Schizophrenia is typically characterized by all of the following EXCEPT
   a. loss of contact with reality.
   b. perceptual, emotional, and intellectual deficits.
   c. a sense of hopelessness.
   d. an inability to function in life.

3. Which of the following statements regarding schizophrenia is TRUE?
   a. Researchers do not agree on what subtypes exist.
   b. Researchers universally recognize spectrum disorders.
   c. Schizophrenia is related to multiple personality disorder.
   d. There is little evidence for a genetic basis of schizophrenia.

4. Schizophrenics with _____ symptoms are more likely to recover.
   a. chronic
   b. negative
   c. violent
   d. acute

5. 20 years after first hospitalization, what percentage of schizophrenics seem fully recovered?
    a. 12%
    b. 22%
    c. 35%
    d. 56%

6. In the 1940s, most researchers believed that schizophrenia was a disorder of primarily _____ causes.
    a. genetic
    b. physiological
    c. hormonal
    d. social

7. When spectrum disorders are NOT considered, the concordance rate for schizophrenia among identical twins is
    a. 48%
    b. 17%
    c. 89%
    d. 28%

8. Jerry and Jason are identical twins. Jerry has schizophrenia, but Jason does not. Which of the following statements is correct?
    a. Jerry's children are more likely to develop schizophrenia than Jason's children.
    b. Jason's children are more likely to develop schizophrenia than Jerry's children.
    c. Jerry and Jason's children are equally likely to develop schizophrenia.
    d. Jerry and Jason's children are no more likely to develop schizophrenia than any member of the population.

9. Which of the following is an example of a negative symptom of schizophrenia?
    a. hallucinations
    b. delusions
    c. bizarre behavior
    d. lack of emotion

10. Which of the following symptoms is/are most likely to respond to treatment with antipsychotic medication?
    a. hallucinations
    b. delusions
    c. poverty of speech
    d. a and b
    e. b and c

11. Traditional antipsychotic drugs such as spiroperidol are
    a. dopamine antagonists.
    b. dopamine agonists.
    c. serotonin antagonists.
    d. serotonin agonists.

12. Which of the following is most likely to cause tardive dyskinesia?
    a. Clozapine
    b. Risperidone
    c. Chlorpromazine
    d. Olanzapine

13. Glycine may be an effective treatment for
    a. acute onset schizophrenia.
    b. negative symptoms of schizophrenia.
    c. positive symptoms of schizophrenia.
    d. a and c.

14. Enlarged ventricles is associated with
    a. schizophrenia.
    b. Alzheimer's disease.
    c. Huntington's disease.
    d. a and b.
    e. a, b, and c.

15. Hypofrontality is most closely associated with damage to the _____ prefrontal cortex.
    a. dorsolateral
    b. subgenual
    c. ventral
    d. anterior

16. Auditory gating is improved in schizophrenics by which substance?
    a. antipsychotics
    b. nicotine
    c. anxiolytics
    d. monoamine oxidase inhibitors

17. All of the following are linked to the brain defects associated with schizophrenia EXCEPT
    a. prenatal exposure to influenza.
    b. premature birth.
    c. prolonged labor.
    d. prenatal exposure to alcohol.

18. Which of the following statements regarding the development of schizophrenia is true?
    a. Gray matter deficits become more pronounced with age.
    b. Cortical neurons fail to migrate to the appropriate locations in the second trimester of pregnancy.
    c. Ventricle enlargement is evident at birth.
    d. Brain damage associated with schizophrenia always appear in adolescence.

19. According to the integrative theory of schizophrenia, positive symptoms are caused by
    a. a decrease in subcortical DA activity.
    b. improper connections between prefrontal and temporal limbic areas.
    c. heightened sensitivity of subcortical DA receptors.
    d. b and c.
    e. a, b, and c

20. Which of the following is not a symptom of major depression?
    a. decreased need for sleep
    b. hopelessness
    c. loss of energy
    d. restlessness

21. Women are more likely than men to suffer from
    a. unipolar depression.
    b. bipolar disorder.
    c. both unipolar depression and bipolar disorder.
    d. neither unipolar depression nor bipolar disorder.

22. The concordance rate for depression among identical twins raised apart
    a. is about the same as for those raised together.
    b. is much lower than for those raised together.
    c. is about the same as for fraternal twins raised together.
    d. none of the above.

23. The first prescription drug used to treat depression was
    a. Prozac.
    b. Iproniazid.
    c. Chlorpromazine.
    d. Nicotine.

24. Prozac is a
    a. monoamine oxidase inhibitor.
    b. trycyclic antidepressant.
    c. second generation antidepressant.
    d. none of the above.

25. Reduced norepinephrine is associated with
    a. sleep.
    b. sexual activity.
    c. body temperature regulation.
    d. lack of motivation.

26. The drug of choice for treating bipolar disorder is
    a. Lithium.
    b. Iproniazid.
    c. Prozac.
    d. Haloperidol.

27. Which of the following is NOT true of ECT?
    a. It typically involves profound memory loss.
    b. It must result in a brain seizure in order to be effective.
    c. It must be repeated several times over the course of 3-4 weeks.
    d. Its therapeutic effects are as good as or better than antidepressant drugs.

28. Which of the following brain changes is/are associated with ECT?
    a. Increased sensitivity to serotonin
    b. Decreased sensitivity at β-noreadrenergic receptors.
    c. Global synchronous neural firing.
    d. a and c
    e. a, b, and c

29. Depression is associated with
    a. a phase-advanced circadian rhythm.
    b. REM sleep deficit.
    c. a heightened sense of arousal in the evenings.
    d. a and b.
    e. b and c.

30. Which of the following statements regarding SAD is TRUE?
    a. It is always unipolar.
    b. It only affects people in the winter.
    c. It can be treated by changing behavior.
    d. It is always bipolar.

31. Regarding phototherapy as a treatment for SAD,
    a. the length of exposure to light is more important than the amount or intensity of light.
    b. the amount or intensity of light is more important than the length of exposure to light.
    c. it only works if it is used early in the morning.
    d. it is less effective than drug therapy.

32. People with SAD self-medicate by
    a. eating a lot of carbohydrates.
    b. smoking.
    c. chewing nicotine gum.
    d. all of the above.

33. Which of the following brain areas shows heightened activity in depressed people?
    a. caudate nucleus
    b. dorsolateral prefrontal cortex
    c. subgenual prefrontal cortex
    d. ventral prefrontal cortex

34. Which of the following groups is most at risk for suicide?
    a. People with unipolar depression
    b. People with bipolar disorder
    c. People with substance abuse
    d. People with schizophrenia

35. Trevor becomes anxious whenever he gets around water, so he avoids going to lakes, rivers and other large bodies of water. What type of anxiety disorder does he most likely have?
    a. Generalized anxiety disorder
    b. Phobia
    c. Panic disorder
    d. OCD

36. _____ relieve anxiety by enhancing GABA activity.
    a. Selective serotonin reuptake inhibitors
    b. Neuroleptic drugs
    c. Haloperidol
    d. Benzodiazepines

37. Anxiety is associated with increased activity in the
    a. prefrontal cortex.
    b. locus coeruleus.
    c. hippocampus.
    d. basal ganglia.

38. The millionaire Howard Hughes was suffering from
    a. generalized anxiety disorder.
    b. phobia.
    c. panic disorder.
    d. OCD.

39. Which drug is most likely to be effective in treating OCD?
    a. Prozac
    b. Benzodiazepines
    c. Haloperidol
    d. Monoamine oxidase inhibitor

40. Tourette's syndrome probably results from increased _____ activity in the
    _____ .
    a. dopamine; prefrontal cortex
    b. serotonin; prefrontal cortex
    c. serotonin; basal ganglia
    d. dopamine; basal ganglia

Answers & Explanations

Guided Review

1. intellectual
2. 1
3. reality
4. schizoid
5. acute
6. physical
7. 60-90
8. adoption
9. spectrum
10. discordant
11. vulnerability
12. positive
13. negative
14. 1950s
15. amphetamines
16. block
17. 2-4
18. autoreceptors
19. serotonin
20. tardive dyskinesia
21. NMDA
22. ventricles
23. gray matter
24. hypofrontality
25. dopamine
26. disruption
27. frontal
28. auditory gating
29. birth complications
30. influenza
31. before
32. integrative
33. subcortical
34. prefrontal
35. dopamine
36. decreases
37. glutamate
38. unipolar
39. Bipolar

40. women
41. identical
42. monoamine
43. increase
44. Serotonin
45. Norepinephrine
46. β-noradrenergic
47. monoamine oxidase inhibitor
48. bipolar
49. manic
50. lithium
51. seizure
52. 6-8
53. schizophrenics
54. suicidal
55. serotonin
56. synchronize

57. circadian
58. REM
59. inhibit
60. seasonal affective disorder
61. women
62. carbohydrate
63. light
64. summer
65. phototherapy
66. circadian rhythm
67. serotonin
68. caudate
69. subgenual
70. 5-HIAA
71. antidepressants
72. phobia
73. fear
74. major depression

75. GABA
76. serotonin
77. locus coeruleus
78. Obsessive-compulsive disorder
79. ritualistic
80. basal ganglia
81. accidents
82. high
83. acral lick syndrome
84. Tourette's syndrome
85. tics
86. childhood
87. males
88. genetic
89. caudate nuclei
90. dopamine

Short Answer & Essay

1. Because the children of each twin were equally likely to develop the disorder, genes are clearly involved in the disorder. It is not something one gets exclusively from the environment; otherwise, the children of the normal twin would be normal. At the same time, because the "normal" twin possesses the same genes as the schizophrenic twin, the differences in environmental factors between the twins must account for the fact that one of them is more affected than the other.

2. The vulnerability model suggests that schizophrenia develops as a result of the combined influence of genetic and environmental factors that reach or exceed some threshold. This model explains that someone with a low genetic predisposition may become schizophrenic if environmental factors, in particular stressors, are strong enough to trigger the disorder. It also explains that someone with a high degree of genetic predisposition may not develop the disorder if s/he lives in a relatively stress-free environment.

3. The mechanism by which DA blockers relieve the symptoms of schizophrenia involves more than just blocking DA receptors. After DA receptors have been blocked for several days, the accumulation of DA in the synapse is detected by autoreceptors on the presynaptic membrane, which leads to a reduction in presynaptic DA release.

4. When it was discovered that amphetamines, which elevate dopamine activity, can produce the same symptoms as schizophrenia, the dopamine hypothesis of schizophrenia was developed. This discovery was important because it suggested that drugs that block DA might be useful for treating schizophrenia. The effects of PCP use also mimic schizophrenia, and it is known that this drug inhibits NMDA glutamate receptors. This suggests that a glutamate deficiency may be involved in schizophrenia as well.

5. A functional deficit is a dopamine deficiency in the prefrontal cortex. One of the most obvious anatomical deficits is enlarged ventricles, which results from loss of cortical gray matter and limbic area volume, and enlarged fissures and sulci. Also, several areas have disordered connections, such as between the prefrontal cortex and hippocampus, and between the frontal areas and other areas involved

in sensation. Finally, there is some evidence that cell migration is abnormal, particularly in the temporal and frontal lobes.

6. According to the integrative theory, the positive and negative symptoms occur for separate, but related reasons. It is believed that the prefrontal cortex controls the release of dopamine to subcortical areas, and that in the schizophrenic, this control is faulty because of improper connections between the prefrontal cortex and subcortical areas. This results in less DA release into the subcortical areas, which respond by producing more receptors, and thus this area becomes more sensitive to DA. Stressors, particularly those experienced in adolescence and early adulthood, result in massive DA release onto highly sensitive areas. This precipitates the positive symptoms. Later in adulthood, DA levels decrease in the cortex and subcortical areas, and the negative symptoms emerge as a result of hypofrontality.

7. Monoamine oxidase inhibitors work by preventing the breakdown of monoamines in the synapse. Tricyclics prevent reuptake of the monoamines. Second generation antidepressants affect one specific neurotransmitter, rather than all of the monoamines; for example, many of these drugs prevent the reuptake of serotonin.

8. Many depressed people smoke, and an ingredient in tobacco smoke has been identified that acts as an MAO inhibitor. Also, people with SAD often eat a lot of carbohydrates, which increases their serotonin levels, and may produce some relief from their depression.

9. Initially, the person follows the atypical sleep rhythm. Then, sleep can be delayed by 30 minutes each night until the person is going to bed and getting up at "normal" times. In addition, preventing REM sleep, especially early in the sleep cycle, may relieve depression as well.

10. Winter-depression SAD may be alleviated by moving to or visiting a region where there is more natural light (people in the northern hemisphere would need to move south, and people in the southern hemisphere would need to move north). Phototherapy also provides relief if the person is exposed to a few hours of bright light during the day in the winter (when days are short and light levels are less intense than in summer).

11. The ventral prefrontal cortex is thought to be a "depression switch" because it is more active during periods of depression and less active when the person is not experiencing symptoms. The subgenual prefrontal cortex may be a bipolar switch because activity levels within it correspond with the manic and depressive states of the disorder; it is more active during mania, less active during depression. Also, it controls the neurotransmitters involved in affective disorders.

12. Low serotonin is a marker for aggression and impulsive behavior, regardless of psychiatric disorder. Both of these probably contribute to suicidal acts. Also, a drug that inhibits the reuptake of serotonin reduces the risk of suicide, even in people who are not depressed.

13. One reason is that heritability studies suggest a link between the two. Generalized anxiety and depression co-occur in families. Also, because antidepressants often relieve anxiety, the two may share a similar mechanism.

14. In some cases of OCD, grooming behaviors and behaviors related to cleanliness are performed excessively. In some animals, hair or feather pulling becomes problematic when bald spots and sores occur. Acral lick syndrome often responds to the same medication used to treat OCD.

15. OCD and Tourette's syndrome are similar in that the behaviors exhibited seem to be compulsions. In Tourette's, a person can control his behavior, but only for a while. The reason why the two are thought to be related is because they co-occur in families.

Post-Test

All page references in this section pertain to the textbook.

1. a. Wrong
   b. Correct; 1 in 5 people are expected to suffer from psychological disorders.
   c. Wrong
   d. Wrong

2. a. Wrong
   b. Wrong
   c. Correct; this is a characteristic of depression, but is not mentioned as being a characteristic of schizophrenia. All of the other choices are characteristics of schizophrenia.
   d. Wrong

3. **a. Correct**; see p. 366.
   b. Wrong; not all researchers recognize spectrum disorders.
   c. Wrong; the "split" refers to a break from reality, not having multiple selves.
   d. Wrong; there is a great deal of evidence for this, including a concordance rate of nearly 50% among identical twins.

4. a. Wrong; these symptoms develop gradually and are more persistent.
   b. Wrong; these symptoms are often long-lasting.
   c. Wrong; there is no mention of violence as a symptom of schizophrenia.
   d. Correct; see p. 367.

5. a. Wrong
   b. Correct; see p. 367.
   c. Wrong
   d. Wrong

6. a. Wrong; while a few researchers believed this to be true, based on twin studies, most were more influenced by Freudian theory's emphasis on social causes of mental disorder.
   b. Wrong; the technology for discovering the physiological basis of schizophrenia did not yet exist.
   c. Wrong
   d. Correct; see p. 367.

7. **a. Correct**; see p. 368.
   b. Wrong
   c. Wrong
   d. Wrong

8. a. Wrong
   b. Wrong
   c. Correct; see p. 369.
   d. Wrong; any child of a schizophrenic is at higher risk for schizophrenia than the general population.

9. a. Wrong
   b. Wrong
   c. Wrong
   d. Correct; all of the other choices represent positive symptoms.

10. a. Wrong; b is also correct.
    b. Wrong; a is also correct.
    c. Wrong; this is a negative symptom, which do not respond to antipsychotics drugs as well as positive symptoms.
    d. Correct; positive symptoms are more likely to be acute, and are more likely to respond to drugs.
    e. Wrong

11. **a. Correct**; these drugs block dopamine receptors, which reduces the effects of dopamine on the post-synaptic membrane. This is one mechanism of drug antagonism.
    b. Wrong
    c. Wrong; the traditional antipsychotics do not directly affect serotonin. However, atypical antipsychotics do have an antagonist effect on serotonin.
    d. Wrong

12. a. Wrong
    b. Wrong
    c. Correct; this is a traditional antipsychotic DA blocker, and has been associated with tardive dyskinesia. The other drugs listed are atypical, and do not directly block dopamine; they are less likely to produce this side effect.
    d. Wrong

13. a. Wrong; it seems to be effective against negative symptoms, which are more often slow to develop (chronic).
    b. Correct; see p. 372.
    c. Wrong
    d. Wrong

14. a. Wrong; b and c are also correct.
    b. Wrong; a and c are also correct.
    c. Wrong; a and b are also correct.
    d. Wrong
    e. Correct; many disorders share this characteristic.

15. **a. Correct**; see p. 374.
    b. Wrong; this area is implicated in bipolar disorder.
    c. Wrong; this area is implicated in depression
    d. Wrong; this area is not mentioned.

16. a. Wrong; the book states that "typical neuroleptics do not improve gating."
    b. Correct; see p. 375.
    c. Wrong; anti-anxiety drugs are not mentioned as being a treatment for schizophrenia.
    d. Wrong; antidepressants are not mentioned as being a treatment for schizophrenia.

17. a.　Wrong
    b.　Wrong
    c.　Wrong
    d.　Correct; although prenatal exposure has been linked to many brain deficits, including mental retardation, schizophrenia is not one of them. All of the other choices have been associated with schizophrenia.

18. a.　Wrong; the deficits are often apparent when the patient is first seen, but do not worsen.
    b.　Correct; see p. 376.
    c.　Wrong; this is not mentioned.
    d.　Wrong; although some teenagers diagnosed with schizophrenia show brain deficits at that time, we cannot logically conclude that this is always the case

19. a.　Wrong; there is a decrease in tonic cortical DA release.
    b.　Wrong; c is also correct.
    c.　Wrong; b is also correct.
    d.　Correct; see p. 377.
    e.　Wrong

20. **a.　Correct**; this is a symptom of mania, but not unipolar depression. All of the other choices are symptoms of major depression.
    b.　Wrong
    c.　Wrong
    d.　Wrong

21. **a.　Correct**; see p. 378.
    b.　Wrong; males and females are equally at risk.
    c.　Wrong
    d.　Wrong

22. **a.　Correct**; according to the text, "the concordance rate drops surprisingly little when identical twins are reared apart (p. 378)."
    b.　Wrong
    c.　Wrong; the concordance rate for identical twins is 69%, and 13% for fraternal twins.
    d.　Wrong

23. a.　Wrong; this is a second generation antidepressant, and much newer than Iproniazid.
    b.　Correct; see p. 379.
    c.　Wrong; this is a traditional antipsychotic.
    d.　Wrong; this is not a treatment for depression (although another component of cigarette smoke may be).

24. a.　Wrong
    b.　Wrong
    c.　Correct; see p. 379.
    d.　Wrong

25. a. Wrong
   b. Wrong
   c. Wrong
   d. Correct; norepinephrine seems to be related to the lack of goal-directed behavior. All of the other choices are related to serotonin.

26. **a. Correct**; see p. 380.
   b. Wrong
   c. Wrong
   d. Wrong; this is an antipsychotic.

27. **a. Correct**; while it may result in some confusion, profound memory loss is not listed as one of its side effects. All of the other choices are true of ECT.
   b. Wrong
   c. Wrong
   d. Wrong

28. a. Wrong; b and c are also correct.
   b. Wrong; a and c are also correct.
   c. Wrong; a and b are also correct.
   d. Wrong
   e. Correct; see pp. 380-381.

29. **a. Correct**; see p. 382.
   b. Wrong; too much REM is associated with depression.
   c. Wrong; people with depression are sometimes very sleepy in the evening.
   d. Wrong
   e. Wrong

30. a. Wrong; sometimes people exhibit depression in one season and mania in another.
   b. Wrong; there are cases of summer depression.
   c. Correct; traveling to more tropical climates can relieve symptoms, as can exposure to more light.
   d. Wrong; antidepressants are not discussed in this section.

31. a. Wrong
   b. Correct; see pp. 383-384.
   c. Wrong; phototherapy at midday is also effective.
   d. Wrong

32. **a. Correct**; carbohydrates increase brain serotonin levels.
   b. Wrong; although a component of cigarette smoke may help alleviate depression, smoking is not mentioned as a self treatment for SAD.
   c. Wrong; using nicotine is not mentioned as a treatment for SAD.
   d. Wrong

33. a. Wrong; activity is decreased in this area.
   b. Wrong; activity is decreased in this area.
   c. Wrong; this area is discussed as being related to bipolar disorder.
   d. Correct; see p. 384.

34. a. Wrong
    b. **Correct**; see figure 13.18 and p. 386.
    c. Wrong
    d. Wrong

35. a. Wrong
    b. **Correct**; because Trevor's anxiety is associated with a specific type of stimulus, it is most likely a phobia.
    c. Wrong
    d. Wrong

36. a. Wrong; these are not discussed as affecting GABA.
    b. Wrong
    c. Wrong
    d. **Correct**; see p. 387.

37. a. Wrong
    b. **Correct**; see p. 387.
    c. Wrong
    d. Wrong

38. a. Wrong
    b. Wrong
    c. Wrong
    d. **Correct**; see p. 388.

39. **a.** **Correct**; the text states that "the only drugs that consistently improve OCD symptoms are antidepressants that inhibit serotonin reuptake," and Prozac is the only drug among these choices that is a selective serotonin reuptake inhibitor.
    b. Wrong
    c. Wrong
    d. Wrong; these drugs work by inhibiting the breakdown of serotonin, not by preventing its reuptake.

40. a. Wrong
    b. Wrong
    c. Wrong
    d. **Correct**; see p. 390.

Chapter 14: Sleep and Consciousness

Chapter Outline and Learning Objectives

As you read the chapter, use these learning objectives to guide your studying. You should be able to define the key terms from the text, which are shown in boldface type below.

1) Sleep and Dreaming
- From the introduction to the chapter, briefly describe the role that the study of consciousness has played in psychology. Why was it virtually ignored in the first half of the 20th century? Why did it become important again in the second half?

- Compare the **restoration** and **adaptive** hypotheses of sleep. What evidence supports each?

- What are some of the negative effects of sleep deprivation, such as from shift work and **jet lag**?

a) Circadian Rhythms
- What is a **circadian rhythm**? What bodily changes follow our sleep/wake cycle? What is the role of the **suprachiasmatic nucleus** in these circadian rhythms?

- What are **Zeitgebers**, and why are they important for our sleep/wake cycle? What happens to our sleep/wake cycles when no Zeitgebers are available?

- What is the importance of exposure to light and darkness for **entraining** the circadian clock?

- How do researchers explain the fact that it is usually easier to adjust to phase delays than to phase advances?

- Discuss the evidence for and against the assertion that the human wake/sleep cycle is on a 25-hour schedule. Why does Czeisler suggest that the cycle is 24 rather than 25 hours?

- What role does **melatonin** play in sleep? How does light affect melatonin?

b) Rhythms During Waking and Sleeping
- What are **ultradian rhythms**? Give some examples.

- Distinguish between alpha and beta waves in terms of the amplitude and frequency of each type. How do they reflect relaxation and alertness, respectively?

- Describe the EEG patterns that correspond to the four stages of sleep.

- What is **rapid eye movement sleep**? Why is it also called paradoxical sleep?

- Compare dreams occurring during REM and non-REM sleep.

i) The Function of REM Sleep
- What happens when a person is deprived of REM sleep?

- According to the **activation-synthesis hypothesis**, what brain activity gives rise to REM sleep and dreams?

- What are the possible functions of REM sleep?

- What are the possible mechanisms by which REM sleep may enhance learning?

ii) The Functions of Slow Wave Sleep
- What are the possible functions of slow wave sleep?

c) Brain Structures and Sleep
- What is the significance of the **basal forebrain area** in sleep and wakefulness?

- What are the components of the POAH? How is this circuit related to sleep? How does caffeine affect this circuit?

- What are **PGO waves**? How do they contribute to REM sleep?

- Define **cataplexy** and **narcolepsy**. How is REM sleep involved in these disorders?

d) Sleep as a Form of Consciousness
- What is lucid dreaming? What does lucid dreaming suggest about a person's potential for awareness or consciousness during dreams?

- Describe REM sleep behavior disorder.

2) The Neural Bases of Consciousness
- How does the author define consciousness?

a) Awareness
- What evidence is there that the thalamus is especially important for consciousness?

- What is the **binding problem**? Why does Crick argue that the thalamus is responsible for coordination of different aspects of awareness?

- To what extent is awareness required for learning? Can learning occur without awareness?

b) Attention
- What is **attention**, and why is it significant for understanding consciousness?

- What does the Cheshire cat effect demonstrate?

- How are changes in attention reflected in changes in brain activity? What mechanism may be responsible for shifting attention among stimuli?

3) The Sense of Self
- How do researchers test for self-awareness in pre-verbal children and nonhuman animals? What do these studies reveal?

a) Some Origins of the Self
- What evidence exists that some elements of the sense of self involve different brain areas?

i) Body Image
- How does the loss of proprioception or limbs affect people's sense of their bodies?

- How is body image thought to be represented in the brain?

ii) Memory
- Why is memory important for our sense of self? What happens to individuals who lose large portions of their long-term memories?

- Why, according to Shallice, is confabulation among amnesiacs significant?

b) Disorders of the Self
  i) The Split Brain and the Self
  - In what ways are split brain patients' behaviors abnormal?

  - What conclusions have researchers drawn about the nature of consciousness based on split brain studies? What, according to Gazzaniga, is the role of the **brain interpreter**?

  ii) Dissociative Identity Disorder
  - What is **dissociative identity disorder**? Why is this disorder controversial?

  - What evidence supports a physiological basis for DID?

  - How may state-dependent learning be involved in DID?

Sleep and Dreaming

Summary and Guided Review

After studying this section in the text, fill in the blanks of the following summary. The answers are found on p. 331.

The study of consciousness within psychology has been controversial. The use of _____ (1) to study consciousness, popular at the end of 19th century, fell out of favor when the _____ (2) attempted to rid psychology of subjective methods during the first half of the 20th century. When _____ (3) psychology emerged in the mid-20th century, mental experiences were once again acceptable to study if they could be examined objectively. However, because of lack of technology, as well as lack of consensus concerning the meaning of consciousness, this topic has remained controversial. Those who do study it often approach the topic from other disciplines, including _____ (4), philosophy, and computer science, and the processes of awareness, attention, and _____ (5) are most commonly studied.

Although sleep is one of our most basic needs, researchers who study it have been unable to fully explain its functions. The _____ (6) hypothesis suggests that sleep allows us to conserve energy and repair our bodies. Because amount of sleep is correlated with a species' body size, food availability, metabolic rate, and vulnerability, the _____ (7) hypothesis suggests sleep is a trade off between needs for energy conservation and safety. There is considerable evidence that getting adequate sleep at the right time is important. People who work _____ (8) or graveyard shifts experience difficulty getting enough sleep during the day. Rates of vehicle and work-related accidents are higher in the early morning hours than at other times. And _____-_____ (9) baseball teams playing games in east-coast cities seem to be at a disadvantage if they are not given adequate time to adjust to the time shift.

Our sleep/wake cycle is an example of a _____ (10) rhythm, and the sleep period corresponds with decreases in several physiological measures such as urine production and body temperature. These cycles are controlled by the _____ _____ (11); rats with SCN lesions no longer exhibit circadian cycles of sleep, _____ _____ (12), steroid production, and drinking. However, they do sleep, so sleep itself is under the control of other brain areas. When daylight cues are unavailable, people's circadian rhythms tend to increase to 25-hour cycles. This suggests that natural light is the critical _____ (13) for entraining the SCN to a 24-hour cycle. Furthermore, being exposed to _____ (14) light during wakefulness and darkness during sleep are important for coordinating the different biological rhythms associated with sleep. The fact that we tend towards a _____ (15)-hour cycle may explain why it is easier to adjust to later times for falling asleep and waking up than it is to adjust to earlier times. Shift workers whose shifts rotate according to phase _____ (16) are able to adjust more easily than those who must accommodate phase advance changes. Chronic _____ (17) who undergo phase delay changes may successfully move their sleeping schedules into a normal range and give up sleeping pills. Although there is evidence to support the existence of a 25-hour cycle, critics argue that phase delay shifts are the result of exposure to _____ (18) late during the waking period. Light controls the sleep cycle through its influence on the pineal gland's secretion of _____ (19); in totally blind individuals, a failure to produce this substance in response to changing levels of light is associated with _____ (20). Blind individuals with normal melatonin cycling probably rely on signals from the _____ (21) pathway to the SCN.

Humans have several bodily rhythms that follow an _____ (22) cycle. Some examples are hormone production, urinary output, and alertness; our rest/activity cycle, which is reflected in changes in brain waves, resets every _____ - _____ (23) minutes. High frequency, low amplitude beta waves are characteristic of _____ (24), whereas lower frequency, moderate amplitude _____ (25) waves accompany relaxation. The EEG patterns of sleep also exhibit a 90 minute rhythm. _____ (26) waves occur during stage 1, or light sleep. During stage 2, we exhibit _____ _____ (27) and K complexes. Slow wave sleep, stages 3 and 4, are associated with _____ (28) waves; movement, including sleep walking, often occurs during this time. Then the EEG activity indicates a reversal of sleep stages until _____ _____ (29) is achieved. REM sleep is characterized by eye movements, alpha-like brain waves, and physiological arousal, although the body is in a state of _____ (30); if the sleeper is awakened, dreaming is likely to be reported.

People deprived of REM sleep will enter it more quickly on subsequent nights and spend more time in this stage of sleep. Researchers have attempted to explain why this stage of sleep is so important for us. The _____ - _____ (31) hypothesis suggests that dreams are the product of spontaneous _____ (32) activity corresponding with REM sleep. According to this hypothesis, dreams themselves serve no specific function; we merely attempt to make sense out of the somewhat random sequence of experiences. Researchers do not agree on the function(s) of REM sleep. One suggestion is that because REM sleep is more common in infants and children than in adults, it promotes neural _____ (33). Another possibility is that REM sleep is important for _____ (34) learning; it corresponds to how much and how well an individual learns. It may also be involved in memory _____ (35), as rats subjected to brain stimulation during REM sleep improved on a learning task more than those who received it during SWS. The _____ _____ (36) hypothesis suggests that the function of REM sleep is to streamline our neural connections, and eliminate those that are not needed.

Because amount of SWS is associated with _____ (37) within the brain, it has been suggested that SWS is more important for brain than body restoration. It may also be involved in cognitive functioning. Individuals given _____ (38) prior to a nap experienced less SWS and poorer cognitive performance following the nap than those given a placebo. Also, reduced memory for word lists following SWS deprivation suggests it plays a role in _____ (39) memory consolidation.

The _____ _____ _____ (40) contains sleep-related cells, which send signals to cortical and limbic areas and receive in put from the locus coeruleus and _____ _____ (41), and waking-related cells, which inhibit activating systems in the hypothalamus and brainstem and receive input from the

POAH. _____ (42) cells are responsive to temperature; warming them increases SWS.

_____ (43) receptors in the preoptic area are inhibited by caffeine, which reduces sleepiness. REM sleep is accompanied by _____ (44) waves, which being in the pons, travel to the LGN, and then go to the occipital cortex. These patterns of activation begin about 80 seconds prior to the onset of _____ (45) sleep. Muscular paralysis during REM sleep results from signals from the _____ (46) to the magnocellular nucleus in the _____ (47). Disorders of REM sleep include _____ (48), in which a person becomes suddenly paralyzed but remains conscious, and _____ (49), in which a person enters REM sleep suddenly and directly from full consciousness.

How conscious are we during dreams and sleep? _____ (50) dreamers report awareness of their dreams as they happen, and also seem to be able to control the content of their dreams. On the other hand, people with _____ _____ (51) behavior disorder lack atonia and may act out their dreams. Perhaps consciousness exists on a _____ (52), and different states such as wakefulness, sleep, and dreaming, reflect different levels of awareness.

Short Answer & Essay

Answer the following questions. See p. 332 for sample answers.

1. Why did the study of consciousness fall out of favor among psychologists in the early 20th century?

2. How may jet lag account for the fact that west-coast baseball teams playing in east-coast cities lose more often than east-coast teams playing in west-coast cities?

3. Jackie is an industrial consultant. A company recently hired her to help them improve productivity in their night shift employees. The company's factory has many windows, and although the night workers are exposed to the same level of artificial light as the day shift workers, their overall working conditions are not as bright. What recommendation do you think Jackie would make to the company? Why?

4. Why do some blind people suffer from insomnia, whereas other blind individuals do not?

5. What underlying brain activity do alpha and beta waves reflect? How are these brain wave patterns related to the states of arousal associated with them?

6. According to the reverse learning hypothesis, what is the function of REM sleep? What evidence supports this hypothesis?

7. What connections does the basal forebrain area contain that make it critical for sleep and wakefulness?

The Neural Bases of Consciousness

Summary and Guided Review

After studying this section in the text, fill in the blanks of the following summary. The answers are found on pp. 331-332.

Although experts disagree as to a specific definition of consciousness, most would probably concur that being conscious includes awareness, _____ (53), and a sense of self.

Consciousness probably depends on a number of different brain areas. However, the _____ (54) is especially important. When we are unconscious, thalamic activity is depressed; thalamic lesions, especially in the _____ _____ (55), result in loss of consciousness. These effects are independent of arousal. Francis _____ (56) suggests that the thalamus is more than just a _____ (57) for awareness; he proposes that it is responsible for coordinating separate areas processing separate components of a stimulus so that we experience these components as a unit. _____ (58) is apparently not necessary for processing all information, and unconscious learning may be more efficient than conscious learning. For example, research participants who learned to _____ (59) the location of a target were unable to explain how they could make the predictions.

_____ (60) is the brain's means of allocating its limited resources. Consequently, much of the stimuli around us go unnoticed, although highly relevant stimuli such as one's name may be attended to. _____ _____ (61), which occurs when the brain is presented with two different visual stimuli apparently in the same location, results in attention being alternately focused on each object, as demonstrated in the _____ _____ (62) effect. The changes in attention correspond with shifts of activity in the _____ (63) cortex. PET scans reveal that when participants are instructed to attend to an object's color, _____ (64) becomes more active, and when told to attend to the object's shape, the _____ (65) cortex becomes more active. Control of attentional focus may reside in the _____ (66) of the thalamus.

Short Answer & Essay

Answer the following questions. See pp. 332-333 for sample answers.

8. What role does the thalamus play in awareness?

9. Describe a research study that indicates we can learn without being aware of what we have learned.

10. How is binocular rivalry, such as the Cheshire cat effect, achieved? What does this tell us about brain activity underlying attention?

The Sense of Self

Summary and Guided Review

After studying this section in the text, fill in the blanks of the following summary. The answers are found on p. 332.

Our sense of self includes identity and _____ (67), by which we are able to understand the consequences of our actions on external objects and events. Children over _____ (68) months of age and chimpanzees appear to recognize themselves in mirrors, indicating that they have a sense of self.

The sense of self is not represented in a single brain area, but probably results from several distributed functions. Studying individuals who lose proprioception, are paralyzed or have undergone limb _____ (69) reveals that bodily sensory feedback provides one basis for our sense of self. For example, the majority of amputees experience some manifestation of _____ _____ (70), such as the sense that the missing limb is stuck in a particular position or that one still has control over it. Because phantom limb occurs in people with spinal cord damage and is accompanied by spontaneous _____ (71) activity, researchers believe it is a brain-based phenomenon. Melzack argues that several brain areas, including the _____ (72) system and parietal lobe, form a network responsible for body image, and that this network is operational at birth. This is supported by the fact that individuals born with missing _____ (73) may also experience phantom limb.

_____ _____ (74) memory is also a source of our sense of identity. People with severe retrograde _____ (75) may become withdrawn. Others engage in _____ (76), which may result from a failure to suppress irrelevant information. However, Shallice suggests that they are attempting to integrate the isolated memories that they do have with their current circumstances.

Studies of split-brain patients can tell us something about consciousness and the self. Although most of the time people whose hemispheres have been disconnected perform normally, occasionally they act as if they have two selves. For example, _____ (77) describes a patient whose two hands simultaneously performed tasks at odds with each other. In laboratory studies, when information is presented only to the nonverbal _____ (78) hemisphere, the person is unable to identify it verbally; and the left hand (controlled by the right hemisphere) must sometimes be restrained to prevent it from helping the right hand perform a _____ (79) task. While some researchers speculate that each hemisphere is capable of a separate sense of consciousness, others such as Gazzaniga argues that the left hemisphere is the brain _____ (80) that integrates cognitive functions occurring throughout the brain. An alternative perspective is that because the right hemisphere lacks _____ (81) ability, it is simply unable to report on its own contents, and therefore appears to be less conscious or aware than the left hemisphere.

Cases of multiple personality or _____ _____ (82) disorder are provocative. Diagnosis of this disorder is controversial. Some experts believe that patients who display it are conforming to their therapists' expectations, but credible evidence for a _____ (83) basis of the disorder does exist in some cases. For example, some studies indicate that DID patients manifest different physiological profiles (heart rate, immune functioning, EEG activity) when different "personalities" are present. One explanation is that DID represents a case of _____ - _____ (84) learning, although thus far this phenomenon yields more subtle differences in "state" than are suggested by cases of DID.

Short Answer & Essay

Answer the following questions. See p. 333 for sample answers.

11. How can we test for self awareness in preverbal children and non-human animals?

12. What evidence is there that one does not need to learn body image?

13. Why does Gazzaniga argue that the left hemisphere is more highly conscious than the right hemisphere? What is the significance of the brain interpreter in his argument?

14. What is state-dependent learning? How might state-dependent learning explain the occurrence of DID?

Post-Test

Use these multiple-choice questions to check your understanding of the chapter. The answers, along with explanations, are found beginning on p. 333.

1. In the late 19th century, consciousness was studied primarily
   a. by using introspection.
   b. with The EEG.
   c. by examining sleep and dreaming.
   d. by observing others' behavior.

2. Currently, brain researchers
   a. are interested only in studying sleep as a form of consciousness.
   b. agree on a definition of consciousness.
   c. integrate philosophical, biological, and computer science perspectives to study consciousness.
   d. agree that consciousness cannot be studied objectively.

3. Which of the following animal species probably sleeps the LEAST?
    a. bats
    b. humans
    c. lions
    d. cattle

4. Which of the following statements regarding shift work is TRUE?
    a. Night shift workers perform their jobs as well as day shift workers.
    b. Night shift workers sleep less than day shift workers.
    c. Night shift workers generally sleep through the day on their weekends or days off.
    d. Job related accidents are most likely to occur between 10:00 pm and midnight.

5. Which of the following baseball teams is LEAST likely to win a game?
    a. The Boston Red Sox playing at the Houston Astros
    b. The Houston Astros playing at the Boston Red Sox
    c. The San Francisco Giants playing at the Atlanta Braves
    d. The Atlanta Braves playing at the San Francisco Giants

6. Circadian rhythms are controlled by the
    a. suprachiasmatic nucleus.
    b. lateral geniculate nucleus.
    c. pineal gland.
    d. pulvinar nuclei.

7. The most significant Zeitgeber for sleep/wake cycles appears to be
    a. moonlight.
    b. sunlight.
    c. clocks.
    d. social contact.

8. Research suggests that in order to increase worker productivity, night shift workers should
    a. sleep in complete darkness.
    b. work in very bright light.
    c. take naps every 2 hours while working.
    d. a and b.
    e. a, b, and c.

9. Assuming that the day shift is from 8:00 am to 4:00 pm, the swing shift is from 4:00 pm to midnight, and the night shift is midnight to 8:00 am, which of the following shift-rotation schedules would be MOST beneficial to workers?
    a. day shift → swing shift → night shift
    b. day shift → night shift → swing shift
    c. swing shift → day shift → night shift
    d. night shift → swing shift → day shift

10. Which of the following statements regarding the body temperature cycle is/are TRUE?
    a. It is a circadian rhythm.
    b. It always matches the sleep/wake cycle.
    c. Body temperature is usually lowest when we are asleep.
    d. a and c
    e. a, b, and c

11. _____ is a hormone released by the pineal gland that induces sleepiness.
    a. Melanopsin
    b. Adenosine
    c. Melatonin
    d. Oxytocin

12. Which of the following cycle lengths could be considered an ultradian rhythm?
    a. 24 hour
    b. 12 hour
    c. 48 hour
    d. 36 hour

13. An EEG pattern showing low amplitude, high frequency (13-30 Hz) waves corresponds with
    a. a state of alertness.
    b. relaxation.
    c. light sleep.
    d. slow wave sleep.

14. Delta waves are most likely to be observed in
    a. REM sleep.
    b. stage 4 sleep.
    c. stage 2 sleep.
    d. stage 1 sleep.

15. Which of the following is NOT a typical characteristic of REM sleep?
    a. low amplitude, moderate frequency EEG
    b. eye movement
    c. arm and leg movement
    d. genital erection

16. Dreams
    a. occur only during REM sleep.
    b. are more vivid in slow wave sleep.
    c. have no personal meaning.
    d. probably occur in all people.

17. Someone who is deprived of REM sleep will
    a. spend more time in REM and slow wave sleep when allowed to sleep without interruptions.
    b. develop narcolepsy or cataplexy.
    c. come to understand the symbolic contents of her dreams.
    d. spend more time in REM sleep when allowed to sleep without interruptions.

18. Infants spend about _____ % of their total sleep time in REM sleep.
    a. 10
    b. 50
    c. 20
    d. 75

19. Which of the following statements regarding REM sleep and learning is FALSE?
    a. Declarative learning is disrupted by REM sleep deprivation.
    b. Procedural learning is disrupted by REM sleep deprivation.
    c. During extended training, REM sleep peaks just before a peak in correct performance.
    d. REM sleep enhances memory consolidation.

20. Which of the following mammals does not experience REM sleep?
    a. elephant
    b. whale
    c. echidna
    d. feline

21. Which of the following hypotheses suggests that inappropriate neural connections are discarded during REM sleep?
    a. neural development
    b. learning
    c. reverse learning
    d. activation synthesis

22. Slow wave sleep is LEAST likely to increase if a person
    a. swims 25 laps in a chilly pool.
    b. runs 10 miles on a hot day.
    c. has a fever.
    d. visits tourist attractions while on vacation.

23. Which brain area contains both sleep-related and waking-related cells?
    a. raphe nuclei
    b. preoptic area
    c. basal forebrain area
    d. lateral geniculate nucleus

24. Caffeine affects sleep by
    a. facilitating the effects of adenosine in the preoptic area.
    b. stimulating the cells of the POAH.
    c. inhibiting the cells in the POAH.
    d. inhibiting the effects of adenosine in the preoptic area.

25. Muscular paralysis accompanying REM sleep is moderated by the
    a. magnocellular nucleus of the medulla.
    b. lateral geniculate nucleus of the thalamus.
    c. occipital cortex.
    d. basal forebrain area.

26. Narcolepsy is a condition in which a person
    a. suddenly goes from being awake directly into slow wave sleep.
    b. falls directly into REM sleep from wakefulness.
    c. suddenly becomes paralyzed while remaining conscious.
    d. is able to control the content and outcome of his dreams.

27. Someone who literally act outs dreams is probably experiencing
    a. lucid dreaming.
    b. cataplexy.
    c. REM sleep behavior disorder.
    d. insomnia.

28. Lesions in which of the following structure will cause a loss of consciousness?
    a. lateral geniculate nucleus of the thalamus
    b. preoptic area of the hypothalamus
    c. magnocellular nucleus of the medulla
    d. intralaminar nuclei of the thalamus

29. Explaining how different elements of a stimulus are experienced as a unitary whole is known as the
    _____ problem.
    a. reverse learning
    b. binding
    c. interpreter
    d. activation-synthesis

30. Which of the following is evidence of learning without awareness?
    a. recognizing that our unconscious mind is capable of motivating our behavior
    b. following a coach's instructions for hitting a ball with a bat
    c. correctly using the grammatical rules of one's native language
    d. reading instructions for assembling a computer prior to putting it together

31. The Cheshire cat effect is an example of
    a. binocular rivalry.
    b. lucid dreaming.
    c. binocular disparity.
    d. unconscious learning.

32. Shifting attention in the presence of distracting stimuli seems to be controlled by the
    a. lateral geniculate nucleus.
    b. magnocellular nucleus.
    c. intralaminar nuclei.
    d. pulvinar nuclei.

33. Which of the following is LEAST likely to recognize herself if a mirror?
    a. a 16-month old human
    b. an adult rhesus monkey
    c. an adult chimpanzee
    d. a 24-month old human

34. Phantom limb sensations may be experienced by
    a. amputees.
    b. people with spinal cord injuries.
    c. people born with missing limbs.
    d. a and b
    e. a, b, and c

35. Which of the following statements regarding confabulation is FALSE?
    a. It often includes elements of real memories.
    b. It is often consistent and meaningful.
    c. It is usually intentional.
    d. It is associated with long term memory loss.

36. Split-brain patients
    a. are unable to perform behaviors requiring coordination both sides of the body.
    b. are usually able to give verbal descriptions of objects presented in the right visual field.
    c. clearly demonstrate that the left hemisphere is more highly conscious than the right.
    d. seem to perform spatial tasks better with the left hand than the right.

37. Which of the following statements regarding dissociative identity disorder is FALSE?
    a. It is not included in the APA's *Diagnostic and Statistical Manual*.
    b. It was formerly called multiple personality disorder.
    c. It is believed to result from childhood abuse or trauma.
    d. Individuals exhibit different physiological patterns when manifesting different identities.

38. State-dependent learning
    a. occurs only with drugs and alcohol.
    b. occurs with different mood states.
    c. is the best explanation of dissociative identity disorder.
    d. can be produced only in a laboratory setting.

Answers & Explanations

Guided Review

1. introspection
2. behaviorists
3. cognitive
4. biology
5. sleep
6. restorative
7. adaptive
8. night
9. west-coast
10. circadian
11. suprachiasmatic nucleus
12. body temperature
13. Zeitgeber
14. bright
15. 25
16. delay
17. insomniacs
18. light
19. melatonin
20. insomnia
21. retinohypothalamic
22. ultradian
23. 90-100
24. alertness
25. alpha
26. Theta
27. sleep spindles
28. delta
29. REM sleep
30. atonia
31. activation-synthesis
32. neural
33. development
34. procedural
35. consolidation
36. reverse learning
37. temperature
38. caffeine
39. declarative
40. basal forebrain area
41. raphe nuclei
42. POAH
43. Adenosine
44. PGO
45. REM
46. pons
47. medulla
48. cataplexy
49. narcolepsy
50. Lucid
51. REM sleep
52. continuum
53. attention
54. thalamus
55. intralaminar nucleus
56. Crick
57. switch
58. Awareness
59. predict
60. Attention
61. Binocular rivalry

62. Cheshire cat	70. phantom limb	78. right
63. visual	71. thalamic	79. spatial
64. V4	72. limbic	80. interpreter
65. inferotemporal	73. limbs	81. verbal
66. pulvinar	74. Long term	82. dissociative identity
67. agency	75. amnesia	83. physiological or
68. 15	76. confabulation	biological
69. amputation	77. Gazzaniga	84. state-dependent

Short Answer & Essay

1. The behaviorists, in their attempt to make psychology a completely objective discipline, found fault with studying consciousness because the primary method was introspection, which was inherently subjective.

2. One possible explanation is that because when we travel from west to east, we must adopt a phase advance schedule; this results in sleep loss because we have to get up earlier than we are used to. Traveling east to west requires a phase delay change, or getting up later, a shift that is much easier to accomplish. Baseball players traveling east to play may be at a disadvantage because they are less rested than those traveling west to play.

3. She should tell the plant managers to increase the lighting intensity for the night shift workers, as this may help their bodies adjust to working when they would normally be sleeping. Also, she should recommend that the workers sleep in the darkest conditions possible.

4. Blind people who show melatonin suppression by light are less likely to suffer from insomnia. Light triggers the release of melanopsin by retinal ganglion cells, which in turn controls melatonin cycling via the retinohypothalamic pathway. Blind people who suffer from insomnia probably do so because of some disruption cells in this pathway.

5. Alpha waves are associated with relaxation; these brain waves are of moderate amplitude and lower frequency than beta waves. Beta waves, which are low amplitude and high frequency, are associated with alertness. The beta waves probably reflect more asynchronous neural activity, whereas alpha waves represent more synchronous activity.

6. According to this hypothesis, REM sleep serves to eliminate neural connections that are not useful, and conserve the connections that are useful. This hypothesis is supported by neural net simulations in which reverse learning enhances performance. Such a process may allow smaller brains to be more cognitively sophisticated. Mammals that do not undergo REM sleep have larger brains relative to their body size than mammals that do undergo REM.

7. Certain cells in the basal forebrain area receive input from the locus coeruleus and the raphe nuclei and relay signals to the cortex, limbic areas, and thalamus; these connections are associated with wakefulness. Other cells receive input from the preoptic area and anterior hypothalamus, and inhibit activating systems in the hypothalamus and brainstem; these connections are associated with sleep.

8. The thalamus seems to be important for awareness. During periods of unconsciousness or anesthesia, it is relatively inactive. Lesions of the intralaminar nuclei produce unconsciousness.

9. The book describes two studies. In one, participants behaved as if they had learned to predict where a target would appear on a screen, although they were unable to verbalize how they were predicting its location. In another study, people formed associations between facial features and personality characteristics, even though many denied making such generalizations.

10. If two images can be made to look as if they are in the same location, binocular rivalry occurs. When this happens, a person's attention is drawn alternately to one image and then to the other. While these attentional shifts are occurring, activity also shifts between different groups of neurons in the visual cortex, suggesting that attention is "caused" by neural activation.

11. Self awareness can be tested for by applying coloring to the face and then observing if the child or animal notices the spot in a mirror. Also, examining one's body using a mirror suggests self awareness.

12. Young children and people born with missing limbs experience phantom limb sensations, which suggests that body image is not necessarily learned.

13. Gazzaniga argues that because the left hemisphere shows evidence of language, inferential capacity, and the characteristics of a brain interpreter, it is more highly conscious. The role of brain interpreter is significant because split-brain people will confabulate reasons for behaviors performed by the left side of the body (and therefore controlled by the right, nonverbal hemisphere). This suggests that at some level the left hemisphere is aware of what the left side of the body is doing, and is attempting to explain it.

14. State-dependent learning is demonstrated when an individual in a particular state of consciousness (such as under the influence of alcohol, or in a particular emotional state) exhibits better recall for information learned in that state as opposed to some other state. Bower suggests that stress such as abuse (which is thought to sometimes give rise to DID) induces an altered state of consciousness, including thoughts and memories, that develop into a distinct personality.

Post-Test

All page references in this section pertain to the textbook.

1. a.   **Correct**; see p. 397.
    b.   Wrong; this is a late 20th century tool.
    c.   Wrong
    d.   Wrong; introspection is inherently subjective.

2. a.   Wrong; although this is one route for studying consciousness, awareness and attention are also ways in which researchers examine consciousness.
    b.   Wrong; there is no universally accepted definition of consciousness.
    c.   **Correct**; see p. 397.
    d.   Wrong; while some scientists may agree with this, not all do.

3. a.   Wrong; bats sleep long hours, perhaps because they are able to hide from predators in caves.
    b.   Wrong; humans eat larger meals than many animals, and we sleep longer than many species, including cattle. Also, we take shelter, so we are somewhat protected during sleep.
    c.   Wrong; lions are considerably less vulnerable to predation, and they tend to eat large meals at irregular intervals.
    d.   **Correct**; because this is a species that eats a low-nutrition food source, it must spend a good deal of time eating, and is also somewhat at risk from predation.

4. a. Wrong; night shift workers perform more poorly than day shift workers.
   b. Correct; see p. 398.
   c. Wrong; often they attempt to conform to the "normal" sleep schedules of others.
   d. Wrong; 2:00 am seems to be the most critical time for such accidents.

5. a. Wrong; in this case, the Boston team would probably be getting up an hour later than usual, which would not put them at a disadvantage.
   b. Wrong; although the Houston team would be traveling east and having to get up earlier, the time zone difference is only one hour, compared to three hours between San Francisco and Atlanta.
   c. Correct; the San Francisco team would have to go to sleep and get up much earlier (up to three hours), both of which are difficult. This may leave the players feeling less rested, which may result in poorer performance.
   d. Wrong; the Atlanta team would have little trouble altering their sleep schedules to awaken later in the day.

6. **a. Correct; see p. 399.**
   b. Wrong; although visual information is projected here from the retina, it is then relayed to the occipital cortex.
   c. Wrong; although the pineal gland is involved (it releases melatonin, which produces drowsiness), it is itself under the control of the SCN.
   d. Wrong; activity in this portion of the thalamus is involved in attentional shifts, and is unrelated to circadian rhythms.

7. a. Wrong
   b. Correct; see p. 400.
   c. Wrong
   d. Wrong

8. a. Wrong; b is also correct.
   b. Wrong; a is also correct.
   c. Wrong; this was not mentioned in the book (and taking naps every 2 hours while working might be counterproductive).
   d. Correct; this is based on the study described on p. 400 in which workers in the light-discrepant condition (with bright lights at night and complete darkness while they slept) performed better than those in the similar-light condition (with normal lighting at night and reduced light when they slept).
   e. Wrong

9. **a. Correct; this schedule conforms to phase delay – in changing shifts, the workers go to sleep later and get up later, which is easier to do than going to sleep earlier and getting up earlier.**
   b. Wrong; this requires phase advance changes.
   c. Wrong; this requires phase advance changes.
   d. Wrong; this requires phase advance changes.

10. a. Wrong; c is also true.
    b. Wrong; body temperature does not follow the sleep/wake cycle when it is lengthened (see p.401).
    c. Wrong; a is also true.
    d. Correct; see pp. 399-499.
    e. Wrong

11. a.   Wrong; this is a light sensitive protein..
    b.   Wrong; although this is a neuromodulator that accumulates while we are awake, and is believed to be involved in sleep, it is not released by the pineal gland.
    c.   Correct; see p. 401.
    d.   Wrong; this is a hormone related to sociability that is released by the pituitary. It is not mentioned as being related to sleep.

12. a.   Wrong; this would be a circadian rhythm.
    b.   Correct; a rhythm whose cycle repeats in less than 24 hours is considered ultradian.
    c.   Wrong; this is even longer than a circadian rhythm.
    d.   Wrong; this is even longer than a circadian rhythm.

13. **a.   Correct**; see p. 402.
    b.   Wrong; alpha waves are characteristic of relaxation, and they exhibit moderate amplitude and lower frequency.
    c.   Wrong; theta waves, which are even lower frequency than alpha waves, correspond with light sleep.
    d.   Wrong; delta waves, which correspond with SWS, are among the lowest frequency brain waves.

14. a.   Wrong; REM sleep is characterized by alpha-like waves.
    b.   Correct; see pp. 403-404.
    c.   Wrong; this stage is marked by sleep spindles and K complexes.
    d.   Wrong; theta waves occur in this stage.

15. a.   Wrong
    b.   Wrong
    c.   Correct; although people with REM sleep behavior disorder may exhibit this, normally we experience atonia during REM sleep. All of the other choices are true of REM sleep.
    d.   Wrong

16. a.   Wrong; they also occur during SWS.
    b.   Wrong; they may be more vivid during REM sleep.
    c.   Wrong; although there is no scientific way of interpreting them, they may have meaning to the individual.
    d.   Correct; even people who say they don't dream apparently do, since participants in sleep research report dreams when awakened during REM sleep.

17. a.   Wrong; the text states that they will spend more time in REM and less time in SWS.
    b.   Wrong; these disorders are related to REM sleep, but do not result from being deprived of it.
    c.   Wrong; there is no scientific basis for interpretation of dream symbols.
    d.   Correct; see p. 404.

18. a.   Wrong
    b.   Correct; see p. 405.
    c.   Wrong; this is about how much time adolescents and adults spend in REM sleep.
    d.   Wrong

19. **a.** **Correct**; declarative learning is apparently not affected by REM sleep deprivation, although it may be enhanced by SWS. All of the other choices are true.
    b. Wrong
    c. Wrong
    d. Wrong

20. a. Wrong
    b. Wrong
    c. **Correct**; only two species of dolphins and the echidna are known NOT to undergo REM sleep.
    d. Wrong

21. a. Wrong; this hypothesis suggests that neural maturation occurs during REM.
    b. Wrong; this hypothesis suggests that procedural learning is consolidated during REM.
    c. **Correct**; see p. 406.
    d. Wrong; this is a hypothesis that suggests dreams represent our attempts to make sense out of unrelated, spontaneous neural activity we encounter during sleep.

22. **a.** **Correct**; SWS increases under all of the other conditions. Although swimming is exercise, the critical relationship is with body temperature, and exercising in a pool of chilly water would prevent one from overheating.
    b. Wrong
    c. Wrong
    d. Wrong

23. a. Wrong; cells in this structure, located in the midbrain, send signals to the waking-related cells in the basal forebrain area.
    b. Wrong; cells in this hypothalamic area send signals to the sleep-related cells in the basal forebrain area.
    c. **Correct**; see p. 407.
    d. Wrong; this are is not mentioned as being associated with waking and sleeping.

24. a. Wrong; the accumulation of adenosine is associated with sleep, and since caffeine inhibits adenosine, it has the opposite effect.
    b. Wrong; caffeine is not mentioned as affecting cells in the POAH.
    c. Wrong
    d. **Correct**; see p. 408.

25. **a.** **Correct**; this area is "downstream" from the pons, and the connection between the two is responsible for atonia.
    b. Wrong; this area is stimulated upstream from the pons during PGO waves.
    c. Wrong; this area is stimulated upstream from the pons during PGO waves.
    d. Wrong; this area is not mentioned as being involved in REM sleep in particular.

26. a. Wrong
    b. **Correct**; see pp. 408-409.
    c. Wrong; this occurs in cataplexy.
    d. Wrong; this is lucid dreaming.

27. a. Wrong; lucid dreaming involves awareness that one is dreaming and possibly controlling the contents of one's dreams.
    b. Wrong; cataplexy involves paralysis.
    c. Correct; see p. 410.
    d. Wrong; insomniacs have difficulty sleeping, and someone who is not asleep cannot be dreaming.

28. a. Wrong
    b. Wrong
    c. Wrong
    d. Correct; this is the only area in which damage is specifically mentioned as causing loss of consciousness.

29. a. Wrong; this is a hypothesis of REM sleep.
    b. Correct; see p. 412.
    c. Wrong; this refers to Gazzaniga's assertion about the role of the left hemisphere in consciousness.
    d. Wrong; this is a hypothesis of dreaming.

30. a. Wrong; this is a Freudian idea, and is not empirically testable.
    b. Wrong; this is an example of learning with awareness.
    c. Correct; this is the best answer because one does not have to formally learn grammar in order to construct grammatically correct sentences.
    d. Wrong; this is an example of learning with awareness.

31. **a. Correct**; see p. 414.
    b. Wrong
    c. Wrong; this is the result of our eyes seeing the same image from slightly different angles.
    d. Wrong

32. a. Wrong
    b. Wrong
    c. Wrong
    d. Correct; see p. 415.

33. a. Wrong; while babies under 15 months do not pass the "mirror" test, older children do.
    b. Correct; the book presents evidence that monkeys, even with extensive experience, will not learn to recognize themselves in mirrors.
    c. Wrong; chimpanzees demonstrate self recognition in mirrors.
    d. Wrong

34. a. Wrong; b and c are also correct.
    b. Wrong; a and c are also correct.
    c. Wrong; a and b are also correct.
    d. Wrong
    e. Correct; see pp. 416-417.

35. a. Wrong
    b. Wrong
    c. Correct; there is no evidence presented that amnesiacs' confabulations are intentional. All of the other choices are true of confabulation.
    d. Wrong

36. a.   Wrong; most of the time they are able to do this.
    b.   Wrong; they are able to verbally identify objects presented to the left visual field.
    c.   Wrong; the textbook suggests that although many scientists believe the left hemisphere is more highly conscious than the right, this may be a function of the right hemisphere's lack of verbal ability.
    d.   Correct; see p. 418.

37. **a.   Correct**; DID is included in the DSM. All of the other choices are true.
    b.   Wrong
    c.   Wrong
    d.   Wrong

38. a.   Wrong; it may occur in emotional states as well.
    b.   Correct; see p. 420.
    c.   Wrong; it is a possibility, but cannot account for the extent to which people with DID display different "personalities."
    d.   Wrong; this is not mentioned in the book.